knowing truth, doing good

knowing truth, doing good

ENGAGING NEW TESTAMENT ETHICS

Russell Pregeant

Fortress Press
Minneapolis

KNOWING TRUTH, DOING GOOD
Engaging New Testament Ethics

Excerpts from *Then the Whisper Put on Flesh,* by Brian Blount © 2001 by Abingdon Press. Used by permission.
Excerpts from *The Moral Vision of the New Testament,* by Richard Hays © 1996. HarperCollins Publishers. Used by permission.
Excerpts from *The Moral Teaching of Paul,* by Victor Furnish © 1985 by Abingdon Press. Used by permission.
Excerpts from *The Earth Story in the New Testament,* ed. Norman C. Habel and Vicky Balabanski © 2002 by Sheffield Academic Press and The Pilgrim Press. Used by permission.

Cover image: Parable of the Good Samaritan, Domenico Fetti (1589–1624).
Photo © Cameraphoto / Art Resource, NY.
Cover design: Kevin van der Leek
Book design: The HK Scriptorium, Inc.

Library of Congress Cataloging-in-Publication Data

Pregeant, Russell.
    Knowing truth, doing good : engaging New Testament ethics / by Russell Pregeant.
        p. cm.
    ISBN 978-0-8006-3846-7 (alk. paper)
    1. Ethics in the Bible. 2. Bible. N.T.—Criticism, interpretation, etc. 3. Christian ethics. I. Title.
BS2545.E8P74 2007
241—dc22   2007040660

Manufactured in the U.S.A.

12   11   10   09   08   1   2   3   4   5   6   7   8   9   10

While the disciples were asleep,

> The people's bread was stolen to buy instruments of war
> And line the pockets of the ones who dress in purple and adorn
> themselves with gold;
> The trees were cut, the wetlands filled;
> So carbon caked upon the firmament and made the planet boil,
> While levees lay untended, weak, decaying;
> And in high places care was nowhere to be found.

> Thus, when Katrina came, with fury fueled by simmering seas,
> The wind and water washed the poor away,
> And the sacred place where jazz was born and soulful music always
> filled the air
> Became a bloody sacrifice to the god of human greed.

But when the sleepers are at last awake,

> What thoughts will occupy their minds?
> Will they waste their time by hunting witches?
> Or will they stand beside the one they claim to follow,
> Who even now in agonizing prayer must contemplate his death,
> Because he made the Empire tremble as he cast his lot
> With those neglected by false shepherds of the sheep?

[T]he moral life is not a compartment alongside economic, political, or religious life; it refers rather to what one values deeply enough to live by and, if necessary, die for because one is convinced that it is both right and true. The moral life is both broader and deeper than morality (patterned behavior) or morals (actions deemed right by a community), for it has to do with the sort of person one is (the doer) as well as the grounding of what is to be done (the deed). To speak of the moral life is to draw attention to one's responsibility, however circumscribed, for the shape of one's life, including what one allows and refuses to allow to influence it. Also, the moral life is more than decision making, for it has to do with what becomes habitual and so exposes one's character. It refers to life actually lived, whereas the word *morality*, being an abstract noun, signals that the subject matter has been detached from life so that it can be analyzed as a self-consistent whole.

—Leander E. Keck (2000, 152)

It has proved the task and the responsibility of marginalized readers today, both female and male, to restore the voices of the oppressed in the kingdom of God. In order to do this, they have had to be able as much as possible to read and hear the text for themselves, with their own eyes and their own ears. And in the final analysis, they have had to be prepared . . . to resist those elements of the tradition that have sought, even in the name of revelation, to diminish their humanity. In so doing, African American women have continued to read the Bible in most instances because of its vision and its promise of a world where the humanity of everyone will be fully valued. They have accomplished this reading in spite of the voices from within and without that have tried to equivocate on that vision and promise.

—Renita J. Weems (1991, 76–77)

Do not be conformed to this world, but be transformed by the renewing of your minds, so that you may discern what is the will of God—what is good and acceptable and perfect.

—Romans 12:2

contents

PART IV

ENGAGING NEW TESTAMENT ETHICS

preface

Before I turn to more personal matters, a word about terminology is in order. I am well aware of the current tendency to distinguish between ethics and morality, with the former pertaining to theoretical reflection and the latter to matters of actual conduct. In the present work, however, I have used the terms more or less interchangeably. I readily grant that it is debatable whether the New Testament actually contains ethics as theoretical reflection, but it is also apparent to me that in various ways it does manifest forms of moral reasoning, most particularly in the letters of Paul. I do not consider any of the New Testament writers to be theologians in the narrow sense of constructors of systems of thought, but neither are they (for the most part) mere conveyors of injunctions. As I hope to make clear, at least in the grander materials I will be surveying, moral teaching is intimately bound to theological convictions.

If I were to write my own version of the parable of the sower, I would add another category of soils: the kind that receives the seed but takes an uncommonly long time to produce the grain. My passion for the ethical dimension of Christian faith is not new, but it is only in recent years that it has expressed itself in a course in New Testament ethics and only now that it manifests itself in a published work. The seeds were there from "the beginning"—that is, from the time of a pre-adolescent religious "awakening." And they received ample nurture from teachers at various stages in my education, as I wrestled with the moral dimensions of social and political questions, but most especially from two of my many instructors in biblical studies over the years: Victor Furnish and Leander Keck, for whose scholarly work New Testament ethics has always been central. So I want to offer a special word of thanks to both of them for their early inspiration and guidance. Of course, neither they nor any of the persons I mention below are responsible for whatever deficiencies this book may have. Another important moment was the appearance of Richard Hays's *The Moral Vision of the New Testament.* With the prospect of doing some work in the field of New Testament ethics already forming in my mind, I read this book with great enthusiasm and deep appreciation and eventually made it the foundation of a seminary course. However, I also found myself thinking rather differently about how to approach the topic and in enough disagreement on some fundamental points to be inspired to respond to Hays's invitation for others to "join [him] in the discipline of listening closely to the New Testament witnesses and to offer their own readings for the edification of the church" (1996, 11). I hope that my many "conversations" with him in this book are such that those who read it will sense the collegial spirit in which they are intended.

I am deeply indebted to my colleagues in religion and philosophy at Curry College—Bette Manter, Les Muray, and Alan Revering—for enjoyable and enlightening conversations, over a period of several years, on matters theological and in particular for raising my consciousness with respect to virtue ethics. More recently, Rob Smid has joined and invigorated these sessions, often held over dinner. Les and Bette (each in turn as area coordinator) also merit thanks for allowing an emeritus professor to continue to wander in from the pasture to teach biblical studies. Ann Levin, in sociology and women's studies at Curry, was of great help in my efforts to evaluate the various claims made with respect to the issue of homosexuality, and a conversation with Allen Callahan of the Seminário Theológico Batista do Nordeste was helpful to me in thinking through the treacherous issues regarding the Jesus tradition and Israel's purity laws. I also want to express my gratitude to Sze-kar Wan—who chaired the New Testament department at Andover Newton Theological School for many years and is now embarking on a new adventure at Perkins School of Theology—for the great freedom he allowed me for over a decade as visiting professor in New Testament at ANTS. It took him less than a nanosecond to agree to my creation of a course in New Testament ethics, and he has encouraged me to offer it on a regular basis. As a result, I have been able to inflict my ideas on several different groups of bright, interested, and thoughtful seminary students and get their reactions; and I would like to offer my thanks to these students also.

Several colleagues and friends have done me the honor of reading all or parts of my manuscript, and I am particularly grateful for this service above and beyond the call of duty. John Hill, a Curry professor in politics and history, with whom I co-taught a course in religion and politics for many years, read the entire work and pushed me at numerous points to make a greater effort to communicate with those outside the fields of biblical and theological studies. Les Muray also read each chapter as it appeared, and Ron Farmer of Chapman University read many of the early chapters. David Lull of Wartburg Theological Seminary read the chapter on the undisputed letters of Paul; and Bill Herzog, dean of the faculty at Andover Newton, read portions of chapters 3 and 4 and has helped me navigate through an area of biblical studies in which I am very much a neophyte. The Rev. Scott Campbell and several laypersons from Harvard Epworth United Methodist Church in Cambridge, Massachusetts, provided stimulating discussions in a study group based on several chapters. Nancy Nienhuis of Andover Newton and Marlene Samuelson of Curry read parts of chapter 12; and Sandy Poole—a recently rediscovered friend from my high school days—read that entire chapter. Betty Mandell and Marvin Mandell, co-editors of *New Politics* (a true oasis in a political desert) and long-time friends and conversation partners regarding many of the topics that inhabit these pages, also read chapter 12. Our lunch-time "seminars" have potentially solved most of the world's problems.

I would also like to express my appreciation to the staff at Fortress Press for the collegial atmosphere with which they approach the publishing venture and especially to Neil Elliott for his suggestions regarding the shape of this project. It is a great honor and pleasure to work with this organization that has produced so many important materials in the field of biblical studies over the years.

I close with two special words of gratitude. The hermeneutical perspective I bring to the New Testament owes much to William A. Beardslee, whose scholarship has been so important in fostering dialogue between our own contemporary world and that of the Bible and whose life was a shining testimony to the power of the New Testament's moral witness. And, finally, I am indebted in a very different way to Sammie Maxwell, whose conversations over the years, through the many twists and turns of our lives, have fed both my mind and my heart in irreplaceable ways. She has always known the shallowness of the "matters of consequence" that Antoine de Saint-Exupéry lampooned in *The Little Prince*. In the words of the fox that inhabits that same profound little story, "you [are] to me unique in all the world."

the bible in babylon

Of what use is the New Testament in making ethical decisions or in living a moral life? To many morally sensitive persons in our time, the Bible provides a solid foundation for constructive values in a society they consider at best confused and at worst corrupt to the core. For others, however—persons of equal but radically different moral sensitivity—the Bible is the enemy. It is a bastion of reactionary thought enshrining innumerable oppressive social patterns from a hopelessly outdated past, such as the subordination of women and the hierarchical ordering of society.

Of course, there are also many in our contemporary world for whom the Bible is neither friend nor foe but simply irrelevant. These are not, however, the only ones who fit neither the first nor the second category. For there are yet others who view the ethical teachings of the biblical writings with decided ambiguity. They have a strong sense that the sacred Scriptures of Christians and Jews have a role to play in contemporary moral reasoning, but they are unsure how to apply specific biblical teachings to the complex issues of our time. It is this fourth group that I have most particularly in mind in writing this book on New Testament ethics, although I would also hope that it could engage others as well. My intention, in any case, is to take seriously the concerns of persons in each of these disparate groups.

The fact that the Bible receives such starkly different evaluations is a sign of the complexity of the social situation that persons of Christian faith or interests confront in twenty-first-century Western civilization. Not only do the cohesive bonds of medieval Christendom lie in a now-distant past, but in the more recent past we have experienced the break-up of the lingering vestiges of that heritage. This reality has affected the United States more slowly than it has Europe.

Nevertheless, North American Christians at the dawn of this century experience a very different environment than did those living at the beginning, or even the middle, of the preceding one. On the one hand, there are vast numbers of persons who seem content to live purely secular lives, whether supported by strong humanistic values or merely devoted to mindless forms of consumerism and pleasure seeking. On the other, religions that once played only marginal roles in Western society—most notably Islam and Buddhism—have made remarkable inroads into it. In addition, innumerable forms of spirituality, often drawing upon ancient sensitivities to nature, abound. The Bible, once indisputably a foundational document for European and American societies, has become one among a bewildering host of voices.

This is not to say that the Jewish-Christian Scriptures are no longer influential. No one familiar with their role in the "culture wars" of the past several decades or the phenomenal growth of the ranks of conservative Christians in the United States could seriously argue that. But the fact remains that the Bible is no longer an unquestioned frame of reference for society as a whole—as anyone who has taught biblical studies in a secular environment of late knows all too well! Thus, despite the enormous political power of the "religious right," persons of this persuasion feel largely alienated from the wider community. And they have much to lament—not only the rise of alternative forms of religious consciousness and dramatic changes in sexual mores but also the perceived betrayal of the faith by liberal Christians under the influence of the likes of Charles Darwin, Karl Marx, and Sigmund Freud.

It is not only conservative Christians, however, who feel at odds with contemporary values. Persons with progressive religious leanings also experience alienation, in ways that both parallel and contradict the perceptions of their counterparts. They might well agree that current television, movies, and other forms of entertainment reflect a debased sense of values. But they also perceive the alliance that some religious conservatives have forged with laissez-faire capitalism, corporate America, and other aspects of the agenda of the political right wing to be a betrayal of the biblical mandate for social justice. And that mandate is something they find increasingly rejected in the United States in recent years.

Whether conservative or progressive, then, many contemporary Christians in Western society have a strong sense of exile. For their experience is in some ways parallel to that of the people of ancient Judah held captive in Babylon—an experience encapsulated in the plaintive cry of Psalm 137: "How could we sing the LORD's song in a foreign land?" Those ancient displaced persons responded to their crisis by collecting and shaping their traditions as a basis of community solidarity. And much that has come down to us through the centuries as classical Judaism took shape during and immediately after this crucial period. Christians of various persuasions are likewise aware that the current situation of the church calls for a similar effort. The problem, however, is the lack of consensus on how to accomplish the task of bringing the ancient traditions to bear on current issues. Because the adherents of various theological perspectives remain worlds apart on this issue, the Christian community finds itself not only in "Babylon"—an alien environment—but also tragically divided.

The Bible stands at the very heart of the struggles among competing groups within the Christian community. The issue is not whether the biblical writings should play a central role in the effort to relate Christian tradition to contemporary issues, but what that role should be. And this is why I have conceived this work not simply as a descriptive discourse on the ethical perspectives of the New Testament. It is also an exercise in hermeneutics—both a reflection on the nature of biblical interpretation and an attempt to render the New Testament writings meaningful in our contemporary world. The point is not simply to understand the biblical writings but to engage them. It is to enter into genuine conversation with them in order to discover the relevance they might have for the actual lives we live as individuals, as members of a religious community, and as participants in a civilization and a world.

If it is necessary, in discussing New Testament ethics, to reflect on the theory of interpretation, it is equally necessary to take account of three additional factors. First, the New Testament (as its name clearly attests) does not stand alone; it is intelligible only against the background of the Hebrew Bible. Any treatment of New Testament ethics must therefore in some sense also be a treatment of biblical ethics more generally.

Second, within the New Testament itself, the ethical teachings are grounded in the broader theological perspectives of the various writings. The reader will therefore note frequent attention to those foundational perspectives.

Third, there is no neutral standpoint from which to view the issues. Recognition of this fact is a crucial component of our particular historical situation in general. And the emergence of the various theologies of liberation—such as African American, Latin American, feminist, and Asian—over the last half century has underscored the point within the theological community. All thought is conditioned by the context of the thinker, and pretense of neutrality can only create a false and dangerous illusion of universality. In terms of the present work, this means that I do not hesitate to pose the issues largely in terms of Western (and particularly North American) social realities, since that is the context within which I think and write. But it also means that I understand my responsibility to be conscious of the limitations of my own perspective and therefore to be attentive to other points of view, from both within and beyond this particular context.

The purpose of this book is to explore ways in which the ethics of the New Testament might legitimately inform the attempts of contemporary Christians to apply their faith to the difficult issues confronting them in a very confusing environment. That environment is one in which, despite the strong influence of Christianity, wildly divergent value systems compete. It is also one in which different Christian groups derive contradictory positions from their biblical faith on issues such as economic and social policies, war, the status and role of women, divorce and remarriage, capital punishment, homosexuality, and abortion. Looking outward, serious Christians feel besieged by mindless consumerism, rampant greed, and shallow hedonism. Looking within their communities, they find themselves burdened with disturbingly bitter disagreements as to the nature of the alternative value systems that biblical ethics might provide. Moreover, as anyone deeply involved in church life today realizes, the controversies are not merely among the various Christian denominations but also among competing and often bitterly divided factions within them.

It would appear, then, that the task of engaging New Testament ethics—of bringing biblical insights to bear on contemporary issues—is anything but simple. So it seems almost self-evident that in pursuing this topic I have no illusions of providing a definitive answer to the perplexing questions it involves. My hope, however, is to present a perspective that Christians of various theological persuasions might find worthy of consideration and that might move the discussion forward in a constructive way.

Part 1 is a venture into the question of method, an exploration of competing theories of the nature of interpretation. The first step in that venture, chapter 1, treats basic issues and examines several recent thinkers whose approaches to biblical interpretation are relevant to New Testament ethics. Against this background, chapter 2 outlines my own approach. Part 2 is an investigation of traditions that lie behind the canonical Gospels, and part 3 is a serial treatment of the canonical writings themselves. Part 4, consisting of a single chapter, is an effort to bring the results of the investigation to bear more directly on the concrete and often perplexing issues that provide the impetus for writing this kind of book.

PART I

madness in the methods?
on learning to treat the text as subject

CHAPTER 1

wending our way
in the postmodern maze

⊸

HOW SHOULD WE READ THE WRITINGS?

The task of describing the ethical teachings of the New Testament might appear to be a straightforward one, but this impression is deceptive, for several reasons. To begin with, the New Testament is not a single, self-consistent document but a collection of writings expressing various points of view. Although some common threads bind the various writings together, they contain significant differences in theological perspective and ethical teachings. At many points it will therefore be impossible to state "the" New Testament teaching on a specific topic. In addition, since the ethical perspective of a given writing is closely related to its broader theological outlook, it will be necessary to ask how any given injunction functions within that larger framework. Viewed from this wider perspective, it might take on a rather different value than if we were to consider it in isolation. A description of the ethical perspective of a specific writing, or corpus of related writings, within the New Testament therefore entails much more than noting its positions on particular moral issues.

It is also significant that the Gospels are the product of a long process of development beginning with oral tradition. For some interpreters, we need concern ourselves only with the final stage of development—the Gospels as they now stand—since it is these that the church has recognized as authoritative. This is an arguable position, but it is not the only way of viewing the matter. One alternative is to look to the words and deeds of the historical Jesus for a definitive perspective. Another is that the witness of Jesus' earliest followers to him, which some scholars have called the apostolic tradition, should play this role. This is a complex question, which I will explore in more detail later in this chapter. Suffice it to say now that it is not self-evident that the canonical level should take precedence over earlier or later levels of tradition when we ask what is definitive for New Testament theology or ethics.

Even if we concern ourselves only with the canonical level, a problem remains. For a close reading of the various New Testament texts reveals that they are far from self-consistent wholes. Certainly each writing has a high degree of thematic unity—this is a point that recent literary approaches to the Gospels have shown. The Gospels, for example, are stories that we can analyze meaningfully in terms of plots, themes, and characters; and central to the thematic dimension of each is its overall theological perspective. Sometimes, however, the interpreter must recognize thematic clashes within a given writing.

I will note this phenomenon at several points in part 2, but one example should suffice for now. From one perspective, the story of Jesus in Mark seems to be following a predetermined plan. Jesus predicts his death and resurrection, the end of the age, and his eventual return in victory. However, notes of contingency are found in the testing by Satan in 1:12-13 and Jesus' agonizing prayer in Gethsemane in 14:32-42, suggesting the possibility that Jesus might fail the tests. Centuries of Christian teaching, focusing on the role of Jesus' death in atonement theology, have tended to suppress this aspect. But if we allow the hint of contingency to disappear altogether, we deprive the story of much of its dramatic power, and we also obscure the theme of Jesus' obedience to God in the face of death as a moral example.

My point here is not that we should choose one strain of thought over the other but rather that we should recognize the tension the disparate elements create. If a writing contains competing strands of meaning, then any attempt to describe its theological perspective becomes a more complex task than we might have imagined. And if ethics is linked to theology, the possible theological ambiguity might affect what appears to be a clear ethical pronouncement.

THE ROLE OF INTERPRETATION THEORY

Recognition of the possibility of competing meanings within a single writing raises the broader question of interpretation theory, and fundamental to this question is the difference between what a text says and what it means. On one level, this is a point that any reader should recognize. Imagine a character in a novel who makes the remark, "What a lovely day." The most obvious way to understand the statement is as a straightforward expression of appreciation of pleasurable weather. It is possible, however, that the character speaks ironically and the statement means the exact opposite of what it says: the day is in fact cold and dreary or excruciatingly hot and humid.

A reader may be able to discern how the character means the statement from the broader context of the story. Perhaps the narrator has already described the weather as pleasant; or perhaps the reader knows enough about the character to be on the lookout for irony. Such is not always the case, however; and for this reason the literary critic Wolfgang Iser (1974) says that it is impossible for a narrator to do all the work for a reader. That is to say, any story will necessarily leave much to the imagination. For example, no matter how vivid a description of a physical object a reader encounters, she or he will still have to draw on personal experience and make subjective judgments in order to form an appropriate mental image. More importantly, the same applies to plots, characters, and themes. There will always be gaps in the plot for the reader to fill in, and no narrator's development of a character can completely determine how a reader will imagine that character. And it is finally the reader's prerogative to make value judgments about characters, the significance of the events within the context of the plot, and the meaning the story might have for human life. Were all this not so, there would be no need for literary critics or interpreters. We speak of interpretation only because the reading process entails something more than the mere recognition of what a text "says."

It is apparent, then, that meaning is not something that resides simplistically either in the author's mind or in the text of the writing itself; it arises in the interaction of text and reader. This view may be unfamiliar to many readers, and certainly not all biblical interpreters accept it. But mainstream literary critics made similar points long before Iser, and it is a perspective increasingly recognized among biblical scholars as well. It is a matter of dispute, however, among both literary critics and biblical interpreters, just how far one should push this insight. We are at this point deep into the heart of contemporary interpretation theory.

At the center of the debate is a school of thought broadly termed "postmodernism," whose adherents argue that recent experience has led us beyond the modern worldview without returning to the premodern. This modern view was characterized by a confidence in the human ability to gain secure knowledge, largely through science, as well as by a comprehensive understanding of reality. It also entailed the belief in at least the theoretical possibility of attaining an objective, or universal, point of view. Postmodernists, by contrast, stress that all knowledge is limited by perspective and thus tend to deny the possibility of an objective description of reality or, indeed, absolute knowledge in any form.

There are competing schools within postmodernism itself, and it is important at present to mention how one of these schools—"deconstruction"—plays out in terms of the interpretation of texts. This perspective has gained significant support among recent biblical scholars. Its basic contention with respect to literary interpretation is that any text has a tendency to "deconstruct" itself. That is to say, it necessarily contains elements that render it open to various readings. Any attempt to find a neutral standpoint for an interpreter to take is therefore futile, because all perspectives necessarily involve prior conceptions or ideological commitments. Of course, one interpreter can make important points and document them from the text itself, but someone else can always make different points in a convincing way, based on different preconceptions and different elements in the text.

The deconstructionists' concern is not merely to note the impossibility of objective readings but to call attention to the possibilities that the open-endedness of a text presents. What bothers postmodernists in general is that certain readings have become dominant over time and have effectively silenced the voices of those who might offer alternative interpretations. And the most important point is that the standardized readings reflect the power structure of our social worlds and therefore serve the interests of a ruling class and/or a dominant gender, ethnic group, or race. Thus, one of the purposes of a "deconstructive" reading is to subvert ("deconstruct") ways of understanding texts that have become so ingrained in the mind-set of both the professional guild and the general public that they appear self-evident. The further intention is to open the way for other readings from perspectives that those in power traditionally exclude.

Another reason that no reading of a text can be final is that meaning is always "deferred," because any concept that appears in a text is intelligible only in relation to some other concept. For example, we cannot understand the meaning of "night" without understanding the meaning of "day." Virtually everyone recognizes this, but deconstructionists argue rather compellingly that this process of understanding one term in relation to another involves us in an endless process. Each term, in its turn, necessitates referral to yet others. Thus, we never have all the "information" we need to make a final judgment about meaning.

I will return to this issue later in the present chapter and will offer an alternative version of postmodernism in chapter 2. It is important at this point, however, to note one aspect of the postmodernists' claims that I consider valid and of enormous importance. Both the interpretation and the meaningful reading of any text entail something far different from the somewhat mechanical process of grasping the meanings of words and the structures of sentences and paragraphs. Reading always involves in some measure the engagement of the human imagination. In finding a meaning in a text, we necessarily construe it in some particular way, a way that neither the author nor the text itself can fully determine. Interpretation therefore means finding a way to order the various components into a coherent whole.

On the basis of these and other considerations that will appear later I conclude that we must take full account of nine factors in any adequate approach to the ethics of the New Testament:

1. the diversity of thought among the various canonical writings;
2. the various strands of meaning within any given writing or corpus of writings;
3. the wide stream of tradition, both oral and written, that precedes, parallels, and follows the composition of these writings and their designation as canonical;
4. the ongoing character of all tradition—that is, its inherently processive, developmental character;
5. the open-ended character of texts, demanding the participation of the reader in the actual creation of meaning;
6. the limitations that the linguistic structures of texts place on the interpretive enterprise, so that not just any reading is necessarily valid;
7. the fact that all writings are conditioned by the social contexts in which they arise;
8. the equally important fact that some aspects of the tradition transcend their original settings more easily than do others;
9. the role that power imbalances have played in the production, selection, and interpretation of texts.

We may now take a step closer to a more concrete discussion of our primary subject by reviewing the works of several New Testament scholars. Not all of these deal directly with the topic of ethics, and there are several important books on the subject that I will make use of later but will not address at this point. I have chosen these particular materials because each is relevant in some particular way to the preliminary question of method: How should we approach the various New Testament writings in an attempt to engage its ethical teachings? My intention is to identify and evaluate several possible answers to this question before outlining my own approach in chapter 2.

A SURVEY OF POSSIBLE GUIDES

A. K. M. Adam: A "Nonmodern" Approach to New Testament Theology

In his book *Making Sense of New Testament Theology: "Modern" Problems and Prospects,* A. K. M. Adam states his intention to establish "that New Testament theology need not be founded on warrants derived from historical-critical reasoning" (1995, 5). Identifying the historical-critical method—which seeks to understand biblical texts in light of their original historical settings—as a centerpiece of the ideology of modernity, Adam denies that this approach is the exclusive or even the privileged mode of interpretation. He does not reject the method but argues that other ways of deriving meaning from texts can have equal validity within their own frames of reference. Adam's view is influenced by postmodernism, but his agenda is not to replace a modern methodology with a postmodern one. For such an attempt would fall into modernity's pattern of claiming superiority over earlier methods (1995, 2). What he proposes, then, is a "nonmodern" approach that does not reject historical criticism but refuses to look to it for legitimation.

A major objection Adam voices to the exclusive dependence on the historical-critical method in modern biblical scholarship is that it makes biblical interpretation into an elite activity. Only those properly trained in modern techniques of historical investigation can participate meaningfully, and they will naturally reject or ignore readings that do not meet strict historical criteria. Thus, Adam asks why one should not be able to read the Bible with other interests and alternative criteria in mind—such as ethical, aesthetic, or theological/ecclesiastical— and be taken as seriously as the historical critic (1995, 3–4).

There is a simple answer to this question from the historical-critical perspective. If such readings do not meet historical criteria, they do not reflect the meaning that the author intended or that the original readers would have discerned. Adam, however, asks why the author's intention or the meaning likely to be evident to the original readers should be the only meaning a text can have. And the vast majority of contemporary literary critics would support his point; for it is well accepted in literary circles today that a writing takes on a life of its own after leaving an author's hands and that authors are not necessarily the best interpreters of their own works!

We therefore come upon a complex issue regarding the nature of interpretation; for one can argue that readings that do not reflect an author's intentions do not identify the "real" meaning of a text but are only reflections on, and perhaps distortions of, that text. I will return to the issue later but will let this statement suffice for the present: to the extent that we acknowledge that the meaning of a text is to some extent open-ended, making necessary a reader's construal, we must also give at least partial approval to Adam's contentions. The historical-critical method cannot by itself render an exhaustive interpretation of a text.

It is important to note that Adam does not deny that some degree of historical investigation is necessary in biblical interpretation. He can say, for example, that "[o]ne could hardly interpret the New Testament . . . without relying on the painstaking philological and textual research that has produced the standard grammars, lexicons, critical editions, and translations." This concession, however, does not negate either his objection to the dominance of the historical-critical method or his insistence on its limitations. For

> this inevitable reliance upon historical scholarship does not necessitate *exclusive* or even *primary* status for historical investigation. The role of historical judgment is not summed up by a binary choice of "aye" or "nay." Even the most rigorously ascetic historians are involved in the selection and suppression of evidence, and in the construction of persuasive accounts to defend their versions of history. In these (non-"historical") activities, historians elaborate a dialogical relation between the strictly historical aspect of their work and various rhetorical, fictive, and ideological aspects. (1995, 159; emphasis original)

According to Adam, although all interpretations depend at least in some minimal way on historical investigation, when historical critics offer actual interpretations of texts, they inevitably reach beyond the historical method, drawing on their broader knowledge, experiences, backgrounds, and ideological perspectives. This reinforces the point that the historical method is merely one among others, since it cannot stand alone, and it also subverts the historical critic's claims to exclusive rights in interpretation and to pure objectivity.

Those committed to the historical-critical method are of course aware that absolute objectivity is unattainable. They argue with some force, however, that "one can at least try" to attain it, which is better than simply imposing a desired interpretation on a text. Nevertheless, criticisms such as Adam's suggest that the problem is subtler than defenders of this method tend to recognize. Subjective elements affect judgments in ways more difficult to identify than one might first think: even the selection of a subject for study and the formulation of questions for investigation are dependent on the imagination of the critic.

In formulating his "nonmodern" approach, then, Adam writes unabashedly of "making" sense of a text, contending that "sense is something *ascribed to* the text, not a property the text *has*" (1995, 171; emphasis original). It would seem therefore that although historical investigation might be necessary to determine in a preliminary way some minimal foundation for interpretation, the actual process of construing a meaning is finally in the hands of the interpreter. The interpreter "makes sense" of a text by *assigning* it a meaning.

It is precisely this freedom in assigning meaning that bothers historical critics most fundamentally. Is just any meaning legitimate if an interpreter asserts it? It is not only the subjective interpretations of individuals that defenders of the historical method see as a threat, moreover, but also the heavy hand of institutional interpretation. The historical-critical approach appears for many to be an important buffer against the manipulation of the Bible by those who serve the interests of particular ecclesiastical institutions. In their own way, historical critics can claim to challenge power structures.

Adam grants a limited validity to the latter point, but—citing historical Jesus studies as a case in point—reiterates the observation that supposedly ideologically neutral claims too often turn out to "reproduce prior convictions about God and humanity." He then goes on to assert that

> [a]rguments from historical investigation will often provide sufficient leverage to displace particular theological positions, but this does not by any means imply that one must always prefer historical hypotheses that cast doubt upon a particular theological interpretation. (1995, 187–88)

As to whether giving readers the prerogative of "making sense" opens the way for unbridled subjectivity, Adam contends that there can be no "transcendent" criteria for interpretation—that is, no universal rules to which one might appeal to adjudicate competing claims. On the other hand, he sees the necessity for and legitimacy of what he calls "local" criteria (1995, 188). This is his hedge against interpretive anarchy.

But what does he mean by "local criteria," and how might these in fact constitute an adequate antidote to anarchy? Drawing on the work of several literary critics, Adam introduces the notion of interpretive communities formed around particular interests (1995, 177–78). It is to these communities and the criteria they develop that interpreters are responsible. Adam grants that the professional guild of biblical scholars ranks among these and is perfectly justified in making the modern historical-critical method its foundation, but he denies that this particular approach should set the agenda for all biblical interpretation. A different community could as legitimately place interests in the doctrines of a church, women's liberation, or human psychology at the center and derive the criteria for interpretation from these concerns. In a community defined by such a "local" agenda, one would evaluate interpretations of a text not by whether they conform to what historical scholarship deems the original meaning but by whether they serve the community's interests.

Well aware that critics will find this appeal to local criteria an inadequate defense against the charge of interpretive anarchy, Adam argues that the readings of all interpretive communities have some responsibility within the realm of public discourse.

> A pro-apartheid Afrikaaner New Testament theology—however offensive it might be to non-Afrikaaners—is not methodologically illegitimate. At the same time, New Testament theologies that reflect the ethical priorities of the dominant groups in the practice of New Testament interpretation are not thereby removed from the field of ethical debate. (1995, 186)

That is to say, within its own bounds, each community is entitled to its own perspective and criteria. But this does not exempt any community from the questions that one might raise from another perspective. Neither the historical critic nor anyone representing a perspective outside of a racist enclave could challenge its readings on the basis of any universal rules of interpretation. But the racist interpreters would nevertheless remain responsible, in the public realm, for the ethical implications of these readings.

I can agree with Adam that the wider realm of public discourse provides an important counterweight to the interpretations of particular communities. But Adam does not provide an adequate indication of the terms of that debate. If all criteria are ultimately local, then how is the ethical debate to proceed? Are there not in fact also communities of *ethical* concerns, each with its own presuppositions and criteria? If communities of biblical interpretation are shut off from one another by their local criteria, why should they be open to one another or to secular arguments when it comes to ethics? I take these to be crucial questions, and in my own proposal in chapter 2 I will try to formulate an approach that gives more adequate answers to them than I find in Adam's work.

I also find Adam's solution problematic at another level. To refer only to a debate in the realm of public discourse, while leaving each community to its own criteria at the level of actual textual interpretation, seems to me finally to negate even the minimal role that Adam has assigned to historical criticism. If we take seriously his concession that the study of philology is necessary, do we not have to reckon with at least a minimal set of universal rules that no community's interests has the methodological right to rescind? Is there nothing that biblical interpreters outside a racist community can say, on the basis of New Testament texts themselves, to challenge this community's readings?

It is also important to ask whether granting nearly absolute rights to inter-pretive communities subverts the power of the text to overturn prior concep-tions—that is, to "convert" readers. In the end, we come face to face with the question of whether the interpreter has responsibility not only to a community of interpreters but to the text itself. It is one thing to say that readers participate in the creation of meaning in texts, that they must make use of their own imagina-tions and exercise their own judgments in construing that meaning. It is some-thing else again to speak, without serious qualification, of meaning as something a reader simply *assigns* to a text. While there is much, therefore, that I can affirm in Adam's approach, I will in the next chapter seek to formulate an interpretive theory that in granting creative rights to the interpreter does not deprive the text of its own distinctive voice.

Richard B. Hays: Imaginative Application of New Testament Ethics

Richard Hays has received well-deserved accolades for his volume *The Moral Vision of the New Testament: Community, Cross, New Creation; A Contemporary Introduction to New Testament Ethics*; the book has, in the words of one reviewer quoted on the back cover, "neither peer nor rival." No other work I know of takes the reader so competently or methodically from descriptions of New Testa-ment ethical perspectives to application of these perspectives to contemporary life. Because of its central importance but also because of my disagreements on a number of crucial points, I will be in frequent conversation with it throughout the present work. A detailed description is therefore necessary.

The book is divided into four parts. In the first of these, "The Descriptive Task," Hays examines the diverse moral perspectives of the various segments of the New Testament. In the second, "The Synthetic Task," he raises the question of unity beyond the diversity and finds this neither in specific moral commands nor in universal moral principles or a dogmatic system. He does, however, iden-tify "a single fundamental story" having to do with God's salvation of the world.

The third part, "The Hermeneutical Task," is an evaluation of various modes of appeal to Scripture and several approaches to the interpretive task as well as a statement of the author's own proposal. Finally, in the fourth part, "The Pragmatic Task," Hays considers four "test cases"—concrete ethical issues of contemporary import—in light of the preceding investigation.

In the introduction, Hays states his intention to "explicate in detail the messages of the individual writings in the canon, without prematurely harmonizing them." He also notes that his investigation will entail "attention to the developmental history of moral teaching tradition within the canon." And he emphasizes that his task reaches beyond explicit moral instruction, since a full understanding of the ethical implications of a text necessitates a grasp of the whole "symbolic world" of the community that produced it. By this term he means a way of grasping reality that shows forth not only in explicit teaching "but also in the stories, symbols, social structures, and practices that shape the community's *ethos*" (1996, 3–4; emphasis original).

In his descriptions of these writings in part 1, Hays places the ethical teachings within the wider frameworks provided by each writing as a whole. For example, he grounds Paul's ethics in the apostle's total theological understanding and the ethics of the Gospels in their thematic structures and plots. He does not, however, pursue a comprehensive treatment of the entire New Testament. He seeks to provide "sketches" of the moral perspectives of the texts he deems most important "by virtue of their substance and historic influence." His descriptive section thus consists of chapters on Paul, letters in the later Pauline tradition, the Synoptic Gospels and Acts, the Gospel and letters of John, and Revelation. And he inserts, after his chapters on the Gospels, an excursus entitled "The Role of 'the Historical Jesus' in New Testament Ethics."

In my own treatment of specific New Testament writings later in this text, I will have frequent occasion to refer to Hays's treatments of this material. At present I will confine my discussion of part 1 of his text to his handling of the "historical Jesus" question, which reveals much about his overall perspective. He does not begin his work with Jesus, in part because it is not his intention to "trace the history of early Christian ethics," and he notes that scholarly reconstructions of the Jesus "behind" the canonical texts vary widely and are "beset by subjectivity and cultural bias." While there is disagreement among scholars regarding the interpretation of canonical texts, he notes, the range of possible meanings of these writings "is narrower than the range of possible critical reconstructions of Jesus" (1996, 159–60).

Most important is the way in which Hays appropriates Rudolf Bultmann's famous contention that the preaching of Jesus is not part of New Testament theology but rather its presupposition. "Jesus is, after all," Hays argues,

> not one of the New Testament writers. His life and death constitute the subject matter of the New Testament's narration and reflection, but if the aim of our inquiry is the ethics of the New Testament, the ethical teaching of the historical Jesus will enter the picture only indirectly, as it is filtered through the compositional purposes of the evangelists. (1996, 160)

It is not merely Hays's agenda in his book that lies behind the status he assigns to the historical Jesus, however. For it is clear that he defines his agenda as he does precisely because of his view of the authority of canonical texts:

> The theological function of the New Testament canon is to designate precisely these interpretations of Jesus as authoritative for the continuing life and practice of the community. Therefore, the historian's reimagining of Jesus, however informative and interesting, can never claim the same normative theological status as the four diverse canonical accounts. (1996, 160)

It is clearly the New Testament texts in their final or canonical forms, rather than the "actual" words and deeds of Jesus or any intervening level of oral or written tradition, that Hays regards as authoritative for Christian faith.

Hays does not oppose historical Jesus studies altogether, however. Although historical inquiry cannot prove the Christian witness to Jesus to be true, it could in principle show Jesus to be completely different from the New Testament depictions of him. Hays therefore deems it important to investigate "what can be known historically about Jesus, even if our historical knowledge is subject to serious limitations." And he cites, with apparent approval, Ernst Käsemann's contention that (in Hays's words) "the Jesus of history must ultimately serve as a criterion against which the New Testament's diverse formulations of the kerygma must be measured . . ." (1996, 160, citing Käsemann 1964, 15–47). Presumably, then, historical Jesus studies can serve to assure Christians that the Gospel accounts are not complete distortions of what Jesus actually said and did and can also perhaps offer an outside point of reference when the Gospels disagree with one another. The results of such study, however, do not constitute an independent witness to the fundamental meaning of the Christian faith; and they do not carry the authority of Scripture.

Within the common story that Hays describes in part 2, he identifies "three focal images"—community, cross, and new creation—shared by "all the different canonical tellings" of that story (1996, 193–94). He has chosen these on the basis of three criteria. They have "textual basis in all of the canonical witnesses"; they "highlight central and substantial ethical concerns of the texts" in which they occur; and they do not "stand in serious tension with the ethical teachings or many emphases of any of the New Testament" writings (1996, 195). Hays fleshes out these images in ways that give important previews of how they function on a concrete ethical level in the New Testament and how the contemporary church might appropriate them in wrestling with specific issues:

- Community

  The church is a countercultural community of discipleship, and this community is the primary addressee of God's imperatives. The biblical story focuses on God's design for forming a covenant *people.* Thus, the primary sphere of moral concern is not the character of the individual but the corporate obedience of the church . . . the coherence of the New Testament's ethical mandate will come into focus only when we understand that mandate in ecclesial terms, when we seek God's will not by asking first, "What should *I* do," but "What should *we* do?" (1996, 196–97; emphasis original)

- Cross

  Jesus' death on a cross is the *paradigm for faithfulness to God in this world.* . . . Jesus' death is consistently interpreted in the New Testament as an act of self-giving love, and the community is consistently called to take up the cross and follow in the way that his death defines. (1996, 197; emphasis original)

- New Creation

  The church embodies the power of the resurrection in the midst of a not-yet-redeemed world. . . . In Christ, we know that the powers of the old age are doomed, and the new creation is already appearing. Yet at the same time, all attempts to assert the unqualified presence of the kingdom of God stand under the judgment of the eschatological reservation; not before the time, not yet. (1996, 198; emphasis original)

It is also important to note the two candidates for unifying themes in the New Testament that Hays explicitly rejects—love and liberation. Regarding love, which many Christians would instinctively identify as the bedrock of New Testament ethics, Hays notes that it fails to meet the first criterion. "For a number of the major New Testament writers," he notes, "love is not a central thematic emphasis." In Mark, for example, the command to love God and one's neighbor in 12:28-34 "stands as an isolated element, not supported by other references to love in the story" (1996, 200). And "[n]owhere in Mark's Gospel does Jesus teach or command his disciples to love; discipleship is defined not by love but by taking up the cross and following Jesus." Hays also finds the love theme present only peripherally in Hebrews and Revelation and totally lacking in the Acts of the Apostles: "Nowhere in [Acts] does the word 'love' appear, either as a noun or as a verb." In addition, he argues that love is not an image but "an interpretation of an image" and that "[w]hat the New Testament means by 'love' is embodied concretely in the *cross*." And, finally, he finds that the concept "has become debased in popular discourse . . . having become a cover for all manner of self-indulgence" (1996, 202).

Although the image of liberation, according to Hays, has "a broader base of textual support than does love," it "does not represent a ground for synthesis." For he finds it to be in significant tension with some New Testament witnesses. "Ephesians and the pastoral Epistles," he writes, "would be particularly resistant to a reading through the lens of liberation." And "Matthew also presents a vision of the Christian life that is oriented more toward orderly obedience than to deliverance from oppressive powers" (1996, 203).

Hays does find that the term "liberation" has some advantages. It offers "a more specific image than the term 'love'"; it is "theologically potent because its allusive appeal to the Exodus story is so richly evocative"; and it is "unlikely to fade into a conceptual abstraction, because it points resolutely to social and economic realities." He also sees in it a potential danger, however. Liberation "can easily be understood in a purely immanent sense as a political term, thus losing touch with the New Testament's emphasis on the power of God as the sole ground of hope and freedom." As with love, then, Hays argues that we should understand liberation in conjunction with another image—in this case, new creation (1996, 203).

The specific ways in which Hays applies New Testament ethics to concrete ethical questions in part 4 will be best addressed later. And as for the five "hermeneutical strategies" he discusses in part 3, I see no need to review his treatments in detail but will later make reference to some of his most important judgments as they appear relevant. It is essential at this juncture, however, to give account of his hermeneutical principles, formulated in the chapter with which he concludes that discussion: "How Shall We Use the Texts? Normative Proposals." His decisions at this point are in my estimation largely determinative of the conclusions he reaches on particular issues.

Hays summarizes his approach in ten "Proposed Guidelines for New Testament Ethics" (1996, 309–10). My discussion has already touched on several of these. Hays seeks "to listen to the full range of canonical witnesses" (#2). He acknowledges "substantial tensions within the canon" (#3), but finds unity among the various materials in the three focal images of "community, cross, and new creation" (#4). He also identifies a basic story of God's redemptive action running throughout the Bible and consequently identifies "narrative texts as fundamental resources for normative ethics" (#6).

In addition, Hays argues, study of New Testament ethics presupposes "serious exegesis" (#1), and this means that writings "used in ethical arguments should be understood as fully as possible in their historical and literary context." It also means reading these texts "with careful attention to their Old Testament subtexts." Having earlier identified several different modes in which ethical material occurs in the New Testament, Hays now (#5) offers a formulation regarding the interpreter's task in correlating them. Because of its central importance, I quote it in full:

New Testament texts must be granted authority (or not) in the mode in which they speak (i.e., rule, principle, paradigm, symbolic world).
a. All four modes are valid and necessary.
b. We should not override the witness of the New Testament in one mode by appealing to another mode. (1996, 310)

The force of this guideline becomes clear in an example Hays provides. Reinhold Niebuhr, he argues, engages in an illegitimate "hermeneutical trumping" of a New Testament theme in his classic piece "The Relevance of an Impossible Ideal." Niebuhr does so, specifically, "when he argues that fidelity to the ideal of love exemplified in Jesus sometimes requires us to use violence to seek justice." This would mean that "adherence to Jesus' love ideal requires rejection (in practice) of Jesus' explicit but unrealistic teaching against violence in the Sermon on the Mount." Hays counters forcefully:

A community that has been taught to see the world through Matthew's eyes . . . will sense that something has gone awry here. In fact, Niebuhr's argument is finally a sophisticated dodge of Jesus' call to costly disciple-ship, allowing us to call Jesus "Lord, Lord," without doing what he commands. (1996, 294)

If one mode of ethical presentation (rule, principle, paradigm, or symbolic world) may not overrule another, however, Hays nevertheless grants "hermeneutical primacy" to the overarching story of God's redemptive action and hence to the narrative aspect of Scripture. Here again he illustrates his point by reference to Niebuhr's treatment of the Sermon on the Mount, this time referring to the plot of Matthew that includes the passion narrative.

Anyone who reads Matthew's Gospel all the way to the end . . . will see that nonresistant love of enemies is not an "impossible ideal." It is, rather, a horrifyingly costly human possibility. A hermeneutic that attends to the narrative form of the gospel message will insist that Jesus' disciples are called to follow him in the suffering love of enemies. Thus, the meaning of love as an ideal or principle is specified for us in and through the story. For Christian theology, rules and principles must find their place within the story of God's redemption of the world through Jesus Christ, and the symbolic world of the New Testament finds its coherence only in that story. (1996, 295)

Another of Hays's guidelines is that "[r]ight reading of the New Testament occurs only where the Word is embodied" (#10). Interpretation, in other words, is a function of a Christian community, not an enterprise of individuals heeding their own particular insights. And it is only as such a community seeks to allow the Word to shape its fundamental identity and guide its decisions that it is engaging in faithful interpretation.

It is not the Bible alone, however, that the church has employed in seeking truth; Hays clearly acknowledges the place of tradition, reason, and experience. He is explicit, nevertheless, in granting the Bible a privileged place and asserting that "[e]xtrabiblical sources stand in a hermeneutical relation to the New Testament" and are "not independent, counterbalancing sources of authority" (#7). He sees the New Testament writings as "the original and uniquely authoritative witnesses" and Scripture as "the wellspring of life, the fundamental source for the identity of the church" (1996, 296).

Hays stresses the culturally conditioned nature of the biblical texts but rejects the popular notion that we can separate aspects of the writings that contain "timeless truth" from those that remain bound to an ancient worldview (#8). "Even the most fundamental theological affirmations of the New Testament writers are intelligible," he notes, "only within the framework of first-century Judaism." And as for its ethical norms, their "continuing normativity cannot depend upon their ahistorical character," since "[t]heir roots are in the earth, not the air." We should therefore "value rather than denigrate the particularity of the New Testament texts . . ." (1996, 299–300).

This latter judgment might seem illogical, since one might well conclude that such pervasive cultural conditioning would render the New Testament's ethical norms irrelevant to experience in our contemporary world. For Hays, however, it is rather an indication of the necessity of "an integrative act of the imagination" (#9) that involves the process of making analogies between the world of the New Testament and our own. The very act of understanding, in fact, proceeds in precisely this way:

> To "understand" any text is to discover analogies between its words and our experience, between the world that it renders and the world that we know; thus, the mere act of reading is already a rudimentary exercise of the analogical imagination, even when the world of the text is very close to our own. (1996, 298)

Application of the New Testament's ethical teaching to the life of the contemporary church is therefore not a mechanical process. It is neither the separation of the timeless elements from the culture-bound nor the simplistic attempt to impose every aspect of that teaching on the present. The distance between the ancient world and our own and the variety of thought within the New Testament itself call rather for "a discernment about how our lives, despite their historical dissimilarity to the lives narrated in the New Testament, might fitly answer to that narration and participate in the truth that it tells." The process is therefore one of "*metaphor-making, placing our community's life imaginatively within the world articulated by the texts*" (1996, 298–99; emphasis original).

Acknowledgment of the imaginative aspect of making use of Scripture in normative ethics is one of the many strengths of *The Moral Vision of the New Testament*. It distinguishes Hays from all who seek to apply specific biblical teachings to contemporary issues in a simplistic fashion without regard to the problems created by divergent worldviews and the variety of thought within the New Testament. It is to Hays's credit that he takes seriously the diversity within the canon and the historical gap between the biblical world and our own.

I also view positively Hays's strong endorsement of the necessity of serious exegesis grounded in historical criticism, which protects him from the dangers that attend Adam's "nonmodern" approach. This emphasis serves as an important counterweight against the whims of the faith community. For Hays, the community is the locus of interpretation, but it cannot legitimately make a text say what it clearly does not say. From my perspective, then, Hays presents a model of interpretation and contemporary reflection grounded in Scripture that is more workable than Adam's. There are some aspects of his approach, however, that I find highly problematic. To begin with, it is significant that Hays's acknowledgment of the role of the imagination arises in the section of his book that makes the transition from descriptive exegesis to practical application. The way in which imagination might already be at work in exegesis itself thus remains less explicit. This is not to suggest that Hays denies the open-endedness of biblical texts. It is far from clear, however, that he allows sufficient room for the reader's participation in the actual creation of meaning. Certainly, we find no acknowledgment of competing points of view *within individual writings* parallel to his frequent notation of a variety of perspectives *among the various writings*. If Adam presents a model of interpretation that is in danger of an excessive subjectivity, then, we must ask whether Hays errs in the opposite direction. Might he not be at risk of placing too severe a constraint on the imagination? The problem should become clearer as we pose some specific questions regarding Hays's proposed guidelines for New Testament ethics.

Hays's intention to listen to "the full range of canonical witnesses" (#2) appears from one vantage point an important hedge against a pick-and-choose approach to New Testament ethics. Certainly, the church's long history of sects based on pathological interest in a limited number of passages or themes justifies the concern. A rigid insistence on grounding in the entire scope of the canon involves its own difficulties, however, and one question to raise in that connection is whether guideline #2 means that all New Testament writings are of equal worth. Apparently not, since Hays himself claims to treat the "most important" materials (1996, 13). If not, however, we must reckon with the possibility that a theme present in a small number of very important writings but absent in others might appear compelling enough to claim a central place in an accounting of New Testament ethics and in consideration of contemporary issues. But it is unclear whether this is a point Hays would acknowledge.

We also need to ask, in relation to guideline #2, whether Hays's emphasis on the full range of the canon diverts attention from some important questions. Does it matter whether placing materials in a particular historical situation might shed light on the reasons behind its particular theological and ethical formulations? If, for example, a specific sociological dynamic appears to be at work in the production of a text, should we not take this factor into account when weighing that text's potential normativity in the present? Thus, when Hays cites Colossians and Ephesians to demonstrate the limited representation of the liberation theme in the New Testament, when in fact that theme is so evident in other writings, might one not want to ask about the reasons for its absence in these?

I do not intend to dissent from Hays's guideline #8—"It is impossible to distinguish 'timeless truth' from 'culturally conditioned elements' in the New Testament." I take it as axiomatic that all writings of any sort are culturally conditioned to the core. But it is equally clear to me that some elements in a text can more easily transcend their original contexts than can others. Certainly Jesus' injunction against retaliatory violence (Matt 5:39-40) would seem to have relevance and appeal in a far wider range of cultural contexts than the prohibition in Leviticus against sowing two kinds of seed in the same field (Lev 19:19). Jesus' statement, no less than the Levitical pronouncement, undoubtedly arose against the background of some specific social situation and in response to some specific issues, but it has resonated with persons in radically diverse circumstances throughout the centuries and in that sense transcends its original setting. It therefore becomes important to ask in each individual case about the extent to which a passage or theme in the New Testament remains bound to a specific cultural milieu.

Another potential problem with guideline #2 arises when we consider it in relation to #7: "Extrabiblical sources stand in a hermeneutical relation to the New Testament; they are not independent, counterbalancing sources of authority." The question is whether Hays gives adequate weight to the observable fact of the development of biblical tradition. He is well aware of this development, but his emphasis on the primacy of the canon over tradition, reason, and experience on the one hand and over the precanonical stages of the New Testament materials on the other risks creating the impression of texts untouched by historical contingency. Such an impression is certainly not his intention, given his clear acknowledgment of cultural conditioning. But I must question the investment of such a high degree of authority in the canonical texts, which are in fact the solidification of a complex process that both precedes them and continues after their production. As Roman Catholic thought has long argued against the extreme Protestant formula "Scripture alone," Scripture is itself part of the wider stream of tradition—a point that many contemporary Protestants now recognize. The question is therefore whether it is wise to tie ourselves to the notion that the authority of tradition (along with reason and experience) has no independent standing but can always be overruled by Scripture.

This problem becomes more acute when we consider guideline #5b: "We should not override the witness of the New Testament in one mode by appealing to another mode." Not only does Scripture hold the upper hand against all other potential sources of authority, but the real thrust of this guideline—although it is framed in a neutral way, applying to all modes of signification—is to give rules a kind of immunity over against criticism based on principles. The example given above regarding Niebuhr's stand on the use of violence is by no means a random choice on Hays's part. I do not mean to deny the danger of wholesale rejection of concrete rules on the basis of abstract principles, and the potential for misuse of the love principle in this way is real. But the question is whether the problem is best solved by proclaiming from the outset that a principle must never override a rule. Ethical injunctions on specific issues, I would argue, are among those elements in a text least likely to have great potential for transcending their social and cultural contexts. Thus, in granting them the immunity Hays's view implies, we place severe limitations on the process of imaginative metaphor making Hays himself envisions.

These limitations, moreover, have crucial implications with respect to the issue of power relationships that are so central to the postmodernists' concerns. The more narrowly we confine authority to Scripture over against tradition, reason, and experience, and the less we attend to precanonical materials and countercurrents within the writings, the more we risk allowing mere social-political power to control what is counted as authentically Christian. For if we take seriously the observation that it is the winners who write history, we cannot easily dismiss the charge that many factors other than theological soundness and genuine efficacy in conveying the truth of the gospel were at work in the formation of the canon.

There are two further aspects of Hays's view, beyond his ten guidelines, that we also need to examine with great care. The first is his choice of three images as the unifying threads within the New Testament. I find each of these unexceptionable, but the question is whether in confining himself to these three Hays has not once again set too many constraints on the imaginative process. Had he not insisted so adamantly on the quantitative criterion of across-the-board representation in the New Testament and had he not rejected themes in favor of images, then certainly the very traditional notion of love as central to the Christian ethic might have appeared more credible.

One final question has to do with the other element to which Hays looks for a unifying factor—the story of God's redemptive action. Certainly, this story is central both to the Bible as a whole and to the New Testament. But the interpreter who is sensitive to countercurrents both within individual texts and among the various writings might want to question the notion that the biblical witnesses find their validity solely through their role in that story. One thinks first and foremost of the wisdom tradition. Characterized in part by its sense of a direct apprehension of God through an intuitive mode of thought, it has in itself no inherent relationship to covenantal thought grounded in God's specific actions in history and special relationship to Israel.

At some points, to be sure, wisdom speculation is drawn into covenantal thinking, so that in some writings wisdom is equated with the Torah. At other points, however, one discovers a rather resilient speculative sense only tangentially connected to the biblical drama of God's actions in history. The book of Job, in fact, relates to the traditional story primarily in a critical way, as a head-on challenge to the notion that God rewards the good and punishes the wicked. And if we allow ourselves to take full account of motifs within individual writings in the New Testament that resist the dominant strains of thought, some interesting and provocative counterstrains become evident there as well. Consider, for example, the nature analogies of the Sermon on the Mount: "Look at the birds of the air . . . consider the lilies of the field . . ." (Matt 6:26-28). Hays would insist that we read such passages in the context of Matthew's total narrative, which is very much an expression of the overall story of God's redemptive action. I would agree with that insistence, as long as our agenda is to understand the dominant theological perspective of the Gospel of Matthew. I would argue with equal force, however, that we can also read that narrative with an ear open to less dominant themes—undercurrents of meaning that might take us in rather different directions.

In summary, Hays's book is an important resource that any serious attempt to engage New Testament ethics must take seriously. I value, in particular, its attempt to balance historically grounded exegesis with the exercise of the imagination in making use of the New Testament in contemporary normative ethics. In the end, however, it appears to me to place far too narrow a set of constraints on the imaginative process. Therefore, in formulating my own approach, I will look for another, more open-ended way of conceiving that process without denying the writings of the New Testament their own distinctive voices over against what any interpreter or community might wish to impose on them. I would like, however, to add at this point one additional word of appreciation. I find Hays's characterization of the church as inherently countercultural to be a faithful appropriation of an important aspect of the biblical witness. It is an insight that will inform my own approach, although at some points it will lead me to conclusions rather different from those Hays draws.

Willi Marxsen: A Criterion for the Authentically Christian

Willi Marxsen's *New Testament Foundations for Christian Ethics* provides a stark contrast to Hays's approach. Although the two share a recognition of significant diversity within the canon, Marxsen responds to this phenomenon with a move Hays rejects. He seeks a single vantage point "behind" the canonical texts—that is, in the precanonical tradition—as a criterion for evaluating the diverse perspectives of the various writings. His book is not therefore an "ethics of the New Testament" but the search within the tradition for a "center" that defines what is authentically Christian.

Marxsen's criterion, however, is not the "historical Jesus." Like Hays, he is skeptical about reconstructing an accurate picture of the actual person Jesus, but his alternative is to seek the earliest level of the Jesus tradition found in the Synoptic Gospels. Rejecting the widespread view that Christianity began with Easter (or Pentecost), he argues that the pre-Easter Jesus tradition was already a form of proclamation with Jesus as its subject. In probing behind the written Gospels we can never isolate Jesus himself, "because we always keep coming upon people who in their stories present Jesus they way they understood him." The earliest level of tradition does not disclose a purely objective account of Jesus' words and deeds but rather "images of Jesus" reflecting what others thought of him. "Thus," Marxsen argues, "in our historical quest for Jesus it is always the proclaimed Jesus we find." That is to say, the earliest traditions are in fact christologies, faith statements about Jesus (1993, 39).

Even at this earliest level, however, Marxsen does not find a fully consistent set of images. Since Jesus spoke and acted in many different circumstances, people must have responded to him and understood him in different ways. And, as a result, "at first there was no way for a consistent image of Jesus to come about," and it became necessary to identify a "center"—a self-consistent image that could serve to define what was authentically Christian. The early Christians did this, Marxsen argues, by constructing summaries of what Jesus was all about. And the overall image of Jesus that emerged from this process is what he accepts as the center of Christian tradition (1993, 59–60).

As examples of these summaries, Marxsen discusses Mark 1:14-15, Matthew 11:2-6, and the Synoptic Son of Man sayings (1993, 59–86). Common to them, he contends, is the image of Jesus as both manifesting and calling his followers to "eschatological existence"—that is, existence in the present age lived in light of the age to come. This Jesus appears as one who is shaped by God and who then shapes others. And it is this process of being shaped by God through Jesus that defines Christian ethics, rather than obedience to commands. For in the eschatological mode of existence that Jesus manifests and proclaims, God appears not as lawgiver but as the Father whose desire is to give the *basileia* (God's rule) to people. Thus, for example, for those who follow Jesus, "love of enemies is not something they are ordered to do by commandments and therefore must do. Love of enemies is something they do because they can" (1993, 105–6).

To say that ethics has to do with being shaped by Jesus means that Jesus has diverted attention from deeds to the doer. We must therefore not designate any specific deeds as Christian in themselves, for the Christian quality of the deed depends rather on the person who performs it. Living eschatologically means that those who would follow Jesus never simply *are* Christians. They are rather sinners, living in the old age (as Jesus himself also lived in the old age), who may nevertheless become Christians momentarily and then await the possibility of becoming Christians again in another moment. Faith is thus a matter of continual decision making on the part of those who would be Christians. And this means that "the God of Jesus is not at their disposal": their status as Christians is not a possession (1993, 129).

Nevertheless, Marxsen notes, "they still must act." Therefore, "they need orientation models" (1993, 129). And one can find such models in one's own past—in the occasions in which one momentarily became Christian. But one can also draw on the experiences of others, and it is in this connection that the images of Jesus function. "For the Jesus images that speak of concrete actions express experiences that people had earlier when there was an inbreaking of God's lordship into their lives." These images, however, provide "orientation *models* and nothing more." For to understand the concrete actions of Jesus that we observe in these images as instructions to be obeyed literally would be to "end up with a law" and thus forfeit the immediacy of decision before God that Marxsen associates with eschatological existence. And this would mean allowing the text to replace God (1993, 130–3; emphasis original).

Those who would be Christians, then, must accept ambiguity and realize "that people will make different decisions" and forgo judging one another in the knowledge that all are sinners. They must also accept that attempts at the ethical life inevitably involve conflicts of duties. In such circumstances it becomes necessary to weigh alternative consequences in the knowledge that what is actually right will remain an open question. For, Marxsen says boldly, "God's will cannot be concretely determined" (1993, 133).

In his delineation of the nature of exegesis, Marxsen appears considerably more distanced from postmodernism (and Adam) than is Hays. This is hardly surprising, since he wrote before this school of thought had exerted much influence on biblical studies. While Hays can separate the exegetical and hermeneutical tasks, it is unlikely that he would make the unqualified claim that Marxsen does: "Exegesis is only the restating of an old statement in an understandable way and nothing more" (1993, 12). Despite Marxsen's treatment of the ethical content of the writings in a nonliteral way, he seems to deny altogether the role of the reader/interpreter in the creation of meaning. The interpreter's translation apparently conveys what the text *really* means, albeit in a way that contemporary persons can grasp.

After locating the image of Jesus that will function as the center of Christian tradition and the criterion for what is authentically Christian, Marxsen turns to Paul. The ethic we find in Paul's writings "cannot," he maintains, "be a norm for judging whether an ethic is Christian—at least not directly—because the apostle was already living in the Christian tradition and was not part of its beginning." But Paul is the earliest representative in the New Testament of a christology fundamentally different from that found in the pre-Easter levels of the Synoptic tradition. It is therefore important to ask whether this later christology—grounded in Easter rather than the images of Jesus—"also brings with it a different ethic" (1993, 142). Marxsen concludes however, that Paul's Easter-based ethic bears an essential similarity to the pre-Easter ethic oriented toward Jesus.

Central to Paul's letters is the notion of "imitator." As Paul is an imitator of Christ, so he urges his readers to become imitations of him so that others, in turn, can imitate them. But this does not mean "imitating the behavior seen in a model." For Paul's words are always addressed to "changed people," who are already under the influence of Christ. Once again, as in the image of Jesus, we find the notion of being shaped. As Paul is shaped by Christ, so those whom he addresses will be shaped through him and become shapers of others. Thus, the actions of Christians are ultimately acts of Christ, since the new life is a gift of God through Christ (1993, 190–97).

Here again, we find an ethic that cannot be formulated in terms of concrete demands. Of course, Paul gave instructions on various issues. But, for Marxsen, we misuse these instructions if we generalize them. For the individual problems in the churches were different, and since in the case of several letters to the same church the problems changed (at least in regard to their focus), Paul had to respond in entirely different ways. With his specific ethical instructions he tried to deal with the difficulties that were immediate. Thus we can say that the more concrete the imperative is, the more situational it is and the less suitable it is for presenting and understanding the character of the Pauline ethic. Hence the imperatives in the letters are useless for resolving concrete ethical problems. (1993, 184)

In the final analysis, this means that "for Paul there can be no material Christian ethic; that is, we cannot specify in detail how Christians should live their lives as Christians, so that their actions can be labeled Christian and can be unmistakably distinguished from the actions of other people" (1993, 215).

It is clear, once again, that no deed as such can be labeled Christian; the issue is whether it is performed by a person who has been shaped by Christ. And although love is central to Paul's ethics, the question always remains as to what concrete form it will take. We can say that for those "doers" shaped by Christ "love always means self-renunciation but never self-realization." However, "self-renunciation as such is not necessarily a Christian act," since, as Paul says in 1 Cor 13:3, even giving one's body to be burned is not always motivated by love (1993, 217). But if no specific act can in and of itself be named Christian, what then is Christian ethics for Paul? It is simply "the worship of God in everyday life" (1993, 225), the turning over of the moments of one's life fully to God, so that all of one's actions become God's own. And this is something—as with ethics oriented toward Jesus—that must take place again and again (1993, 225–27).

The remainder of Marxsen's book is devoted to an analysis of "Developments and False Developments" in other New Testament writings. The specific question he poses for each segment of material is whether it retains the connection between christology and ethics found in the early Jesus tradition—that is to say, whether it retains its understanding of eschatological existence.

This understanding is a modification of the standard apocalyptic expectation. Although the framework of apocalyptic thought remains in the sense that a future event is still expected, the date of the expected event now becomes irrelevant. For "people now *always* live in imminent expectation, for the possibility of eschatological existence *always* awaits them." But it is possible to lose this sense of being confronted with the eschatological expectation moment by moment in all of one's life by reverting to the apocalyptic mode of thought in which the focus is on the future rather than the present. And to do this is to sever ethics from christology and hence to fall away from the authentically Christian ethic (1993, 229–30).

I will note only two examples to illustrate Marxsen's application of his criterion, and these very briefly. Later, however, I will have occasion to discuss his treatments of various New Testament writings.

Matthew's ethic, Marxsen maintains, is not authentically Christian; it is, rather, "a relapse into the Pharisaic ethic" (1993, 246). In Matthew, Jesus appears as the teacher of a new righteousness, and a key issue is the precise meaning of the "better" righteousness of 5:20. If we could understand the difference between it and that of the Pharisees as qualitative, this would indicate a "different kind of doing," and that would indicate that "there are *different doers* who perform the deeds" (1993, 238). This would mean that the imperative would be preceded by an indicative that would signal the enablement of the doer. But Marxsen finds no such indicative in Matthew, and he points to passages such as 5:18-19 and 6:14-15 as indications to the contrary. In the former, Matthew's Jesus speaks of the continuing validity of all the details of the law. And in the latter, according to Marxsen, he speaks of God's forgiveness in such a way as to make it "conditional upon the people forgiving their debtors first" (1993, 238–40).

Marxsen also claims that the Sermon on the Mount falls short of a genuine Christian ethic, because he reads it as a set of entrance requirements for the kingdom of heaven, and this means that Matthew's concern is with a salvation that is future rather than present. "For the sake of this future salvation people are to do the new righteousness now" (1993, 245). This does not, in Marxsen's terms, constitute a Christian ethic.

By contrast, the Gospel of John does present such an ethic. The community of disciples, in John, "give form to exactly what Jesus lived," and "without Jesus the disciples can do nothing" (15:5). Just as they "do as Jesus has done to them" (13:15), so Jesus himself "can do nothing on his own" but "only what he sees the Father doing" (5:19). We have, then, a circular movement showing that "ethics and Christology are identical in John" (1993, 290). This is clear also in the way John uses the term "love" not as "an exclusively ethical term" but to indicate a mutual relationship. "The Father loves the Son, and the Son loves the Father. The Son loves his disciples, and the disciples love the Son" (1993, 287–88).

The authenticity of John's ethic is also apparent in John's transformation of futuristic eschatology into a realized eschatology:

In the "church" of his time eschatology had again become a "doctrine of the last things." Parousia, resurrection, and judgment were expected in the future. . . . John has Jesus announce what is expected as already present for the faithful, and he realizes that he is in contradiction with the widespread belief of his time. (1993, 292)

The great value in Marxsen's approach to New Testament ethics is his treatment of the early Jesus tradition as an independent testimony, apart from the final versions of the canonical writings. This appeal to an external point of reference is one way of dispelling the notion that all canonical writings are of equal worth. It also gives voice to perspectives that might have been excluded during the more formal stages of the canonization process and thus has potential for speaking to the problem of power imbalances during that process.

Marxsen's view also has advantages over against the appeal to the historical Jesus. On the one hand, it avoids some of the difficulty involved in determining the actual words and deeds of Jesus with a high degree of certainty. On the other, it avoids the problem of making something completely outside the faith tradition—a set of mere historical facts—the criterion for authentic Christianity. For it is essential to Marxsen's view that the early tradition to which he looks is already a proclamation of faith. It is thus in principle of the same order as the canonical materials themselves.

In fact, there is a sense in which the early tradition is actually canonical. For an accurate accounting of the development of the canon will stress that the finalization of the list of authoritative writings was only the culmination of a long process that began at the oral stage. The act of passing on stories of what Jesus said and did was already a process of selection for use in the proclamation. And the same is true of the later stages of collecting these materials in both oral and written forms. Granted that the shift to written forms and the selection of whole writings as authoritative were important moments, we should understand the process primarily in terms of continuity rather than momentous changes.

While I approve in general terms of this aspect of Marxsen's view, however, there are several points at which I must register dissent. First, I am not convinced that it is either necessary or helpful to make the early tradition as he defines it into an absolute norm. I will explain my position more fully in chapter 2, but the basic point is that if we accept canonization as process, then no one moment should have absolute hegemony over others. It is important, however, to have a counterweight outside the finalized canonical writings, and I would agree that we should pay close attention to the earliest level.

My second point of dissent is that I would direct this attention to the very earliest traditions—despite the diversity Marxsen finds at that level—rather than to the second level, at which the various images of Jesus are pressed into a single mold through what Marxsen calls summaries. In doing this, we will move even farther away from any hint of power relationships determining the content of the faith. By attending to the earliest traditions we seek to hear an even wider range of voices.

There are other problems also with Marxsen's view, not the least of which issues from his designation of the exegetical task as "scientific." If this term means only that it is important to seek a degree of objectivity in interpretation through the use of the historical-critical method, I can applaud him for maintaining a principle that Adam is in danger of forfeiting. As I suggested above, however, he seems in fact to treat meaning as residing simplistically in a text rather than something that arises in the interaction of text and interpreter. And this is one point at which I think we need to take the postmodernist insight seriously.

Marxsen's understanding of exegesis becomes doubly problematic when one examines closely his actual attempts at restating the meaning of text. When, for example, he describes Jesus' view of eschatological existence in a way that deemphasizes the actual futurity of the expected event, it is clear that he is drawing heavily on his teacher Bultmann's existentialist approach to New Testament interpretation. That approach, in brief, is to strip away the supernatural or mythological elements in the New Testament message, which are characteristic of an ancient worldview, in order to identify its true intention. And that intention, according to Bultmann, is to express a human self-understanding that is not bound to that worldview but is applicable to life in any time and place. Thus, the real meaning of the proclamation of a future end of the age, for example, is not that God will in fact one day supernaturally bring human history to a conclusion with the literal return of Jesus as judge. It is rather that all human beings stand in every moment of decision before a God who confronts them with both grace and demand (see, for example, Bultmann 1958 and 1984).

It is not that I object to Bultmann's program or even to Marxsen's use of existentialist categories in describing Jesus' view of eschatological existence. I would agree that these categories put one in touch with important aspects of New Testament texts. It is something else again, however, to claim that this "translation" captures the true intention of the original. For the clear implication is that this terminology, and only this terminology (at least in our present situation), conveys what the texts *actually* mean. My own alternative will be to seek a way of understanding such an interpretation as one means among others of interacting with the texts in order for a new articulation of meaning to emerge but without falling into Adam's trap of regarding interpretation as simply *making* meaning.

Although existentialist interpretation is in touch with some aspects of New Testament texts, it filters out others. In particular, as many critics have noted, it tends toward an individualistic and abstract understanding of the human possibility that the New Testament offers. That is to say, it tends to ignore the concrete dimensions of that possibility that are defined by the social environment. The earliest Jesus tradition, for example, appears in a rather different light when viewed against the background of the Roman occupation of Jewish Palestine and the economic structure of that society than it does when described in purely existentialist terms.

One final problem with Marxsen's approach is that it reflects a long-standing tendency in Protestant biblical scholarship to draw a sharp dichotomy between the message of Jesus and the teachings of his Jewish contemporaries to produce something of a caricature of the latter. While scholarship in this mold is generally complimentary when describing the Hebrew Bible and early Israelite religion, it tends to view Judaism in the time of Jesus as a degeneration into a legalism that in effect denies the grace of God. Marxsen makes an effort to distance himself from the uglier aspects of this view with the claim that he is merely describing different patterns, not making value judgments. His dichotomizing view nevertheless tends toward a serious mischaracterization of Judaism of the New Testament period and an unhelpful distancing of the Jesus of the early tradition from his own heritage.

Elisabeth Schüssler Fiorenza: The Emancipatory Jesus Movement, the Bible as Historical Prototype, and the Community of Women-Church

Elisabeth Schüssler Fiorenza's feminist interpretation, although not focused directly on biblical ethics, is highly relevant to our present search for an adequate guide for dealing with that subject. Her project is similar to Marxsen's in three respects. She rejects the view that simply accepts the canonical texts as normative; she looks behind these texts to a prior history of tradition as a counterweight; and she rejects the historical Jesus, as reconstructed by scholarship, as that counterweight. It is not, however, Marxsen's compendium of early summaries that plays this role for her. Her alternative is to focus on the concrete praxis of the Jesus movement—the early communities of his followers.

The Jesus movement, however, does not function as an absolute norm for Schüssler Fiorenza as the early Jesus material does for Marxsen. Nor does any level of the biblical tradition, since she is critical of the canon-within-a-canon approach, which she identifies with neo-orthodox theology (1984, 12–13). For her, the final arbiter of what is authentically Christian is the contemporary community of faith that she terms "women-church"—a community of women and men dedicated to the emancipation of women and opposition to all forms of oppression. The tradition remains an important resource for that community in its deliberations, although it stands in need of critical evaluation at all levels.

Schüssler Fiorenza criticizes the various quests for the historical Jesus for their inappropriate claims to objectivity. And to this extent her views parallel those of postmodernists. The most recent wave of Jesus studies, she says, promotes a kind of

> scientific fundamentalism, since it generally does not acknowledge that historians must select, reject, and interpret archaeological artifacts and textual evidence and simultaneously incorporate them into a scientific model and framework of meaning. (1994, 87)

She also finds that some versions of the quest reinforce Christian anti-Judaism by understanding Jesus in opposition to the Judaism of his time. And, she argues, the insistence on a scientifically objective reconstruction of Jesus as "the heroic individual" enshrines "the historical 'fact' of Jesus' 'maleness' as an objectified historical-theological given that is constitutive for the faith and identity of Christians in general." She therefore rejects any approach that "abstracts Jesus as a historical artifact from the movement of his followers and separates him from his historical-religious context." Because she believes that such an approach can never achieve certainty, she focuses on the Jesus movement, rather than on Jesus himself: "who Jesus was and what he did can be glimpsed only in the interpretation and memory" of those who formed the communities that followed him (1994, 87–90).

This movement, Schüssler Fiorenza contends, was a "Jewish emancipatory movement of wo/men" that "must be understood as one among several prophetic movements of Jewish wo/men who struggled for the liberation of Israel" (1994,

88, 92). One must therefore not understand it as outside the boundaries of Judaism or set it apart from similar Jewish movements as superior.

Central to this movement was the symbol *basileia tou theou*. Although this phrase has traditionally been translated as "kingdom of God," scholarly discourse in more recent times has generally rendered the term *basileia* as "kingly rule or reign," because when used in relation to God it signifies the act of ruling rather than territory. Schüssler Fiorenza objects to this rendering, however, because it fosters what she terms a "kyriarchal" meaning—that is, an exclusive focus on the authority of a lord (*kyrios*), an inherently patriarchal concept. Such a narrow focus misses the political overtones of the use of this symbol, "which were apparent in a context in which people thought of the Roman empire when they heard the word *basileia*" (1994, 92). She therefore suggests the term "commonweal" as a more adequate translation. And she argues that "Jesus and his first followers, men and women, sought the well-being of Israel," God's people, and proclaimed God's "*basileia*/commonweal/empire" explicitly "as an alternative to that of Rome" (1994, 93).

To say that the phrase *basileia tou theou* is a symbol (Schüssler Fiorenza names it specifically a "tensive" symbol) is to contrast it with a one-dimensional concept. The point is that it draws on a wealth of ancestral lore to appeal to the human imagination—more specifically, "to the oppositional imagination of people victimized by an imperial system." And the use of this symbol by the Jesus communities speaks eloquently of the life they fostered within their fellowship:

> [The phrase *basileia tou theou*] envisioned an alternative world free of hunger, poverty, and domination. This "envisioned" world was already present in the inclusive table community, in healing and liberating practices, and in the domination-free kinship community of the Jesus movement, which found many followers among the poor, the despised, the ill and possessed, the outcast, the prostitutes, and the "sinners"—women and men. (1994, 93)

Schüssler Fiorenza also believes that the figure of personified, female Divine Wisdom (Sophia) was central to the self-understanding of the Jesus communities. Those in the movement thought of Jesus as a prophet of Sophia commissioned to proclaim that Israel's God, interpreted through the image of Divine Wisdom, was God "of the poor, the outcasts, and all those suffering from injustice." And in his prophetic role Jesus stood in a long line of prophets, including John the Baptist, who "were persecuted and killed as the emissaries of Divine Wisdom"

(1994, 140, 142). This understanding of Jesus' role, moreover, emanated from the experiences of the ordinary people in Galilean villages: "Jesus, who like many of these Galilean wo/men had no place to go and had to sustain himself on what was offered to him, was remembered as one of the prophets who was sent by Divine Sophia, who was executed, and who was proclaimed as the Living One by Galilean women" (1994, 147).

First Corinthians 1–4, Schüssler Fiorenza argues, confirms the specific role of women in the development of the understanding of Jesus in relation to Sophia. For here we find clear indication that women functioned as prophets and leaders who identified the risen Christ with both the Spirit of God and Divine Wisdom (1994, 149). Contrary to what some scholars have argued, wisdom speculation was not completely dominated by elite males and did in some instances reflect the empowerment of women (1994, 133–39). And the communities of the Jesus movement apparently stood within such a tradition.

There is a clear parallel between the role of the Jesus movement in Schüssler Fiorenza's approach and the early tradition in Marxsen's. As stated above, however, the Jesus movement does not for her constitute an absolute norm, for it was not free from aspects that are problematic from the perspective of our contemporary concerns. It

> must not be construed as free of conflict and kyriarchal tendencies. From its very beginning, differences and conflicts existed, as the diverse if not contradictory theological articulations of the movement indicate. *In Memory of Her*, for instance, discusses the *basileia* sayings tradition (Mark 10:42-45 and 9:33-37 par.) as an antipatriarchal tradition that contrasts the political structures of domination with those required among the disciples. . . . While this tradition advocates nonkyriarchal relationship in the discipleship of equals, its imperative form simultaneously documents that such relationships were not lived by everyone. The would-be "great" and "first" seem to have been tempted to reassert kyriarchal social and religious status. (1994, 94, citing 1983, 148)

All levels of the biblical witness are therefore subject to critical evaluation by the contemporary community seeking to embody such a discipleship of equals. And it is important to understand precisely how the Bible can function within such a community if it neither is nor contains an absolute norm. The key to Schüssler Fiorenza's position lies in her distinction between the Bible as "mythical archetype" on the one hand and "historical prototype" on the other. She explains the former term in this way:

> As mythical archetype the Bible can be either accepted or rejected, but not critically evaluated. A mythical archetype takes historically limited experiences and texts and posits them as universals, which then become authoritative and normative for all times and cultures. For instance, many scriptural texts speak of God as a male, patriarchal, all-powerful ruler. Therefore, it is argued, feminists have to accept the patriarchal male language and God of the Bible, or they have to reject the Bible and leave behind biblical religion. (1984, 10)

A historical prototype, by contrast, is "open to feminist theological transformation" (1984, 10). It is a "formative root model of biblical faith and life" upon which the contemporary women-church can draw, but it is not the final authority for this community. A "feminist critical hermeneutics" derives its canon "*not* from the biblical writings, but from the contemporary struggle of women against racism, sexism, and poverty as oppressive systems of patriarchy and from its systematic explorations in feminist theory." In its ongoing struggle against oppression, the community's "vision of liberation and salvation is informed by the biblical prototype but is not derived from it." Biblical texts therefore stand "under the authority of feminist experience insofar as it maintains that revelation is ongoing and takes place 'for the sake of our salvation.'" Rather than "identification with certain biblical texts and traditions," Schüssler Fiorenza seeks "solidarity with women in biblical religion." And the task of the "church of women" is "not to reproduce biblical structures and tradition but to remember and transform our biblical heritage" (1984, 14).

Apparently, then, for the Bible to function as prototype means that the community honors it as a generative moment in an ongoing process of continual transformation. It provides a fund from which the community can draw without being bound absolutely to any aspect of it or any historical level of the tradition it incorporates. And just as predecessor Christian communities continually reshaped tradition in light of their own experiences, so now the church that stands opposed to oppressive structures in the world must exercise its critical powers of discernment to produce new transformations. The prototype is a generative force that empowers but is also subject to criticism in the light of contemporary experience.

Schüssler Fiorenza's emphasis on the authority of the contemporary community and her denial of the possibility of full objectivity in biblical scholarship parallel emphases in postmodernism. It is therefore not surprising that A. K. M. Adam's evaluation of her project is largely positive. Adam is distressed, however, that "she insists on the necessity of historical criticism as the basis for the feminist critical hermeneutics she advocates." He thus finds a serious limitation in her attempt at a "feminist critical reformation of biblical scholarship" and concludes that she still operates within "the conditions established by modernity" (1995, 128–29). From my own perspective, however, her desire to retain an important role for historical criticism, even as she understands its limitations, is a strong point in her favor.

Hays is critical of Schüssler Fiorenza on numerous points, most notably her investment of final authority in the contemporary women-church. To him this signals an outright abandonment of the symbolic world of the Bible:

> The historical and cultural distance between the world of the New Testament and our world looms large in Schüssler Fiorenza's work. Consequently, though her historical exegesis seeks to make the symbolic world of the New Testament intelligible, she does not seek to establish that symbolic world as the normative context for ethical reflection. In fact, it might be suggested that her hermeneutic works the other way around: she seeks to show how the historical data can be reinterpreted in terms of categories drawn from the symbolic world of modern social science and political ideology. Her theological anthropology is resolutely modern, conceiving of human beings as autonomous persons whose greatest fulfillment is to be found in freely choosing and deciding their own destinies. She does not even attempt to ground this view in the New Testament; it is simply assumed as a self-evident truth. (1996, 278)

I have quoted this entire paragraph from Hays because it illustrates a problem that I will try to overcome as I formulate my own approach in chapter 2. It does, in my estimation, point to a genuine problem in Schüssler Fiorenza's point of view, similar to the one I find in Adam. If the final authority lies purely and simply within a given community of faith, then the tradition seems to be ultimately at the mercy of the whims of this group. While one might agree with that community's ideology and even find that it reflects aspects of the biblical tradition, it is inadequate for the community to appeal only to itself—its experience and its commitments—for legitimation. For if one community can appeal to its experience and commitments, another community with completely contradictory ideals can do the same. Here again, as in Adam's case, we have to ask whether Schüssler Fiorenza's view subverts the power of the text to challenge the readers' preconceptions.

On the other hand, Hays's statement seems to presuppose that the symbolic worlds of the New Testament writings are beyond criticism. But such an assumption is highly problematic, given what we know about the historical conditioning that lies behind any understanding of reality. What we need, then, is a way to encourage the transformation of tradition in light of contemporary experience without making the biblical perspective subservient to a preconceived point of view. Schüssler Fiorenza lays the groundwork for such a method in her very helpful notion of the Bible as historical prototype, which grants it an important status in the community's deliberations. From my perspective, however, this insight needs qualification through a stronger affirmation of the "rights" of the tradition over against the freedom of interpreters. But I can affirm her contention that the tradition must nevertheless remain subject to criticism and transformation. As I will argue later, the process of transformation is a necessary and unavoidable component of tradition.

There is of course one sense in which contemporary interpreters—whether we think in terms of individuals or communities—must hold sway over any other authority. For it is finally their prerogative to decide whether they wish to remain within a given faith tradition. The question with which we are concerned, however, is whether they can legitimately claim a connection to that tradition if their judgments are no longer somehow responsible to it rather than simply to their own perceptions.

Marxsen's attempt to identify a center amid the variety of early New Testament witnesses, combined with his substitution of "orientation models" for concrete ethical pronouncements, is one way of trying to get beyond the problem I identified above. There is a center of tradition for him in a way that there is not for Schüssler Fiorenza, but all Christians must draw on their own experience in determining how to honor that tradition in any given set of circumstances. If, however, one is convinced, as is Schüssler Fiorenza, that no level of tradition is free from flaws—and it is hard to avoid this conclusion if we accept Hays's premise that all aspects of the biblical tradition are culturally conditioned—then Marxsen's solution becomes questionable. There is in my estimation strength in both these positions, and here again I will try in chapter 2 to formulate an approach that avoids the pitfalls of both.

On some points, however, I find Schüssler Fiorenza's position clearly preferable to Marxsen's. Her focus on the Jesus movement avoids the individualism inherent in Marxsen's existentialist language and opens the way to a discussion of the sociopolitical context of the early witness. Also, by placing that movement squarely within its Jewish context and stressing its continuity with other prophetic movements, she avoids anti-Jewish implications. Yet she retains some of the advantages of Marxsen's position, since the Jesus movement—although it is not an absolute authority—provides another source of understanding the early Christian witness alongside the formalized canon.

Brian K. Blount: An African American Perspective on New Testament Ethics

As the title of his book indicates, Brian Blount explicitly chooses African American experience as the standpoint for his reading of biblical texts: *Then the Whisper Put on Flesh: New Testament Ethics in an African American Context*. His justification for approaching the issue from a predetermined perspective clearly indicates an affinity with the postmodern consciousness. Using the term "space" to indicate a particular location or setting in the world, he justifies the interpreter's use of a given space as "a communal and/or personal lens" through which to grasp the New Testament's moral reasoning.

Blount is well aware that this endorsement of the use of such a lens means that he cannot claim "that there is some objective ethics we can uncover absent the influence of the space we inhabit." In a way closely parallel to Iser's reading theory, he understands the meaning of a text as emerging from the process of interpretation, not as residing simplistically in the text itself:

> It is in the interchange between that space, the Jesus event, and the text that New Testament ethics will *develop*. It is not found; it evolves as a result of an active, dialogical interaction. Our (communal and/or personal) reading lens interacts with the text's shaping (Jesus event) lens in such a way that the text becomes meaningful *for us*. (2001, 19–20; emphasis original)

Sensitive to the issues raised by such a stance, however, Blount adds an important qualification of his endorsement of the prerogatives of the reader or community of readers. Focusing on objections that might be raised against accepting the readings of African American slaves, whose experiences he takes as his starting point, he acknowledges the potential problem: "One could very easily . . . dismiss a slave's unlettered, untrained ethical appropriation of the New Testament as a negatively biased reading that has no merit beyond that particular slave's individual or communal experience." He then proceeds to defend this practice, not simply by an appeal to a community's entitlement to its own perspective but by a refinement of his statement on how reader and text interact:

> If . . . one could show that the New Testament has a vast meaning potential that includes emphases toward social and political concerns, then the case could be made that, because of their unique social and political circumstance, African American slaves were uniquely outfitted to interact with that part of the meaning picture that other communities, because of their space implications (limitations), could not. . . . It could well be . . . that one community has seen something that has eluded another. (2001, 20)

Although meaning arises in the interaction between text and reader, the text itself defines and limits the parameters of meaning. The meaning potential, in other words, is not infinite. The reader's "space" provides an angle of vision from which aspects of that meaning potential can come to light, but it does not simply *impose* a meaning that has no textual warrant. This qualification would seem to set Blount's understanding of the interpretive process apart from Adam's, and it also implies that historical criticism plays a more important role for him than it does for Adam. For the process of validating a given meaning potential of a text, apart from a given community's reading, falls to the standard tools of such an approach.

It is central to Blount's thesis that African American slaves were generally illiterate and "lived in a contextually sensitive oral culture." They therefore created their own "text," in oral form, from what they heard from the King James Version of the Bible. As Blount quotes from Delores Williams:

> They composed this oral text by extracting from the Bible or adding to biblical content those phrases, stories, biblical personalities and moral prescriptions relevant to the character of the life situation and pertinent to the aspirations of the slave community. (Williams 1993, 188; quoted in Blount 2001, 23–24)

Blount elaborates this point by stressing the compositional process that was at work in the production of this oral text.

Fusing biblical material with their own life situation and concerns, their space, they composed a biblical witness that was uniquely their own and spoke to their uniquely tragic circumstances. In other words, they contextually constructed *their* biblical story. . . . It is no wonder that the "Bible" they ended up "reading" and the "Christ" whom they ended up worshiping and serving were neither the same Bible nor the same Christ proclaimed to them by white slave owners and missionaries. They were a Bible and a Christ borne out of and uniquely responsive to the context into which the slaves were condemned. And since that enslaved space differed so radically from the enslaving space enjoyed by their captors, it is not surprising that what they might have called New Testament ethics also looked and sounded radically different. (2001, 24; emphasis original)

Drawing largely on the work of several scholars on the slave narratives from 1703 to the twentieth century, Blount identifies liberation as a unifying theme throughout three distinct periods, each marked with its own specific concerns. Liberation was, he observes, "the lens that slaves and ex-slaves used to bring focus and clarity to their thoughts about their world" (2001, 28). And he notes three ways in which this emphasis is played out in the narratives. First, in contrast to the wider Southern culture, "the narratives suggest a kind of equanimity between men's and women's roles," although the freedom from patriarchy was far from absolute (2001, 29).

Second, the narratives exhibited a strong tendency toward syncretism. Specifically, "[t]he slaves felt themselves free to merge religious realities from many different West African spiritualities with their understanding of the Christian God." Of particular importance was the West African notion of a high God over all creation who had specific concerns for justice and the plight of the weak. "This traditional belief," Blount observes,

would have had dramatic liberation implications for the African slaves. How could a God who cared about their individual welfare approve of their corporate enslavement? How could such a God be preoccupied with the matter of saving individual souls when the physical bodies that housed those souls were so systematically abused? Such a God could not; the God the slaves brought with them and syncretistically introduced to the Christian God of their master could not. *This* God would have presided over a particular kind of ethics. The "ethical" follower of such a God could not focus exclusively on personal, spiritual salvation. (2001, 30; emphasis original)

Blount's third point follows logically:

in this newly fashioned, syncretized belief, faith and politics were always considered together. . . . It was for this reason that a longing for spiritual liberation and heavenly redemption connected so integrally with the hope for social and political salvation from the clutches of historical slavery. (2001, 30–31)

Not surprisingly, the West African high God's concern for the oppressed dovetailed with the exodus account in the Hebrew Bible, which then became a focal point through which the slaves were empowered to "reconfigure their own reality." They thus appropriated ancient Israel's story as their own: "Moses became *their* liberator too."
And this appropriation

provided the backdrop to the most dramatic reconfiguration of all. Jesus, God's son, was seen not on his own New Testament terms alone, but through the liberating lens of the exodus. We are not just talking spiritual liberation any more. . . . Jesus, all of a sudden, means freedom—social and political freedom. (2001, 31–32)

This interpretation of Jesus in light of the exodus by no means muted the New Testament emphasis on redemption through Jesus' suffering and death, however. It meant that in the slaves' religious consciousness Jesus became "an even closer companion to the slave because Jesus suffered as the slave suffers; Jesus can understand the pain, the tragedy, the hopelessness, the sorrow, and most important, the hope." Not only that, but Jesus' death and resurrection, "while continuing to signal human liberation from sin, take on the added significance of breaking the authority of the principalities and powers who preside over the institution of slavery" (2001, 33).
If the slaves related easily to the story of Jesus, the letters in the Pauline corpus were another matter. Both the slaves and their descendants "looked upon the apostle to the Gentiles with an uneasy sense of skepticism and even outright hostility." And this attitude marks an important aspect of their implicit hermeneutical principles: they maintained the right to a critical appropriation of the

tradition that included the prerogative of rejecting some aspects of it. "This does not mean," Blount comments, "that the New Testament text lost its sense of authority for the slaves." It does mean, however, "that their perception of God in their midst is *more* authoritative" (2001, 33–34).

According to Blount's analysis, the slaves' freedom in interpreting the Scriptures was ironically the result of the way in which the slave owners presented the Bible to them. Because they had no written texts, they experienced a high degree of latitude in how they understood them. "The slaves did not so much read the story as participate orally with it." Therefore, "when the imagery in the story contrasted with experience, a critique was raised" (2001, 34).

The net result of the slaves' freedom of interpretation was a "reconfigured ethics." Conducting their own services of worship and prayer, in defiance of legal prohibitions, they developed "a culture of resistance shored up by a completely reconfigured understanding of ethics." And "they mated their space with their faith in such a creative, defiant way that the biblical ethics they hatched was completely contrary to the biblical ethics they were taught." Their understanding of sin, for example, was broadened from "breaking one's relationship to God" to include "the breaking of relationship with fellow sufferers of oppression" (2001, 40).

They also developed a "code of silence" designed "to protect others who had committed acts the owner or overseer considered unethical." And their reconfigured moral sense could condone such acts as lying, deceit, and stealing in their relationships with whites. "It was wrong to 'steal' something from another slave; it was, however, not only appropriate but also moral to 'take' from an owner." Sheer need was of course a major justification for this development, but Blount argues that the most basic rationale "came from their understanding of a God who could not tolerate the indignity of their oppression and who approved of whatever actions were necessary to survive it, even if human law and ethics understood such behavior to be immoral" (2001, 40–41).

Blount also notes that sometimes the slaves justified violence against their oppressors. And, even here, they found justification in their understanding of the scriptural tradition: "It was the biblical mandate of exodus coupled with the story of Jesus' life, death, and resurrection that not only prompted the violence but sanctioned it as well. Ethics, in this case, has been totally reconfigured. Space mattered *that* much" (2001, 41–42).

Having delineated the lens through which African American slaves and ex-slaves appropriated the Bible that the slave holders conveyed to them in oral fashion, Blount proceeds to an analysis of the various segments of the New Testament that employ this lens. He uses it to uncover a "kingdom ethics" in the Synoptic Gospels, a "christology of active resistance" in the Gospel of John, and a "witness of active resistance" in Revelation. He also finds in Paul a "theology enabling liberating ethics" but he acknowledges that the slaves did not generally understand Paul in such a positive light. Blount himself, moreover, finds it necessary to add important qualifications to his appreciative evaluation, in particular on the issues of slavery, the status and role of women, and homosexuality. It is of particular interest, from my own perspective, that Blount attributes the complexity of his evaluation to "the fact that [Paul's] ethics are enabled by his theology, and his theology is also not monolithic" (2001, 150). I take the latter part of this statement as a recognition of the presence of multiple strands of meaning within any given segment of the biblical canon.

In his concluding chapter, Blount notes a change in his own perspective that the process of writing his book effected. His original intention was to examine biblical texts relevant to concrete ethical issues and then to suggest "the proper ways in which Christians should behave." In the end, however, he concluded that to attempt "such universally normative ethical directives for living would contradict everything for which" his book eventually "came to stand." Now, he says, he is "less interested . . . in arguing for or against the most biblically appropriate way of governing ourselves ethically on any particular issue." He is in fact "more and more interested in provoking a discussion of New Testament ethics from the many different cultural perspectives that characterize contemporary Christians" (2001, 185–86).

The conclusion Blount draws is similar to that of Marxsen in that he does not find it possible to derive universal concrete directives from the New Testament. Whereas Marxsen bases his view on the ethical perspective of the early Jesus traditions, Blount's insight issues from his understanding of the nature of interpretation. His particular sensitivity to the role of culture in shaping the interpreter's perspective also reflects his affinities with postmodernism. And his emphasis on the "place" of the interpreters links him with both Adam and Schüssler Fiorenza.

It would seem relevant, then, to ask of Blount the same question I asked earlier of both Adam and Schüssler Fiorenza—whether the interpretive community is in fact to hold absolute sway over the tradition. I find Blount considerably more nuanced on this issue than Adam, however. In formulating his understanding of the role of perspective or place in the interpretive process, he clearly distances himself from Adam by couching that role in terms of providing a perspective for uncovering elements that are apparently objectively present in the texts. As we have seen, the interpreter apparently does not simply "ascribe" meaning, and Blount's actual treatment of the New Testament writings bears this out. On the other hand, the question of limits on the creativity of interpreters such as those represented in the slave narratives remains unresolved. Granted that we should not simply dismiss these interpreters out of hand, is there any sense in which we can say that at some points they might in fact be violating texts, however understandable their motives might be?

It is not that I find Blount objectionable on this point, but that I think his approach could profit from further methodological clarification. If his interest is more in a conversation among various perspectives on New Testament ethics based on differences in place than on identifying universal norms, then it is fair to ask him as well as Adam about the terms of this conversation. Granted that attention to the slave narratives can sensitize the interpreter to the liberative content of the New Testament, how do we proceed when confronted with the claims of slave owners who approached the texts from a perspective defined by their own place, or even the claims of nonracist readers whose experience tends to limit them to the other-worldly aspects of the writings? Blount's balanced statement on the way in which meaning arises from interaction with a text is a good beginning; but his insight needs elaboration.

These questions aside, Blount's bold use of the slave narratives sheds new light on some important aspects of the hermeneutical discussion. If we accept the postmodern insight that all attempts to state the meaning of a text are selective, then we must also recognize that there is a sense in which all interpreters or communities of interpreters create their own texts. And if this is so, then it is not so huge a leap to take seriously the oral texts created by groups such as African American slaves as genuine biblical interpretation.

The oral "texts" remind us that behind the entire written biblical tradition lies a long process of oral tradition. More importantly, they remind us that oral tradition does not disappear with the advent of written texts. There is therefore a strong sense in which the experiences on which the slaves drew were not simply external to the biblical tradition; they were to some extent engendered by the continuing oral telling of the biblical story. And this insight should caution us against playing tradition, reason, and experience off against Scripture when we attend to the question of authority. In some instances, at least, we are speaking of sources of understanding that are deeply rooted in a consciousness that is already informed by a Christian perspective.

Attention to the syncretism involved in the slaves' use of their native tradition, such as that of the West African high god, should also sensitize us in another way. It should remind us of the degree to which syncretism was in fact at work in the biblical tradition itself from the very beginning. And if we take this insight seriously, the distinctions between biblical and nonbiblical tradition between what is authentically Christian and what is not begin to look less absolute.

Daniel Harrington and James Keenan: *The New Testament and Virtue Ethics*

The last among our potential guides is a joint venture by a New Testament scholar (Harrington) and a moral theologian (Keenan): *Jesus and Virtue Ethics: Building Bridges between New Testament Studies and Moral Theology*. Their contention is that the category of virtue ethics is peculiarly well suited both to the nature of the New Testament texts and to the challenge of relating these two fields, which, they lament, have shown a surprising lack of mutual contact.

Virtue ethics concentrates on the building of human character rather than on the actions themselves. We can thus note a point of similarity between this approach and that of Marxsen, who found the notion of the believer's being shaped by Christ to be fundamental to New Testament ethics. In both cases, the emphasis is on the doer rather than the deed. Harrington and Keenan, however, draw on the rich tradition of Roman Catholic moral theology to flesh this notion out, whereas Marxsen's frame of reference is an existentialist perspective inherited from Bultmann. And this difference is by no means insignificant. For Marxsen's contention that one must become Christian, over and over again in every new moment, stands in marked tension with the classical notion of shaping a character from which concrete actions flow.

On another note, Harrington and Keenan do not, as far as I can see, join Marxsen in a complete denial of the possibility of a material Christian ethic. But their focus on virtue rather than specific deeds distinguishes their approach from that of Hays in subtle but important ways. Notable is their reaction to Hays's proposal of the three images of community, cross, and new creation as the basis for synthesizing the moral aspects of the various New Testament materials. Referring to these images as "master lenses," they make the following comments:

> But Hays, unlike the feminists and liberationists, ignores the social location of the one using these master lenses. It is as if any of us could look at the texts through these lenses and see the same thing in the same way for the same end. But since Aristotle, we have recognized that the ability to

recognize the good depends on the ability of the agent—the one looking. Whatever we see depends upon our own ability to see.

Hays's three lenses have three virtues correlative to them: reconciliation, mercy, and hope. And these virtues, because they engage the very person of the one who is reading scripture, serve to guide us more accurately in our biblical evaluations and syntheses. The community we envision is a reconciled one that in Christ reconciles us to God and one another through Christ. The cross is always for us a symbol of God's mercy and the eternal willingness of God to be merciful; that is, to enter into the chaos of another. By the cross, we are called to be merciful as God is merciful. The new creation is that for which we are a community of hope. Thus not only should we be attentive to the lenses through which we read the texts, but more importantly we must recognize that insofar as reconciliation, mercy, and hope constitute us as disciples, to that extent we will grasp the meanings of scripture. (2002, 29–30)

This statement is not a denial of the validity of Hays's three images as lenses through which we can approach the New Testament writings, but a reminder that they do not automatically insure a right understanding. For if these images point beyond themselves to virtues, and readers truly understand the text only to the extent that they themselves become engaged by these virtues, the process of interpretation remains on the surface level unless such an engagement takes place.

In all fairness, it is doubtful that Hays would object to the way in which Harrington and Keenan expand on the significance of his three images. The missing element in his account, however, is a sufficient recognition that it is after all the reader who must discover and to some extent shape their significance. And if we do recognize this point, then it would appear that the most important element in the hermeneutical process is in fact the fundamental claim that the images make on the being of the reader, not its demand for specific action.

As the quotation cited above reveals, the approach of Keenan and Harrington has important points of contact not only with Marxsen but also with feminist and liberationist perspectives. Their emphasis on the importance of the reader's perspective opens up the way for a discussion of "politics from a marginal perspective," for example. Also, their concentration on the category of virtue allows them to restore, against Hays, the centrality of love in New Testament ethics, treating it as the primary virtue. *Jesus and Virtue Ethics*, in my estimation, provides an important corrective to approaches to New Testament ethics that are focused too narrowly on deeds rather than on the virtue of the doer.

CHAPTER 2

making meaning in the mists of babylon

—◉—

TOWARD A MODEL FOR INTERPRETATION:
PARAMETERS AND PRINCIPLES

Interpretation is never a simple matter. But the "mists of Babylon"—the aspects of contemporary culture that set it so severely apart from the New Testament world—render the church's task of deriving relevant meaning from its inherited texts particularly complex. It is therefore necessary to explain in some detail the model of interpretation I am proposing, drawing on my evaluations of the approaches discussed in chapter 1. I begin by restating in summary fashion the set of *parameters* within which an adequate method must operate as it takes full account of these nine factors:

1. the diversity of thought among the various canonical writings;
2. the various strands of meaning within any given writing or corpus of writings;
3. the wide stream of tradition, both oral and written, that precedes, parallels, and follows the composition of these writings and their designation as canonical;
4. the ongoing character of all tradition—that is, its inherently processive, developmental character;
5. the open-ended character of texts, demanding the participation of the reader in the actual creation of meaning;
6. the limitations that the linguistic structures of texts place on the interpretive enterprise, so that not just any reading is necessarily valid;

7. the fact that all writings are conditioned by the social contexts in which they arise;

8. the equally important fact that some aspects of the tradition transcend their original settings more easily than do others;

9. the role that power imbalances have played in the production, selection, and interpretation of texts.

In order to meet the requirements of these parameters, I propose the following eleven *principles.* They will receive considerable elaboration as I try to show how the interpretation theory I propose will incorporate them.

1. All levels of the canonical tradition have some claim to validity, not simply the final versions of the texts.

2. The earliest level of the Jesus tradition—understood as disparate and as reflecting an entire movement and not just an individual—has a special, although not absolutely normative, status.

3. Both the writings of the New Testament and the traditions that precede, parallel, and follow them must be interpreted in light of the Israelite traditions out of which they grew.

4. The New Testament canon holds a special, but not absolute, position within the broad stream of tradition. The distinction between Scripture and tradition is therefore a relative one, as is the distinction between officially sanctioned tradition and those elements ignored or branded heretical at any given point in history.

5. Themes that are pervasive, rather than peripheral, in the New Testament have a presumptive special status; but this does not mean that they must always take precedence over countercurrents of meaning.

6. The historical-critical method is an indispensable means of determining basic parameters of meaning potential in a text. This does not mean that other approaches are illegitimate, only that they are subject to the basic determinations of this mode of investigation in areas such as philology and social context.

7. There is much in a text that stands outside the provenance of historical-critical study. Some aspects of literary criticism, for example, offer important avenues for interpretation.

8. It is not only legitimate but necessary to approach a text from some particular point of view—in other words, to bring to it certain questions

and presuppositions. Such interest is the tool for transforming potential meaning into actual meaning.

9. The method with which we approach the writings must be truly interactive; that is, it must recognize the rights of both the text and the interpreter. We must allow each to challenge the other.

10. Respecting the text means that we must find some means of evaluating various readings that go beyond "local criteria"; and if this entails public discussion, we must stipulate the terms of this discussion.

11. Respecting the rights of the reader means recognizing that meaning arises only when someone orders the potentialities of a text in some particular way that is always informed by interests.

OUTLINE OF A HERMENEUTIC FOR NEW TESTAMENT ETHICS

With the preceding parameters and principles in the background, I will now propose a theory of interpretation suited to help contemporary Christian readers and communities of readers engage the ethical teaching in the New Testament writings. The components of this theory are a perspective on the nature of language, involving both the imprecision of language and its systematic thrust toward understanding, and a perspective on the nature of tradition and interpretation. These components are expressions of an alternative postmodernism from which we may approach the biblical texts.

A Perspective on the Nature of Language

The most fundamental question we can ask when reflecting on the question of what it means to interpret any text—including a biblical text—is how language actually operates. That is, what is happening when one person speaks or writes and another hears or reads and understands? How, in other words, does understanding take place?

The specific hermeneutic that I propose is based on insights from Alfred North Whitehead's "philosophy of organism," most particularly his theory of language. This understanding of language is an important aspect of Whitehead's whole cosmology, which rests on the intuition that all reality is at base both processive, or dynamic, and relational. The use I will make of it in the present context, however, does not necessitate an acceptance of that larger framework of thought, for his analysis of language is able to stand on its own. This is so, however, precisely because Whitehead's insight about the dynamic and relational character of reality is consonant with the experience of many people in the late modern and postmodern eras. But the appropriate question for the readers of this chapter to ask is not whether they accept Whitehead's entire system of thought—which I will not, in any case, seek to describe—but whether the specific aspects I invoke illumine their experience of the phenomena of hearing or reading and understanding.

The central insight of this understanding of language is that it has a dual nature. On the one hand, all linguistic formulations are necessarily fragmentary and open-ended. They are inherently imprecise, making necessary an act of interpretation in which the recipient of a signification construes it in a particular way and places it in a particular context for a particular reason. On the other hand, all such formulations necessarily contain a systematic thrust, a drive toward a comprehensive understanding. Both of these points stand in need of considerable elaboration and justification.

The Imprecision of Language

It may at first seem extreme, even to someone who acknowledges that texts are subject to a variety of valid readings, to say that *language itself is fragmentary and open-ended* (Whitehead 1933, 291–93). Certainly, we can make very simple statements that seem definite and precise. Whitehead's most fundamental point regarding language, however, is that the impression of definiteness is ultimately illusory, since all language involves a degree of abstraction that is so subtle as to generally escape notice (1938, 48, 54–55). To apply a name to an object, for example, entails the process of abstracting some of its aspects out of the web of complex relationships in which it exists. And to emphasize some aspects is to ignore or play down others (Lundeen 1972, 29; Pregeant 1978, 36; Farmer 1997, 94–99).

We can best illustrate the point by focusing on the smallest unit of signification within a language system—the individual word. Let us imagine that one person enters a room and sees another person, sitting behind a desk, who points to an object in the corner and says, "Bring the chair over here." The reference of the term "chair" seems definite and concrete, and the person entering the room will presumably know what is meant. But if there is more than one empty chair in the room, the act of pointing is essential to the definiteness that is achieved.

And even if there is only one empty chair, the meaning of the sentence depends on that fact. It is therefore neither language itself nor the inherently precise meaning of the term "chair" that creates precision but language in combination with various nonlinguistic factors (Lundeen 1972, 48, 71, 103; Pregeant 1978, 37).

And if this chair is made up of several parts, when I treat this conglomerate as a single object, I do so only because of convention: I live in a culture in which "chairs" have a known function, and I speak a language that has a word for objects that fulfill that function. Thus, once I realize that it is the human mind that creates the notion of "chair" out of a conglomeration of objects, my decision to treat that conglomeration as one object appears somewhat arbitrary. But it is also arbitrary to isolate the chair from the other objects in the room and, indeed, from the room itself. To an insect crawling on the rug, the chair is no more a discrete entity than a hill is really a discrete object in a landscape. Of course, it is necessary, in ordinary communication, to delineate "objects" such as "chairs" and "hills," yet it is a mistake to ignore the degree of abstraction in the designations we take to be concrete. For what we actually do when we speak of a "chair" is to abstract certain elements out of a very complex set of experiences and ignore others.

Now, if even the simplest language involves some degree of abstraction, it follows that *persons who use language are constantly engaged in a process of valuation* (Lundeen 1972, 71, 103–4, citing Whitehead 1958, 13; Pregeant 1978, 37–38). The choice to treat a "chair" as a chair and not as a pile of firewood is a choice to value what is before me in one particular way. And, to go one step further, *language is also participatory:* it necessarily entails the demand to engage the subject matter of an utterance on a deeper level than that of bare information. For value judgments do not flow automatically from recognition of fact. They are rooted in a person's subjective experience of the world—the way a person "feels" her or his environment. Even at the level of perception itself (Whitehead 1933, 232), we grasp the world around us in terms of our own subjective immediacy. And on the level of language, we can understand others only to the extent that we in some measure share a world of feeling with them. I cannot communicate the horror of murder to someone who does not "feel" the value of human life. Nor could I understand the meaning of an invitation to sit in a chair apart from a degree of participatory knowledge, since even the concept "chair" depends on my pre-intellectual, value-laden experience of what a chair is.

In summary, language is necessarily imprecise, fragmentary, and participatory. *Its open-ended quality makes meaning dependent in part on the hearer in a particular situation,* which is fraught with nonlinguistic factors, as well as on the way it is specifically configured in spoken or written form. And what is true on the level of an individual word or sentence is multiplied exponentially when small units of signification come together to form larger blocks. If a single sentence remains imprecise, how much more so a discourse, a poem, a novel, a parable, a gospel, or a letter.

The Systematic Thrust of Language

If, for Whitehead, language is imprecise and fragmentary, it nevertheless contains *a drive toward systematic, comprehensive understanding within the total world of experience.* Thus, "every proposition refers to a universe exhibiting some general systematic metaphysical character" (1978, 11). This point is considerably more difficult to illustrate concretely than is the fragmentary character of language, but I think we can understand this claim in the following way.

All cultures exist within the larger world of human experience. Although each culture has its own worldview, and competing worldviews can differ radically, each must in some way take account of that larger world. There is great leeway in the ways persons or groups can interpret experience, but experience for Whitehead is not merely a function of language or perception. The world outside the person or the group delivers data, and the data have resilience over against the worldview of the culture. Thus, *the intelligibility of language depends not only on a world of meaning created by a culture but also on the larger world of human experience in general, which in turn exists within the universe itself.*

Ultimately, then, for a statement to be intelligible it has to make sense within these broader contexts. Of course, we do not have direct access to these larger contexts as such. We have only our own experience, not "human experience"; and we have only fragmentary experience of the universe as a whole. For Whitehead, however, language rests on some level of universal human awareness of the broader contexts; and the desire to communicate meaningfully presupposes the intelligibility of the world in which we live. Although language cannot convey reality in an unadulterated fashion, it pushes toward systematic, comprehensive, universal understanding. It is always doomed to failure because of its fragmentary character and the limitations of our own experience, but we miss an important aspect of its nature if we do not recognize the metaphysical thrust it also contains.

If, then, we must take into account the impreciseness of language, we must also recognize its drive toward systematic and comprehensive understanding. And one test of an adequate hermeneutic will be the extent to which it is able to respond to both these characteristics.

A Perspective on the Nature of Tradition and Interpretation

The preceding account of the nature of language has important implications regarding the nature of tradition. To say that language is valuational and participatory is to offer an explanation of what takes place when tradition undergoes changes as it moves through time and geographical space. New circumstances bring new needs and perceptions, and modifications of prior tradition are responses to these new realities. What Whitehead's perspective adds to this analysis is to ground this insight in the very nature of signification itself. A new circumstance does not create the need for a change in something that is theoretically self-contained and stable. *It is in the very nature of tradition that persons and groups receive it only in terms of their own subjective immediacy.* The drive toward modification is built into the process. Every single appropriation of an element of tradition is always a reappropriation, a revaluation. And this is true even when the same person considers one particular element a number of times. Like language itself, tradition is a participatory venture.

This reappropriation, moreover, is always a matter of a kind of "negotiation" between the world of a person or group on the one hand and the world of the received tradition on the other. It is helpful in this connection to apply the concept of a "contrast," drawn from Whitehead's metaphysical system, to the phenomenon of tradition (Whitehead 1978, 228; Farmer 1997, 115). When something new emerges, it draws together disparate causal elements from its relevant past into a higher unity. Because some aspects of those realities remain incompatible with one another, the new reality must "select" some and leave others aside. The richness and value of this new reality, however, depends in part on its ability to hold together a wide variety of different elements. Hence the term "contrast."

If we understand the traditioning process in terms of this model of a "contrast," we can gain some insight into what actually takes place when modifications occur. Every social situation brings with it a complex of factors that make it distinctive, and every individual's experience functions similarly. We have already seen that the subjective immediacy of a person or group affects the way in which a given linguistic formulation will be grasped. What the notion of contrast adds to this is an account of the role played by tensions among the various strands of tradition and between the world of the received tradition and that of the recipients.

Here, then, is a way of comprehending the traditioning process. A tradition, perhaps containing numerous elements held together in tension, enters a community or the life of an individual. It brings with it certain presuppositions, elements of a worldview that belonged to its prior context. Inevitably, however, the new context entails different presuppositions, which are elements in a world-view that is also different. Hence the "negotiation," which takes place largely on an unconscious level. The recipients find their own worldview challenged by the presuppositions of the tradition, but they also allow their own worldview to challenge and modify the presuppositions that underlie the tradition. They thus "negotiate" a new version of what is received, creatively transforming it by blending it with elements from their own prior understanding. And this often means revaluing or reordering the tensive strands within it.

To say that the traditioning process entails a creative transformation of received materials, however, is not to say that all such transformations are of equal value. On the one hand, it is possible for an individual or community to become so tightly bound to the past as to stifle the creativity of the process. The result in such a case will be that the tradition remains relevant only to a sectarian group severely cut off from the wider culture. Communities of this nature can rightly claim counterculture status, and they achieve a high degree of internal solidarity by branding the larger culture totally corrupt. But the question is whether they do so by denying features of the broader world of experience they share with the larger community and therefore sacrificing intelligibility in the outside world. If so, they risk requiring their members to bifurcate their very lives, living in two worlds on the basis of two sets of incompatible presuppositions at the same time. Or, alternatively, they cut themselves off from the world at large so severely that they move beyond counterculture to fanatical sect.

The irony, however, is that no matter how dedicated a group is to maintaining the patterns of the past, it is fighting a losing battle; for we are never able to repeat the past entirely. Even the most committed forms of fundamentalism remain hybrids—negotiated settlements between the world of the past and the world of the present. The self-conscious biblical literalism of Christian groups in our own era rests on a rationalistic base, focused squarely on assent to doctrine, that is simply not characteristic of the faith of the earliest followers of Jesus, the Gospels, or the authentic letters of Paul.

It is possible, on the other hand, for an individual or community to distort a tradition beyond all recognition by simply shaping it to fit an ideology born of its own contemporary situation. When this happens, the tradition loses its prophetic status—its ability to challenge the values of the culture in which it finds itself. Among the more notorious examples of such distortion is the phenomenon of *Deutschechristentum*, "German Christianity," the movement that proclaimed Hitler as "God's man of the hour."

We must not, however, allow our disapproval of a movement such as this to obscure the possibility that there might be times in which contemporary experience could legitimately call some aspects of tradition into question. That is to say, we should be prepared to acknowledge that there might be values that seem on the basis of our experience to be worthy of embrace but are simply not supported, and are perhaps even contradicted, by the tradition. Any such cases, of course, will force the honest person either to admit the inadequacy of the tradition on some particular issue or to reexamine the perceived value.

Both the stifling of the creativity of tradition by refusal to allow its development and the distortion of tradition through the imposition of alien values upon it can result from an imbalance in power among adherents. That is to say, when one group within a community gains undue power over the process, many factors other than genuine meaningfulness and salutary effect can enter in. In such a case, both the potential of the tradition and the needs of the present become subordinate to specific agendas that serve the interests of a limited group, whether it is a minority or a majority. Thus, what would ideally serve to challenge, enlighten, and empower members of the community becomes a means of dominating and disempowering some while serving the narrow interests of those in control.

From a theological perspective, the ultimate issue is not whether a particular development in a tradition reflects the views of the membership but whether it represents an authentic response to the Spirit. Since we have no access to the mind of God apart from the various human claims to discernment, however, the stifling of any segment of a community without fair hearing is a potential stifling of the Spirit. Nor does an uncritical acceptance of the canon solve the problem, since the definition of canon is itself necessarily a human enterprise.

It is clear, then, that the traditioning process is subject to various types of corruption, a fact that gives rise to the continual need for reformation. If such reformation is not to be one-sided, however, it must find a way to honor both the needs of the present and the integrity of the tradition itself. If the Christian community should not allow the formulations of the past to obliterate contemporary insight, neither should it allow the worldview of the present to completely change the nature of what the past has delivered to us if it wants to lay legitimate claim to its heritage. However, the subtle pitfall in trying to honor the past is that it is notoriously difficult to separate that heritage from the ways in which powerful groups within the community have been able to manipulate the process of interpretation.

In order to be true to the tradition, then, those who seek to interpret it for the present must be continually in search of a "center" in that tradition, a core that resists transformations that would render it completely unrecognizable. Because of the ongoing nature of human experience and the problem of power imbalances, however, it is self-defeating to try to define that center, once-for-all, as a stable essence that will hold valid for all time. On the one hand, new angles of vision will inevitably bring new insights; what appears "essential" from one perspective may appear peripheral from another. On the other hand, new perspectives will often uncover power relationships unnoticed by earlier generations. In the end, then, we must recognize that the process cannot be simply mechanical. There is no conceivable way to avoid the risk entailed in a process of discernment. Neither counting passages that support one view over the other nor identifying one aspect of canon or tradition that retains absolute veto power over all the rest can save us from the inherent subjectivity of bringing the world of the past into conversation with the present.

This does not mean that the process is futile. For we still have both the actual formulations of the past and the insights of contemporary experience, to which we can hold all attempted solutions accountable. And in this respect religious tradition is no different from other dimensions of our lives together. In no case can we resolve our conflicting judgments in these spheres mechanically; yet we do not therefore cease to enter into serious discussion about them.

If we narrow our focus from the broad category of tradition to biblical interpretation, two points need emphasis. First, *the biblical writings are themselves a part of ongoing tradition.* As noted previously, tradition precedes, parallels, and follows them. They grow out of prior tradition, feed future tradition, and stand both in continuity and discontinuity with tradition, which continues on its way beside them. Chronological analysis of the various writings also reveals the process of tradition at work in the way in which later writings draw on and modify earlier ones. Matthew and Luke, for example, draw both on Mark and on the pre-Gospel source we designate as Q. The letters many scholars designate as Deuteropauline, produced by a later generation of Paul's followers, draw on Paul's own letters, transforming his thought in both subtle and blatant ways. In addition, we can observe in the later writings a strong tendency toward the definition of a definite body of doctrine, which is not evident at earlier stages. The canonical writings, then, are very much a part of tradition and share its general characteristics. So it is highly misleading to split them off from the broader stream and treat them as an entirely different category. Scripture and tradition belong together as facets of the same general phenomenon.

The second point is that *interpretation of texts is itself a part of tradition.* Both the later Gospel writers and those who wrote in Paul's name after his time were interpreting, and thereby transforming, what he had written. And what applies to ancient interpreters applies also to those in our era. This is self-evidently true of biblical interpretation carried out explicitly in the service of the church, but is it true of interpretation that self-consciously seeks to avoid value judgments in favor of pure historical reconstruction of events or meaning? To begin with, we may point out that a totally value-free interpretation is impossible. More important in the present context, however, is the fact that many seemingly neutral aspects of "purely historical" research find their way into the life of the church. Consciously or unconsciously, all who pursue biblical interpretation offer potential contributions to the ongoing tradition.

An Alternative Postmodernism

As indicated in chapter 1, the model of interpretation I am developing has strong affinities with the school of postmodernism I discussed primarily in relation to the work of A. K. M. Adam. Both models recognize that language is inherently subject to a variety of interpretations, because meaning arises from the interaction of text and interpreter rather than from the text itself in isolation. Both, moreover, recognize the role of power relationships in establishing standard interpretations that silence the readings of the less powerful. At two significant points, however, my perspective differs significantly from this type of postmodernism, a fact that leads me to adopt David Griffin's (1989) designation *constructive postmodernism* for the perspective that informs my method.

The first way in which the approach I am suggesting differs from what we might call "deconstructive" postmodernism is the place I make for the systematic thrust of language—the recognition that all language presupposes a systematic universe. The difference, however, is far from absolute. To be sure, deconstructive postmodernism denies the ability of human thought or language to puzzle out the nature of reality, since any attempt to do so remains radically limited by the perspective of any thinker or community and distorted by an imbalance in power relationships. This does not mean the total rejection of all metaphysical thought, however, but a recognition that all arguments for a systematic understanding of reality are "deconstructed" by counterarguments, with the result that neither perspective can command full credibility in itself. It may be that human beings necessarily construct worldviews, but the problem is that all such constructions are ultimately negated by competing perspectives, so that they can never claim anything other than local and limited loyalties. Thus, metaphysical and antimetaphysical interpretations of reality coexist in a kind of tensive symbiosis. There is therefore a real sense, however limited, in which the deconstructive postmodernist can affirm the metaphysical enterprise.

The other side of the matter is that a Whiteheadian approach to metaphysical thought also carries with it a self-limitation. Fully committed to an understanding of reality as processive and dynamic, Whitehead insisted that his own system of thought remained open to revision. It can have only a provisional character. Nevertheless, the difference between the two schools, although relative, is real and important. The emphasis in deconstructive postmodernism is on the way in which competing strains of thought subvert one another, leaving those who seek to make ultimate sense of things caught in the paradox of the tensions between them. For Whitehead, however, it remains important to propose systematic understandings of reality and to test them out against experience, even in the knowledge that they inevitably remain incomplete and subject to revision.

The implications for biblical hermeneutics are significant. A typical deconstructive interpretation of a text ends with a demonstration of how that text collapses in on itself, that is, how one strain of meaning subverts another. An approach employing a Whiteheadian "contrast," however, entails the invitation to try to embrace the disparate strands of meaning within a higher unity, even though the "negotiated" meaning will remain provisional. Honoring the systematic character of language as well as its fragmentary nature, interpreters working with this model will try to work out the systematic implications of each strain of meaning as the basis for proposing an intelligible way of bringing aspects of each into a new understanding. That is, they will propose a reconstruction of meaning beyond the deconstructive moment. I will elaborate on this point in the section that follows.

The second way in which a constructive postmodernist approach will differ from that of deconstructive postmodernism has to do with some important aspects of Whitehead's epistemology. For Whitehead, although there is a strong subjective element in all perception, it is nevertheless grounded in our experience of an actual world. Sense data come to us from an "external" environment, and perception consists in relating these data to a prior, nonsensuous awareness that we have of our own bodies and internal experience. The fact that I process the data on the basis of my own nonsensuous awareness means that my perception will always be value laden and subjective, never merely an objective and mechanical appropriation of "what is out there." The original data I receive, however, do in fact stand in a causal relationship to my eventual perception. When any event in the world gives rise to another, successive event, it delivers something of itself over to what is new. The present, in other words, contains something of the past within itself. Thus, when sense data enter my experience they convey something actual from the world "outside." Although there is a strong sense in which I "create" that world through interpretation, I do not create it out of nothing. If I see a train coming down the track about to collide with my automobile, I am guilty of genuine misperception if I interpret the approaching object as a cuddly puppy. And the immediate future will in fact make the point for me, whether I recognize it or not.

When we apply this insight to the phenomenon of language, we may say that it does not operate—as some recent schools of thought would claim—within a closed world of signification in which signs refer only back and forth to one another, not to an external world at all. And the first implication this has for biblical hermeneutics is that texts are capable of reflecting events in the actual world of the past. This does not mean that all biblical claims regarding actual historical events are true, but only that texts have the capacity to convey information from the world of actualities.

The second implication is that if data we receive convey an actual world outside our own experience, then texts not only open up potential meaning but also impose certain limitations on legitimate interpretation. Wholly apart from its reference to an actual world in the past, a text delivers to us the data that constitute its own internal "world" of potential meaning. For the actual written entity—with its use of specific words, grammatical constructions, and the like—consists of a definite, specific configuration of signifiers. This configuration may be viewed from innumerable angles based in a variety of human experiences, but any angle of vision, any interpretive scheme, remains bound to take serious account of what it actually says and does not say in the process of deriving meaning from it. We do in a sense create the meaning, but we do not create it out of nothing. Thus, as Leander Keck observes, "because we are as contingent and biased by our preoccupations as the writers, editors, and canonizers, what we owe the text is willingness to listen and learn by trying to see what *they* saw before telling the text what we would have said had its writers been as wise and moral as we are" (1996, 6).

Rejecting both an objectivism that imagines meaning to reside in a text itself and a subjectivism that gives sovereignty to an interpreter or community of interpreters, then, I am arguing for an approach that treats the text as "subject."[1] By this I mean an entity possessing its own integrity in the form of voices to which the interpreter is obligated to attend—an entity that constitutes one pole in a process of "negotiation" from which meaning emerges.

APPROACHING BIBLICAL TEXTS

We are ready now to think more explicitly about how the proposed model of biblical interpretation will work out in practice. I suggest that we recognize five components in the process of interpreting a text:

1. using the historical-critical method in order to establish a baseline of meaning determined by philology and attention to broad historical context;
2. reading the text as a whole in order to determine the basic patterns of meaning potential it contains;
3. attending to ambiguities, gaps in meaning, the presence of undercurrents and countercurrents of meaning, and other aspects of the text that might disclose a wider range of potential meaning;
4. tracing out, as far as feasible, the logical implications of various competing strands of meaning that might appear under analysis and testing them against the background of human experience in general;
5. proposing a way of relating various strands of meaning that does the greatest justice to the range of meaning potentials; that is, offering a specific way of shaping these potentials into actual meaning, which is to say, a "reconstruction" of meaning in which the interpreter's worldview and that of the text are brought together in genuine interaction.

The final three components will not apply to every text, because in many cases the inevitable ambiguities will be relatively insignificant for any particular investigation. It is nevertheless important to give a fuller account of each at this point.

1. Employing the Historical-Critical Method

In making a prominent place for the historical-critical method, I do not mean to suggest that no one can gain legitimate meaning from a text apart from the use of a technical apparatus. As even Adam admits, however, philology is necessary simply to determine the range of meanings a word can legitimately have. And at least a minimal sense of the broad historical context is important in determining how the original readers of a text would have understood a given linguistic signification. In some cases, specific historical events form the background of a given scriptural passage. One thinks immediately of the role the Roman destruction of the Jerusalem temple in 70 C.E. plays in the Gospels. In other cases, social codes provide the relevant background. If, for example, we were unaware of the patriarchal structure of ancient societies, we would miss much of the significance of materials relating to women. Or if we were unaware of the ways in which various literary genres and rhetorical devices functioned in a given ancient environment, we might seriously misunderstand the way in which a given writing might strike the original readers.

This is not to say that the meaning the original readers or the author would have assigned to a text defines the text's meaning for all time. I have already argued for the open-endedness of meaning and the role of the reader in creating meaning. The point is rather that the broad outlines of original meaning form a kind of baseline for later interpretation. If we know, for example, that the parable of the Good Samaritan presupposes the bitter hatred between Judeans and Samaritans, then the disruptive effect of the parable's device of making the Samaritan the hero of the story needs to figure into any later reading of the story if we are not to ignore the significant contours of its meaning potential. Certainly, there is much one can gain from the parable without this knowledge, but in such a case something important has been lost.

2. Determining the Basic Patterns of Meaning Potential

Beyond the specific contributions of the historical-critical method, we must read the text in the light of its genre and specific linguistic configuration. Historical issues are still in the background here, but the interpreter must read the text as a reader seeking meaning; and this is a task that knowledge of the ancient world simply cannot supply in an exhaustive way. A degree of personal interest becomes necessary in order to glimpse the possible emotional tones a text might be capable of evoking. Thus, the interpreter's task is closely akin to that of a literary critic reading a work of contemporary literature. When interpreting one of the Gospels, we need to take account of plot, themes, and characters. In reading a letter of Paul, we must pay attention to the apparent intentions of the various modes of address he uses—argumentation, rebuke, comfort, exhortation, and the like.

3. Attending to Signs of Wider Meaning Potential

Recognizing the open-endedness and fragmentary character of language, it is essential to pay close attention to the various ways in which any particular set of significations, whether on the level of an individual sentence or a writing as a whole, might legitimately evoke a variety of responses. In some cases, this might simply mean that we can imagine a range of specific meanings, different but in no way incompatible, that one might derive from a linguistic configuration. In other cases, however, we might discover a number of perspectives, claims, or lines of logic that appear in tension or even incompatible with one another. And we will almost certainly find ambiguities and gaps, whether in the plot of a story or in a letter's argumentation, that encourage the reader to make a decision as to how to construct meaning. Sometimes, of course, knowledge of the ancient world can suggest the most likely way an original reader would carry out the task. But that will not be true in all instances, and in any case it is not self-evident that it is the contemporary interpreter's task to make the same decision. If the ambiguity is real, then the text has in fact issued an invitation to the reader to play a role in the making of meaning.

4. Tracing Out Ultimate Implications

In cases in which we find competing strains of meaning, we should be prepared to follow through the implications of each competing strain as far as thought allows us. If, for example, we are confronted with two conflicting images of God, we will need to ask about the ultimate implications of embracing either. To some extent, this process will involve comparison with other biblical materials—that is, asking which image is most securely grounded in the broader range of scriptural witness. Ultimately, however, we will have to move beyond the world of Scripture into the wider world of human experience and thought in general. We will need to be attentive to both the moral and the logical consequences of each and to ask the question of relative adequacy.

5. Proposing a "Reconstruction" of Meaning

If we do find competing strains of meaning in a text, and if we are in fact able to trace out their respective implications in a satisfying way, the remaining task is to propose a way of ordering the disparate materials that does the greatest possible justice to each. Presupposed in such a move, however, is the belief that all strains contain some meaning potential that we deem worth saving. We should also be open to the possibility that we will find some strands so completely out of tune with either the overall thrust of biblical thought or the constraints of contemporary knowledge and experience that we cannot honor them on any level.

And it is important to make this point in order to avoid the rather poignant criticism that some have directed against the entire hermeneutical enterprise—that it always saves the text at all costs. That is to say, it offers a way of affirming any text, no matter how reprehensible it might appear from a particular perspective, thus depriving the interpreter of the right of rejection. Aside from this possibility, however, it is legitimate for the interpreter within a faith community to approach scriptural texts with the general expectation that they will be able to speak meaningfully to believers in the contemporary world. And the model of the Whiteheadian contrast, which I elaborated above, is designed to find that potential for salutary meaning even in the face of problematic aspects.

In the end, the interpreter's task is to bring the world of the text into a genuinely two-way conversation with the world of the present. By this I mean a conversation in which each world is allowed to challenge the presuppositions of the other and in which the interpreter seeks a higher unity on the basis of which to transform the disparate elements into a coherent whole that speaks meaningfully to a contemporary faith community.

As I proceed through the individual New Testament materials in part 2 and part 3, I will give explicit attention only to steps 1–3. Here the emphasis will be on identifying the main contours of potential meaning as well as undercurrents and tensions. The final two steps, of tracing out the ultimate implications of various strands of meaning and of reconstructing meaning in dialogue with our own worldview, will be the subjects of part 4.

PARTICULAR EXPERIENCE AND SHARED EXPERIENCE: THE STATUS OF READING PROPOSALS

The final two elements in the approach outlined above will presumably appear problematic to proponents of deconstructive postmodernism and others who emphasize the role of the particularity of one's situation in the interpretive process. For attempts to speak from a universally human perspective have been notoriously guilty of imposing the perceptions and values of one culture on the entire human race. It is therefore important to clarify how I envision this process of tracing out implications. My intention is not to deny the ultimately "local" character of any attempt at general characterization of human experience. I grant from the outset that the way I will try to trace out the implications of any given signification and evaluate it in terms of its universal adequacy is very much a product of my own particular life situation. So let me at this point offer a brief indication of that situation.

I am a white, middle-class, native-born North American—of mixed European extraction—who grew up in a small town in the deep South. I was heir to white privilege but born in a family of relatively limited financial means and thus aware of the reality of economic injustice from an early age. My worldview has been shaped by my lifelong membership and active participation (as well as ordination) in the United Methodist Church, eventual and dramatic "conscientization" through major cultural upheavals, beginning with the civil rights and peace movements, formal education, and contact with persons of diverse backgrounds, interests, and commitments. For better or for worse, my reading of the writings of the New Testament will reflect these influences—even if some aspects of them now function primarily as reminders of values I have come to reject.

My situation, however, is not my destiny. Unless those who read the New Testament from "local" perspectives are willing to risk attempts to speak in broader terms, there is no way to communicate with those representing other perspectives. If someone reading from another perspective thinks that my readings are far too limited by my background, it is of scant value to a conversation if the only response is to negate these readings with other, equally insular, interpretations. The way beyond the impasse is rather for all parties to submit their proposals for meaning to a wider set of criteria—even as we understand that the criteria themselves are part of what stands in need of negotiation! Here again, the process cannot be mechanical, because we have no given criteria to start with; but that is not to say that it is fruitless.

The key to such a meaningful discussion is that we treat all proposed readings as precisely that—as proposals rather than claims to objective truth. They must, however, try to say something that both accurately reflects the material being interpreted and speaks to a wide range of shared human experience, not *only* to one group's experience—as necessary as the latter is as a starting point.

It is also important to remember that one's "location" in life is neither one-dimensional nor stable. Each of us plays numerous roles in life, and our perspectives are constantly changing. So my point is not that we try at the outset to define the components of a shared word of human experience, as if any of us had an objective understanding of what it would entail. It is rather that each of us, drawing on the complex particularities of our own experiences, advances proposals from those perspectives, fully expecting to have those perspectives transformed in the process. In simpler terms, our world of experience is expanded through encounter with other worlds of experience. But this will not work unless we take the risk of trying to say something that applies beyond the various territories we occupy at any given moment.

BEYOND SCRIPTURE:
TRADITION, REASON, AND EXPERIENCE

The criticism that hermeneutics always saves the text at any cost is one we should take very seriously. It is therefore important to affirm the prerogative of those who engage in theological reflection on behalf of the church to reject a given text or strand of meaning. And we must also recognize that the hermeneutical enterprise will sometimes involve an appeal to sources of potential authority outside the canonical texts—that is, to tradition, reason, and experience. Having said this, however, it becomes important to clarify how I would envision the relationships among the various potential sources of authority.

I noted earlier that the distinction between Scripture and tradition is relative. The canonical texts not only draw on prior tradition, whether oral or written, but also feed into future tradition; and they stand within a broad stream of tradition, both oral and written, that parallels them. Scripture is therefore but one element within a broader phenomenon, a point dramatically illustrated by the fact that the canonical status of any text is the product of tradition. It is the community alone that can deem a text canonical.

What is true of the relationship between Scripture and tradition is equally true of the other relationships among Scripture, tradition, reason, and experience. Behind both Scripture and other forms of tradition stands experience; it is only on the basis of human experience that tradition comes into being in the first place. Those who first encountered Jesus, for example, began to pass on his words and deeds only because they experienced them as meaningful—that is to say, in at least some broad sense, salvific. And the experience of meaningfulness, or salvific potential, is dependent upon prior experience. No person or group receives a religious testimony unless it somehow speaks to the specific conditions under which the person or group exists. The message must somehow illumine actual life situations in order to evoke a response. This is not to deny that the testimony can redefine those situations or evoke unnoticed existential needs, but it is to claim that without the prior existential need the testimony would be meaningless. It does not *create* the need to which it speaks. We may say, then, that we cannot legitimately understand either Scripture or tradition as totally distinct from experience. And the case is no different with respect to reason. Whenever we translate experience into meaning complexes, human reason is at work. Thus, neither Scripture nor the other forms of tradition come into being apart from the operation of reason.

Clearly, then, the distinctions among the four sources of potential authority are relative. This is not say, however, that these distinctions are not real and important. So it remains necessary to reflect on the implications of possible conflicts among them. On the one hand, most important in the present context is the question of whether it is legitimate to overrule Scripture on some particular point in the light of testimony from one or more of the other sources, or even to overrule Scripture in combination with tradition on the basis of experience and/or reason. Such a move is in fact legitimate but is so only if we can find some justification for the move by appeal to the broader witness of Scripture itself. If we allow tradition, reason, or experience to rule without qualification, we may in fact be siding with the truth; but if we cannot *in some way* link that truth to Scripture, we have clearly moved beyond the bounds of the community of faith that claims Scripture as authority. On the other hand, if we categorically deny tradition, reason, or experience the power to overrule Scripture on a given issue, we are clearly denying its inherent relatedness to the other modes of authority. In light of that relatedness, we are granting it a quality of absoluteness that is simply unjustified. We must therefore be careful not to define too narrowly the *way* in which judgments to overrule Scripture must themselves be grounded in Scripture. We must be prepared, in other words, to pay attention to some very *broad* scriptural warrants when considering certain specific issues.

NEW TESTAMENT ETHICS AND NEW TESTAMENT THEOLOGY: KNOWING TRUTH, DOING GOOD

One final, brief word is necessary as I approach the New Testament materials. My primary interest is in New Testament ethics. Because the ethical perspectives of these materials are closely related to their broader theological orientations, however, significant attention to the latter will also be necessary. As Keck comments, "Morals can be taught, and usually are, without making explicit the sapiential judgments and the ideas that inform them; but there is no ethics without theological ideas" (1996, 8). And attention to the theological dimensions is particularly necessary because the competition among various strains of meaning is often more evident at the theological level than it is at the ethical. But the inseparability of theology from ethics raises an important question: Does theology arise as a sanction for ethics, or is it in fact the foundational element from which ethics is derived? I will not propose an answer to that question until part 4, but it is important at this point to affirm the inseparability of these two dimensions within the biblical witness. For the biblical writers and their original readers, there is no question but that doing the good was integrally related to knowing the truth.

PART II

the ethics of the jesus movement

CHAPTER 3

the context of the jesus movement

⟿

The subject of part 2 is the Jesus movement. By this term I mean the movement constituted by Jesus and his followers during his lifetime. I will therefore treat the earliest stage of the Jesus tradition—that is, materials that go back to the pre-resurrection period—as relatively privileged over against later tradition. I will not try to isolate the actual words of the historical Jesus but will seek rather to describe the movement he founded. In an attempt to identify the theological and ethical beliefs of his followers, I will investigate, in chapter 4, the traditions the people passed on regarding the words and deeds of Jesus.

Neither Jesus himself nor the Jesus movement, however, existed in a vacuum. It is therefore important to preface the treatment of that movement with a discussion of the environment within which it existed, including its social, political, and religious aspects. In the present chapter I will therefore seek first to describe the social location of the movement and then to characterize the strains of tradition to which it was heir.

THE "WORLD" OF LOWER GALILEE

The unanimous testimony of the Synoptic Gospels is that Jesus carried out his ministry in the villages and towns of Galilee, the northernmost section of the old northern monarchy, Israel, which had separated from Judah following the reign of Solomon. The northern nation, which included Samaria, shared a broad Israelite heritage with its sibling to the south. From early times, however, it had fostered traditions somewhat distinct from those in Judah, particularly with respect to the place of Jerusalem and the ideology surrounding the Davidic line. The split between north and south resulted in large measure from Solomon's policies of impressed labor and heavy taxation that financed the building of the temple and his luxurious palace. Thus, when the north established its own monarchy, it did so on the basis of a covenant theology with a different understanding of God's promise to stand by the chosen people. In contrast to the unconditional promise regarding the perpetuity of David's line and the inviolability of Zion, the northern ideology involved the notion of a conditional covenant. Rooted in the ancient Mosaic tradition, it stressed that possession of the land was contingent on the obedience of the king and the people to God.

When the Assyrian empire attacked the northern monarchy in 733–732 B.C.E. and eventually brought an end to the nation in 722–721, large numbers of people were taken into exile. Some scholars think that the north was virtually stripped of its population and remained devoid of Israelite culture for centuries. By other accounts, however, it was primarily the ruling classes and those immediately associated with them that were involved (Horsley 1995, 26). Either way, by the time of Jesus the majority population in Galilee was once again Israelite, because the region underwent significant Judean colonization during the Hasmonean period, although there is evidence of other ethnic groups living alongside and interacting with the Israelites.

If a significant Israelite population remained in Galilee following the eighth-century deportations, the Galileans of Jesus' time were probably privy to ancient traditions rooted both in the old northern monarchy and in their own local communities. Although they now understood themselves as part of an Israelite nation that included Judea to the south and shared a wealth of traditions with the people of that region, they also fostered traditions of their own. And these, in some instances, would almost certainly have conflicted with those based in the south. Most particularly, the Galileans of Jesus' time would have been less inclined to accept the pronouncements of the temple-based hierarchy—the priestly aristocracy and those associated with them.

Some scholars argue against the continuity of tradition in Galilee, contending that the beliefs of the Galileans would have been essentially the same as those of Judeans. Their case hinges largely on the claims of archaeologists that "the region was almost completely abandoned at the close of the Iron Age . . ." (Pearson 2004, 491, citing Reed 2000, 23–62). As Richard Horsley points out, however, such evidence is by nature fragmentary and cannot in and of itself settle the issue. The more likely scenario is that "the deportations were mainly of officials and skilled personnel," while others "remained in their villages or perhaps withdrew into the rugged interior" (1996, 23). Assyrian records, moreover, attest a population significant enough that the conquerors created "a province with their own administrative officers to gather taxes and keep order in the area." And there is some indication that many of those deported from Galilee were not Israelites but Syrians (Horsley 1995, 27).

The question of historical continuity with the old northern kingdom is, in any case, not the only relevant factor in identifying the traditions that informed the Galilean peasantry in the time of Jesus. To begin with, we may note that the literary traditions of the north did not simply vanish altogether. The legal traditions of the northern Levites found their way to Jerusalem in the form of an early version of Deuteronomy. It would therefore seem highly likely that some of the Galileans displaced during the conflict would have also found their way south and brought their oral heritage with them.

In addition, it is important to recognize that written tradition is very much the provenance of an elite class. The rate of literacy was low among the peasantry, and written materials were not easily accessible. We must therefore imagine that in rural Galilee most teaching and learning took place on the basis of oral tradition, which is subject to far less control than its written counterpart. Thus, quite apart from the question of north versus south, we must take account of the almost inevitable difference in traditions between rural and urban, elite classes and the peasantry, and educated and illiterate. Even if the Galilean population in the time of Jesus for the most part traced its ancestry to Judea, they would likely have nurtured traditions that would have been distinct from those perpetuated among the ruling classes in Jerusalem and would likely have paralleled those from the north in some respects, despite the strong influence of the temple hierarchy. And if Galilean traditions did in fact find their way south after the deportation, they could very easily have found their way north again when Galilee was resettled.

In any case, we should recognize what social scientists have termed a "Little Tradition," fostered among the lower, largely illiterate classes, which stood alongside the "Great Tradition," fostered by the ruling classes and eventually encoded in the written texts of Scripture.[1] Although it undoubtedly shared much with the latter, and the two would have interacted with each other over the centuries, the Little Tradition was undoubtedly subversive of some aspects of it. And because Galilee lacked an "indigenous aristocracy corresponding to those in Jerusalem and Shechem," the Galileans apparently produced no sacred literature of their own, so that the Little, or popular, tradition would almost certainly have flourished (Horsley 1995, 33).

In sum, then, whether or not the Galilean peasantry of Jesus' time had access to an unbroken chain of tradition going back to the old northern monarchy, they most likely fostered a parallel stream with similar grounding in the ideals of the Mosaic covenant. And we may certainly assume that the themes expressed by Amos in the north (although he was Judahite in origin!) and Micah in the south were strong elements in that stream: not only economic justice but a critical attitude toward the ruling classes and the "official" religion they sponsored.

Much of the tension between the Great Tradition and the Little Tradition would have focused on the rule of the temple elite in Jerusalem. For the temple was responsible not only for the collection of tithes and offerings that supported its operations and the priests who carried them out but also for the collection of the tribute paid to the successive empires, including Rome, by whose sanction it continued to exist (Horsley 1996, 77). This situation changed when the Romans placed Galilee under the rule of separate governance from Jerusalem following the death of Herod, whose son Antipas found his own way of draining the Galilean economy in the elaborate reconstruction of the city of Sepphoris. Resentment would therefore have shifted focus somewhat, but the memory of oppressive imperial control linked to Jerusalem and the temple would have remained. And although scholarly opinion is divided on the issue of Galilean loyalty to the temple,[2] it is inherently likely that the resentment of regulations emanating from that quarter would have been stronger in a region so distant from that center of power. In any case, loyalty to the temple in principle would not preclude sharp criticism of those currently in charge of it.

Rome, for its part, was quite diligent in exacting its demands. As Horsley comments, the empire "considered nonpayment of the tribute tantamount to rebellion" (1995, 217). After all, a main purpose of imperial rule was to collect "surplus" produce to feed the Roman populace. And although there are varying accounts of the seriousness of the Galilean peasantry's plight, there is good reason to think that a style of life that was precarious under the best of circumstances was made considerably worse by Roman rule. And our sources from the period tend to confirm this judgment.

> Both the synoptic Gospel tradition and early rabbinic literature provide numerous portrayals of people perpetually, even heavily, in debt. The viability of the peasants' tenure on traditional landholdings was thus . . . undermined by the imposition of heavy tax burdens. When desperate peasant households were forced heavily into debt . . . they or the produce

of their fields would come increasingly under the control of their credi-
tors. (Horsley 1995, 219)

The threat of the loss of land was one of enormous proportions in ancient
agrarian societies. For the basic social unit was the patriarchal, intergenerational
family; and for a family to lose its land was to lose its ancestral inheritance and
an essential part of its identity. Indeed, the identity of the individual was inseparable from that of the family.

The family, moreover, was the focus of much of the inherited tradition mentioned above. And we must not think of this tradition as exclusively "religious"
in the narrow sense. Since what moderns would term "the religious," "the social,"
and the "political" were all parts of an integrated web of social existence, any
sharp distinctions among them would seriously distort the way these people
understood their lives. Thus, Horsley notes, the sum and substance of the Mosaic
covenant had to do largely with familial matters:

> The basic covenantal principles of social policy governing the relations
> between God and the society and social-economic relations within the
> society, in form addressed to the male heads of household, focus on the
> matters of most importance for social life: relations between generations
> within the family, the sanctity of human life, the sanctity of (patriarchal)
> marriage, the inviolability of moveable property, dealings with other
> heads of household, and the inalienability of the members of households
> and the principal instruments of economic viability (ox and ass) as well as
> the house (or whole estate) itself (Exod. 20:12-17). Of those six principles
> of social policy governing relations within society, all but (perhaps) "thou
> shalt not murder" protect the continuing viability of the family/house-
> hold. (1995, 196)

Since families lived in villages, concerns regarding the interactions among
families and of life in a larger communal setting were also important. The villages of Galilee enjoyed a relatively high degree of autonomy in dealing with
local matters (Horsley 1995, 276–77), and it is with this in mind that we should
understand the local institution of the synagogue. As a number of scholars have
argued in recent decades, the term *synagogue* in all probability originally referred
not to a building but to an institution—that is, to a local assembly concerned
with the full range of community concerns, not simply those of a "religious"

nature. Nor did these assemblies operate under the authority of the Pharisees, despite a long-standing strain in scholarly opinion. The Pharisees seem rather to have had their power base in Jerusalem, where, according to Anthony Saldarini, they probably functioned as "retainers," a social class that served the interests of the temple leadership, which formed the governing class (2001, 277–97, esp. 284, 296). The Pharisees would likely have visited the synagogues in Galilee, perhaps trying to exert influence over them on matters of religious observance (Herzog 2005, 74–79, contra Horsley 1995, 232). Far from an avenue for Pharisaic teaching, however, synagogues were probably more broadly based and community-oriented entities that functioned as forums for dealing with a broad range of local concerns (Horsley 1995, ch. 10).

The relative autonomy exercised by the people in dealing with many community concerns, however, would have had limited effect in dealing with the economic hardships wrought by the cycle of excessive taxation and indebtedness within the context of foreign rule. And there is little question but that such a situation would have had a detrimental effect on the social fabric as a whole. "It has become a standard generalization of modern social science," Horsley writes,

> that subject peoples, whether in colonized countries or metropolitan ghettos, develop an anxious distrust even of their brothers and sisters. Indeed, since any active expression of resentment against the dominant system or society is blocked by institutionalized repressive measures, subject peoples tend to vent their frustration in attacks against one another. (1987, 255)

It is against such a background that we should interpret Gospel reports of Jesus' sayings regarding enemies, accusers, and the settlement of disputes. We must therefore imagine the context within which the Jesus movement arose as one characterized not only by resentment against imperial rule and the Jerusalem leadership but also by a significant measure of internal strife.

Although the people could not change the political and economic landscape, they could draw on a rich fund of tradition in order to understand their situation and clarify the bases of their complaints against their various overlords. Among the strands of this fund would have been the Great Tradition, encoded in Scripture, to the extent that they knew and had access to it, although they would have known it largely through oral recitation. It would also have included, however, the Little Tradition, which was rooted both in the needs and problems of everyday life and the memory of the ancient Mosaic themes. It is from such sources that we must imagine that Jesus and his first followers drew as their ideological base and to which they could refer as they sought to draw others into their circle.

The Jesus movement was centered in Lower Galilee, which was somewhat different from its more northern counterpart. While Upper Galilee remained more rural and isolated, the lower region was closer to urban centers of Hellenistic culture. Indeed, two major urban centers that served at some points as centers of government administration were located within the region. Sepphoris, the site of recent archaeological activity, was in the heart of Lower Galilee, in close proximity to Jesus' hometown of Nazareth; and Tiberias lay on the western shore of the Sea of Galilee.

There is a strain of recent scholarship that places a great deal of weight on our new appreciation of the centers of urbanization and Hellenization in Lower Galilee in characterizing Jesus and his followers. The presence of Sepphoris and Tiberias in Lower Galilee, however, does not mean that the entire region was urbanized or thoroughly Hellenized or that the vast majority of peasants had very much interaction with these cities. The pattern of Hellenization throughout the lands conquered by Alexander, in fact, was that although Greek culture flourished in the great urban centers, the hinterlands were less deeply affected by it. And it is entirely consistent with this pattern that Sepphoris is never mentioned in the Gospels, which depict Jesus' activities as focused on the towns and villages of the region.

The peasantry would certainly have been aware of the Hellenized cities and would likely have had some interaction with them, but they would undoubtedly have viewed them as in many ways alien and allied with the forces that oppressed them. It therefore seems probable that Jesus, his original followers, and those with whom they interacted lived primarily within the "world" of Israelite tradition. As one final step before attempting to characterize the ethics of the Jesus movement, then, it is important to look more closely at the ethical aspects of that tradition.

TRAJECTORIES IN ISRAELITE ETHICAL TRADITION

The ethics of the Israelite tradition may appear at first glance to be a consistent ethics of divine command, expressed in the laws of the Torah and elaborated in various ways in other scriptural texts, most especially the prophetic writings. There is important truth in this characterization, but the actual situation is more complex. What we actually find, on close examination of the tradition, is a long process of development with many competing strands. Because an understanding of that complexity is important for grasping the import of the ethics of the Jesus movement, we turn now to two works that have particular relevance to our present interests: Erhard Gerstenberger's *Theologies in the Old Testament* (2002) and John Barton's *Understanding Old Testament Ethics: Approaches and Explorations* (2003).

Erhard Gerstenberger: The Origin and Development of Ethical Traditions

"The long, prehistoric period of humankind was presumably an age of small groups and hordes." Thus begins Gerstenberger's chapter on the social history of Israel. It was from such "groups and hordes" that closely knit clans emerged in the Near East—kinship networks that were autonomous in matters of economics, law, and religious observance. They were also, despite their patriarchal structure, relatively democratic. Each community was devoted to group survival, which necessitated the sharing of goods and attention to the welfare of all its members (2002, 19–22).

It is within this local context that both religious observance and ethics had their original provenance. With specific regard to the land that became known as Israel, the incorporation of the vast majority of the people into an Israelite community devoted to the exclusive worship of Yahweh was a long and gradual process.[3] Prior to the ascendancy of Yahwism, each family worshiped its deity with the most basic needs of the group in mind: survival and prosperity (2002, 23–35). In this original context, ethics was very much a matter of local custom oriented toward the goal of internal cohesion and well-being. "Family respect, the mutual solidarity of all, an alliance to provide protection and resistance against outsiders, are the basic values" (2002, 62). At this level, custom suffices and law is unnecessary. The family passes on values in the raising of children, and it enforces the rules when necessary.

At the level of towns and villages, the direct and relatively democratic process of decision making remained, but the larger environment required additional elements.

> A system of jurisdiction developed in law. In religion and the cult, common obligations towards the higher powers were recognized, e.g., in the celebration of rites of passage (puberty; resettlement) or the ceremonies of seasonal work in the fields and the harvest. In the military sphere, protection against enemies had to be organized. . . . Interests which transcended

the family or arose out of an accumulation of common efforts had to be looked after by local authorities. . . . The elders of the city or the locality were given the authority to find the right solution in the common interest (cf. e.g. Ezek 14:1; 20:1). (2002, 20–21)

The tribes that eventually formed in Israel functioned in a rather different way from families and clans or villages and towns. The tribe is "predominantly a grouping which presents itself to the outside world, leaving the families and clans quite untouched."[4] Its structure was loose, and its primary responsibilities had to do with defensive war and the cultic actions associated with it (2002, 122–38). And because of the tribe's war-making function, devotion to a common deity became important at this level of organization. Thus, Yahweh originally entered the religious consciousness as the war god of a specific tribe, who eventually became ascendant in a tribal alliance (2002, 138–56).

Because of the inherent weakness of the tribal structure in the face of organized, external military threat, it eventually gave way to monarchy and a fundamental transformation:

By contrast with the tribal society, the monarchical state of the ancient Near East was a bureaucratic, centralized system. All the authority emanated from the king (and court). The segmentary groups (large families, villages, cities, tribal alliances, semi-nomadic shepherds and itinerant workers) had to submit to the royal authority wherever the well-being of the state as a whole or the leading dynasty was at stake. (2002, 163)

With the monarchical state came a royal theology, which understood the king as acting on the deity's behalf and participating in divine power: Yahweh became the state deity, who was worshiped in an official cult and represented by the king. This did not mean permission for purely arbitrary rule, however, since the king had responsibilities. These were essentially such matters as preserving the law, securing justice for the poor and marginalized, punishing transgressors, protecting the people from external enemies, and making secure their land and prosperity (2002, 183–85). Monarchical rule, however, provides few visible structures for holding the king accountable. In particular, the poor and marginalized have limited avenues for the presentation of their concerns. So it is hardly surprising that royal theology never completely dominated the lives of ordinary people but was, from the beginning, unable to overcome popular belief. And as kings and the aristocracy continually pursued policies that worked against the interests of the lower classes, this subterranean tradition found powerful expression through the voices of the prophets: "the prophetic opposition during the time of the monarchy came predominantly from marginalized social peripheral groups or represented their interests. The critics accuse the ruling groups in the name of Yahweh of flagrant violation of their duty to care for the weak and the poor." The ethic expressed in such opposition, moreover, "is none other than the principle of solidarity which is customary in clan and village communities. Concern for the weak is imposed on the community by virtue of God's command and the very natural will of the group for self-preservation" (2002, 195–96).

The survival of local tradition was not limited to matters of ethics. We have clear evidence of the persistence of local shrines, despite the centralized worship of Yahweh, that undoubtedly perpetuated domestic cults that reached back to ancient times (2002, 182). The canonical tradition understands the prophets as uniformly speaking in the name of Yahweh, but it is not clear that this was always the case. For it is difficult to separate the original prophetic traditions from the editing carried out in later times by those who sought to portray a unified history and theological perspective (2002, 197). What seems certain, though, is that "the temple cult in Jerusalem or Bethel or Dan hardly played any role for the normal citizen (perhaps on the occasional pilgrimage?, 1 Sam. 1f.). The sacrificial feast of the tribe is more important than presence at the royal court (1 Sam. 20:6, 29)" (2002, 202).

Particularly with respect to ethics, aspects of local religion persisted even after the Babylonian Exile:

> The traditions which were saved from the past in the early Jewish communities . . . in part came from the old family and village tradition. In all matters pertaining to everyday life it was easier to begin there than with the tribal and state traditions. So it is only natural for us to find in the sphere of social ethics that the central problems of the ethic of the time were the care of the weak and poor; the humanitarian protection of women, slaves and foreigners (though in some respects this was only rudimentary); incorruptible justice and honest trade; and an attempt at compensation in civil disputes (bodily injury, killing, crimes against property and so on). All the texts are far removed from any kind of state ethic. (2002, 221–22)

This is not to say that the postexilic community rejected the fundamental tenet of monarchical religion in favor of local tradition. For the ascendancy of

Yahweh as the sole deity of the people became even more entrenched in this formative period of Judaism. Nevertheless, according to Gerstenberger, in the religion of the postexilic community "belief in Yahweh took on very personal features, in contrast to the theologies of tribe and state." A social ethic therefore developed that applied the concept of solidarity that once reigned in the families and tribes to the larger community as a whole. All members of that community were brothers and sisters, so that one could think of Yahweh "as the 'Father' of all" (2002, 223), and the commandment to love Yahweh was paralleled by the injunction to love one's neighbor as oneself (Lev 19:18) (2002, 268).

Cohesion was thus a primary value, and the formation of Scripture was a major means of achieving it. The Torah took shape in the form of "stories and rules for behaviour," with even the narrative sections serving primarily as catechetical material. And the prophetic writings probably served as commentary on the Torah, rounding out a theologically constructed understanding of God's relationship to the people (2002, 211–15).

The Scriptures as a whole clearly identify God's will and action in terms of justice and peace (2002, 234–42), and this definition of the interests of God also defines ethical norms. Every individual is entitled to justice, and a hallmark of the prophetic materials is the relentless emphasis on justice specifically for the poor. But this theme is not limited to the prophetic books. Examining the canon as a whole, Gerstenberger comments that "we note with amazement at how many points God's power for the weak and the sufferers appears" (2002, 249).

Alongside this concern for community solidarity there was another aspect of what was perceived to be God's will, and this was found in the elaborate traditions regarding purity. These traditions "issue from a great anxiety about anything like an uncontrolled mixing of substances" and express the pervasive consciousness in the ancient world that "nature was everywhere ensouled and animate." As central as purity concerns are to the postexilic community, they paradoxically illustrate the survival of popular belief in the face of the ascendancy of Yahwism. For Gerstenberger finds them to be in tension with the central notion of the goodness of God's creation (Gen 1:3) and speculates that their origin is either in "alien" theological perspectives or early traditions "which did not yet know of the one good creation of Yahweh" (2002, 267). However, whereas these elements of ancient tradition find a place in the new system of belief, there is a concerted effort to suppress other elements. Among these are beliefs and practices branded as "Canaanite," including those pertaining to goddesses and women's participation in the cult. The effort is not fully successful, though, because popular religion is still discernible in the texts (2002, 258–62).

An important result of Gerstenberger's investigation is the clear picture of ethics at all levels as fundamentally rooted in the concern for community survival and cohesion. The tradition supports ethical norms by referring to God's will, but it tends to identify God's will with values that promote community survival and cohesion. "The good," in other words, is anything but arbitrarily defined, as if it were the good simply because God commands it. To the contrary, the tradition defines God's will precisely in terms of a notion of the good that seems ultimately to be based on an intuitive grasp of what promotes community solidarity and makes life livable for all.

John Barton: The Basis of Ethics in the Hebrew Bible

John Barton's work reinforces the notion that the tradition understands God's will not as arbitrary command but as rooted in values promoting the good of the community. Barton identifies three bases of ethics in the Hebrew Bible: obedience to God's declared will, natural law, and the imitation of God. Fundamental to his concerns is the issue of whether the biblical ethic is simply "a jumble of isolated precepts with no underlying rationale" or is "generated by deeper and more fundamental structures of ethical thinking, even if these are relatively inarticulate by comparison with those of western philosophy" (2003, 46).

The first of Barton's categories, obedience to God's declared will, might seem to confirm the notion that the ethics of the Hebrew Bible is in fact a simple ethic of divine command. As Barton himself acknowledges,

> Many *people* in ancient Israel in various periods seem to have thought . . . that human beings, and Israelites especially, should do as God told them; and many of the texts they produced, which now form our Bible, operate with the same assumption. . . . Ordinary Israelites and those who wrote the biblical books alike regarded "the good" as that way of life which God enjoined. There were no doubt levels of sophistication in thinking about the matter, but there was no essential disagreement. (2003, 47; emphasis original)

Barton argues, however, that the matter is not so simple, since God's demands appear not as divine whim but as grounded in God's own moral character. That is to say, there is a direct correlation between God's actions toward Israel and what God demands of the people (2003, 48).

In any case, the obedience model is not the only model present in the Hebrew Bible. With respect to natural law, a term that Barton uses only reluctantly, he identifies two forms that such a basis for ethics takes. The first is the presence of norms that pertain to human beings as such, apart from any particular injunctions given either by God or human beings. To substantiate this type of natural law, Barton first refers to the wisdom tradition, citing Job 31:13-15 as an example of an appeal to a common humanity as a basis of human solidarity. Job justifies his listening to the complaints of his servants not on the basis of a commandment but because the same God fashioned them all in the womb. And Barton contrasts this appeal "to the Deuteronomic exhortations to be kind to slaves, which appeal rather to the Israelites' own experience of slavery and to the response-evoking kindness of God in setting them free" (2003, 33).

Even more significant is the presence of an appeal to a common humanity in Gen 9:6, which prohibits murder on the basis of humanity's creation in the image of God. For despite the fact that God is the source of the commandment, "the prohibition of murder is not seen by the writer as a potentially arbitrary commandment . . . but as simply an explicit statement of what is held to be evident in any case from the existence of humans as made in God's image, namely their essential sacrosanctity."[5]

As a third example, Barton cites the oracles against the foreign nations in Amos 1–2, which, he notes,

> notoriously represent a difficulty for any view of the ethical tradition in ancient Israel which sees it as exclusively tied to law and covenant, since the nations here accused of war crimes cannot be thought of as standing in a covenant relationship with Yahweh such as would entail the acceptance of Israelite norms of conduct in war. (2003, 34)

When in 2:16 Amos turns his ire on the Israelites themselves, the intended effect is clearly one of surprise, and such a tactic presupposes that his audience assumed that the nations would know that their behavior was unacceptable to Yahweh. Thus, "we should have to say that the atrociousness of certain kinds of war crime was an established point which everyone could be assumed to agree about" (2003, 35).

The second form of natural law Barton identifies hangs on the notion "that a certain kind of ethical system is somehow built into the world or to the nature of things. . . ." Following C. S. Rodd (2001), he finds one example in Abraham's challenge to God regarding the destruction of Sodom (Gen 18:16-33). When Abraham confronts God with a standard of justice (18:25), the unavoidable implication is that he identifies an ethical standard that stands over against God as a basis of evaluation (2003, 35).

Still stronger examples, Barton contends, are found in the prophets. Isaiah, in particular, identifies the people's sin in terms that are not derived from the law. In this category are his condemnations of drunkenness, "the excessive luxury of the rulers of Judah," and such attitudes as folly, stupidity, and pride. Thus, "somewhat in the manner of Proverbs, he is concerned with false attitudes, a wrong and inflated sense of one's own importance, a selfish lack of concern for others, and (in the case of political alliances) a tendency to rely on the unreliable rather than on God, the source of true strength" (2003, 36).

Barton is sensitive to the possible objection that on the canonical level all such instances of natural law have been embraced under the category of obedience to God's law. He by no means grants this premise, but he argues that even if it is so it is of limited importance: "But this will be a truth, if it is a truth, about late postexilic Judaism, or about the hermeneutical problem of the Old Testament, not about the thought of Israel's prophets in the eighth century . . ." (2003, 39). At the very least, in other words, the natural law element stands as a significant undercurrent within a canon dominated by an understanding of ethics as obedience to divine command.

The imitation of God, Barton argues, is a strong theme in the Hebrew Bible that can in some sense hold together the two other ethical models. Building on Johannes Hempel's (1964) contention that we should not view the Decalogue as arbitrary commands but as expressions of how "natural law is to be applied in practice," he proposes that God is equally bound by the laws God underwrites. "Yahweh is a *good* God, a designation which is not incompatible with what people in Israel would have meant by good; thus it made sense for them to imitate God." Barton then suggests that such a notion might express one dimension of the declaration that human beings are made in God's image. Thus, "Yahweh and humanity share a common ethical perception, so that God is not only the commander but also the paradigm of moral conduct" (2003, 52; emphasis original).

Barton is clear that the Hebrew Bible is far from consistent on this point, since God does in fact appear to act arbitrarily in some instances. But this does not negate the widespread "assumption that God acts according to moral standards that human beings also share." For it is only such an assumption that makes intelligible the passages in which God is "upbraided for failure to do so" (2003, 52).

These reflections lead Barton to raise the question of whether the ethics of the Hebrew Bible is primarily deontological or teleological—that is, whether it is a duty ethics focused on God's commands or an ethic of goal or consequences, which judges actions as right or wrong by their effects. The importance of our discovery of the elements of natural law and imitation, he argues, is that it exposes, alongside the more commonly recognized model of divine command, "a strongly teleological character to much of the ethical teaching in the Hebrew Bible" (2002, 52). And this insight is all the more significant when we remember Gerstenberger's location of the origin of biblical ethics in the need for cohesion and solidarity in ancient local communities.

SUMMARY

What can we now say, in summary, about the "world" within which the Jesus movement arose? It was the world of a people in possession of a rich cultural and religious heritage that was of vital importance in their lives, but it was also a world in which strands of that heritage played complex and sometimes contradictory roles. The Great Tradition that held the entire Israelite community together conveyed grand themes of God's gracious action in history as well as laws promoting community solidarity. Yet those who were its official arbiters sometimes wielded power in ways that created significant hardship for the lower classes. For the effects not only of Roman domination but also of the lifestyles of the indigenous aristocracy took an enormous economic toll on the lives of the poor majority. Thus, although there was much in the Great Tradition that spoke to the needs of ordinary people, from the perspective of those struggling for subsistence, some aspects of that tradition, as well as their implementation by the official power structure, would have appeared as part of the problem rather than a solution. It would therefore hardly be surprising that, in a movement generated from the heart of the peasantry, people would look to the Little Tradition as a resource for challenging existing, formalized norms.

CHAPTER 4

the ethics of the jesus movement

⟨⟩

Before turning specifically to the topic of ethics, I will attempt an overall characterization of the Jesus movement. My intention, as stated earlier, is not to try to isolate the actual words of Jesus. It is rather to identify materials that reflect in a broad, thematic way the preresurrection situation, even though the specific formulations might date from a later stage in the movement. Then, with this general picture in the background, I will turn to specific texts that can flesh out in some detail the fundamental beliefs and ethical concerns that were current among Jesus and his original followers. In all of this, I presuppose the two-document hypothesis, according to which Matthew and Luke are dependent on Mark and also on a common source, designated by the symbol Q, which is roughly defined as the material found in Matthew and Luke but absent from Mark.[1] Because of the pervasive ethical content of Q, as well as the likelihood that it is our earliest source among the strands of the Jesus tradition, my initial attempt to characterize the ethics of the movement will involve a close examination of key Q passages.

THE ETHOS OF THE MOVEMENT

Jesus, John the Baptist, and the Rule of God

Few aspects of the Jesus tradition are more securely established than the connection between Jesus and John the Baptist. It is attested not only by Mark and Q but also by the Gospel of John and the book of Acts. Both Matthew and Luke adopt Mark's story of Jesus' baptism by John (Mark 1:9-11; Matt 3:13-17; Luke 3:21-22), and the Q material in Matt 3:7-10 and Luke 3:7-9 provides a description of John's message that would be irrelevant except as an introduction to Jesus' own ministry and message. The Gospel of John, moreover, gives a parallel account

(1:19-34) of John the Baptist's testimony to Jesus that in its own way affirms the connection; and in 1:35-42 we hear that Andrew and another unnamed disciple of John become followers of Jesus. To all this we should add Matt 11:2-6//Luke 8:18-23 (the inquiry of John's disciples to Jesus) and Matt 11:7-19//Luke 7:24-25 (Jesus' words about John).

The Matthean and Johannine accounts of John's testimony to Jesus, in particular, show that the connection to John, far from a motif that later tradition might have invented, presented something of a difficulty for Jesus' followers of another generation. John's protest in Matt 3:13-15 that he is unworthy to baptize Jesus is clearly an attempt to speak to the problem of Jesus' apparent subordination to John. In addition, John 1:19-23, with the Baptist's fulsome denials that he is the Christ, makes clear his lesser status and suggests a rivalry at some point between Jesus' later followers and a movement that remained focused on John even after Jesus' death.

Clearly, then, there is strong indication that the movements founded by John and Jesus were known to have been intimately connected. And the apparent fact of Jesus' baptism by John is best explained by the thesis that Jesus' movement grew out of the prior movement spearheaded by John—that Jesus in fact was once a follower of John. In addition, I concur with Ekkehard and Wolfgang Stegemann against John Dominic Crossan that we need not conclude that the separation of the two movements resulted from "a break between Jesus and John," since the Gospels hold John in high regard (Luke 7:24ff.; Matt 11:7ff.) (1999, 196). However, the fact that John's movement continued alongside that of Jesus shows that John did not understand himself as a precursor to Jesus. This motif probably arose as a way of explaining the relationship between John and Jesus, which was problematic for Jesus' later followers.

According to the Q account in Matt 3:7-10 and Luke 3:7-9, John issued a dramatic call for repentance in the face of God's impending wrath, and his witness to Jesus in Mark 1:7-8, Matt 3:11-12, and Luke 3:15-18 adds forceful imagery to the notion of a coming judgment. Only Matt 3:2 describes John's preaching explicitly in terms of the announcement of the coming *basileia*— the rule of heaven/God. Nevertheless, the pervasive eschatological tone of the cumulative description of John shows that he did proclaim the imminence of the age to come.

Mark 1:15, paralleled by Matt 4:17, describes Jesus' own message similarly as a call for repentance in the face of the rule of God/heaven that has drawn near, and the theme of Jesus' proclamation of God's rule pervades the entire Synoptic tradition. The motif of repentance is less well attested, and the fact that it is stronger in Luke than in Mark and Matthew indicates that the author of Luke has expanded it. Nevertheless, passages such as Luke 10:13-15//Matt 11:20-24 (the woes on unrepentant cities), Mark 2:13-17//Matt 9:9-13//Luke 5:27-32 ("I have come to call not the righteous but sinners"), and Matt 18:12-14//Luke 15:3-7 (the lost sheep) are strong evidence of its authenticity.

On the other hand, repentance seems to have functioned rather differently in the Jesus movement than it did for John. The distinction appears both in the contrast between the comportment of John and that of Jesus and in practices attributed to their disciples. Matthew 11:18-19//Luke 7:33-35 portrays John as an ascetic but describes Jesus as radically different. Whereas "John came neither eating nor drinking," Jesus "came eating and drinking," so that people criticized him as "a glutton and a drunkard, a friend of tax collectors and sinners" (Matt 9:14-17//Luke 5:33-39). Consistent with this, Mark 2:18-22 has John's disciples fasting but Jesus' disciples not doing so. Although this passage may be the product of postresurrection tradition, it is almost certainly reflective of preresurrection practice.

This stylistic difference between John and Jesus presumably grew out of an important aspect of Jesus' approach to repentance. As E. P. Sanders notes, "there is no instance in which Jesus requires the wicked to do what the law stipulates in order to become righteous." Although this omission might seem insignificant on the grounds that fulfilling the formal requirements of repentance is assumed, Sanders finds an alternative more likely:

> that Jesus thought and said that the wicked who followed him, though they had not technically "repented," and though they had not become righteous in the way required by the law, would be in the kingdom and, in fact would be ahead of those who were righteous by the law. (1993, 235)

This view makes Jesus' conflict with the Jewish leadership more intelligible than does the notion that he assumed all the legal requirements surrounding repentance. We must not, however, think of repentance in a narrowly individualistic or "religious" sense. To begin with, the call to repentance was directed not merely to individuals but, in typical prophetic fashion, to communities as such. We can see this clearly in Luke 10:10-12//Matt 9:7, 14-15//Mark 6:10-11:

> But whenever you enter a town and they do not welcome you, go out into its streets and say, "Even the dust of your town that clings to our feet, we

wipe off in protest against you. Yet know this: the kingdom of God has come near."

A similar theme appears in Luke 10:13-15//Matt 11:21-23, where Jesus pronounces woes on Chorazin and Bethsaida for their failure to repent in the face of his "deeds of power." Some scholars consign this latter passage to a later expansion of the original version of Q, but there is no consensus on dating the supposed "strata" of Q. And, in any case, there is no reason to deny that the general theme of judgment against the unrepentant belongs to the preresurrection situation.[2]

If Jesus' call to repentance involved collective as well as individual responsibility, it also embraced a sociopolitical dimension. We can see this, above all, in his demonstration in the temple, which many scholars now interpret as a symbolic destruction rather than a "cleansing" with a view to reform. This interpretation is suggested by the disruption of the activity of the money-changers, whose role was necessary for the functioning of the sacrificial system, and reinforced by the traditions about Jesus' predictions of an actual destruction (E. P. Sanders 1985, 61–76). But if Jesus' action was not a mere "cleansing," neither was it a rejection of Israelite tradition. It was in all probability a prophetic symbol pointing to God's coming eschatological action, the dramatic closure of the old age and the beginning of the new.[3]

The question, though, is why the eschatological age should require the temple's destruction. For Sanders, the reason is simply that the new age required a new temple (1985, 73–77). And he seems to deny that Jesus had specific criticisms of the current operation of the temple, noting that the usual criticisms of it had to do with matters "about which the gospels are silent"—that is, matters related to the purity of the priests (1985, 65). Jesus' criticisms need not have been the same as those made by others, however; and if we remember the role of the temple in the overall economy of Jerusalem and Jewish Palestine we should be wary of understanding them in narrow religious/cultic terms. Since the temple functioned by the sanction of a succession of imperial rulers, to symbolize its destruction was also to signal the end of imperial rule in the face of the coming rule of God. Jesus' demonstration was therefore probably an indictment of both the indigenous religious leadership and the rule of Rome.

One saying of Jesus widely accepted as authentic might seem to call this judgment into question, however—Jesus' reply to the question about paying the Roman a poll (or head) tax, which was required of every adult male (Mark 12:17//Matt 22:21//Luke 20:25): "Give to the emperor the things that are the emperor's, and to God the things that are God's." Early on, the tradition understood the statement to mean that Jesus' followers should pay the tax, and in later times it became the cornerstone of a doctrine of two realms, that of God and that of Caesar, each supported by divine sanction.

The saying, however, does not endorse payment any more than it sanctions refusal to pay. It is rather "a masterful bit of enigmatic repartee" (Funk and Hoover 1993, 102), a cagey formulation designed to disorient the hearer by refusing to take a definite position. Also, we must interpret it against the background of a worldview in which there is no clear separation between politics and religion. The notion of two separate realms of authority would have been unthinkable in this context. And, finally, we need to understand it in light of a peasant consciousness grounded in the Little Tradition. As James C. Scott has shown, among such populations, it is a common practice to foster a "hidden transcript,"[4] a way of speaking and acting that communicates subversive ideas without alerting the power structure.

Drawing on Scott's work, William R. Herzog II argues convincingly that Jesus' response to the attempt to trap him into taking an explicit stance against the Roman occupation was a deliberate way of delivering a "coded message" through which he offered "both an inducement and the encouragement to resist by using the full arsenal of what Scott calls 'the weapons of the weak'" (Herzog 2005, 190; see also 2004). One key point in his treatment is his observation that the Roman demand was not a tax in the sense we generally imagine, but the payment of tribute, which signified loyalty to the empire. Another key point is the nature of the denarius, which Jesus asks his questioners to show him. Bearing an image of the emperor wearing a laurel wreath, which signified divinity, along with an inscription that made an explicit claim of divine status, it constituted "a blasphemous statement and an idolatrous claim" (Herzog 2005, 186), for it violated not only the prohibition against graven images (Deut 8:5) but also "the first and the second commandments of the Decalogue (Exod 20:1-16)" (2005, 187). It was therefore "no ordinary Roman coin" but rather "a piece of political propaganda that staked Rome's claim to rule the cosmos" (Herzog 2005, 185).

When Jesus demands that one give to God the things that belong to God, his Israelite audience will already know that all things in fact belong to God. But if that is so, then what remains to be rendered back to the emperor? "One thing only," Herzog says. "The coin which he minted in his own image and likeness. That can be returned (paid back) to Caesar because it came from Caesar. Indeed, it must be paid back because it is blasphemous and idolatrous" (2005, 189). Jesus can say none of this explicitly without being arrested, however; thus he offers an "aphorism that acts like a riddle" and constitutes "a disguised, ambiguous, and coded form of speech dedicated to maintaining the hidden transcript of resistance while leaving a public transcript that is in no way actionable" (2005, 189). But what, then, did this subtle act of resistance accomplish? "True," Herzog muses, "the peasants still had to pay tribute, but now they could pay their poll tax or *tributim capitis* not as an act of acquiescence but as an act of resistance, even defiance" (2005, 190).

Whether or not those in the Jesus movement generally paid the tax, they can hardly have done so out of acceptance of the rule of the empire. Like the saying itself, such compliance could only have been a survival tactic. For what is "hidden" in the statement is precisely a strong declaration of the sovereignty of God over all human pretensions to power. And against the background of a proclamation of God's imminent rule and Jesus' demonstration in the temple, such a declaration would have been anything but an acknowledgment of the legitimacy of Roman rule. Had this been the intention of Jesus or his followers, there would have been no need for an "enigmatic repartee"; they could and would have made the point directly and unambiguously.

To return to the matter of Jesus' action in the temple, the eschatological implications of this event combine with his connection to John the Baptist to suggest that the rule of God in Jesus' proclamation cannot be reduced to a present reality that the individual can enter. Although such a description contains an important element of truth, the futuristic, social, and public aspects of the coming rule of God are too deeply imbedded in the early tradition to ignore. I take Crossan to be correct, therefore, in stating that Jesus' acceptance of John's baptism implies his initial acceptance of John's apocalyptic eschatology. But I take him to be off the mark in arguing that Jesus then abandoned this eschatology in favor of a fully present rule in the mode of wisdom thought (1991, 237–38). And I join with many scholars in understanding Jesus' healings and exorcisms (however we might want to explain such phenomena) as signaling the imminence of the coming age. In casting out demons, Jesus was—precisely as the Beelzebul controversy (Mark 3:22-27//Matt 3:24-29//Luke 11:15-29) indicates—binding up Satan in order to plunder his house. In his healings he was symbolizing that ultimate *shalom*, or total well-being, that belongs to the new age and also, by restoring individuals to the life of the community, establishing a beachhead of that new age. And therein lies the truth in the claim that for Jesus and his first followers the rule of God was already present. For it was in fact available for entrance *proleptically* to those who followed him, and in their life together they were already experiencing a foretaste of what was yet to come.

The Social Structure of the Movement

If the Jesus movement understood itself as a foreshadowing of the new age, what can we say about its social structure? First, it seems to have had two foci. Most visible in the tradition are the twelve, an inner circle of disciples clearly symbolic of the twelve tribes of Israel and presumably signs of the coming renewal of the Israelite community. There are indications, however, that there were others who traveled with Jesus on his journeys and that among these were a number of women.[5] There is also evidence of persons who remained in their villages but were part of the movement and who formed communities of some sort there. As Horsley notes, "[t]he 'Jesus movement' must have had some economic base in Palestine other than a few dozen propertyless missionaries and converts in the 'Jerusalem community,' and that base must have put down roots prior to the crucifixion and resurrection-exaltation of Jesus" (1987, 210). Luke 10:3-12, which gives instructions to missionaries, seems in fact to presuppose that those who respond positively to their preaching will remain where they are, as was apparently the case with the sisters Mary and Martha in Luke 10:38-42. The healing stories provide a similar testimony, since those who are healed have already heard about Jesus from friends and family, and Jesus generally sends them back to their homes (Horsley 1987, 227–28). Beyond all this, many of Jesus' instructions presuppose life in a settled community.[6]

There has been much discussion, particularly in light of the recent excavation of the city of Sepphoris, about the social class of Jesus and his followers. A number of scholars think that the availability of work for artisans in an affluent Hellenized setting a few miles from Nazareth indicates that Jesus and his inner circle were considerably better off that has generally been thought. Wolfgang Stegemann, however, argues that Matt 6:25 ("do not be anxious about your life, what you shall eat or what you shall drink") and other texts presuppose an audience in dire economic circumstances (1984, 161–62). Along similar lines, many scholars have made much of the fact that the word for "poor" in the first beatitude (Luke 6:20) is *ptōchos*, which refers to the destitute rather than the relatively deprived. So we may say at the very least that Jesus directed his message largely at the very poor and that his movement almost certainly embraced persons of the lowest economic status.

A broad social inclusiveness, moreover, seems to have been a major characteristic of the movement. Jesus' offer of easy access to repentance resulted in the acceptance of persons generally deemed morally unfit for social interaction, and the depiction of him as consorting with sinners[7] suggests that he included such persons in his fellowship. On another note, the parable of the great supper in Luke 14:15-24 (even apart from v. 21, which may be a Lukan addition) creates the image of a meal attended by members of various classes. To invite people randomly encountered on the "streets and lanes of the town" is to make such mixing virtually unavoidable. Thus Crossan's reading of the accusations made against Jesus in such passages as Matt 11:18-19//Luke 7:31-35 seems justified: "He makes . . . no appropriate distinctions and discriminations. He has no honor. He has no shame" (1991, 262).

Indicative of yet another dimension of inclusiveness is the portrayal, at various levels of the tradition, of Jesus' interaction with women.[8] Gender roles were apparently undergoing significant modification in the Jesus group, as was also the case in some other Jewish groups of the time (Schüssler Fiorenza 1994, 9; Brooten 1982; 1986). Such modification, moreover, seems to have been at some stage of the movement a matter of explicit policy rather than an unreflective development. Indeed, the community's practice seems to have challenged patriarchal customs at their core. This is evident, as Schüssler Fiorenza has argued, from the combined force of two striking Synoptic passages. The first is Matt 23:9: "And call no one on earth your father, for you have one Father—the one in heaven." The second is Mark 10:29-30: "there is no one who has left house, or brothers of sisters or mother or father or children or fields who will not receive a hundredfold now in this age—houses, brothers and sisters, mothers and children, and fields. . . ." Thus, the title "father"—a key element in the patriarchal system—is forbidden, and those who leave everything to follow Jesus do not regain fathers even though every other item in the list is restored to them: "Insofar as the new 'family' of Jesus has no room for 'fathers,' it implicitly rejects their power and status and thus claims that in the messianic community all patriarchal structures are abolished" (1983, 147). This theme, moreover, becomes explicit in Mark 10:42b-43: "You know that among the Gentiles those whom they recognize as their rulers lord it over them, and their great ones are tyrants over them. But it is not so among you; but whoever wishes to become great among you must be your servant, and whoever wishes to be first among you must be slave of all."

SUMMARY

In conclusion, the Jesus movement was a prophetic movement that took shape against the background of some degree of economic deprivation in the context of Roman rule. It drew on ancient Israelite traditions, both written and oral, in heralding God's imminent rule, which would bring a *shalom* that would entail great social upheaval and the destruction of many aspects of the current order. As they anticipated this rule, the communities of Jesus' followers understood themselves as called to practices of radical inclusiveness, mutual care and cooperation, and forgiveness that transcend all individual or family striving for honor or wealth at the expense of others. That, at least, is the picture that emerges from a broad reading of key elements in the Jesus tradition that are likely to reflect the preresurrection tradition.

What remains is an examination of specific texts with an emphasis on ethics. We will begin with a detailed treatment of a select group of Q texts and then broaden our vision with a brief look at the wider Jesus tradition.

A PROPHETIC ETHIC

Q as a Window on the Jesus Movement

Q as a whole exhibits both thematic and formal diversity. Most importantly, there are some materials that we can classify as fitting a "wisdom" mode and others that are "prophetic" in orientation. The wisdom materials consist largely of maxims, anecdotes, and the like that stand on their own as valid observations or sound advice, having little if any inherent connection to the grand themes specific to an Israelite worldview. Taken by themselves, they present a view of Jesus largely as a sage. The prophetic and apocalyptic materials, by contrast, focus on such distinctively Israelite themes as God's judgment and God's coming rule. In them, Jesus assumes the roles of prophet, exorcist, and even the eschatological Son of Man who will one day return to preside over the judgment of the world.

According to such scholars as John Kloppenborg, Burton Mack, and Leif Vaage, the diversity within Q is to be explained in terms of a developmental model. They argue that the Original Q, a thoroughly sapiential document in which Jesus functions as a sage, was subsequently edited to include the prophetic and apocalyptic materials.

What these scholars generally identify as Original Q, however, is a rather small amount of material that is difficult to interpret apart from the provision of a specific social context. Much of it, in fact, can be—and traditionally has been—interpreted in light of the more prophetic and apocalyptic materials found in other parts of Q. Especially for Mack and Vaage, however, we should turn not to the thoroughly Israelite context that these latter materials would provide but to the Hellenistic environment for an interpretive key. Finding parallels to the materials of Original Q in the sayings and actions of Cynic sages, they envision the Q community as a countercultural movement critical of the existing social order but not the arbiter of God's judgment or the advocate of a program of social renewal. In the spirit of the Cynics, the original "Q people" rejected social convention but did not herald God's coming rule as an upheaval in the present order. The rule of God they envisioned was an inward attitude adopted by the individual, and their entire ethic was a strategic way of removing themselves from the ill effects of a corrupt and degenerate society. Thus, even the injunction to love one's enemies was not altruism but simply a strategy for developing certain character traits that would help one handle hostility "with notable restraint and calculated inversion" (Vaage 1994, 48).

I do not deny that some of the Q materials bear a certain resemblance to Cynic philosophy, nor do I reject all aspects of the reconstruction of Christian origins that scholars such as Mack and Vaage propose. The very existence of Q is testimony to a type of early commitment to Jesus centered not on resurrection faith but on Jesus' words and deeds. I depart sharply from those scholars, however, in my understanding of the character and meaning of those words and deeds attributed to Jesus that formed the basis of the group's ideology.

My initial contention is that there is something fundamentally wrong headed about the entire procedure that lies behind the "Cynic hypothesis." To begin with, it rests on the delineation of a supposedly earliest stratum of Q, which is in itself a rather tenuous move that has failed to convince all Q scholars. Even if we accept the arguments for Original Q, however, difficulties remain. To say that this material was the first to be gathered together in documentary form is not necessarily to say that it is chronologically prior in origin; it is possible that the additions to Original Q were drawn from traditions (perhaps those of other segments of the Jesus movement) that are as early as those first put together. So it is by no means self-evident that we should accept the supposed Original Q as somehow the definitive component in our reconstruction of Christian origins.

In addition, there is reason to see the interpretation of Original Q in terms of a Cynic-like ideology as a grand illusion made possible by the ambiguity of the material and lack of specific indicators of social context. It is largely because the supporters of the Cynic hypothesis presuppose a strongly Hellenistic ethos, based on their view of Lower Galilee as thoroughly Hellenized, that such a move seems logical to them. But it is precisely such presuppositions that I questioned in chapter 3 in discussing the world of Lower Galilee.

As an alternative to the Cynic hypothesis, then, here is the procedure I will follow in making use of Q as one window into the Jesus movement. I will focus on selected portions of the material generally designated as Original Q. Although I remain unconvinced by attempts to identify discrete strata in Q, my intention is to meet the proponents of the Cynic hypothesis on their own ground and show that even the supposed earliest level of this tradition is compatible with an understanding of the Jesus movement as prophetic in orientation. Then, in a subsequent section, I will draw on other elements in Q and the wider Jesus tradition to present a fuller initial characterization of the ethics of the movement.

In citing specific Q passages, I will follow the generally accepted practice of giving the chapter/verse designations found in Luke. For example, the designation Q 6:20 refers to a passage that is found in Luke 6:20 and paralleled in Matt 5:1-3. When I quote a passage, however, I will make use of *The Critical Edition of Q* (Robinson 2000), an attempt to reconstruct the original text of Q; so the wording may differ slightly from that in the standard translations of Luke. There are two reasons for this. First, the editors of *The Critical Edition of Q* have provided their own translations of the passages. Second, and more importantly, the Q text will be a reconstruction based on the comparison of the different versions.

Q 6:20-21. Scholars who identify strata in Q regard the three beatitudes in Luke 6:20-23 as standing at the beginning of the original document, following a brief introduction that is now lost. The reconstructed text is as follows: "Blessed are you poor, for God's reign is for you. Blessed are you who hunger, for you will eat your full. Blessed are you who mourn, for you will be consoled" (Robinson 2000, 48).

In commenting on these verses, Vaage argues that the first beatitude "is not primarily about the kingdom of God but rather, is a statement about the status (that is, happiness) of the poor, just as the two subsequent sayings in 6:21ab address those who are hungry and weep." The function of the reference to God's kingdom/rule is to explain how it is that the state of poverty, generally associated with misery, could generate contentedness (1994, 56).

On this reading, the beatitudes have nothing to do with a coming eschatological upheaval but are statements that support a Cynic attitude of detachment from riches and other conventional components of a happy and fulfilled life. One gains the kingdom inwardly by rejecting the illusory and fleeting signs of worldly success. "In 6:20b, the kingdom of God is precisely this ability—call it wisdom, if you will, to incorporate adversity into the enjoyment of contentment" (1994, 57).

We need not deny that the sayings function to make the Kingdom/rule present in the life of the individual or that they constitute a call to a kind of contentment that incorporates adversity. But these sayings are also compatible with the Israelite notion of a rule of God that comes precisely as an answer to the unjust and oppressive structures of present society. Certainly, the future tense can as easily signal an imminent event of dramatic proportions as it can the inevitable rising and falling of human fortunes in daily life. Wholly apart from the clearly prophetic verses that follow immediately in Luke 6:22-23, the Lukan beatitudes are at least susceptible to an interpretation that sees in them the dramatic theme of eschatological reversal, which Vaage rejects. Such a reading, moreover, coheres with the theme of God's preference for the poor and oppressed that is so pervasive in the Israelite tradition—a theme that is severely undercut if we accept Vaage's comments on the happiness of the poor.

Q 6:27-38. The heart of the Q ethic appears in Q 6:27-38. Here we find the most radical injunctions in the entire Jesus tradition, beginning with commands to love one's enemies, to return curses with blessings, to turn the other cheek, and to give one's shirt (inner garment, worn next to the skin) to anyone who seeks to take one's coat (outer garment). Verses 32-33 elaborate the logic of loving enemies, and vv. 34-35 extend that logic to the practice of lending. The result is a systematic condemnation of reciprocity as a motive for positive actions toward others: to love or to lend with the hope of reward is in no way meritorious behavior. Verses 35-36 reiterate the commands on love and lending, now supplementing them with a turn in the logic. A reward for the recommended behavior will in fact be forthcoming—not from human beings but from God. Then the sequence closes in vv. 36-38 with recommendations on how to imitate the impartial mercy of "the Most High," who "is kind to the ungrateful and the wicked" (6:35). Since God acts in such a radical and unexpected way, Jesus' followers too must extend Godlike kindness and mercy even to those who mistreat them: "Be merciful, as your Father is merciful" (6:36).

Recognizing that the "unresolved hostility and sporadic military repression" characteristic of Roman-dominated Galilee must have presented enormous barriers to personal happiness, Vaage interprets these verses as a recipe for "'liberation' of some sort" in these difficult circumstances (1994, 42). He understands them, however, as more a survival strategy than as an ethic in the sense of a statement of

what is in itself right. Regarding vv. 29-30, he therefore draws the following conclusion: "To turn the other cheek and give up both cloak and tunic were hardly
expressions of 'universal love,' but just 'smart moves' under the circumstances"
(1994, 40). As for the lead statement on loving enemies, which in fact seems to
state a universal principle, he views it as a secondary formulation, derived from
the more concrete injunctions that follow rather than vice versa.

> The particular phrase "love your enemies" should not . . . be understood
> as ever having been itself the operative mainspring of the *modus vivendi*
> it now introduces. The opening exhortation in 6:27 is simply a second-
> ary conceptualization of the specific acts referred to in 6:28-30. (1994,
> 43–44, citing Ricoeur 1974, 211–22)

In making his case for the injunctions in vv. 29-30 as practical strategy,
Vaage cites Robert Tannehill's classic study *The Sword of His Mouth*: "The commands are not based upon prudential considerations as to what will result in the
greatest good for the other" (Vaage 1994, 50, citing Tannehill 1975, 71). This use
of Tannehill, however, is somewhat misleading. Tannehill discusses this passage,
in its Matthean version, under the rubric of "focal instance." Matthew 5:39b-
42, he argues, presents a series of commands that are topically diverse but share
a rejection of the principle of self-protection. Precisely because of the diversity
of subject matter, "the similarity in meaning for which the similar form sets us
seeking is found not at a superficial level of topic but at the deeper level of our
tendency to put self-protection first." The extremity of the demands, moreover,
is a clue that they point beyond their immediate, literal meanings to suggest an
entirely different approach to life as an alternative to what is generally accepted.
The Greek term translated as "shirt," for example, referred to the inner garment,
worn next to the skin, so that anyone losing both "shirt" and "coat" would be
left "not only penniless but naked." The series of sayings thus function as "focal
points" within an open-ended field of situations that reach far beyond those specifically addressed (Tannehill 1975, 70–72).

There is a clear parallel between the way Tannehill understands the force
of the rhetoric of such passages and Vaage's reading of this passage in light of a
Cynic rejection of convention. In both cases, the extreme commandments call
social convention into question, and in neither case does the welfare of the other
come directly into consideration. Tannehill's point, however, is not that the
commands can be reduced to practical strategy. It is rather that the rhetoric of
the focal instance lures the hearer/reader into a process of open-ended reflection

that moves beyond obedience to specific rules. The commands do not deliver prepackaged answers to moral questions, but they do point to the direction in which the reflection should proceed. They create a shock that "arouses the moral imagination," fostering a new way of understanding the possibilities for action in any given situation. And the ability to do this, Tannehill comments, is the root of the power this type of command has "to speak again and again to new situations" (1975, 73–74). To exercise moral imagination in this way, to engage in this kind reflection, is to consider something other than a strategy for survival; it suggests a genuine engagement with issues of ultimate right and wrong, beyond the conventional definitions.

With respect to the command to love one's enemies, Vaage treats it not only as secondary to the specific commands that follow but also as an oxymoron, which is "literally quite impossible" (1994, 43). Only the concrete injunctions could have any direct practical application. The distinctive quality of the demand to love one's enemies, however, marks it as bedrock tradition, whether or not it was originally attached to the verses that follow (see Funk and Hoover 1993, 145–46, 291). And this is an injunction that has to be taken seriously as a central component in a definition of ethical behavior. Nor do I see the justification for Vaage's claim that it "depends upon the preexistence" of the concrete demands that follow (1994, 44).

In light of the complaint of some ethicists that "love" is a vague notion, easily sentimentalized, that offers little help as the basis of an ethic, it is important to address the issue of its precise meaning in the context of the Jesus movement. We may begin by asking whether Vaage is justified in treating the command to love one's enemies as an oxymoron, incapable of literal application. It appears to me that his claim rests on an overly individualistic and psychological understanding of what constitutes an "enemy." Vaage would apparently think of my enemy as a person whose relationship to me is characterized by mutual hatred and rejection—someone whom I would hate rather than love. Is this, however, an adequate understanding of the term within the environment of the Q material?

Although persons living in first-century Galilee would undoubtedly have had individual relationships characterized by bitter animosity, "enemy" would also have had a more social reference in that environment. Family was the basic unit of human association and self-identification, and there are specific concerns that would have been central to the maintenance of family well-being. Most basically, the family's honor was a core element in its standing in the community. And land, which was an indispensable measure of well-being, was a matter not merely of individual possession but of family inheritance. Possession of one's ancestral property was an essential component in the family's ability to survive and prosper.

Against this social background, we can imagine that the designation of an "enemy" had to do largely with feuding among various families and clans. Many of these would have involved controversies over land and other issues with an economic dimension, while others might have had to do with the way in which one group impaired another's honor. Such controversies arise in all societies, but anthropological studies suggest that the entire ancient Mediterranean culture was particularly "agonistic" in nature: families, groups, and individuals constantly struggled for competitive advantage. At the base of this struggle was the concept of "limited goods": people thought of all the components of human well-being—including not only land and other commodities but also honor—as quantitatively fixed. One family could gain honor only at the expense of another's honor, and one person's increase in wealth was perceived as the decrease of someone else's. And of course such competitive struggle would have escalated in proportion to the social and economic difficulties that plagued a given society.

In such an environment, the enemy would likely have been a person from another family locked in a bitter feud with one's own. Thus to love one's enemy would be to transcend the bitter rivalries that disrupted the social fabric and adopt a cooperative attitude (see Horsley 1987, 255–73). In the radical form presented in Q, it would mean a willingness to forgo the "normal" means of achieving competitive advantage, even to the point of suffering financial loss on the one hand and loss of honor on the other. The command to love one's enemies was thus a difficult challenge, to be sure, but not an oxymoron.

If we recall Gerstenberger's location of the genesis of ethics in family solidarity, we see that to love the enemy would have meant the expansion of this solidarity to a wider circle. On the level of village and town, law and custom held the social fabric together despite the competing interests of different families. The Q ethic, however, proposed an alternative system of self-identification that created a deeper, more internalized bond to play this role. Already familiar with the notion of God as father of all within the community, those confronted with the radical demands of Q would have felt a challenge to appropriate this ideology in a fuller way. As we will see in more detail below, this new understanding sharply relativized the family loyalty that had its roots in the most ancient traditions.

More than a strategy for personal survival through withdrawal from convention, this radical ethic drew on precedents in the Israelite tradition even as it brought them to an excruciating level of application. The demand to love one's neighbor (Lev 19:18) was an important component of covenant thought that lent motivating force to the various commandments regarding merciful action toward widows, orphans, and the poor. Beyond that, the command against oppressing foreigners (Exod 23:9) had early on extended human concern beyond the bounds of the covenant community, and the Israelite tradition was rife with expressions of God's concern for all people.[9] To call for the love of enemies thus had both a narrowing and a broadening effect. The somewhat abstract sense of God's universal care for humankind was now focused on those closer at hand in one sense but more distant in another. The enemy was a fellow Israelite, but one made socially distant through institutionalized grudge.

Q 6:32-36, which reiterates and elaborates on the demand to love one's enemies, reinforces the internalization of the demands in important ways. The references to the actions of Gentiles (Matt 5:47; Luke: "sinners") as a negative example, to "reward" as a motivation, and to the goal of becoming children of God suggest a type of virtue ethic. As Vaage comments, the goal is to become like God (1994, 41). This emphasis on virtue, however, is by no means antithetical to the Israelite focus on just action and community solidarity. To lend without expecting anything in return (v. 35) is not only to cultivate a personal lifestyle at odds with conventional behavior but also to act out of concern for the neighbor. At this point, concern for the other is in fact clearly in view: it is action done without hope for human reward that merits divine reward. As we have seen, John Barton finds the demand to imitate God in one's actions to be an important theme in the Israelite ethical tradition. In these verses, virtue ethics and the demand for just action toward the other coalesce.

Q 9:57-60; 14:26. The sayings in Q 9:57-60 present a radical portrait of Jesus as a homeless wanderer and a radical characterization of the conditions of discipleship. The statement with which Jesus rejects the potential follower's request "first to go and bury" his father is genuinely shocking: "Leave the dead to bury their own dead." Given the importance in the Israelite tradition of performing proper burial rites for parents, it has the feel of an outright assault on social convention. And the same is true of the statement in 14:26 in which Jesus demands that his followers hate their fathers and mothers. Both passages are amenable to an interpretation along the lines of the Cynic hypothesis, but another reading is possible if we view the sayings as hyperbolic accompaniments to the proclamation of God's rule. The point would be that something dramatic is happening in the present that takes precedence over all else, even family obligations.

More than social convention is at stake in the saying on burying the dead, however. As E. P. Sanders notes, it stands in opposition to "the Mosaic legislation as it was understood throughout Judaism" and thus reveals at least one instance in which "Jesus was willing to say that following him superseded the requirements of piety and Torah" (1985, 252, 255). This does not mean a wholesale rejection of the Law, but it does indicate a certain looseness toward it, which, combined with Jesus' demonstration in the temple, gives credence to Sanders's judgment that although Jesus did not oppose the Law neither did he regard it as a final dispensation (1985, 267). Such a view is quite intelligible against the background of a prophetic eschatology that envisioned the rule of God as already breaking into history.

Q 11:2b-4. The reconstructed Q version of the prayer Jesus taught his disciples is as follows: "Father—may your name be kept holy!—let your reign come. Our day's bread give us today; and cancel our debts for us, as we too have canceled for those in debt to us; and do not put us to the test" (Robinson 2000, 206).

Although proponents of the Cynic hypothesis reject the traditional eschatological interpretation of the prayer, there is good reason to accept it. To begin with, many scholars interpret the Greek *epiousios,* translated here as "day's" (more usually, "daily"), as a reference to bread for the expected eschatological banquet. Many also understand "the test" as the time of trial associated with the dissolution of the present age and the beginning of the new. Wholly apart from these disputed readings, moreover, to counsel prayer for the coming of God's rule suggests that it is not something attained by individuals but depends on the dramatic action of God.

The case becomes even stronger when we place the petition for "day's bread" and the forgiveness of debts against the social background described earlier. The petition for God's cancellation of debts is no doubt a plea for forgiveness of sins. That does not mean, however, that the declaration of the cancellations of debts owed to oneself should be reduced to the level of the forgiveness of personal affronts only. We are dealing with a society in which literal, financial debt is an all-pervasive negative fact of existence. In such a context, to say that "we too have cancelled debts owed to us" would almost certainly include literal, financial obligations. The juxtaposition of the two senses of "debt," in fact, has the dramatic effect of drawing a close analogy between God's forgiveness of one's sins and one's own forgiveness of another's debt. This reduces the significance of what the other owes by reminding the one who prays of the much greater debt all owe to God and elevates the forgiveness of the other's debt to the level of the imitation of the action of God.

There were, of course, types of debts that were not financial, given the all-pervasive character the client-patron system. Jesus' call for radical forgiveness thus undermined the whole system of debt that in its own way contributed to hierarchical social relations. To be indebted was to be subordinate to another and thus subject to the other's demands. Wholesale cancellation of debts thus implied the cancellation of the system itself in favor of the values inherent in God's coming rule.

Q 12:22-31; 12:33-34; 13:18-21; 14:16-24. There are significant blocks of material designated as Original Q that, taken in isolation, fit nicely into the Cynic hypothesis. Among them are the injunctions against worrying about material goods in Q 12:22-31 and the call to sell one's possessions in Q 12:33-34. In the parable of the great supper (Q 14:16-24), however, the polemic against concern with worldly affairs has a more prophetic character. Even deleting the explicit mention of "the poor, the crippled, the blind, and the lame" in Luke 14:21 as an addition, the theme of reversal seems central to the parable's meaning. The original hearers would have known that only the affluent would be invited to a "great banquet" in the first place. Thus, their replacement by people from the streets would suggest that the new guests were far from peers of those on the original guest list. As Robert Funk comments,

> There are those . . . whose mouths water at the thought of so sumptuous a repast. They secretly aspire to be of sufficient social standing and afflu-ence to be the recipients of invitations. But they know they will not be invited. . . . Only in fairy tales do beggars sit at the tables of aristocrats. (1964, 191)

We need not allegorize the banquet into a cipher for an apocalyptic sorting out of those worthy of a heavenly kingdom, as Matthew has done,[10] to see here a strong note of judgment involving a reversal of status. In the context of a com-munity with a sense of prophetic mission that took the part of the marginalized poor, it would constitute a powerful expression of their conviction that God was inaugurating a rule that would stand the existing social order on its head. And the same may be said of Q 13:18-21, the parables of the mustard and the yeast. In neither case do we have parables of "growth," as earlier interpretations supposed, but rather the symbolization of a rule that springs up unexpectedly from appar-ently insignificant beginnings. The Jesus movement might not have seemed like the dawn of God's promised rule, but the future would reverse that judgment in dramatic fashion. In addition, the figures of mustard and yeast suggest that God's coming rule will be subversive of the present order. For mustard was so notoriously difficult to control that there were prohibitions on planting it in a garden, and yeast was widely used as a symbol of corruption (B. B. Scott 1989, 375, 324).

The parable of the yeast, especially when it is considered in concert with the parable of the lost coin (Q 15:8-9), may also hint at another aspect of the social attitudes of the Q community. The use of the figure of a woman to make the parabolic point in each case is a possible reflection of an attitude of inclusiveness toward women. Although only a hint in itself, it supports the stronger indications of such inclusiveness noted in the preceding section.

Q 6:41-49. This group of sayings manifests the same ambiguity we have seen in other material designated as Original Q. Verses 41-42 present an ethic of nonjudgmentalism toward one's neighbor, and vv. 43-45 trace ethical action to the heart. The point is that one must cultivate a good heart in order to produce good works. Such injunctions promote a virtue ethic quite compatible with the Cynic hypothesis but also with a prophetic context. Verses 46-59 are likewise compatible with either mode of thought. The implicit warning regarding the consequences of building one's house on a weak foundation could mean only that evil deeds have a way of subverting one's plans for survival, but it could also take on a prophetic character if understood in light of God's coming rule. And if my earlier characterization of the Jesus movement is accepted, vv. 46-59 should in fact be interpreted in precisely that way.

The Witness of the Wider Jesus Tradition

Confirmation of the Q Ethic

Many of the themes present in the material designated as formative Q receive significant reinforcement in the wider tradition. And among the more vivid instances of such reinforcement are some of the longer parables of Jesus, which are generally accepted as belonging to the earliest level of the tradition.

The parable of the prodigal son (Luke 15:11-32) is a powerful portrayal of unconditional forgiveness. In addition, the power inherent in the bare plot is increased exponentially by the extravagant details of the father's acceptance, which flies in the face of social convention, and also by the scene with the older brother, which builds in a response to possible criticisms of that acceptance. And that very response suggests another dimension of inclusiveness. For, as Dan Via notes, "The father not only goes out to the prodigal son; he also goes out to the elder brother" (1967, 171). If we take this aspect seriously, then, we will have to imagine that Jesus' call to repentance is directed not only to those considered sinners and marginalized by conventional society but also to those elements in society whose loyalty to convention separates them from some of their neighbors. The image of Jesus as mediating a radical forgiveness on God's part, in any case, suggests an ethic of similarly radical forgiveness on the part of the community of Jesus' followers.

The Good Samaritan (Luke 10:25-37, with vv. 25-29 and at least v. 37b usually considered secondary) is an equally dramatic reinforcement of the theme of inclusiveness. Crossan rightly claims that it illustrates the nature of God's rule by shattering one's "world" and subverting conventional wisdom by forcing the listener to pronounce the hated Samaritan "good." However, his contention that the parable does not teach mercy but rather assumes it needs qualification. The freedom that opens up when conventional wisdom is shattered is precisely a freedom to move beyond narrow definitions of neighbor and broaden one's base of solidarity. A story that uses the Samaritan as a positive symbol is clearly an extension of the command to love one's enemies. It is also, by implication, a statement about the inclusiveness of God's love, a point that we found also in Q 6:35 (see also Matt 5:45), where Jesus points to God's kindness toward the wicked.

Another dimension of human solidarity appears in the Workers in the Vineyard (Matt 20:1-16). As B. B. Scott notes, although the landowner in no way violates the agreement he made with the all-day workers, "the parable's skillful strategy still maneuvers him into the appearance of injustice" (1989, 297). After all, a sense of basic fairness would suggest that those who worked longer should be paid more. But the impact of the final scene is precisely that it questions conventional human wisdom regarding "fairness" through the unexpected treatment of the latecomers as if they had worked all day. If the landowner's action portrays some aspect of God's rule, it is a sign that its advent has the character of gift. And if this is so, then the attitude of the grumbling workers mirrors human resentment of such grace. Thus, as Luise Schottroff comments, "The parable has two foci—the goodness of God and—as a consequence of this goodness—the solidarity of human beings" (1984, 138). Because Jesus manifested such solidarity, the community is clearly expected to follow suit.

A Specific Issue: Divorce and Remarriage
There is one position of Jesus on a specific ethical topic, unusually well attested as belonging to the earliest tradition, which merits special attention: his

prohibition of divorce. The multiplicity of versions, however, makes it difficult to know the exact nature of or reason for the prohibition. Mark 10:11, which forbids a man to divorce his wife and marry another woman, is partially paralleled in Luke 16:18a and in Matt 5:32 and 19:9. The two Matthean passages, however, make an exception in the case of *porneia*. This term is usually interpreted as adultery on the part of the wife, although some suggest that it refers to premarital intercourse, in which case "the exception clause would refer to the situation described in Deuteronomy 22:13-21, in which the husband finds his new bride not to be a virgin." Yet another possibility is that it has to do with "marriage within degrees of kinship prohibited by Jewish law, as outlined in Lev 18:6-18" (Hays 1996, 2000). Whatever the specific meaning of the term, the exception undoubtedly refers to the violation of laws pertaining to sexual relations.

The matter is further complicated by the fact that Matt 5:32 and Luke 16:18 add a prohibition against marrying a divorced woman, and Matt 5:32 lacks the qualification "and marries another" found in all the other forms. Also, only Mark 10:11-12 forbids a wife from divorcing her husband and remarrying. All forms of the saying, however, link divorce in some way to adultery. The Lukan and Markan forms, as well as Matt 19:9, view the man's divorce and remarrying as adultery; and Matt 5:31 claims that the divorce itself causes the wife to commit adultery.

The agreement of Matt 5:32 and Luke 16:18, against Mark, in adding the prohibition of marrying a divorced woman, indicates that some form of the saying on divorce existed in Q as well as in Mark, which means that we have two independent attestations within the Synoptic tradition. And we also have the testimony of Paul, who alludes to a saying of Jesus in his command that a wife should not separate from her husband—to which he adds the stipulation that if she does, she should not remarry (1 Cor 7:10).

The majority of scholars view the application of the prohibition to women as well as to men in Mark 10:12 as secondary, since Jewish women in Palestine did not generally have this right. As Eugene Boring comments, "[t]he only instances of Jewish women divorcing their husbands are among the nobility, who live by Gentiles standards and were considered scandalous exceptions (cf. Josephus, *Ant.* 15.259; 18.136 . . . 20.141-43)" (2007, 287–88). Likewise, Matthew's qualifier regarding *porneia* is doubtless a concession arising at a later stage of tradition. We should probably discount also the statement in Matt 5:32 that the divorce causes the woman to commit adultery. It is only here that the prohibition takes this particular form, and it is likely that the author of Matthew has constructed this version of the saying, on the basis of the Markan form he adopts in 19:9, in order to flesh out his set of "But I say unto you sayings" in 5:21-48 (Hagner 1993, 123). Further, it is only in Matt 5:32 that the woman's remarriage after her husband has divorced her is (apparently) assumed. We are therefore left with two declarations likely coming from an early stage of tradition: (1) a man commits adultery when he divorces his wife and marries another (Mark 10:11 and Luke 16:18); (2) a man commits adultery when he marries a divorced woman (Matt 5:32 and Luke 16:18).

Both of these declarations cut against the patriarchal system, but in different ways. The second curtails the man's right to marry, but it remains within a patriarchal structure in that the adultery is against the woman's first husband. The first declaration, however, breaks radically with tradition by proclaiming that the husband who divorces his wife and marries another commits adultery against his first wife. Mark's inclusion of "against her" makes this explicit, but even without this phrase the clear meaning is that it is the divorced wife who is the offended party. Since Jewish law recognized only adultery against a man, such a declaration would entail the extension of a man's right in this matter to a woman. Thus, the prohibition of divorce appears to many interpreters as a defense of women, who would be left in a precarious position when divorced by their husbands. And John Kloppenborg has taken this line of reasoning to its logical conclusion. The point is not just the protection of a woman from economic vulnerability but the intentional subversion of the androcentric honor-shame system itself; for the effect of divorce and remarriage would in fact be to rob a woman of her honor (1990, 197, cited by Crossan 1991, 301).

Some scholars, however, have challenged the notion that the protection of women is in view. E. P. Sanders (1985, 256–60) thinks the prohibition of divorce had to do with the imminence of God's reign. Thus, the reason was comparable to that of Paul, for whom this command was related to the notion that one should not change one's status in view of the "impending crisis" (1 Cor 7:24-31). This makes sense in light of Jesus' general proclamation, but it has no explicit support in any of the Synoptic texts. And, in any case, a focus on the imminence of God's rule is not necessarily incompatible with the view that the prohibition is intended to protect women.

Ulrich Luz, focusing largely on the second declaration, points out that since a divorce would leave a woman in a precarious situation, the prohibition of marrying a divorced woman could, by cutting off the possibility of her coming under the protection of a new husband, have a devastating effect on her. Like Sanders, he denies that the motive is protection of women and argues that the prohibition is a function of Jesus' sense of the "pure, unconditional will of God" (1989, 302).

It is still relevant to ask, however, what the logic behind such a reading of God's will might be. And it is also relevant to note that the cumulative effect of the two declarations would have been to reaffirm the integrity of families. Divorce disrupts the family, and marriage of a divorced woman contributes indirectly to the dissolution. (We should therefore be clear that criticism of the androcentrism of the family system did not imply an attack on the institution of family itself. Thus, the issue at stake in the radical saying in Matt 8:22//Luke 9:60 would be whether an *absolute* attachment to family prevented one from responding to the demands of God's coming rule, not whether family loyalty itself is valid.) Even if a broader interest such as reaffirmation of the family is in view, however, it seems undeniable that the first declaration both increases the rights of women and undermines aspects of the androcentric system of honor and shame. And what we have already seen about the status and role of women within the Jesus movement makes such motivation seem likely.

One question remains about the specific meaning of the first prohibition: Are men prohibited from divorcing their wives at all, or only from divorcing and remarrying? It is important to note that the divorce would in itself work hardship on the woman. And since the purpose of divorce was generally remarriage (Luz 1989, 302), the distinction begins to fade. The phrase "and marries another" becomes a point of clarification, almost redundant. So it would appear most likely that in the Jesus movement divorce was prohibited altogether, at least in principle.

A Broader Issue: The Jewish Law

The sayings on divorce and on burying the dead (see above on Q 9:57-60) involve us in a long-standing controversy: the question of the relationship of Jesus and his disciples to the Jewish Law. It is a controversy that raises issues of a sensitive nature in light of recent attempts to avoid the caricatures of Judaism that prevailed for so long in popular Christian thought, the official theologies of Christian denominations, and Christian scholarship from both liberal and conservative quarters. And it is one of the ironies of the present situation that it is primarily the statements of some liberal Christian scholars that others, both Jewish and Christian, find to perpetuate—however unintentionally—the age-old stereotypes.

How did Jesus and his disciples regard the Jewish Law in general? Were they fully observant of it? More specifically, how did they relate to the laws of purity? These are difficult questions, because the evidence is ambiguous. What is most important is that we pay attention to that evidence itself. This means, on the one hand, avoiding the temptation to insure Jesus' special character by drawing a sharper contrast between the Jesus movement and other Jewish groups than is warranted. On the other hand, it means not glossing over whatever tensions the evidence does in fact indicate in order to avoid the appearance of anti-Jewish sentiments. Needless to say, such a task presents us with a fine line to walk and calls for extreme caution. My intention, therefore, is to depend as little as possible on speculation on this point.

I have already noted, in connection with Q 9:57-60, E. P. Sanders's comment that this saying shows that Jesus did not regard the Mosaic dispensation as final. This does not mean that Jesus denied the validity of the Law, and Sanders goes to great lengths to call into question the image of Jesus as one who flaunted disobedience to the Law's requirements. Regarding the prohibition of divorce, for example, he points out that it does not overturn a Mosaic demand but merely forbids something that the Law allows: "It is a general principle that greater stringency than the law requires is not illegal" (1985, 256). With respect to the controversy stories in the Gospels, he makes three points. First, the stories themselves involve "extraordinarily unrealistic settings," such as a group of Pharisees lurking in cornfields in the hope of identifying transgressors. Thus, we should question not only Jesus' transgression of the Law but even that he had significant disputes with the Pharisees. As scholars have widely recognized for some time, the Gospel stories of such disputes generally reflect a later situation in which the followers of Jesus are competing with other groups to determine the future shape of the Israelite heritage. Second, the disputes regarding handwashing are not disputes about the Law per se, since this ritual was required only of priests, although some particularly pious groups among the laity took obligations such as this upon themselves. And, finally, the stories of healing on the Sabbath do not involve transgression of the Law, since they do not entail actual work (1985, 264–66).

There is little doubt that later tradition has exaggerated whatever controversies Jesus had with the Pharisees. Accounts of such conflicts pervade the tradition so thoroughly, however, that it is difficult to imagine that they have no historical basis at all. As we saw in the preceding chapter, the Pharisees were probably based in Jerusalem, as "retainers" who served the interests of the temple leadership, and were not in charge of the synagogues. It is likely, however, that precisely because of their connections to the temple hierarchy, they would have visited Galilee for the purpose of promulgating the interpretations of the Great Tradition fostered in Jerusalem. It is therefore probable that Jesus and his followers, as proponents of the Little Tradition, would have entered into some disputes with them. Herzog summarizes the point as follows:

> Although the Pharisees were centered in Jerusalem, they had reason enough to travel to Galilee to maintain their networks of agents and supporters. In this role, either they or their proxies could very well have entered into conflict with Jesus over the interpretation of the Torah. This means that Jesus' conflicts with the Pharisees are not to be understood as a Christian theologian (Jesus) fighting against a legalistic Judaism (Pharisees) but are better understood as arguments about the application of Torah for Galilean villagers and its implications for the meaning of a covenant community. (2005, 79)

We cannot know the exact terms of these disputes, but it is important to address the much debated issue of the purity codes. For many scholars, Jesus' willingness to forgo these regulations was a distinctive trait of his ministry that was a prime illustration of his inclusiveness and compassion. Paula Fredriksen among others, however, has objected to this line of argument. Impurity, she notes, is a temporary rather than a permanent state, and the purity system involves regular means of purification. For some scholars, then, the purity code, far from something that divides people along class lines, is actually a leveling agent. Everyone, from priests on down, goes through a constant cycle of impurity and purification. Thus Jesus' touching of a leper is something that could be taken care of through the prescribed rituals. And, as Fredriksen further notes, the tradition itself gives a few glimpses of Jesus' deference to these rituals, as when he tells the leper to show himself to the priest (1999, 105–10, 197–214).

So do we, then, have genuine evidence that Jesus and his disciples violated or subverted the purity laws? It is notable that the tradition never depicts Jesus or the disciples engaged in any acts of observance. Such an argument from silence is not irrelevant but cannot be taken as determinative in itself. Another body of material often cited in this regard is the Gospels' portrayal of the Pharisees attacking Jesus for associating with "tax collectors and sinners."[11] The usual assumption is that this charge was provoked by the inclusion of common people, who habitually ignored the laws of ritual purity out of ignorance or the difficulties that plague the lives of the poor. E. P. Sanders, however, notes that we have no indication that either the Pharisees or any pious groups took upon themselves the purity laws of the priests or "that they aimed at the exclusion of the common people from worship or study" (1985, 198). He suggests, rather, that we understand the term "sinners" not as the merely nonobservant but precisely as the "wicked" and that Jesus' "offense" was offering them fellowship "without requiring repentance as normally understood . . ." (1985, 199–206; quotation from 206).

A passage of particular importance in this connection is Mark 7:15-19, including the narrator's interpretive comment in v. 19. In the sayings themselves, Jesus states that nothing that comes into a person can defile, although what comes out of a person can—that is, evil thoughts. Whatever we make of such a pronouncement in itself, the narrator's comment clearly rescinds the entire set of dietary regulations: "Thus he declared all foods clean." The problem with giving full credence to this material, however, is that it very likely, at least in part, reflects the postresurrection situation, in which Jesus' followers were gradually moving away from the larger Israelite community and the ritual requirements of the Law had become a matter of debate. This is almost certainly the case with the narrator's comment, since—as many scholars have noted—had Jesus made such an explicit statement we would not have had the controversy over the Law that is visible at so many points in the New Testament.[12] And we can say that for similar reasons the sayings themselves were probably not originally understood as a systematic denial of the food laws per se. There is, however, some force to the Jesus Seminar's acceptance of the saying in v. 15 ("There is nothing outside a person that by going in can defile") as representing in substance an authentic theme in Jesus' teaching: not only does it stand out as distinctive over against the cultural background, but it is "independently attested in" the *Gospel of Thomas* 14:4 "in a different configuration," which suggests that it "once circulated independently" (Funk and Hoover 1993, 69). On the other hand, the saying also serves the interests of a community that is beginning to embrace Gentiles.

So where, then, does this leave us with respect to the attitude of the Jesus movement to the laws of purity? We know that in the postresurrection situation, those laws were eventually abandoned, but our evidence regarding the preresurrection situation remains ambiguous. The few indications of deference to these requirements are hardly enough to substantiate Fredriksen's portrayal of Jesus as fully observant, but neither can we find unambiguous evidence of a systematic denial of the purity system per se. It is fair to note, however, that the fact that the later community debated the issue cuts both ways. Although it indicates that Jesus probably never attacked the purity system systematically, it also suggests that there was something about the teachings (whether or not we accept Mark 7:15 as authentic) and practices in the Jesus movement that led later followers to think he had done just that.

To some extent, the question of the Jesus movement's relationship to the purity codes hinges on how we understand their relationship to the Pharisees. For Sanders, purity was simply not an issue among them. His view, however, depends largely on an argument from silence—that is, the absence of clear evidence that in the pre-70 C.E. situation the Pharisees were in fact largely concerned with purity rules surrounding table fellowship (1985, 187–88). And his view also requires that we see the Gospel accounts of Jesus' controversies with the Pharisees as having practically no historical basis at all. However, granted that these accounts are greatly exaggerated and reflect the interests of the church in the post-70 period, one must ask whether Sanders is right in discounting them to the degree he does. As Jacob Neusner notes, "the Gospels' picture conforms to the rabbinical traditions about the Pharisees, which center upon the laws of tithing and ritual purity, defining what and with whom one may eat, that is, table-fellowship" (1979, 80). To be sure, the rabbinic sources are late and reflect the interests of those who apparently succeeded the Pharisees, so we cannot accept them uncritically any more than we can the Gospels. But it does not seem sound to neglect the correspondence between two of our ancient sources, especially when our third source—the Jewish historian Josephus—does not explicitly contradict the impression that they give on the matter of purity.

It therefore seems likely that purity was, indeed, an issue between Jesus' group and the Pharisees, but that does not mean that we must see the latter as hard-hearted bigots eager to exclude others from salvation. With Herzog, we may understand their motives as "shaped by the imperial situation to some extent, for [they] were trying to isolate and create an area of life that the colonizers could not easily control or undermine because they did not have easy access to it." On this interpretation, they wanted to foster a "politics of holiness" for all Israel by replicating "in their houses the meals that occur in the temple." However, "the very conditions that led to pure table companionship excluded the peasants of Galilee and created an assortment of outcasts and outlaws identified in the Gospels by phrases like 'toll collectors and sinners'" (Herzog 2005, 195–96).

We need not deny that among the marginalized folk included in the Jesus movement's fellowship were those whom Sanders terms the "wicked," but it is hard to avoid the conclusion that this pejorative designation was also directed at those among the peasantry who did not comply with the Pharisees' high standards of purity. We may thus imagine that the Jesus movement, informed by the Little Tradition, included a wide range of persons who were marginalized for various reasons and who thus manifested in graphic terms "an alternative political vision for the renewal of Israel that includes the ingathering of those who were made outcasts by the propaganda of the great tradition of the elders" (Herzog 2005, 196).

Summary

The ethic of the Jesus movement took shape against the background of Jesus' proclamation of the coming rule of God. It was a radical ethic, calling for devotion from the depths of one's heart and a willingness to break with social convention. The commitment it demanded entailed an explicit detachment from anything that might stand in the way of following Jesus—be this family obligations or an attachment to the goods of the world. This ethic cannot, however, rightly be termed an "interim ethic," as if the demands placed on the followers of Jesus issued solely or even primarily from the crisis created by the imminence of the new age. For the demands were, at least in some instances, grounded explicitly in the character of God. Those who followed Jesus were called to act toward their neighbors in a way that imitates God's own actions both in the natural world and in the treatment of persons. The ethical injunctions therefore have for the most part nothing to do with eschatology per se, although they may be made urgent by it. Reference to the character of God also means that the ethic was not one of sheer divine command. For imitation of God is a matter of virtue and not simply action, and it is a response not merely to a command but to a recognition of the very nature of the good, seen above all in God's own embodiment of it.

The "truth," therefore, that grounded the call to do and be the good in the Jesus movement was the goodness of God and the imminence of God's rule. Those who followed Jesus believed that God was in the process of creating among them the rule of peace and justice envisioned by the prophets, most particularly justice for the poor and those otherwise marginalized. They understood their role as not only to proclaim that rule but to begin to live their lives, collectively and individually, as a proleptic manifestation of it. Yet even as this ethic anticipated a future ideal state, it was also in some sense a restatement of the age-old ethic of community solidarity fostered within families and small communities early in Israelite history. It also stood in a long trajectory of the reformation of that ethic insofar as it reached dramatically beyond the traditional boundaries within such solidarity is generally defined.

This ethics meant first of all to allow a change in one's own heart that would effect a change in behavior toward others. And this behavior involved a radical love of others that went so far as to embrace the enemy, putting behind oneself all competitive striving for wealth or honor at the expense of others. It necessitated a rejection of violent retaliation and all forms of feuding based on family or clan histories or a personal sense of affront. It meant embracing the other in a new sense of community and cooperation. To embrace the other, moreover, entailed rejection of the entire system of social ranking and a nonjudgmentalism that overlooked the past lives of those whose actions were perceived to be outside the pale of religious or social acceptability. It even embraced those among the heirs of the Israelite heritage traditionally considered enemies of the true people of God, although we have no clear evidence that it dealt explicitly with Gentiles, the people beyond the bounds of that heritage.

We may say, then, that the Jesus movement was an alternative community within the larger Israelite society. It did not negate the heritage or fundamental values of the larger group, but it did challenge some social norms in light of its own appropriation of elements within that heritage. If it was an ethic of love, then, it was also an ethic of liberation, because it offered a radical form of inclusiveness. By prohibiting divorce, it offered protection for women. But the liberative aspect of the community's practices was not exhausted by the inclusiveness of its internal life. For those very practices, if we take them seriously as signs of the proleptic rule of God, also constituted a form of nonviolent resistance to the hierarchical, violent, and oppressive governance of the empire in which the entire Israelite people, along with many others, were ensnared. The ethic of the Jesus movement was therefore also an ethic of communal self-liberation empowered by God's own liberating action. In their commitment to the rule of God in their own internal life, they both proclaimed and lived out a challenge to the rule of Rome that, although in some sense "hidden" and implicit, was nonetheless real. For it created, for those who embraced it, an alternative reality.

HERMENEUTICAL QUESTIONS

The ethic of the Jesus movement, as I have described it, is a relatively self-consistent way of life. There is, however, a subtle point of tension between the ethic proper and the set of beliefs that support it. This tension is a function of the eschatological orientation of the movement. On the one hand, the primary force of the proclamation of God's rule is an affirmation of the justice of God and a declaration of hope for human beings in oppressive situations. In an eschatological context, however, the hope for justice is also wed to confidence in a coming judgment, a point underscored by Jesus' prophetic action that symbolized the expected destruction of the temple. There can be no justice apart from the dismantling of the orders of society that make for injustice. The execution of final judgment, however, stands to some degree in tension not only with the ethic of inclusiveness commended to human beings but also with the radical inclusiveness of God, who is "kind to the ungrateful and the wicked" (Q 6:36). Although the ethic forbids human violence, hope for the triumph of justice seemingly necessitates the violence of God. In a sense, then, we can say that the ethic of radical nonviolence and inclusion resists the very sanction the tradition gives it. And yet it remains unclear what basis there is for hope apart from belief in just such an act of God.

For many Christians throughout the centuries, this tension has presented no problem at all. After all, those subject to God's eschatological judgment are precisely those who have stubbornly resisted God's will. We should note, however, that those who embrace this logic often do so not in the name of an ethic of love, justice, and liberation but on doctrinal grounds. In their eyes, many of those subject to judgment, along with "evildoers" within the community, are not necessarily the unjust but rather the unconverted. So the question is whether acceptance of the eschatological sanction might violate the very heart and soul of the ethic of the Jesus movement. This is a question that cries out for hermeneutical reflection, and one that we will have to pursue in some detail in part 4.

Another point of tension might seem to arise when we consider the apparent limitation of the vision of the movement to the renewal of Israel, without any explicit consideration of the Gentile world. Over against this absence stand such passages as Q 12:24, which depicts God's universal care: "Consider the ravens: they neither sow nor reap, they have neither storehouse nor barn, and yet God feeds them. Of how much more value are you than the birds" (see also vv. 27-28). We should probably assume, however, that a notion such as is found in Isa 2:1-5 and numerous other places in the Israelite tradition was presupposed. In the coming age the Gentiles would in fact be somehow included in God's community.

There is, on the other hand, an undeniable tension that arises in any attempt to render the ethic of the Jesus movement relevant in our own world of experience. Like so many throughout the ages, we in our time are often brought up short when confronted with the extreme nature of some of the demands: nonretaliation, radical detachment from wealth, an apparently absolute prohibition of divorce. Indeed, the ethic of the Jesus movement can strike us as simply unworkable in the actual world. Of course "workability" is hardly the point with respect to the demands of God's rule, but the differences between the ancient world and our own, as well as the complex character of human existence generally, once again drive us to recognize the need for hermeneutical reflection. In fact, if we take the issue of divorce as a test case, when we turn from the Jesus movement to the canonical tradition, we can already see such reflection at work.

One important issue that we need to keep in mind as we pursue this reflection is the question of the nature of the language employed in the materials before us. We have seen some specific cases of modes of expression that are clearly intended to be more imaginative than literal, to provoke deep reflection rather than rote compliance. The parables of Jesus are inherently of such nature, and along with them stand such materials as the "focal instance" discussed in relation to Q 6:27-38 and blatantly hyperbolic statements. Such clearly open-ended pronouncements force us to ask about the most appropriate way of responding to the entire range of ethical instructions, even the elements that seem to be absolute and call for literal application.

There are, consequently, complex issues that face any interpreter seeking to explore the relevance of the ethic of the Jesus movement for our own time. What is the appropriate Christian response on the issue of divorce? Does faithfulness to Jesus demand pacifism, a rejection of war or, indeed, any kind of violence, under any circumstances? What about self-defense, or the defense of others? What should the call to detachment from worldly goods mean in our specific circumstances? How, more generally, do we appropriate Jesus' "preferential option for the poor"? And, finally, what are the implications of his proclamation of the coming of God's rule for our social, political, and economic institutions? I will try to write more concretely about such questions in part 4, but my point at this juncture is that we need to accept hermeneutical reflection as a necessary and appropriate response to tradition, both generally and in relation to ethical issues. So the question is not whether contemporary Christians should become a part of an ongoing process of reinterpretation but only what type of reflection is appropriate in any given set of circumstances.

PART III

the ethics of the canonical writings

CHAPTER 5

the gospel of matthew

There is no segment of the New Testament in which ethical injunction is more prominent than the Gospel of Matthew. As explicit and all-pervasive as the ethical dimension of this Gospel is, however, it is not the central focus of the writing. For Matthew is, above all, a story—a narrative construction in which plot, characters, and themes are the primary conveyors of meaning. And this story presents itself as the denouement in the larger drama of God's ongoing redemptive relationship to Israel and the world. The Matthean ethic therefore takes shape within the context of an explicit theological point of view or understanding of ultimate truth. From the perspective of this story, the God who made a covenant with the people of Israel acted in the birth, life, death, and resurrection of Jesus to bring salvation to the people of Israel and, through them, to the world at large. The resurrected Jesus, moreover, is spiritually present with those who follow him as they carry out the mission of making disciples "of all nations" (28:19). And this mission will remain in effect until his eventual return in glory to judge the world and bring the fullness of God's rule.

This Gospel's distinctive narrative structure and characterization of Jesus do, however, create a vehicle particularly well suited for ethical instruction. Jesus' role is defined largely in terms of teaching, and the appearance of five major teaching discourses as the story unfolds gives him occasion to make explicit pronouncements on numerous issues.[1] The first of these discourses, moreover—the Sermon on the Mount in chapters 5–7—is an extended articulation of the ethic of the rule of heaven (Matthew's circumlocution for rule of God). Explicit teaching, however, is not the only way in which the story conveys an ethical point of view. For Jesus himself models ethical actions, so that his deeds as well as his words are an important means of instruction.

Clearly, then, the figure of Jesus is central to the story that is told. As Messiah and Son of God, Jesus is God's representative; he speaks with God's authority, which he in some sense passes on to his disciples, and, through them, to the church he has founded. Yet, the effect of this presentation of Jesus is not merely to grant him an exalted status. It is also to make specific declarations about the character of God. As the one who is named "God is with us" in 1:23, Jesus stands in God's stead. Since he speaks and acts for God, his words and deeds are God's own words and deeds: to obey his commands is to obey God, and to imitate his actions is to imitate God. And much of the plot of the Gospel has to do with the conflict between competing evaluations of Jesus' status and between opposing understandings of who God is and what God requires.

THE AUTHORITY OF JESUS

In the final scene of the Gospel, Jesus makes an explicit claim to God's authority as the basis of the missionary commission he delivers to his disciples: "All authority in heaven and on earth has been given to me" (28:18). This is not, however, the first time the reader of Matthew has encountered such a declaration. Jesus has already stated in 11:27 that "all things have been handed over" to him by his Father and concluded the declaration by grounding this claim in his exclusive relationship with God: "and no one knows the Son except the Father, and no one knows the Father except the Son and anyone to whom the Son chooses to reveal him." In addition, Jesus' status and authority are supported by the direct testimony of God. At his baptism, a heavenly voice declares that "This is my Son, the Beloved, with whom I am well pleased" (3:17). And in the transfiguration scene, a voice from a cloud repeats the declaration with the addition, "listen to him" (17:5). All this testimony, moreover, takes place against the background of Jesus' genealogy, which establishes him as a descendant of both Abraham and David (1:1-17); his miraculous birth through the action of the Holy Spirit (1:18-24); the testimony of divinely guided magi from the East (2:1-12); and repeated references to the fulfillment of Scripture (for example, 1:22; 2:15, 17, 23; 4:14).

The divine authorization of Jesus' status is only half the picture, however; his obedience to God's requirements is the necessary complement to that authorization. Thus, his reply to John's reluctance to perform the baptism provides the initial justification for God's approving evaluation of him: "Let it be so now; for it is proper for us to fulfill all righteousness" (3:15). In addition, Jesus further demonstrates his obedience in the scene where he is tested by the devil (4:1-11) and again, dramatically, in his agonized submission to God's will in Gethsemane (26:36-46).

When Jesus begins the Sermon on the Mount in 5:1, his status as Son of God and Messiah is already well established. Likewise, the general thrust of his preaching has been delineated: at 4:17 his message is defined as repentance in the face of the nearness of the rule of heaven. So as the sermon opens with references to that coming rule (5:3), it becomes clear that the instruction that follows defines an ethic specifically for it. Indeed, the rule of heaven is, in Keck's apt phrase, the "master" image of this Gospel (1984, 47, cited by Blount 2001, 67). The teaching, however, does not stand alone; for the reader is also aware of certain fundamentals regarding Jesus' character. Not only has he demonstrated obedience to God, but in 4:23-25 his ministry of deeds appears precisely as a ministry of compassion and liberation from suffering: he cures all manner of diseases and demon possession. Therefore, when he commands mercy in 5:7, he does so as one who has already extended mercy himself. His authority comes from God, but it is supported by his own compassionate action, which is self-validating as the manifestation of the good.

JESUS' DEFINITIVE INTERPRETATION OF THE LAW

Central to the Matthean understanding of Jesus' teaching is the programmatic statement in 5:17-20. Jesus declares that he has not come to abolish the Law and the prophets but to fulfill them: the Law in its entirety will stand "until all is accomplished." And in anticipation of later encounters with the scribes and Pharisees leading up to his bitter denunciation of them in chapter 23, Jesus closes the statement with this warning: "For unless your righteousness exceeds that of the scribes and Pharisees, you will never enter the kingdom of heaven."

These verses abound with exegetical difficulties, not the least of which has to do with the precise meaning of the verb "to fulfill" (*pleroun*).[2] It seems clear, however, in light of the contrast ("but I say unto you") sayings that follow immediately in vv. 21-48 that the verb refers primarily to Jesus' interpretation of the Law, which brings out its true intent. But since Jesus fulfills both the Law *and the prophets*, we must also recognize a salvation-historical dimension alongside the normative aspect (Trilling 1974, 174). Jesus' definitive exposition of the deeper meaning of the Law belongs explicitly to a particular stage in God's ongoing relationship with Israel. As the constant references to fulfillment of prophecy throughout the Gospel make clear, what the prophets had foretold is now coming to pass, and God's plan is reaching its penultimate goal. All that remains at the end of the Gospel is for the mission to the world to proceed in anticipation of Jesus' eventual return.

The term "righteousness" (*dikaiosynē*) in v. 20 has been the subject of some debate, but it is now widely accepted[3] that in Matthew the term usually refers to human action in accordance with God's will. As we will see later, this is not always the case, but it is clear that in this verse Jesus tells those who would follow him that their obedience to God's commands must be better than that rendered by the scribes and Pharisees. For this reason, some interpreters, notably Willi Marxsen (1993, 237), interpret the demand for a better righteousness in purely quantitative terms. However, the first two contrast sayings (5:21-30) suggest otherwise. By forbidding anger as well as murder and lust as well as adultery, Jesus is clearly asking for an obedience that goes deeper than adherence to external commands. He is calling for what Hays terms "the transformation of character and of the heart" (Hays 1996, 98), a point Jesus makes explicitly at the end of the discourse on church life when he demands forgiveness "from the heart" (18:35).

The qualitative character of obedience is also apparent within the Sermon on the Mount in 6:19-34, where Jesus continually stresses one's fundamental orientation as the basis of ethical action. To say that "where your treasure is, there your heart will be also" (6:21) or to call for a healthy eye as the "lamp of the body" (6:22-23) is to recognize that one's inner attitude is the root of all ethical action. Similarly, the injunction against serving two masters is a call for wholeheartedness in one's devotion to God (6:24). And the demand for radical dependence on God for the necessities of life (6:25-34) likewise addresses one's fundamental motivations. Those who trust God in the depths of their being will not be distracted from righteous behavior by attachment to worldly goods.

That Jesus' teaching is an interpretation of the Law is evident in the contrast sayings in 5:21-48. The emphatic use of "I" (*egō*) is a sign of Jesus' sovereign authority: he speaks as Messiah. In light of v. 17, however, the "but" (Greek *de*; a weak negative) cannot indicate an abrogation of the Law as such. Nor do any of the contrasts actually entail the overturning of a commandment. The sayings on anger and lust simply deepen the injunctions against murder and adultery, and the same is true of the prohibition of all swearing in vv. 33-37. The saying on divorce, while it forbids something the law permits, does not permit anything the Law forbids. And this is true even in the parallel saying in 19:7-8, where Jesus attributes the permission for divorce to Moses' concession to the people's hardness of heart. The contrast sayings thus bring out the true meaning of the Law by giving its definitive interpretation. And the explanatory statement in 19:8 only makes explicit what is implicit in 5:21-48: Jesus' interpretation recovers God's primordial will and actual intention in giving the commandments.

God's primordial will, moreover, is summarized in the two great commandments—love of God and love of neighbor—that Jesus endorses in 22:34-40. And the programmatic character of this endorsement is insured by v. 40: "On these two commandments hang all the law and the prophets." Here Jesus states unequivocally the principle at work in his interpretation: these dual commands constitute the hermeneutical key for unlocking the true meaning of all else in the Law. And this principle is clearly at work throughout the Gospel. To begin with, an equivalent of the command to love one's neighbor appears in the golden rule at 7:12, which closes the ethical teachings of the Sermon on the Mount. Then, in the judgment scene in 25:31-46, it is precisely one's performance of or failure to perform deeds of compassion that is the basis of the separation of the sheep from the goats. In addition, on two occasions (9:10-13 and 12:1-8) Jesus quotes Hos 6:6 as justification for his actions: "I desire mercy, not sacrifice." In both cases, Jesus' compassionate behavior provokes controversy. In the first, it is his acceptance of tax collectors, and in the second, it is that he allows his disciples to pluck grain on the Sabbath because they are hungry.

The use of the quotation shows in both cases that Jesus derives the notion that mercy trumps a narrow reading of the Law from Scripture itself. And in 12:1-8 he underscores the point with an illustration from the life of David, making the matter even more explicit with his question, "Have you not read in the law . . . ?" Immediately after this incident, moreover, we find Jesus defending the practice of healing on the Sabbath by elevating compassion in the face of human need to the status of an interpretive principle. For he follows his declaration that a person is of greater value than a sheep with the pronouncement that "it is lawful to do good on the sabbath" (12:12).

It is thus clear that in Matthew Jesus is the definitive interpreter of the Law, using the love command as the hermeneutical key to discover its deeper intention, or God's primordial will. Equally clear is that Jesus does not appear as the giver of a new law: as 5:17-18 shows, the Law in its original form still stands. In practical terms, however, it is Jesus' messianic interpretation that will be functional for the new community he founds in 16:16-20 and on whose behalf he gives the discourse on church life in chapter 18. For in the scene that concludes the Gospel in 28:16-20, it is to his own teaching that he refers as he sends the disciples out to all the world in mission: "Go therefore and make disciples of all nations . . . teaching them to obey *everything that I have commanded you.*"

The primacy of Jesus' messianic interpretation, however, has the actual effect of loosening, rather than tightening, the process of deriving concrete guidance from scriptural prescriptions. For it is clear from the fragmentary character of the "but I say unto you" sayings in 5:17-48 that they are illustrations of the nature of messianic interpretation rather than an exhaustive restatement of the details of the Law. The same must be said of the Sermon on the Mount itself, as well as the cumulative ethical teaching of the Gospel as a whole. We do not in Matthew come anywhere near the formulation of a new Law or complete rendering of the meaning of the full range of Mosaic legislation.

Where, then, does this leave the Matthean community? On the one hand, it inherits a pronouncement of the continuing validity of every detail of the Law. Alongside it, however, stands Jesus' fragmentary messianic reinterpretation of that Law, based on the hermeneutical principle of the love command, which suggests a much more open-ended process of applying the Law to concrete situations. The implication is that the community must continue the process of reinterpretation rather than simply reiterate the details of Jesus' own readings.

What is implicit throughout the Gospel, moreover, becomes explicit in the church discourse in 18:15-20. After outlining a procedure for dealing with church members who "sin against" other members[4] and then granting the power to exclude from the community, Jesus acknowledges the decision-making power of the body itself: "whatever you bind on earth will be bound in heaven, and whatever you loose on earth will be loosed in heaven." The immediate context of this pronouncement shows that the power of exclusion is the focus of attention, but the parallel statement in 16:20, when understood in the light of rabbinic usage of the terms "bind" and "loose," suggests a broader reference.

Although traditional interpretation of 16:16-20, where Jesus founds the church and gives Peter the "keys of the kingdom," has fostered the image of St. Peter as the gatekeeper of heaven, more recent exegesis reveals a different possibility. In rabbinic thought, the terms "bind" and "loose" referred to legal interpretation. To "bind" was to state that a regulation must be followed; to "loose" was to declare the opposite. And if we understand that in Matthew *the kingdom of heaven* is not a synonym for heaven itself but is a reality that is already breaking into the present world, then it is clear that the power Peter is given—and that is given to the church as a whole in 18:18—is "the power to open the gates of God's Rule to persons here and now" (Pregeant 2004, 114; see Davies and Allison 1991, 634). But how do Peter and the church exercise this power? Precisely by "binding" and "loosing," which is to say by interpreting the Law, deciding what is permitted and what is not permitted. Thus, when Jesus follows the statement on binding and loosing in 18:18 with the promise that he will be with his followers (v. 20) and will give them whatever they ask, we can see that much more than the issue of exclusion from the fellowship is at stake. Jesus promises his presence to those in the community precisely as they wrestle with how to apply the Law to the concrete issues of their ongoing communal life. And although the parallel promise at 28:20 surely involves broader notions, such as empowerment for mission, the reference to teaching in the first part of the verse shows that his presence is also guidance in the process of teaching, which necessarily involves interpretation.

In sum, Jesus' definitive interpretation of the Law is more illustrative than legislative. He establishes a hermeneutical principle and applies it in a few instances but then passes on to the community the ongoing task of reapplication of the principle to new circumstances. There is therefore an open-ended quality to the interpretation of the Law, which is consonant with the open-ended quality of some of the specific teachings Matthew incorporates. We have already noted (see above, 102) the phenomenon of the "focal instance," illustrated in the radical sayings on nonviolence (Matt 5:38-42), the effect of which is more to foster reflection than to legislate specific behavior. And the imaginative character of such material is not lost when it becomes part of a Gospel that recognizes the necessity of ongoing interpretation.

This does not mean that Matthew leaves us with nothing but the broad principle of love. The illustrations are many, and the substance of the ethic is not in doubt. The Sermon on the Mount incorporates much of the Q material treated in chapter 4, so that we find strong statements on nonviolence (5:38-42) and love of enemies (5:43-48), along with an expanded version of the beatitudes, which I will treat in some detail below. Nor can the attentive reader of Matthew miss Jesus' teachings on forgiveness (6:14; 18:21-35), mercy and compassion (5:7; 9:13; 12:7), and detachment from worldly goods (6:25-34). Nevertheless, for Matthew, all the specifics of the ethical life are in some way derivative from the two great commandments.

ETHICS IN THE SOCIAL SPHERE:
THE MATTHEAN SENSE OF JUSTICE

Justice Themes in the Sermon on the Mount

The emphasis on personal behavior in Matthew can easily obscure the subtler social dimension, and recent exegesis has revealed a somewhat unexpected focal point of such an element in the Matthean beatitudes (Powell 119–40; Hagner 1993, 89–96; Pregeant 2004, 45). The newer reading, which I find extremely well founded, hinges on the rendering of four key terms and a judgment about the rhetorical structure of the passage.

Traditional exegesis has usually claimed that the first term, "poor in spirit" in v. 3, is a spiritualization of Luke's "poor" and that it refers to those who are conscious of their need for God rather than to the literally poverty stricken. People who are literally poor, however, are likely also to be broken in spirit, and attention to the background of the term "poor in spirit" shows that it was used synonymously with "the poor" (Hagner 1993, 91). We need not exclude the notion that the referents are in fact aware of their need for God, since the poor have hope in nothing else. The likelihood, however, is that the term indicates those who have been beaten down by economic deprivation, and an examination of the probable meanings of the other terms supports this suggestion.

In v. 4, the verb *penthein* means "to mourn" or "to grieve," but the question is what causes the grief. The frequent assumption is that the cause is simply life's inevitable sorrows. However, if "poor in spirit" refers to those who have been beaten down by oppressive social structures, then we may see the reference to grieving or mourning as an elaboration of the inner feelings of the oppressed. And that possibility is supported by an examination of vv. 5 and 6. In v. 5, the term *praus* has usually been rendered "meek" and interpreted as referring to humble, nonviolent people. Matthew 5:5, however, is a near quotation of Ps 37:11. Here the Hebrew term translated "meek" in the NRSV is *ănāwîm*, which is often rendered "poor" and in Isa 61:1 clearly means "the oppressed" (NRSV). It is, moreover, peculiarly appropriate that "the humiliated" or "oppressed" inherit the "earth" (*gēs*: earth, land, soil, and so on) in the rule of heaven if they are in fact those who have been deprived of their land! Why the "meek" should receive this particular compensation, on the other hand, remains puzzling.

So far, then, it would appear that Matthew's first three beatitudes promise relief by way of reversal of status to oppressed persons in the coming rule of heaven. And if we understand *dikaiosynē* in the fourth (v. 6) not as "righteousness" in the sense of piety but as "justice," then the case is virtually clinched. The notion of "hungering and thirsting" for piety, in fact, is a rather odd notion. But to hunger and thirst for justice is precisely what we should expect from those humiliated by their experience in an unjust system. To translate *dikaiosynē* as "justice" means that it has a somewhat different sense than it does in 5:20. The action in this case seems to be primarily God's rather than that of human beings, since it is God who initiates the rule of heaven. But the reference is still to right action, and the establishment of a just society on the earth would necessarily entail human justice as a reflection of the justice God establishes.

In light of this reading, we must be careful in describing the ethical content of the first four of Matthew's beatitudes, which is only implicit and indirect. The pronouncement that humiliated, downtrodden people are blessed is in no way a recommendation that persons should seek such a status! It is rather a word of comfort that carries with it the implicit imperative to revive and maintain hope in the face of genuinely disastrous circumstances. It also implies a condemnation of the social system that creates those circumstances.

When we turn to the remaining four beatitudes and the summary statement in vv. 11-12, we find a basic shift in point of view. For here the pronouncement of certain persons as blessed is based not on their circumstances but on their attitudes and the actions that flow from them. As Mark Powell notes, the second set describes "those who help to bring to reality the blessings promised to others in 5:3-6" (1995, 130). It will be important to look briefly at each of the four.

"Blessed are the merciful, for they will obtain mercy." If Jesus' own actions make the rule of heaven manifest, then it is clear that mercy is one aspect of that rule. His inclusion of outcasts (9:13), his concern for human hunger (12:7), his acts of healing (9:27; 20:30, 31), and his exorcisms (15:22) are all explicitly presented as acts of mercy. And it is not difficult to see mercy at work, as Powell does, in the image of the cancellation of debts (6:12). When Jesus blesses the merciful, he is congratulating those who extend his own ministry of mercy. So we may agree with Powell that "'the merciful' (5:7) are healers, people who seek to put right that which has gone wrong. They favor the removal of everything that prevents life from being as God intends: poverty, ostracism, hunger, disease, demons, debt" (1995, 131).

"Blessed are the pure in heart, for they will see God." Purity of heart describes an inner attitude, what Donald Hagner terms "a consistency between the inner springs of one's conduct and the conduct itself" (1993, 94). It is, in other words, a whole-heartedness or single-mindedness with respect to doing God's will. By itself, the saying might seem difficult to assimilate to Powell's reading, but if we allow the context to determine the specific meaning, this reading makes good sense: "in context, the blessing is primarily for those who, with integrity, exhibit such virtues as showing mercy (5:7) and making peace (5:9)" (Powell 1995, 133).

"Blessed are the peacemakers, for they will be called children of God."
Central to the whole Hebrew tradition regarding the rule of God were the concepts of peace (*shalom*) and justice (*mishpat*). The terms overlap significantly, and *shalom* has a much wider range of meaning than the mere absence of conflict: it describes all the blessings entailed in the fullness of life that God desires for human beings. The Greek term for peacemaker (*eirēnopoios*) in Greco-Roman literature "applies to rulers who establish security and economic well-being" (Powell 1995, 134). We may therefore understand the term, in this context, as a reference to people who seek to establish *shalom*, or total well-being, in the world of human affairs—those, in other words, who work to make the rule of heaven manifest.

"Blessed are those who are persecuted for righteousness' sake, for theirs is the kingdom of Heaven." If we understand *dikaiosynē* as "justice" in this verse as in 5:6, then we can see a parallel between the last beatitude in each set. Those persecuted for the sake of *dikaiosynē* are those who seek justice on behalf of those who hunger and thirst for it—those to whom it has been denied. The persecuted are the courageous people who, in the face of personal rejection and danger, imitate God's own justice in bringing the rule of heaven by seeking to implement it.

Following the second set of beatitudes, Jesus adds a ninth (5:11-12), in a different form. Now he turns from the third person to the second, addressing his disciples directly, and pronounces them blessed precisely when they suffer persecution. The emphasis shifts at this point by virtue of the phrase "on my account," which makes Christian witness the cause of the persecution. However, by drawing a parallel to the persecution of the prophets, Jesus maintains the link with the emphasis on justice in the first eight beatitudes. And, of course, the Jesus of the Christian witness is one who himself performs deeds of justice.

As to whether the call to establish *shalom* applies only within the church community, there is nothing in these verses that demands or even suggests such a narrow reading; and we may also note that it would be quite out of keeping with Jesus' own inclusive ministry as depicted in Matthew. The reference to society at large, moreover, is unmistakable when we turn to the verses that follow (5:13-16). Here, Jesus challenges his followers with the terms "salt of the earth" and "light of the world," metaphors that clearly define the disciples' mission in terms of society as a whole. Some interpreters argue that the activity implied in these terms is intended only to convert others or to create an alternative society in the midst of unjust structures. Powell rejects these readings, however, and also dismisses the notion that the church's role is to set an example for the world, since "Matthew's Gospel betrays no notion that the world will ever improve based on what it learns from Jesus' followers." As an alternative, he suggests that the church is "called to perform justice in a world that itself remains untransformed." In support of this view he notes that it is consistent with "Jesus' commission to his disciples to proclaim the imminence of God's rule by healing the sick, raising the dead, and casting out demons (10:7-8)" (1995, 142–43). Although explicit witness to Jesus is a major aspect of the disciples' mission, then, we cannot fully subsume the call to do deeds of mercy under this banner.

The Challenge to Social and Political Structures

By treating the materials examined in the preceding section under the rubric of "social justice," I do not mean to imply that the original readers of Matthew would have understood this Gospel as a call to reform or revolution—that is, to social action in our contemporary sense of altering social and political structures. Not only were the tiny communities of Jesus' followers in the first century helpless in the face of Roman power, but the apocalyptic framework of their thought would have rendered such a thought almost unintelligible. The "social action" envisioned here is therefore a matter of *doing* justice. This means, on the one hand, creating just structures within the community itself, but, on the other, ministering as far as possible to the overwhelming needs of suffering humanity. It does not mean an attempt either to overthrow Rome by force or to somehow "humanize" its policies.

This is not to say that the Gospel endorses the notion that Rome was God's legitimate agent for the governance of the world or that it counseled acquiescence in Roman policy. It presents God's rule neither as the ultimate foundation of the empire nor as a parallel and complementary realm, but rather as the antithesis of worldly political power. The proclamation of a new rule is necessarily a herald of the end of the existing order and a condemnation of it. But it is God and not the community of Jesus' followers who will initiate this coming rule. We therefore do not find Jesus in the Gospel of Matthew commanding overt subversion of Roman power. We do, however, find indications of God's own subversion of that power and the obligation of those who follow Jesus to base their lives on a radically different loyalty. They are to live in conformity with God's rule, not Rome's.

This political dimension appears early in the story. There is a subtle hint in the fact that the genealogy and birth stories present Jesus as Messiah Son of David—a royal designation—and as savior (1:21), a status also claimed by the Caesars. But the matter comes to the foreground in Herod's reaction to the magi's inquiry regarding "the child who has been born king of the Jews" (2:2). This is Herod's own title, and his fear is clearly that Jesus will replace him. He appears, moreover, not only as fearful but as devious and cruel. He lies to the magi about his intentions and is the perpetrator of a brutal murder of children.

Herod is not a Roman, and within the context of the story he in some sense symbolizes the power of the Jewish establishment as well as that of the empire. The readers of Matthew, however, would have known that the Jewish people as a whole did not accept him as authentically Jewish and despised him. They would also have known that he ruled as an agent of Rome. Thus the thoroughly negative depiction of him in the story is more clearly a critique of Roman power than of the Jewish leadership.

The depiction of Pilate is more complex, but we should not allow the story about Barabbas and the hand-washing incident to mislead us—as they have many interpreters—into thinking this Gospel exonerates him from Jesus' unjust condemnation. The function of these scenes is to underscore Jesus' innocence and play up the guilt of the Jewish leadership and the crowds, not to present Pilate in a positive light. The implication of his reluctance in 27:18-19, 23, to condemn Jesus is that he recognizes Jesus' innocence. He knows the unworthy motivation of those who have brought Jesus to him, and he presumably accepts the validity of his wife's vision. But out of fear of a riot (27:24), he acquiesces. This is not a sympathetic portrayal. Far from an act of repentance for what he is about to do (repentance in advance would be a self-contradictory notion indeed!), it is an ironic self-indictment. As Warren Carter comments,

> Pilate, who is in charge of events, pretends that he is not. But a quick hand washing and a few words cannot remove the legal responsibility with which Pilate is charged as governor and agent of Roman power. Nor can they absolve him of his guilt in the murder of an innocent man or transfer it to a faceless crowd. Roman justice is all washed up. It is not exonerated but exposed as expedient, allied with and co-opted by the religious elite who manipulate a crowd to accomplish its own ends. (2000, 527)

The "washed up" character of Roman justice, thus of the empire itself, is not negated by the pericope on paying taxes to Caesar in 22:15-22. We have already seen (see above, 94–95) that Jesus' statement in v. 21 does not clearly endorse payment. But even if the implication in Matthew is that Jews should pay the Roman tax, this by no means implies an acceptance of the validity of Roman power. We may take our clue from the similar exchange in Matt 17:24-27 regarding payment of the half-shekel temple tax.

In this latter scene, Peter gives an unequivocally positive answer when the collectors of the tax ask whether Jesus pays it. The meat of the story, however, is in the interchange between Peter and Jesus. By referring to the "kings of the earth," Jesus deflects attention from the temple and frames the issue in terms of the broader question of worldly—and implicitly imperial—power. And by accepting Peter's declaration that such kings tax not their own children but "others" and then pronouncing that "the children are free," he subverts the entire ideology behind the tax collection. As Carter notes, the king's children are not the king's nation but "the ruler's direct physical offspring . . . the apparently inevitable successors to and ominous continuation of the ways of the kings of the earth." The point is therefore that the ruling class "privileges its own at the expense of the rest," which shows that "[t]he 'kings of the earth' . . . act in a manner contrary to God's purposes" (2000, 358–59). The tax itself is thus the product of a corrupt system, and it is only in order to avoid offense (v. 27) that Jesus sends Peter on the journey to get the denarius from the fish's mouth.

It is crucial, in determining the significance of this story in its Matthean setting, to remember that the original readers lived in a post-70 C.E. world, after the temple's destruction (by Rome!). The Romans now collected the tax, which had once supported the operation of the temple, for purposes that should have been offensive to any Jew.

> The emperor Vespasian co-opted it to rebuild and sustain the temple of Jupiter Capitolinus in Rome. That which had formerly proclaimed the Jewish God now provided a rebuilt temple for the triumphant Jupiter, patron god of the Flavians and the empire. . . . The tax had punitive and propaganda value. Its payment reminded Jews of Roman political, military, economic, and religious sovereignty and superiority sanctioned by Jupiter. (Carter 2000, 347)

According to Carter, when Jesus tells Peter to pay the tax, he means for him to pay it "subversively." Refusal to pay would amount to an incitement to violent rebellion. The pronouncement that "the children are free," however, shows that the story is not an endorsement of accommodation to Roman power. Its point is rather that "a tax can be paid without being a vote of support for Rome." With respect to 22:15-22, then, the interchange regarding the tribute tax and the coin with Caesar's image, Carter argues that the same principle applies: one can pay the tax within the context of "nonviolent subversion of Rome" (2000, 440).

These indications of a subversive attitude toward the empire are much less in the forefront of the narrative than is Jesus' interaction with Jewish authorities. The reasons should be clear. First, the historical reality was that Jesus in all probability had very little direct contact with Roman power until his final days. Second, although the Gospel of Matthew subtly counsels nonviolent subversion of Roman power, we cannot deny the tendency to shift the blame for Jesus' death from the Romans to the Jewish authorities. This is seen above all in 27:25, the notorious passage, unique to Matthew, in which the Jewish crowd shouts, "His blood be on us and on our children." This verse does not—as many interpreters through the centuries have thought—connote the guilt of the Jewish people as a whole for all time. The more likely reference is to those who rejected Jesus and those who do so later in the time of the Matthean community (Saldarini 1994, 32–34). But the effect of this and many other passages in Matthew is to play up the guilt of the Jewish leaders. We may regret this move, but we can also understand it in light of the Matthean community's struggle in their own time with the leaders of majority Israel for the hearts and minds of the populace.

In any case, we find Jesus in conflict with Jewish leaders, more specifically the scribes and Pharisees, throughout the Gospel. And because he challenges both their scriptural interpretations and their character (see especially ch. 23) he is an affront to their power and authority. His quarrel is not with the people per se, although he can in fact speak of an "evil and adulterous generation" (12:39) when his message is rejected. Nor is it with Israelite tradition as such, since he upholds the validity of the Law (5:17-20) and defends his actions on the basis of it. But his actions sometimes not only offend the scribes and Pharisees but also cut against the social grain. We see this, for example, when he eats with tax collectors and sinners (9:9-13) and tells a would-be follower to "let the dead bury their own dead" (8:22).

As Elaine Wainwright shows, the narrator also cuts against the social grain in listing within the patrilineal genealogy four women, each of whom is in some way an anomaly when viewed from the perspective of the dominant patriarchal system (1998, 56). Nor is this the only place we find challenges to the patriarchal structure. At two points women are portrayed more positively than the disciples—the anointing at Bethany (26:6-13) and the story of the Canaanite woman (15:21-28), whose "great" faith stands in implicit contrast to Jesus' designation of the disciples as persons of "little faith" (8:26; 14:31;

16:8; 17:20). Also, by inserting herself into the male world of honor competition by engaging Jesus in a game of challenge/riposte (Wainwright 1998, 86), the Canaanite woman transgresses a social boundary, as does the woman who touches Jesus' garment in 9:20-22.

Finally, the most dramatic instance of Jesus' confrontation of social and political structures is his demonstration in the temple. Just prior to this action, the narrator applies the title *king* to Jesus, interpreting the event as a fulfillment of Scripture (21:4-5). His action is therefore a specifically messianic deed and a sign of the coming rule of God. Later, in the discourse on judgment, Jesus predicts the destruction of the temple (24:1-2). And although he distinguishes that destruction from the end of the age (a necessity in the context of a post-70 c.e. situation), it is clearly part of the eschatological scenario and signifies God's judgment.

It is thus evident that the coming rule of heaven is in Matthew a force that is disruptive of the present social-political order, and that both Jesus' actions and elements of the narrator's commentary image what it means to live on the basis of the emerging new reality. It is not always easy to tell to what extent those actions of Jesus are to serve as models, however. His demonstration in the temple, for example, is a singular, unrepeatable event; but it is clear that Matthew contains an aspect of character ethics in that it invites readers in some measure to imitate the actions of both Jesus and God. This is only an aspect, however. For, as Hays rightly states, "the power of Matthew's vision is generated precisely by the paradoxical tension between his stable deontological moral categories and his message that the kingdom transforms everything, including the people who live under accountability to those categories" (1996, 98).

It is clear, nevertheless, that the transformation of human character in light of the character of both Jesus and God plays a central role in this Gospel. And to that theme I now turn.

THE QUESTION OF CHARACTER: GOD, JESUS, DISCIPLES

The conflict between Jesus and the Jewish leadership in Matthew is ultimately rooted in their differing representations of God. Jesus' teaching and deeds manifest an understanding of God that stands at a polar opposite from the representation of God by the scribes and the Pharisees. The Matthean characterization of these groups should not, of course, be taken as historically accurate, but our concern at present is with them as characters within the plot of Matthew. Here they appear as utterly intransigent, never open to Jesus' message, hard hearted and merciless, and focused on the externals of the Law and their own traditions rather than on the will of God. Jesus, by contrast, understands God's true will in terms of the love command, mercy, inclusiveness, and compassion. Within the framework of the narrative, then, Jesus presents God as possessing precisely these same qualities, whereas the God implied by the scribes and the Pharisees mirrors their own rigid and hard-hearted attitudes.

Jesus describes his own character, in summary fashion, at 11:29: "for I am gentle and humble in heart. . . ." The Greek term rendered "gentle" in the NRSV is *praus*, which, as noted above, takes on the sense of "humiliated" or "oppressed" in the third beatitude. In 11:29 it has a slightly different nuance, as it probably does in the quotation from Zech 9:9 in Matt 21:5, describing a character trait contrasted with proud or arrogant. But we need not reduce the meaning in the latter instances to mere gentleness. Since he has sided clearly with the outcast and oppressed both in the beatitudes and in his ministry of mercy in chapters 8 and 9, Jesus' self-characterization as *praus* almost certainly embraces a sense of solidarity with the poor in 11:29. Not only does his humility contrast with the arrogance of those who attacked him for his compassionate deeds, but those deeds themselves place him spiritually alongside those who suffer. Thus, even when he enters Jerusalem as king in 21:5, he does so as a king who ranks himself among the poor and despised.

Jesus clearly expects his disciples to imitate his own character. In the church discourse in chapter 18, the emphasis is on humility (18:1-6), wholeheartedness (18:6-9), and forgiveness of others (18:21-35); and the empowerment to cast out demons and to heal in 10:1 is also a commission to continue his ministry of compassion. Insofar as Jesus stands among his followers as the one called "God is with us" (1:23), moreover, imitation of his character is also imitation of the character of God. In addition, the notion of *imitatio Dei* comes out explicitly in 5:44-45, where Jesus bases his command to love one's enemies on the beneficent "neutrality" of God's own behavior; and here, interestingly, it is neither Jesus' own example nor Scripture that is invoked but the natural world as a venue of God's activity. As in 6:25-34, one can discern the character of God from the nurturing quality of the world that is a divine creation.

These references to the natural world are signs of God's universal concern, a notion that is evident also in the theme of the inclusion of Gentiles in the coming rule of heaven. Both Jesus' own ministry and that of his disciples are programmatically limited to Israel during his lifetime (10:5). Yet that restriction is dramatically lifted in 28:16-20, and in fact Jesus extends himself to Gentiles when occasion demands (8:5-13; 15:21-28). That the salvation Jesus brings has always been intended for Gentiles as well as Jews, moreover, is indicated from the outset in the visit of the magi (2:1-12) and in the quotation from Isaiah in Matt 4:15. In fact, even the missionary discourse that limits the initial mission to Israelites hints that the restriction is temporary (10:18). The God of Jesus, whom the disciples are to imitate, is a God of universal care.

"THE LILIES OF THE FIELD": INTIMATIONS OF ECOLOGICAL THEOLOGY IN MATTHEW 6:24-34

Recent concern regarding the ecological/climatological crisis has sparked renewed interest in passages, such as Matt 6:24-34, that express God's care for the natural world as potential sources for an ethic of ecojustice. The main message of this passage is that God will care for those who give God's rule first priority in their lives, and the argument hinges on the observation that God cares even for birds, grass, and lilies—that is, for the plants and animals that inhabit the earth along with human beings. The logic of the passage thus suggests that in God's eyes the natural world has intrinsic value apart from the instrumental value it accrues in its contributions to human life.

It is generally recognized that as an observation of the ordinary working of the world, the passage belongs to the wisdom tradition and thus stands outside the more typically biblical focus on covenantal themes. I believe that this judgment is largely justified, but Adrian M. Leske has successfully demonstrated the presence of covenantal and prophetic dimensions that provide important insights beyond the more obvious point regarding God's care for the natural world. In this passage, he notes, "Jesus is addressing people . . . who have earlier been described as members of the new kingdom, as 'the salt of the earth' and 'the light of the world' (Mt. 5.13-16)" and "is reminding them to live now as the restored covenant people." The injunction against anxieties over food, drink, and clothing "relate to the summary of the covenant curses in Deut. 28.48, which warns the people of God" that failure to serve God "with joyfulness and gladness of heart" means that they will "serve their enemies 'in hunger and thirst, in nakedness and want of all things.'" Also in the background is Second Isaiah's declaration that the deliverance of the people from exile means that they need no longer "experience hunger and thirst because they would be led by springs of water (Isa 41.17; 49.10; cf. Ps 1.3; Jer 17.8)" (2002, 21).

Leske also contends that another passage in Second Isaiah is relevant to the interpretation of Matt 6:33 ("But strive first for the kingdom of God and his righteousness, and all these things will be added to you"). In Isa 45:8, we find a statement in which the masculine term for "righteousness" (*ṣedeq*) refers to God's action ("And let the skies rain down righteousness"), whereas in a later statement the feminine form (*ṣedeqah*) indicates human response to that action: "And let [the earth] cause righteousness to spring up also." Leske argues that "righteousness" (*dikaiosynē*) in Matt 6:33 reflects the meaning of the masculine form in Isa 45:8—that is, it refers to God's gracious act of covenant faithfulness. Thus "Matthew 6.33 is really a declaration of the fulfillment of the prophetic longings for future restoration and a complete reversal of Deut. 28:48. No longer is there to be hunger, thirst, or nakedness" (2002, 22–23). Here again, we find that *dikaiosynē* departs from its sense as human action but remains consistent with one dimension of its meaning in 5:6: the justice of God, for which human beings long.

When we place Jesus' statements on God's provision for the birds of the air and the lilies of the field against this background, it becomes apparent that they describe the world as God intended it to be, which is what the coming of God's rule now restores. Human beings will no longer be prey to the destructive forces of a natural world whose harmony has been disrupted. Thus, Leske notes, "Restoration of relationship with God would also mean a return to the proper relationship between humanity and the animal world as partners in Earth community . . ." (2002, 24). And by linking God's care for human beings to God's care for plants and animals, the passage illumines what that proper relationship is and what it means:

> God's caring for Earth community members, be they birds of the air or flowers of field, is strong indication that God also takes care of all those who are members of God's kingdom. The implication of the interrelationship between human beings and the rest of Earth community is thus made clear. Human beings are . . . of Earth and cannot survive apart from Earth. The healing of Earth comes with the healing of humanity. When that happens the one serves the other in divine harmony. (2002, 26)

I am uncertain whether Leske rejects the wisdom reading of this passage altogether in favor of his covenantal/prophetic interpretation, but in any case I do not find the two incompatible. On the one hand, God cares for all creation, as nature itself should make plain to any observer; and this care extends not only beyond the covenant people but beyond the human community as well. On the other hand, the coming of God's rule enables those who embrace it to participate in the healing that will mean the end of the distortions that have come through human departure from God's intended way of life—hunger, thirst, and nakedness. There are thus two intimations of a nascent ecological theology in the passage: God's universal care, manifest in the operations of the natural world, and God's specific acts of covenant faithfulness that restore the primordial harmony among God's creatures.

HERMENEUTICAL QUESTIONS

Marxsen excludes Matthew from his list of materials in the New Testament that he considers authentically Christian on the grounds that its christology is not integral to its ethics. As we have seen, he thinks that the "better righteousness" of the Sermon on the Mount differs from that of Matthew's scribes and Pharisees only quantitatively. He also points to 6:14-15 as evidence that God's judgment of human beings is dependent on their deeds. God forgives only those who forgive others. The original intent of the statement in the Lord's Prayer regarding forgiveness, Marxsen argues, was that God's forgiveness enables human forgiveness. But in Matthew's interpretation this grounding of the imperative in the indicative has been negated. Thus, although Matthew has a christology, "it does not help people to act," and people are left to earn their status before God (1993, 239–40).

I have argued above that Marxsen is wrong in thinking that the "better righteousness" is merely quantitatively different from that of the scribes and Pharisees, and I think it can be shown that Matthew is not devoid of the notion of grace. The phrase "until all is accomplished" in 5:18 on my reading means that Jesus' fulfillment of the law will bring about true obedience (Strecker 2004, 104; Pregeant 1978, 68–69). And because Jesus' announcement of the coming rule of God precedes the Sermon on the Mount, Jesus' commands take on the character of a response to God's prior action. With respect to the Lord's Prayer, moreover, 5:13—the petition to be delivered from evil—"rules out any sense that those who pray the prayer can do what is right(eous) by sheer force of will" (Pregeant 2004, 52). Thus, the relationship between divine and human actions here is not that human forgiveness merits God's forgiveness but that each form of forgiveness presupposes the other. We find in the epilogue to the prayer in 6:14-15, however, that for grace to continue to operate, human action is indeed required—a point reinforced by the parable of the unforgiving servant in 18:23-25. And this raises a hermeneutical problem that I will discuss below.

Despite my disagreement on the issue of grace, I believe Marxsen is correct on two points. Matthew does envision a judgment of human beings based on their deeds, as 25:31-46 and many other passages indicate. And there is indeed a certain disjunction between christology and ethics in Matthew—a point I have argued in detail elsewhere (Pregeant 1978, 107–20 and esp. 121–27). I object, however, to the contention that this disjunction disqualifies Matthew as an authentically Christian ethic.

I observe in Matthew a tension between two currents of meaning. On the one hand, Jesus appears as Messiah, Son of God, who will save the people from their sins and who can even state at 11:27 that "no one knows the Father except the Son and anyone to whom the Son chooses to reveal him." It would not be difficult to derive from such an aspect of the Gospel a doctrine of exclusive salvation.[5] On the other hand, there are several points at which the Matthean soteriology and ethics overrun the christological boundary.

In 25:31-46, for example, it is deeds of mercy that form the basis of eschatological judgment, not relationship to Jesus. In fact, those who perform the deeds of mercy do so in ignorance that he has identified with them. And far from a rhetorical flourish, their ignorance is the point of the story. They are rewarded specifically because their deeds were just and for no other reason.[6] In a similar way, in the explanation of the parable of the weeds among the wheat in 13:36-43 the identification of the field in which both good and bad seed are found as "the world" seems to imply that some good seed is found in the world at large, just as some bad seed is found within the church (Pregeant 1978, 107–13). And, finally, Jesus' references to nature in the Sermon on the Mount suggest that one can in fact know God simply by observing the workings of the physical universe.

Passages such as these, combined with the Matthean presumption that one can simply do the good, create an undercurrent of meaning that stands over against a mainstream of christological exclusivism. But we need not play this undercurrent off against a doctrine of grace, as Marxsen does. The Matthean worldview is significantly different from that of Paul. Both views are set within an apocalyptic framework in which Satan wields power in the present age. In Matthew, however, there is no sense that the human will is held in thrall by that power and therefore no sense that only through a basic cosmic shift can human beings find the freedom to offer true obedience to God. But this does not mean that grace is not operative or that human beings earn their salvation before God.

The coming of God's rule, Jesus' definitive interpretation of the Law, and his abiding presence with his followers are all enabling agents. Both the repentance that integrates and purifies the heart and the deeds that flow from the heart are responses to God's gracious action in bringing the rule of heaven near and sending the Messiah. This schema differs significantly from that of Paul, but in its own way it provides an indicative to ground the imperative.

With this in mind, however, it is important to recognize that the disjunction between christology on the one hand and soteriology and ethics on the other does create a hermeneutical problem. If we follow the dominant strain of meaning through to its logical conclusion, we will likely conclude that the ethic of Matthew operates within the framework of an exclusivist approach to salvation. If we follow the undercurrent, however, a rather different understanding emerges. So we come upon a problematic aspect in the Matthean understanding of "the truth" that impinges significantly on how we define its notion of "doing the good." If we take seriously the possibility of obedience to God wholly apart from the christological witness, we encounter the question of whether there is an enabling grace available in human experience per se. And we also come upon the possibility of an understanding of "the good" that breaks the bounds of Matthew's dominant view of ethical action as response specifically to divine command. Such a possibility, moreover, has important implications regarding how we read Matt 28:16-20, the Great Commission. Viewed from one perspective, this classic mission text is rightly celebrated as a ringing endorsement of inclusiveness. Combined with an exclusivist notion of salvation, however, it has fostered an understanding of Christian mission that—allied with Western imperialism—has served to negate the cultures and religious experiences of non-Western peoples. The question thus arises as to whether it is possible in our time to read this passage in a way that does not enable its use as a tool of colonial domination. All these issues stand in need of hermeneutical clarification in part 4.

There are also points of tension between the Matthean understanding of God on the one hand and Jesus as his representative on the other, as well as within the images of Jesus himself with respect to the notions of mercy and forgiveness. Clearly, both God and Jesus appear in Matthew as supremely merciful and forgiving. Yet God is also depicted as exercising eschatological violence, and Jesus can pronounce judgment on God's behalf in the harshest terms (for example, 11:20-24; 13:40-43; 18:32-35; 23:1—25:46). But this does not negate the tension between such elements and the image of one who shows universal mercy and compassion and who calls for the love of enemies.

One can argue, of course, that given a scheme of final judgment, there is hardly any alternative. Unless all moral standards are to be eliminated, forgiveness must be cut off at some point. And it is along these lines that we must understand the epilogue to the Lord's Prayer and the parable of the unforgiving servant. But to recognize this is only to relocate the point of tension. It is, in the end, the apocalyptic schema itself that causes the difficulty. And it becomes clear just how difficult that problem is when we consider that apocalypticism in general, as well as the text of Matthew specifically, contains an inherently violent element. The question is whether and how we can reconcile the nonviolent teachings and deeds of Matthew's Jesus with his announcement of the eschatological violence that God will eventually bring not simply on the wicked but on those who have rejected Jesus. We might also ask whether the eschatological violence associated with Matthew's apocalyptic scenario, involving as it does indications of the dissolution of the cosmos (24:29), undermines the intimations of the "earth story" we found in Matt 6:24-34. Once again, the apocalyptic framework of the story cries out for hermeneutical reflection.

CHAPTER 6

the gospel of mark

~⊖~

Even more so than with the Gospel of Matthew, it is necessary in dealing with the Gospel of Mark to give primary attention to its literary form as story. Although Jesus' role as teacher is important to the Markan portrayal of him,[1] the actual volume of teaching material in Mark is considerably less than that in Matthew; and some of the most important ethical insights appear only when we take into account the peculiar nature of the Markan story. This is a story of profound irony, mystery, and paradox; and these elements are essential for an understanding of Mark's distinctive moral vision. Most importantly, we must grasp the way in which Jesus' strange concealment and disclosure of his identity and destiny reveal the specific meaning of his messiahship and the nature of the discipleship to which he calls his followers.

THE WAY OF THE CROSS:
THE STRUCTURE OF MARK'S PLOT

Seeing Clearly: Losing One's Life in Order to Find It

In 1:1—8:21, Jesus appears largely as one who performs astonishing deeds of power. He casts out demons, heals the infirm, stills a storm, walks on water, raises a dead girl, and on two occasions miraculously feeds thousands with a few loaves and fish. Mysteriously, however, when the demons recognize who he is, he silences them; and after some of his healings he insists that the witnesses tell no one what has happened. When questioned about the meaning of his parables, moreover, Jesus speaks of the secret of God's rule and sets up a dichotomy between insiders and outsiders (4:10-12). His disciples, to whom he explains the parable of the sower, are supposed to understand its meaning, but for outsiders the purpose of the parables is to confound.

Clearly, then, Jesus treats his identity as a secret and the rule of God that he proclaims as a mystery. Since the narrator identifies Jesus as Son of God at the very beginning (1:1) and this designation is confirmed by the voice of God at his baptism (1:11), the plot takes on a profound irony. The reader knows who Jesus is, but most of the characters in the story do not; and so they remain unaware of the full meaning of the events of which they are a part. And a particularly poignant aspect of the irony is that the disciples themselves are largely unable to grasp the meaning of his words and deeds, show a stunning lack of faith, and remain unclear regarding his identity; but the demons recognize him immediately. Thus, the distinction between insider and outsider seems in some ways reversed.

The secrecy motif prevails throughout the first part of the Gospel but undergoes a shift as the plot takes a new turn. Following a dramatic portrayal of the disciples' lack of understanding in 8:14-21, Jesus heals a blind man in a strange, two-stage miracle. On the first try, the man's sight remains defective; when Jesus makes another attempt, the man sees clearly. Later, in 10:46-52, Jesus heals another blind man, named Bartimaeus, in a single try; and Bartimaeus immediately follows him on his way. The symbolism in the juxtaposition of these two parallel stories and the material in between them is crucial for understanding the motif of secrecy and the nature of discipleship in Mark.

The two stories form an inclusion, a rhetorical device for marking off a thematically unified segment of material. Between the two stories, Jesus predicts his eminent suffering, death, and resurrection three times. And in each case the material that follows the prediction teaches a lesson on what it means to follow him.

The first sequence comes immediately after the first instance of giving sight. Jesus initiates a conversation with the disciples regarding his identity by asking, "Who do people say that I am?" (8:27). This question modifies the pattern of secrecy, but it builds on prior incidents. When Jesus stilled the storm, the stupefied disciples asked, "Who then is this, that even the wind and the sea obey him?" (4:41). And in a preface to the flashback about the death of John the Baptist, the narrator reported the various opinions regarding Jesus' identity: John the Baptist raised from the dead, Elijah, "a prophet, like one of the prophets of old" (6:14-16).

These three possibilities reappear in the disciples' answer to Jesus' inquiry in 8:27 regarding what "people" say of him. But when he then asks who the disciples themselves think he is, Peter makes the dramatic declaration, "You are the Messiah." Strikingly, however, Jesus responds not with a congratulatory statement (as in Matt 16:17-19) but with a rebuke, which is obscured by weak translations of the Greek verb *epitiman*—used also by Jesus when he silences the demons—such as "sternly ordered." Jesus' reply is not a direct rejection of the title, but neither is it an acceptance; it is apparently a reprimand of Peter for having spoken it aloud. The secrecy therefore holds as Jesus commands the disciples not to tell anyone about him.

The significance of the harsh response begins to come out in 8:31-33, as Jesus now informs his disciples of his coming death. Horrified at this disclosure, Peter now rebukes (*epitiman*) Jesus; and Jesus, in turn, once again rebukes (*epitiman*) Peter in the sharpest possible terms: "Get behind me, Satan! For you are setting your mind not on divine things but on human things." Following this interchange, Jesus states that those who want to follow him must take up their own crosses, and he adds this explanation: "For those who want to save their life will lose it, and those who lose their life for my sake, and for the sake of the gospel, will find it" (8:35).

At this point, the reader, who has known Jesus' identity all along, can also begin to understand the reason for the secrecy. It is the particular nature of Jesus' role as Messiah, and the corresponding nature of discipleship, that is at issue. Peter's answer is correct on the surface, but he understands neither that the role of Messiah entails death and suffering nor that discipleship entails a similar fate. Impressed with Jesus' miraculous deeds, the disciples understandably expected a "straightforward," triumphant Messiah. Instead, they are given one whose triumph is paradoxical and ironical, shrouded in mystery.

Two more times Jesus predicts his death and suffering, and two more times he speaks of discipleship in response to disputes among the disciples. In 9:33-37, an argument among the disciples about who is the greatest leads to extended teaching, beginning with the declaration that those who want to be first "must be last of all and servant of all." Then in 10:35-45, the request of James and John for special positions in God's rule leads to the question of whether they are able to share his cup and his baptism—obviously, in context, symbols of his coming death. When they answer, naively and ironically, "We are able," Jesus replies by stating that they will indeed suffer his fate but that he cannot grant the favor they request. Then, when the disciples become angry with James and John,

Jesus makes another paradoxical statement, declaring that the way to greatness is through servanthood.

The healing of Bartimaeus follows immediately (10:46-52) and closes off the central section of Mark. What the reader can now "see" is precisely what Peter and the others could not. Like the first blind man who was healed only partially at first, the disciples understood that Jesus was the Messiah. But they did not grasp the paradoxical, ironical nature of that office, nor did they understand what it would really mean to follow him. And herein lies the heart of Markan ethics: to be a disciple is to accept the cross of Jesus as one's own. It is to accept suffering on his behalf, to be last of all rather than first, and to find one's life not directly but paradoxically—by losing it for Jesus' sake and for the sake of his gospel. And apart from an understanding of the true nature of both messiahship and discipleship, any proclamation of his identity creates false expectations and is therefore itself false. Herein lies the reason for the secrecy.

In the end, Jesus declares his status openly. When asked by the high priest whether he is the Messiah, Jesus answers unequivocally: "I am" (14:62). And at the moment of his death, the narrator signals that the secret of his identity is out. Observing how Jesus dies, the centurion at the cross utters the first human acknowledgment of who Jesus is that is not rebuked: "Truly this man was God's son." No longer subject to misunderstanding, the declaration of Jesus' messiahship can now be proclaimed without reservation.

The Parable of the Sower, the Characters in the Story, and the Enigmatic Ending

Mary Ann Tolbert has identified the strong role played in Mark's plot by the parable of the sower (4:1-9) and its explanation (4:13-20). In doing so, she has shed important light on the strange way the story ends, with the women at the tomb failing to bring the message of the resurrection to the disciples "because they were afraid" (16:8). In the explanation, the four types of soil that produce varying results represent different types of persons who hear the word.

If we search the narrative for examples of these various types of soil, it is apparent that the scribes and Pharisees correspond to the hardened ground of the path, where seed is sown but never has a chance to take root before the birds (Satan) come and snatch it away. And the reader's natural inclination is to expect the disciples to exemplify the good soil, which receives the seed and bears much fruit. Over the course of the narrative, however, it becomes increasingly clear that the disciples are more like the rocky soil, where the seed springs up but—having only shallow roots—is unable to withstand the scorching sun (trouble and persecutions) and so withers away. They constantly fail to understand; they manifest wrong attitudes; and, in the end, they all fail Jesus, just as he predicts. Their failures along the way, moreover, are accentuated by the ending, which leaves no occasion for reconciliation. When the story comes to a close, they remain alienated from Jesus. They do not play the role of the good soil (Tolbert 1989, 121–24).

The account of Jesus' trial, death, and burial, however, raises another possibility. The women who had followed Jesus do not scatter as the disciples do following his arrest; they look on the crucifixion from a distance. And after the Sabbath, three of them—Mary Magdalene, Mary the mother of James, and Salome—come to the tomb to anoint the body. Given the charge by the figure at the tomb to give a message to the disciples, they represent the reader's last hope for "good soil." When even they fail, however, the reader's hopes are dashed. There is no one to be the good soil—to tell the story. No one, Tolbert notes, "but the audience itself" (Tolbert 1989, 297). The plot therefore draws the reader in as a participant, to play the role of the faithful follower who in fact "sows" the gospel.

It should be apparent that, in terms of ethical models, the disciples do not serve this function in Mark. This does not mean, as some scholars have argued, that the reader is to imagine that their alienation is permanent. The announcement at the tomb that Jesus is going to Galilee to meet the disciples is surely an indication of an eventual reunion that lies beyond the plotted events. And the reader may take this as a sign that forgiveness is always operative in the household of God, just as Jesus has extended it during his ministry. But the fact remains that the actions of the disciples within the plot are largely negative. Jesus is a positive model, but they are not, although their behavior can serve as a warning against the temptation to fall away when circumstances become difficult.

In contrast, as David Rhoads, Joanna Dewey, and Donald Michie have stressed, there are minor characters who do serve as positive models.

> Some emerge from the crowds for healing; others are lifted up by Jesus as examples; still others serve Jesus. Usually, they are marginal people with no power—children, women, a beggar, a foreigner, a poor widow. Many are excluded from common life because of their afflictions. Some are considered unclean—demoniacs, the leper, the woman with the flow of blood, and the Syrophoenician woman. Yet these minor characters constitute the fertile soil for the good news of the Rule of God. (1999, 129–30)

It is noteworthy also that women figure prominently as exemplars, despite their quantitatively minor roles. Among the actions of these positive models are

> the serving of Simon's mother-in-law, the faith of the woman with the flow of blood, the insight and clever wit of the Syrophoenician woman, the self-giving of the poor widow, and the prophetic act of the woman who anoints Jesus. (Rhoads, Dewey, and Michie 1999, 132)

In addition, the three women who come to the tomb—and who are named as having followed Jesus in Galilee—"take risks by being at the crucifixion and by going to the grave, and . . . show their willingness to serve by buying spices and going to anoint Jesus" (Rhoads, Dewey, and Michie 1999, 132–33).

THE LOGIC OF FAITHFUL SUFFERING

Above all else, the ethic of discipleship in Mark entails suffering in the name of Jesus, taking up one's cross in following him. It is important, however, to explore the deeper logic of this call to suffering. It is intimately connected with a number of other motifs, and only by examining these do we get a clear understanding of its meaning and the reason it is necessary. On one level, we may say that discipleship means suffering because Jesus the Messiah himself suffered. But why must Jesus suffer? And why should discipleship necessarily entail imitation on this point?

The Reasons for Suffering and Death

Jesus' three predictions of his suffering and death suggest that this outcome is unavoidable. The Greek verb *dei* ("it is necessary"), moreover, suggests a divinely ordained outcome; and the agonizing scene at Gethsemane (14:32-42) confirms that what is about to take place is in accordance with God's will. In Mark 14:21, moreover, Jesus makes this paradoxical declaration as he informs the disciples that one of them will betray him: "For the Son of Man goes as it is written of him, but woe to the one by whom the Son of Man is betrayed." There is thus in Mark a strong note of foreordination regarding Jesus' fate. If, however, we seek a reason for such a foreordination, the closest we come is in two brief passages that deal with the effect of Jesus' death. He closes the third prediction with this statement: "For the Son of Man came not to be served but to serve, and to give his life a ransom for many" (10:45). And at the final meal he gives the disciples a cup from which they all drink and then tells them, "This is my blood of the covenant, which is poured out for many" (14:24). We can derive from these passages the claim that Jesus' death establishes a covenant among his followers and that it somehow liberates them—which is what a ransom accomplishes. And we can note that in the Israelite tradition blood is used as the ratification of covenant relationships (for example, Exod 24:8). But we cannot—short of illegitimately importing medieval doctrines of atonement—begin to elaborate the "mechanics" of how Jesus' death accomplishes all this.

We can, however, refer back to the cosmic dimension of the conflict in which Jesus is engaged from the beginning of the story. The first opponent he encounters after his baptism is Satan; and his first work of power involves the defeat of an unclean spirit. In the Beelzebul controversy in 4:19b-28, moreover, his ministry of exorcism is portrayed specifically as the binding of Satan in order to plunder his house. If Jesus' suffering, death, and resurrection bring liberation, then, we may assume that this liberation is ultimately from the cosmic powers of oppression. And we may surmise that the covenant he establishes is what binds together a new community that exists in the new, liberated "space."

It thus appears that it is the apocalyptic framework of Mark, with its presupposition of Satan's hold on the world in its present condition, that makes Jesus' death necessary. That death is somehow the means of breaking that hold. The conflict in Mark has two levels, however: Jesus' human opponents are the other face of his cosmic enemies. It is therefore important to consider the argument of Ched Myers, who claims that the necessity of Jesus' death should be understood not as "fate or fatalism" but as "political *inevitability*" (1990, 244; emphasis original). Because Jesus appears as the advocate of true justice, Myers claims, he comes into conflict with the authorities. That is why his death is unavoidable.

I think that Myers is in danger of reductionism, but I also believe that there is a valid aspect to his argument. The distinction that persons in our own time are apt to make between the earthly political dimension and a cosmic dimension was foreign to the biblical mind. To understand Jesus' death as a divinely ordained necessity would not have seemed in conflict with the notion that it was the result of sociopolitical realities. Thus, an analysis of the reasons for Jesus' death should embrace an understanding of what was so offensive about his actions.

We do not have to look very far to find an answer. Jesus appears here as in many ways disruptive of the social fabric. In 1:40, he heals a leper with a physical touch; and although he commands the man to show himself to a priest and bring an offering as prescribed by Moses, Jesus apparently does not himself seek cleansing from the defiling touch. The man, moreover, fails to obey the command and instead goes immediately on his way proclaiming what Jesus has done. Thus, the net effect is a challenge to the system of determining purity and impurity, a system that Jesus explicitly undermines in 7:19: "Thus he declared all foods clean." Although the controversy in Mark 7 is specifically with the Pharisees over their traditions regarding hand washing, 7:19 wipes out the dietary regulations altogether.

More offenses follow quickly after the healing of the leper. Jesus forgives a man's sins, thus incurring the charge of blasphemy (2:1-12). He accepts a tax collector into his fellowship, and he dines with "tax collectors and sinners" (2:13-17). He allows his disciples to pluck grain on the Sabbath, and then he performs a healing on the Sabbath. When confronted with criticism, he defends himself in part by referencing the Law (2:25-27; 3:4), but his use of the Law has peculiar twists. In 3:27-28 he digs beneath Sabbath law per se to ask about its purpose in relation to the human good, and then he asserts his sovereignty over the Sabbath itself. In 3:4, he again looks to the underlying purpose of the Law, while in 2:17 he defends his table fellowship with tax collectors and sinners merely on the basis of human need. And when in 2:18-22 he responds with the saying on new wine and old wineskins to the criticism that his disciples do not fast, he places the set of controversies in the context of the dawning rule of God.

The rule of God that Jesus proclaims is thus the root of social and religious upheaval, and, given the inseparability of religion and politics, this means that Jesus and his disciples are treading on politically dangerous ground. For the most part, the sociopolitical aspect of the narrative is played out against the background of the Jewish leadership rather than against the Roman government. Thus, the first direct indication we have of his eventual fate comes at the end of a series of conflicts with religious authorities, which begins in 2:1. The final story—the healing of the man with the withered hand—concludes with the narrator's dramatic comment in 3:6: "The Pharisees immediately went out and conspired with the Herodians against him, how to kill him." This emphasis on the role of Jewish authorities prevails even at the end. At 14:1 the narrator attributes a death plot to "the chief priests and scribes," and it is a crowd sent from "the chief priests, the scribes, and the elders" who arrest Jesus in 14:43-48. The high priest and the council, moreover, charge him with blasphemy and hand him over to Pilate (14:53-65); and it is the chief priests and scribes who stir up the crowd in 15:11 to demand his death.

It is nevertheless Pilate who issues the death decree, however reluctantly (15:14-15); and there are subtle indications along the way that God's rule challenges the empire itself. To begin with, the inclusion of the Herodians in the plot against Jesus in 3:6 implicates Rome, since the Herods ruled on their behalf. When Jesus asks the demoniac in 5:1-21 his name, the allusion to Rome in the reply, "My name is Legion; for we are many," is unmistakable—as is the prediction of Rome's ultimate fate in the death of the "legion" in the sea (Myers 1990, 190–94). The call to take up one's cross, moreover, cannot be abstracted from its political nuance: it is Rome alone that crucifies. And even the use of the term "good news" (*euangelion*) has potential political consequences, since it was the term used in celebration of military victories (Myers 1990, 122–24).

Despite the strong indications in Mark of the cosmic necessity of Jesus' death, then, we see also a significant strain that justifies the notion of "political inevitability." We cannot adequately state the reason for the crucifixion without taking account of the social and political disruptiveness of both the gospel he preached and the activities he pursued. Nor do we rightly understand the significance of his message and his deeds without taking into account their connection to the theme of justice, which is so essential to the notion of God's rule. And that theme in fact surfaces in the stories of Jesus' socially disruptive actions. Not only do his healings meet human need, but Myers sees his act of forgiveness in the story of the healing of the paralytic in 2:1-12 as a direct subversion of authority:

> The scribes are incensed, and for good reason. Their complaint that none but God can remit debt (2:7b) is not a defense of the sovereignty of Yahweh, but of their own social power. As Torah interpreters and co-stewards of the symbolic order, they control determinations of indebtedness. But as Jesus did with the priestly prerogative, he has also expropriated this function. (1990, 155)

Jesus, in other words, is undermining an entire system in which hierarchical authorities determine the status of people in the general populace by their rulings regarding indebtedness of all types, whether with respect to purity, financial matters, or sin. Within the Markan frame of reference, to challenge such a system is to act on behalf of the justice of the rule of God. And it is significant that, as Myers also notes, the charge of blasphemy, which the scribes level against Jesus in this story, is the grounds on which he is accused at his trial in 14:64. It is "no accident that the next time the scribal authorities appear it is in the person of government investigators" (1990, 155).

If, then, one dimension of the cause of Jesus' death in Mark is political inevitability issuing from his actions on behalf of justice, why must those who follow him suffer also? The unavoidable answer is that they too will perform actions and pass on teachings that are socially and politically disruptive. This is subtly indicated, in fact, in Jesus' interchange with the disciples on the issue of wealth. For in his statement about the motive of those who have left everything behind them, he adds "and for the sake of the good news" (10:29) to "for my sake." The reader may well understand the former phrase to embrace the whole story of Jesus' life, death, and resurrection; but it must also include the "good news of the gospel of God," which Jesus himself proclaimed and which has to do with the coming of God's rule (1:14-15). And those who leave all for Jesus and the good news, we should note, receive not only the blessings of a new community but also persecutions (10:28-31).

Related Motifs

Those who follow Jesus are called not only to suffer for him and his good news but to live humbly by putting others first, accepting lesser status for themselves, and renouncing wealth and all forms of self-seeking. Suffering is thus one of several aspects of the general attitude of abandoning self-interest. And the justice dimension of all these ways in which Jesus' followers must forfeit self-interest appears in his denunciation in 12:38-40 of the scribes, whose comportment is the exact opposite of the ethic he expounds:

> Beware of the scribes, who like to walk around in long robes, and to be greeted with respect in the marketplaces, and to have the best seats in the synagogues and places of honor at banquets! They devour widows' houses and for the sake of appearances say long prayers. They will receive the greater condemnation.

Those who lack the humility Jesus commends seek the best and most for themselves at the expense of others.

The economic dimension of this contrast appears clearly in the story of the rich man in 10:17-31. In listing various commandments, Jesus adds, "You shall not defraud" (echoing Exod 20:17 and other passages) to the ethical injunctions from the Decalogue before he shocks his inquirer with the demand to sell all his possessions. Then, in the saying on the needle's eye, he graphically illustrates the barrier that wealth presents to entering God's rule. The new community that Jesus founds will, however, be distinguished by sharing, as vv. 28-31 show.

This community will also reject hierarchical authority. When the other disciples criticize James and John for their request to sit on his right and his left when he comes into his glory, Jesus turns the criticism back on them by contrasting the way rulers among the Gentiles "lord it over" their subjects with the relationships he expects among his followers: "whoever wishes to become great among you must be your servant, and whoever wishes to be first among you must be slave of all" (10:43-44). The other disciples were critical of James and John because these two "had attempted to maneuver themselves into the favored positions they all wanted" (Boring 2006, 301). And we must not overlook the political implications of the reference to Gentiles. Who more exemplifies hierarchical power than the empire itself? The phrase in v. 42 that the NRSV renders as "whom they recognize as their rulers," moreover, is better translated as "their so-called rulers" (Jerusalem Bible).[2] As Morna Hooker observes, it "is probably intended to indicate that their rule is only apparent and is unreal in the eyes of God" (1991, 247). And its unreality or illegitimacy must be due in part to its inherent injustice, which stands in explicit contrast to the ethic of the new community that manifests the values of the rule of God.

Suffering for Jesus and the gospel, humility, servanthood—all the various forms of self-sacrifice—are related to the love of neighbor, which Jesus endorses alongside love of God in 12:28-34. But how important is the love command in Mark? Frank Matera counts love of neighbor as a central emphasis in this Gospel (1996, 34), but Hays argues to the contrary. While the passage "is certainly an important indicator of Mark's evaluation of the Law," we find that "the concept of love . . . receives very little attention in Mark." The passage itself, he also notes, occurs "in a controversy discourse rather than in Jesus' teachings to his disciples"; and the Markan Jesus never promotes "love as a distinctive mark of discipleship" (1996, 84). What are we to make of these differing valuations of the love command in Mark?

One factor that Hays ignores is the broader context of 12:28-34 in the plot of the narrative. He observes that it occurs in a controversy dialogue but does not comment on its position at the conclusion of a string of disputes that closes off Jesus' conversations with the Jewish leaders. The narrator's comment in 12:34 signals a significant turn of events: "After that no one dared ask him any question." Although spoken to a (presumably) friendly inquirer (Mark lacks the statement found in Matthew and Luke that the question was a test), Jesus' answer thus takes on the quality of a summary statement of the issues between himself and his opponents. And if it does in fact express "Mark's evaluation of the Law,"

Jesus' reply to the scribe's repetition of his own statement suggests that we cannot separate that evaluation entirely from Jesus' understanding of discipleship: "You are not far from the kingdom of God."

Hays also neglects some important elements in the passage. As Dan Via notes, when Jesus replies to the scribe's inquiry with two commandments rather than one, he says "in effect that no one commandment could be marked off as first, but these two together comprise the essence of human responsibility." For Via, this means that faith and ethics are inseparable: ethics is grounded in faith, and nonethical faith is inconceivable. Thus, he concludes, "Love to the neighbor for Mark has a programmatic and encompassing significance because it is an inseparable part of the *first* commandment (1985, 85–86; emphasis original).

It is true that in Mark Jesus never explicitly connects love and discipleship, and that "the single fundamental norm that is laid down in the narrative is Jesus' own death on the cross" (Hays 1996, 84). To weight this observation as Hays does, however, is to ignore the distinctive character of love as a motivating factor rather than as defining a specific behavior, as do such terms as suffering, humility, and giving away possessions. And while Hays is partly correct in saying that in Mark the focus is on "simple external obedience rather than on motivation or the intention of the heart" (1996, 83), we do find an acknowledgment of inwardness in 7:14-23. "It is what comes out of a person that defiles," Jesus says, and he then goes on to list the forms of evil that come from within. And what is true of evil, we may conclude, is also true of the good. In other words, presupposed in all the ethical actions to which Jesus calls his disciples is in fact the motivating factor of love. Thus, Via is surely correct that the content of the second commandment "must be discerned from the totality of Mark's view of ethical obligation, and from the model of Jesus" (1985, 86).

Hays also overlooks a distinctive trait of Mark's version of the pericope. "Only in Mark does Jesus cite the *Shema* (Deut. 6:4) with its emphasis on the oneness of God." On the basis of this observation, Via argues for a close connection between the emphasis on God's oneness and the command to love one's neighbor.

> Only if one is devoted to the one personal Power who is sovereign over all of reality can one love the neighbor as required. Money (11:15-16), political power (12:13-17), and the dead past (12:24-27) are potential gods which can claim the loyalty and restrict the freedom of the disciple. Only if the disciple loves with the whole being the one God over all, who can subordinate such powers and their claims, can the disciple be enabled to

have the freedom to love without reserve. From the other side, only a love for the neighbor without reservation can fittingly correspond to the reality of a God whose sovereignty is unlimited. (1985, 86)

It is true that Jesus' death is never described as an act of love in Mark as it is in Paul and John (Hays 1996, 84–85). But if we accept that the crucifixion results partly from Jesus' actions on behalf of justice, and we remember that these acts are often explicit deeds of compassion, we can also say that love is implicit as a motivating factor. And to the extent that the followers of Jesus are also called to suffer, we may further conclude that their own willingness to suffer is itself an act of love.

EXTRAORDINARY DEMANDS:
REFLECTIONS ON SPECIFIC ISSUES

Divorce

Matera observes that the Markan pronouncements on divorce (10:2-11) stand together in a unit of material with the sayings on children (10:13-16) and possessions (10:17-31). Since both of the latter segments couch Jesus' teachings explicitly against the background of the rule of God, he concludes, we should understand the entire unit as consisting of extraordinary demands that Jesus makes in light of that rule (1996, 28). Similarly, Via understands the call for indissoluble marriage as an "eschatological possibility" (1985, 104–11). I accept these observations, but we must not understand the eschatological sanction for this demand as indicative of an interim ethic. The explicit justification comes in a reference not to the future but to creation: Jesus' commands reflect God's original intention (10:6). The extraordinary demand regarding divorce is not like the injunctions in 1 Cor 7:17-39, which Paul justifies in terms of the "impending crisis" of the imminent new age (1 Cor 7:26). The Markan demand is ideally applicable to life in general and is not simply the function of special circumstances.

This means that the prohibition is presented as an absolute, but Via finds an aspect of the Markan text that mitigates the absoluteness. There are two parts to Jesus' pronouncement on divorce, and they take different forms. In 10:2-8, Jesus speaks in the apodictic, or unconditional, mode. He simply makes a pronouncement. Following his explanation of Moses' concession to the people's hardness of heart, he quotes Gen 2:24 and concludes in 8b-9: "So they are no longer two but one flesh. 'Therefore what God has joined together, let no one separate.'"

In vv. 10-11, however, Jesus speaks in the casuistic, or "if-then" mode, referring to specific, contingent circumstances. A man who divorces his wife and marries another woman commits adultery, as does a woman who divorces her husband and marries another man. Here the act of remarriage after divorce is prohibited on the grounds that it constitutes adultery. The form of the statement, however, presupposes the possibility of divorce. In and of themselves, moreover, these verses do not condemn divorce as such. It is only remarriage that is specifically condemned.

We must of course read vv. 10-11 in light of vv. 2-8, and Via concedes that this means that 10:1-11, taken as a whole, do in fact pronounce all divorce sinful. Nevertheless, by treating the two elements separately, he has uncovered an interesting point of tension:

> Consider for a moment . . . how the juxtaposition of 10:9 and 10:11-12 appears to resolve the question of how sinful divorce is. In 10:9 it is absolutely wrong without qualification. In 10:11-12 it may not be wrong at all, but if it is, it is not as wrong as divorce and remarriage. In 10:11-12 there are, then, degrees of guilt. When the two are put together, divorce is always wrong (the effect of 10:9 on 10:11-12), but not as wrong as divorce and remarriage (the effect of 10:11-12 on 10:9). (1985, 113)

If I understand Via correctly, he does not deny that the Markan text as a whole treats divorce as a violation of God's will. He emphasizes that there is a subtle tension between the two components of the Markan pronouncement on this issue.

Possessions

The story of the man seeking eternal life in 10:17-22, together with the conversation in vv. 23-31, has provoked much discussion on the issue of poverty and riches in Mark. The question is usually posed in terms of whether the demand Jesus makes on the man applies to all who follow him or is specific to this particular person, but I find that such discussion is somewhat misdirected. The first point to be made is that vv. 17-31 constitute a tight thematic unity, as Myers shows by an analysis of the passage's concentric structure. Observe the following pattern leading up to the thematic statement in v. 31.

A   question about eternal life (v. 17)
   B   rich man cannot leave possessions and follow;
      C   Jesus' explanation, disciples' reaction (twice)
   B'   disciples have left possessions and followed;
A'   answer to eternal-life question (v. 30). (1990, 272)

Clearly, the conversation in vv. 23-31 is intended to illumine the story itself. The first segment of this conversation, vv. 23-28, elaborates on the narrator's comment in v. 22 that it is the man's many possessions that stood in the way of his response to the call to discipleship. And the hyperbolic statement about the needle's eye in v. 25 drives the point home with a vengeance. In addition, as Myers notes, Jesus' response also has the effect of overturning a widespread assumption regarding the source of wealth. When the disciples ask, "Who then can be saved?" in v. 26, they reflect the belief that riches are a sign of God's favor. But Jesus rejects this view, "contending instead that the only way to salvation for the rich is by the redistribution of their wealth—that is, the eradication of class oppression" (1990, 275).

The rhetorical structure of the passage thus reveals a biting critique of attachment to wealth as a primary—perhaps even *the* primary—impediment to discipleship. Far from a one-time counsel to a particular person, it says something indispensable about discipleship. Although it may take on metaphorical value, it is evident throughout the conversation that the reader is asked to take the literal level seriously. Apart from such an assumption, neither the disciples' reaction in v. 26 nor their claims regarding their own economic sacrifices in v. 28 make sense.

We must, however, note that the second segment of the conversation, which begins with v. 28, compels the reader to put the entire conversation in the context of the community of Jesus' followers. In the story itself (v. 21), Jesus ends his demand to sell all with the further command to follow him, and his response in vv. 28-30 is clearly a description of life within a communal setting. In context, then, the demand to sell all and follow Jesus is not an abstract call to personal divestment of wealth but a commitment to a fully communitarian way of life that embraces the economic dimension. Thus, to ask whether the passage means that all who follow Jesus in any time and place are required to give up all their wealth is to some extent to miss the point. The passage operates within the framework of an assumption about the nature of the fellowship of Jesus' followers. When time and circumstance have made such a fellowship a historical rarity, the reader is necessarily faced with the hermeneutical task of discerning its import for the new situation. The dramatic force of the passage, however, should warn against any attempt to reduce the call to abandon wealth to a plea for mere charity.

The importance of this passage in the overall structure of Mark is indicated by its presence in an extended teaching section following Jesus' second prediction of his death (9:33—10:31). There is more concrete teaching on specific issues here than in the sections following either the first or the third prediction, which signals an intention to lift up the pronouncements in this section as of prime importance for the later community. Myers, moreover, observes a close connection between 10:17-31 and the parable of the sower, which is so central to the plot. Although Mark's story up to this point has focused primarily on obstructions to the growth of the seeds, in 10:29-31 there is a new turn of events. "Now it is time for the yield of good soil; forfeited homes, lands, and family . . . will be recovered a hundredfold (cf. 4:20)" (1990, 276). As we have seen, the disciples in Mark do not fulfill their role as good soil within the plotted narrative. In chapter 10, however, Jesus looks forward to the new community in which, by God's own power, good soil will emerge and bear fruit in the form of genuinely communal life.

Martyrdom

Jesus' persistent call to share his fate by bearing one's cross takes on a metaphorical dimension at some points in Mark. This is indicated by the fact that the central section in which these calls come includes such emphases as abandoning wealth, becoming like children (10:13-16), and taking on the role of servant (10:41-45). The metaphorical dimension, however, by no means negates the literal. We can see this clearly in Mark 13, which foresees a time of extreme distress and persecution before the Son of Man's return. Although 13:13 assumes that some will survive these terrors, 13:11 reckons with the possibility of literal martyrdom: "Brother will betray brother to death, and a father his child, and children will rise against parents and have them put to death."

This possibility, moreover, is subtly reinforced by Mark's strange ending, in which the reader finds no direct statement, as in Matthew, of Jesus' abiding presence. The fear in which the women leave the tomb is an indication of the expectation that readers must live in a time devoid of tangible signs of hope. They have no guarantees against the possibility of the starkest tragedy—only the word of paradoxical hope that the Gospel as a whole conveys. There is, of course, the promise of ultimate eschatological victory. But in the meantime Jesus' followers must travel the dangerous, foreboding way of the cross.

HERMENEUTICAL QUESTIONS

The three "extraordinary demands" discussed in the previous section raise important questions for hermeneutical reflection. I will begin this concluding section by commenting on them.

The tension Via finds between Mark 10:9 and 10:11-12 is extremely subtle. As we have seen, there is no doubt that the pericope as a whole renders an absolute judgment against divorce. If, however, we allow the latter verses to speak with their own voice, we see a gentle hint of a different perspective in which the only real problem is remarriage. This is not an undercurrent that we can detect anywhere else in the Gospel—which is hardly surprising, since the issue of divorce is far from a central, thematic concern. But it is a point worthy of some attention in a broad hermeneutical discussion of the whole issue of marriage and divorce in the New Testament.

Of much greater significance, for our purposes, is the Markan variation on earlier tradition that is found in 10:12: "and if she divorces her husband and marries another, she commits adultery." This extension of the statement in 10:11 to women likely results from the influence of a more Hellenized environment, in which women had the right to divorce. And it is the very fact of accommodation to a new situation that is particularly of interest from a hermeneutical perspective that seeks contemporary relevance.

With the addition of 10:12, the basic premise of 10:11 remains—marriage after divorce is adultery—but a new set of circumstances has necessitated an extension of its logic. This extension, however, is not as "innocent" as it might seem. For behind it lies a significant change in the social situation. With the extension of women's rights, the institution of marriage itself undergoes fundamental change, since it constitutes a significant modification of the patriarchal structure. So apart from the specific content of the modification, the very fact of modification on the basis of changes in the social environment raises the question of application to yet other situations, far removed from the entire New Testament world. There are good grounds to question whether marriage in the twenty-first-century Western world is in fact the "same" institution that we observe in the New Testament texts. To inquire whether and how the biblical injunctions regarding marriage in general apply to our own world, in other words, involves complex hermeneutical questions.

Jesus' call to divestment of wealth is another issue that deserves hermeneutical reflection. We have seen that Jesus' command to the rich man to sell all his possessions and give the proceeds to the poor presupposes a communitarian setting characterized by some form of shared wealth. Thus, here again we encounter a tension between the ancient context and our own. Should we ask how we might appropriate Jesus' command outside such a communitarian setting? Or should we take this passage as a demand to re-create such a setting? There can obviously be no universally applicable answer to such questions, but they remain important aspects of any attempt to make contemporary use of New Testament ethical norms.

The third "extraordinary" demand—the call to martyrdom—leads more directly into the broader issue of self-abnegation, although that issue is implicit in the other two also. Viewed from one perspective, the demand to find one's life by losing it is extraordinarily powerful and uplifting. The notion of finding meaning in one's life by giving it over to a greater reality carries with it the promise of grounding one's whole life project in the cosmos itself. As demanding and as paradoxical as it is, it has had enormous appeal to many persons through the centuries, even though it remains unintelligible to many others.

The sensitivities to human worth that have developed in our own time, however, have raised serious questions about the morality of the images of carrying one's cross and losing one's life in order to find it. Most significantly, we have been forced to recognize in recent decades the damage done by these images to groups of persons traditionally subject to subordination by others. For they have been powerful tools in the hands of the dominant gender and dominant races and classes in facilitating the internalization of a subservient mentality by the subjugated. And all too often it has not been those in full possession of their own lives and identities but those denied a sense of self-worth who have answered the call to self-sacrifice.

A responsible hermeneutical discussion of this theme, therefore, will have to take very seriously its negative potential and actual historical effect. It will be important to place it in the context of the wider biblical witness and also to bring it into conversation with aspects of our most recently developed sensitivities.

Relevant to such a discussion is Burton Mack's broadside attack on this Gospel (1988, 333–49), in which he characterizes it as a violent and vindictive work that has fed not only anti-Judaism but the military arrogance of powerful nations through the centuries. From one perspective, he concedes, Mark issues a call to humility and self-sacrifice. But its apocalyptic framework, most evident in Mark 13, negates these themes with a strong emphasis on God's vengeance upon those who have rejected Jesus. And the call to service is operative only within the community. Mack's interpretation of Mark is a serious challenge not only to what he calls "pious" readings of this Gospel but also to

Myers's political reading. If we understand this Gospel as nothing more than an encouragement to enduring in suffering while waiting for God's revenge, then what many have seen as its moral force is completely subverted, however we might characterize the nature of that force.

Evaluation of Mack's reading, in my estimation, takes us beyond the exegetical realm and invites explicit hermeneutical reflection. No one can deny the violent aspects of Mark 13 or the negative role such aspects of the Gospels have played in human history. Neither can one deny, however, that the call to humility and self-sacrifice is a central, indeed all-pervasive, theme in this Gospel. The question is how to weigh these competing aspects and relate them to one another. Mack chooses to allow the strain of violence and vindictiveness to cancel out the competing strain of meaning. One can, however, at least as easily choose to weight these elements in the exact opposite way. To the extent that we understand the Jesus of Mark as acting on behalf of justice, along the lines that Myers conceives, then the eschatological recompense that so offends Mack will appear less as mere revenge than as an act of liberation.

Mack's point, of course, is that it is precisely such an identification of Jesus and his followers as the righteous who stand over against the unrighteous who rejected him that has been such a destructive force. To allow this insight to negate the Gospel's undeniable emphasis on serving others, however, is to miss an important potential for meaning in the Markan story. Totally apart from the question of the Gospel's historical "accuracy" or "inaccuracy" in relating the causes of Jesus' crucifixion, it presents a compelling portrayal of the universal conflict between arrogant, oppressive power and human compassion and longing for justice. And it issues a clear invitation to a nonviolent, self-sacrificial lifestyle as a response to the story that it tells.

This is not to say that Mack's criticisms are completely unfounded. But we can evaluate these criticisms fairly only if we take with equal seriousness the competing strains of meaning in an attempt to work hermeneutically with the tension they create. In the end, it would seem that once again much of this tension issues specifically from the apocalyptic framework that is so pervasive within the New Testament.

CHAPTER 7

luke-acts

⌐⊙⌐

The story told in the Gospel of Luke differs from that in any of the other Gospels by virtue of the fact that it is part of a two-volume work that includes the book of Acts. One can make good sense of Luke by itself, but scholars since the time of Henry J. Cadbury's classic treatment, *The Making of Luke-Acts*, have generally preferred to interpret it in concert with Acts. Not only is the common authorship a virtual certainty, but the thematic unity and continuity of plot create a coherent complex of meaning, dimensions of which are lost if either part is read in isolation. We can do full justice neither to the theological nor to the ethical dimensions of either volume without taking account of that essential unity.

THE ETHIC OF GOD'S PLAN:
THE SCOPE AND CHARACTER OF
THE PLOT OF LUKE-ACTS

The story that Luke-Acts tells spans two segments of the history of God's dealings with the world at large and with the people of Israel. These two segments are the story of Jesus and the story of the early Christian community. Bracketing these narratives, however, are allusions to a broader story, signified in various ways within the narration, that begins with creation and ends with the parousia—the anticipated return of the resurrected Christ in glory. The two volumes thus portray a turning point in the larger story of how God makes the redemption promised to Israel available to the world. This larger story is a history of salvation, designated at several points as God's plan.[1] It is within the worldview of that history that the ethical perspective of Luke-Acts takes shape.

The Hope of Israel

The Gospel begins with narratives of the births of John the Baptist and Jesus, followed by the stories of Jesus' presentation in the temple as an infant and his discussion with the teachers in the temple at age twelve. In all these accounts, the narrator forges strong connections to the larger story of the people of Israel. The temple figures not only in the stories about Jesus but in the account of John's birth. John's father, Zechariah, is a priest, and it is in the temple that he hears the angelic promise that his wife, Elizabeth, will bear a son. In addition, both this announcement and that concerning the birth of Jesus relate the coming events to God's dealings with Israel. John "will turn many of the people of Israel to the Lord their God" (Luke 1:16), and Jesus will receive "the throne of his ancestor David" and "reign over the house of Jacob forever . . ." (Luke 1:33). The speeches of the various human characters reinforce this emphasis. Mary's exultation interprets Jesus' birth as God's merciful action toward Israel in accordance with the divine promises (Luke 1:34). And Zechariah speaks of God's people and the house of David (Luke 1:68-69), refers to Israel's prophets (Luke 1:70), and declares John himself to be "the prophet of the Most High" (Luke 1:76). Then, when Jesus is presented in the temple, a man named Simeon—who was "looking forward to the consolation of Israel" and awaiting "the Lord's Messiah" (Luke 2:25-26)—prophesies that the child "is destined for the falling and rising of many in Israel" (Luke 2:34).

This emphasis on Israel goes beyond a sense of continuity with the past, for the divine promise regarding Jesus is that he will fulfill Israel's hope for eventual restoration/vindication/redemption. That is the point not only of Simeon's expectation of Israel's "consolation" (*paraklēsis*), but also of Zechariah's declaration at John's birth that God "has visited and redeemed his people" (Luke 1:68, RSV; NRSV, "looked upon and redeemed"). The theme of Israel's hope also appears in the narrator's description of the audience to whom the prophet Anna speaks about the child Jesus: "all who were looking for the redemption of Jerusalem" (Luke 2:38). And it surfaces dramatically in the climax of Mary's speech: "[God] has helped his servant Israel, in remembrance of his mercy, according to the promise he made to our ancestors, to Abraham and to his descendants forever" (Luke 1:54-55). It is also affirmed near the end of the Gospel in the ironical statement of the disciples at Luke 24:21: "But we had hoped that he was the one to redeem Israel."

This theme continues throughout Acts. In 1:6, the disciples ask the resurrected Jesus whether he will now "restore the kingdom to Israel," and Jesus does not give a negative answer but declares that it is not for them to know "the times and seasons" set by God. Later, when Paul defends himself before King Agrippa, he says that he has been accused because of his "hope in the promise made by God to our ancestors" (26:6-8). And, finally, when Paul preaches to the Jews in Rome at the end of the story, he declares that "it is for the sake of the hope of Israel that I am bound with this chain" (28:20).

Just how this hope of Israel finds fulfillment is a matter of interpretation, because the Gospel makes clear (Luke 19:44) that Jerusalem fails to recognize its "visitation," and the apocalyptic discourse in 21:5-36 predicts the destruction of the temple and Jerusalem. Moreover, Stephen's speech in Acts 7 not only blames the people as a whole for Jesus' death (esp. 7:51) but in 7:48 seems to challenge the very notion of the temple, despite the clear reverence for it evident in Luke 1 and 24. Throughout Acts, moreover, Paul's preaching to Jews produces ambiguous results. Some respond positively to his message, but the majority reject it (for example, Acts 13:42-46; 17:1-15; 28:17-28). Apparently, then, fulfillment of Israel's hope means neither the reestablishment of the Israelite nation as a political entity nor the formation of a community in which the vast majority of Israelites participate.

The remarkable persistence of the theme,[2] however, and the "materialist" aspect of the vision of Luke-Acts with respect to the future hope should caution us against either spiritualizing the hope of Israel or consigning it to a heavenly future. The speeches of both Mary and Zechariah show that this hope is that of an oppressed people for liberation. Preceding Mary's declaration that God has helped "his servant Israel," she proclaims that God "has brought down the powerful from their thrones" (1:52); and Zechariah defines the role of the Davidic savior in terms that reflect the yearning for release from political domination: "that we would be saved from our enemies and from the hand of all who hate us" (1:71). More precise delineation of the character of that expected liberation will be possible as we delve into other dimensions of Luke-Acts below, but pursuit of this issue will take us into hermeneutical questions.

The Inclusion of Gentiles and the Course of the Spirit-Empowered Mission

A central aspect of the plot in Luke-Acts is that the hope for Israel's redemption is paralleled by a strong emphasis on the inclusion of Gentiles in the new community. The latter emphasis in no way negates the former, since there was a significant strain of thought within the Israelite tradition that envisioned an eschatological influx of Gentiles.[3] Within the theological framework of Luke-

Acts, however, there is strong resistance among Jews to such inclusion. In fact, the struggle that it foments—first between Jesus and those who oppose him in Israel, and later between factions within the early Christian community—is a major theme in this two-volume work.

Alongside the strong emphasis on continuity with historical Israel in the opening chapters, there are early hints regarding Gentile inclusion. Simeon speaks of God's salvation not only as bringing glory to Israel but also as "prepared in the presence of all peoples, a light for revelation to the Gentiles"; and the quotation from Isaiah that introduces John the Baptist ends with the declaration that "all flesh shall see the salvation of God" (Luke 3:1). Nevertheless, the opposition to inclusion develops quickly. When Jesus has completed his inaugural sermon in Nazareth, his accounts of the ministries of Elijah and Elisha to Gentile persons (Luke 4:25-30) result in the people's attempt to throw him off a cliff.

Only after the resurrection, however, does the Gentile issue come fully into view, and even then it emerges only gradually into central focus. In his last appearance to his followers, the risen Jesus commands that the message be proclaimed "to all nations, beginning from Jerusalem" (Luke 24:47). The reference to Jerusalem reaffirms the continuity of the Christian movement with its Israelite heritage, even as it indicates the universal scope of the mission. And the same is true of the reiteration of the commissioning in Acts 1:8: "and you will be my witnesses in Jerusalem, and in all Judea and Samaria, and to the ends of the earth." The deacon Philip's preaching in Samaria (Acts 8:4-24)—Israelite, but not Jewish territory—constitutes a bridge to the wider mission, and then his encounter with the Ethiopian eunuch (Acts 8:1-39) serves as a precursor to the Gentile mission and an indicator of its universal geographic scope.

However, it is only with the extended account of Peter's dealings with the Roman centurion Cornelius in Acts 10, reiterated in 11:1-18, that the programmatic inclusion of Gentiles is explicitly affirmed. Peter's vision in 10:9-16 shows that God has made clean all food considered unclean by the Jewish Law (10:15). This eventually leads to Peter's own declaration that no person is "profane or unclean" (10:19) and then to his declaration that "God shows no partiality" but accepts anyone in any nation who "does what is right" and what is acceptable to God (10:34). In the midst of Peter's speech, the Gentiles who are present receive the Spirit just as the Jewish believers did at Pentecost in Acts 2:1-13.

When Peter relates these events to the believers in Jerusalem, however, some object to his having eaten with uncircumcised persons. And although his testimony convinces those present (Acts 11:18), the matter is not fully resolved until chapter 15. By this time, the mission of Paul and Barnabas has resulted in the inclusion of many Gentiles, even though their practice is to bring the message first to the synagogues. There is strong opposition to the acceptance of Gentiles without demanding circumcision, however, and this is the issue at the conference in chapter 15. Only after the testimony of Peter, Barnabas, Paul, and James is there finally an agreement to forgo circumcision and demand of Gentiles only abstention "from things polluted by idols," fornication, meat from strangled animals, and blood (15:19-21). From this point, the mission to Gentiles can proceed without impediment.

The mission is also universal in its geographical scope. It must begin in Jerusalem, which signifies that it remains an extension of God's dealings with Israel, but its ultimate goal is "the ends of the earth" (Acts 1:8; 13:46). The plot line, however, does not trace the mission to its conclusion, for that remains in the narrator's future. It rather takes the reader, through the person of Paul, from the center of the Jewish world to the center of the Gentile world—Rome. This penultimate goal is stated through explicit divine testimony (Acts 23:11), and it is achieved when Paul arrives there as a prisoner. From there, the mission will proceed to the ends of the earth, and its ongoing character is signified by the fact that at the end of the narration Paul is still alive, merely under house arrest, actively preaching the word.

The story told in Luke-Acts is thus the drama of God's ongoing interaction with the world. That interaction begins with creation (Acts 17:24-28), continues with a special relationship to the people of Israel (Acts 7:1-53), and reaches a climactic point in the life, death, and resurrection of Jesus (Acts 2:22-36). It continues in the proclamation to the world at large, and it will reach its conclusion when the mission reaches the ends of the earth and Jesus returns in glory (Acts 1:8; 17:30-31). The narrated portion of the drama is directed by the Holy Spirit. It is the Spirit that engenders the birth of Jesus (Luke 1:34), speaks through the characters in the birth and infancy stories (Luke 1:41, 67; 2:25) and descends on Jesus at his baptism (Luke 8:21-22). It is also the Spirit that descends on the believers at Pentecost (Acts 2:1-4) and throughout Acts and determines the course of the Christian mission (Acts 1:8; 11:12; 13:2, 4; 16:6; 19:21; 21:11), sometimes in strange and unexpected ways (16:6; 21:4). It is therefore the Spirit that implements God's plan for Israel and for all humanity.

The Character of God and the Ethic of God's Plan

The nature and scope of the plan reveal both the character and the ethic of God. To say that God made promises to Israel (Acts 7:2, 17; 13:23, 32-33) and is now fulfilling those promises is to testify to God's integrity, or faithfulness to the people to whom they were made. To say, more concretely, that the fulfillment of those promises entails God's deliverance of Israel from its oppressors means that God desires the people's well-being. It is thus to say that God's action is liberating, enabling the fulfillment of a people's divinely ordained destiny.

God's plan, however, involves a redefinition of the people chosen for this destiny. For to open that destiny to all persons, without qualification, is to say that God's concern for human welfare is without limits, that all persons count equally in God's eyes. If Israel is liberated from its oppressors, Gentiles are also liberated from the barriers that set them apart from the people of promise. The plan of God therefore reveals God's character and ethic as embracing a universal care for human beings and the integrity to implement that care through dramatic acts of liberation.

Implicit already in the portrayal of the character and ethic of God through a rehearsal of the elements of God's plan is the demand to imitate God's actions as well as the promise of empowerment to do so. The ethical responsibility of human beings, however, does not remain implicit; it is made explicit in various ways in the course of the plot.

THE DIMENSIONS OF INCLUSION AND THE NATURE OF LIBERATION

In the preceding section, I treated the broad theme of inclusion under the rubric of the mission to Gentiles because this particular form of inclusiveness is central to the plot of Luke-Acts. Ultimately, however, Gentiles stand under the larger heading of general inclusiveness alongside various other groups, each of which involves its own specific set of issues; and we miss the specific character of this inclusiveness if we do not understand it as liberation. For, in one way or another, Jesus also brings liberation to each of the groups that he embraces. And the programmatic character of the liberation theme is evident in Jesus' own definition of his mission. Immediately following his testing by the devil, he enters the synagogue in Nazareth and applies to himself the scriptural passage he reads, which combines Isa 61:1-2 and 58:6:

> The Spirit of the Lord is upon me,
>   because he has anointed me
>   to bring good news to the poor.

> He has sent me to proclaim
>   release to the captives
>   and recovery of sight to the blind,
> to let the oppressed go free,
>   to proclaim the year of the Lord's favor. (Luke 4:18-19)

This statement describes the ethic of Jesus, and therefore of God; and it becomes clear at several points that the same ethic is expected of Jesus' followers. For example, Luke's version the parable of the great dinner is prefaced by Jesus' instruction that one should invite "the poor, the crippled, the lame, and the blind to one's own banquets (Luke 14:14)—just as the host eventually does in the parable (14:18). In Acts, moreover, the apostles repeat Jesus' healings with parallel miracles of their own (for example, 3:1-10; 5:12-16; 16:16-19; 19:11-12; 20:7-12). They, too, are agents of liberation. So when we observe Jesus including and ministering to the various types of persons who in some way stand in need of liberation, we must also discern an implicit imperative for the disciples and the reader of the story.

The Poor and the Powerless

Among the more persistent themes in Luke is Jesus' "preferential option for the poor"—a phrase I have borrowed from liberation theology that is particularly apt when applied to Luke. The attention devoted to this matter is, in fact, quite overwhelming. Partiality toward the poor surfaces in both explicit and implicit ways early in the Gospel. Mary's speech is stunning in this regard, with its powerful articulation of the theme of reversal. God scatters the proud, brings down the powerful "from their thrones," lifts up the lowly, fills the hungry, and sends the rich "away empty" (Luke 1:51-53). Jesus is born in a manger and is visited not by Matthew's magi but by lowly shepherds. As we have seen, the passage Jesus reads in Luke 4:18-19 mentions first of all the proclamation of "good news to the poor" as the task of the one anointed by God's Spirit. Later, in Luke 7:22, Jesus confirms his messianic status through an allusion to the Isaiah text that highlights the theme of the poor. Together, the two passages frame the components of Jesus' ministry with the commission to preach good news to the poor.

In the Sermon on the Plain, Jesus not only begins with three beatitudes that acknowledge God's blessing on the poor, the hungry, and the grieving but adds three corresponding woes, beginning with "But woe to you who are rich, for you have received your consolation" (Luke 6:24). Here, the reversal theme takes a particularly sharp form, which is parallel in force to the parable of the rich man and Lazarus in Luke 16:19-30. And the contrast between rich and poor is graphically evident when we compare the story of the rich ruler in Luke 18:18-25 with that of the poor widow in Luke 21:1-3. In the latter, Jesus commends the woman, who puts "all she has to live on" in the temple treasury, contrasting her gift to the offerings of the rich. In the former, a rich man balks at Jesus' advice to sell all and give the proceeds to the poor, provoking Jesus' statement on the difficulty of the rich entering God's rule—a point even more dramatically underscored in the parable of the rich fool (Luke 12:13-22). Finally, as Matera notes, it is only Luke who characterizes the Pharisees as "lovers of money," thus placing the issue of wealth and poverty at the very heart of the conflict between Jesus and his opponents (1996, 83).

As noted earlier (see above, 96), the word for "poor" in the Gospels (*ptōchos*) refers to the destitute. Brian Blount, however, draws on the work of Joel Green to show that the poor in Luke are not only economically deprived but persons of dishonorable status within the honor/shame system; they are those who are utterly powerless. This is why we find the term "poor" so consistently associated with parallel terms referring to other forms of social marginalization. Blount therefore concludes that

> Jesus' message in Luke's Gospel is more than a message about enriching those who are presently destitute; it is a message about empowering those who are powerless. It is a message that reverses social, economic, and political status, a message that proclaims the kind of societal transformation that makes those who were formerly cast to the oppressed margins of society the ones around whom the new God-dominated society will revolve. (2002, 81, citing Green 1994, 65)

This is not to deny the economic aspect of poverty in Luke-Acts; it is rather to understand it as a central component in a broader phenomenon of social exclusion and oppression. And it is to reiterate that Jesus' inclusion of the poor and the otherwise powerless is an act of liberation anticipating the reversal that God's rule brings. If we must not reduce the term "poor" to its bare economic dimension, however, there is a clear reason that this term remains so central to Jesus' proclamation. There is an irreducible "materialist" dimension to the liberation Jesus brings; it changes the actual, concrete conditions under which people live on the earth and in society. Images of disease and infirmity complement the references to poverty, but the latter is for good reason the controlling element.

Sinners and Tax Collectors

Another central aspect of Jesus' ministry in Luke is his reaching out to sinners. To begin with, we find him keeping company with persons known to be sinful. Along with Mark (1:13-17) and Matthew (9:9-13), Luke depicts Jesus as incurring the criticism of the Pharisees for eating with "tax collectors and sinners." Jesus refers to a similar charge ("a glutton and a drunkard, a friend of tax collectors and sinners") in Luke 7:34 (//Matt 11:19), and in Luke 15:1 the narrator comments that "tax collectors and sinners were coming near to listen to him." In addition, in Luke 7:36-50, a story parallel to the anointing of Jesus at Bethany in Mark 14:3-9 and Matt 26:6-13, the Lukan narrator (alone) identifies the woman as sinful.

Linked with the depiction of Jesus in the company of sinners is an emphasis on repentance and forgiveness. Although Luke lacks the description of Jesus' own message as a call to repentance found in Matt 4:17 and Mark 1:16 and focuses rather on the proclamation of liberation preached in the synagogue at Nazareth (Luke 4:16-30), repentance remains a central theme. As Matera observes, the statement in Luke 5:32 (//Matt 9:13//Mark 2:17) makes it programmatic: "I have not come to call the righteous but sinners to repentance" (1996, 70). This statement, moreover, is paralleled by Luke 19:10, where Jesus declares that "the Son of Man came to seek out and to save the lost." In addition, when Jesus perceives the discomfort of his host at his willingness to receive the touches of the sinful woman in the anointing story, he launches an extended statement on forgiveness and pronounces the woman's sins forgiven. He also forgives the paralytic's sins (Luke 5:17-26) as in the other Synoptics (Matt 9:1-8; Mark 2:1-12), and in Luke, the parable of the lost sheep (15:3-7//Matt 18:12-14) is followed by two additional parables, the lost coin and the prodigal son, that illustrate the same theme (15:8-32). The Lukan version of the parable of the lost sheep expresses the theme more explicitly ("one sinner who repents") than the Matthean, and the story of the prodigal son provides one of the most graphic and touching illustrations in the entire biblical tradition.

The theme of "repentance for the forgiveness of sins," moreover, spans the entire narrative of Luke-Acts. The angelic announcement to Zechariah in Luke 1:16 defines John the Baptist's role as turning "many of the people of Israel to the Lord their God," and the narrator describes John in Luke 3:3 as "proclaiming a baptism of repentance for the forgiveness of sins." As Jesus is dying on the cross, he (in a passage distinctive to Luke) accepts the repentance of one of the criminals crucified beside him (Luke 23:39-43). Then, following the resurrection, the narrator gives a programmatic definition of the content of the mission proclamation: "repentance and forgiveness of sins is to be proclaimed in his name to all nations, beginning from Jerusalem" (Luke 24:47). This theme is reiterated in Acts 2:38, when Peter urges those present at the miracle of Pentecost to be baptized in Jesus' name and receive forgiveness.

From this point, the theme of repentance/forgiveness becomes thematic in the speeches of the apostles. When Peter makes a defense before the council in Jerusalem in 5:32, he defines God's purpose in exalting the crucified Jesus in terms of fostering "repentance to Israel and forgiveness of sins." He also tells a Gentile audience in 10:43 that those who believe in Jesus "receive forgiveness of sins through his name." Paul makes a similar declaration in the synagogue in Pisidian Antioch (Acts 13:38-39), and in his defense before Agrippa he reports that at his conversion/call he heard a voice defining his mission as bringing a message of forgiveness of sins to the Gentiles (Acts 27:17-18).

With such a strong link between Jesus' association with sinners and the call to repentance, it might seem that we should define this aspect of Jesus' inclusive practice as acceptance of *repentant* sinners. To do so, however, would mute one of the most important aspects of Jesus' teaching and practice in Luke. In the parable of the lost sheep, the shepherd goes looking for the sheep, and in the parable of the lost coin the woman mounts a relentless search that does not end until she finds what she is looking for. In the story of the prodigal son, most dramatically, the father goes out to meet the son before the errant one has had a chance to say a word. There is therefore no question as to how to interpret Jesus' association with sinners. Although directed toward repentance, it precedes repentance. Jesus extends the grace of God to those who are lost in order to reach them; he does not offer it merely to those who have come seeking it. In other words, he includes sinners *as* sinners, with a view to their transformation.

The charge that Jesus eats with "tax collectors and sinners" occurs following Jesus' call of Levi the tax collector in Luke 5:27, at a banquet to which Levi invites Jesus, along with "a large crowd of tax collectors and others" (5:29). We also find Jesus, in a story found only in Luke, eating with Zacchaeus, a "chief tax collector," who was rich (19:1-10). As Robert Tannehill observes, the story of Zacchaeus, following closely on the story of the rich ruler in chapter 18, answers "the question of whether and how a rich man can be saved (see 18:24-27)." Tannehill also notes that the parallel statements of Jesus in 5:32 and 19:10, passages noted above that define Jesus' role in terms of calling sinners/seeking the lost, create an inclusion that serves to sum up his entire ministry (1986, 107).

Zacchaeus's wealth, however, is not the only impediment to his salvation. The pairing of tax collectors with sinners is surely an indication of their entirely negative status. And this insight makes the images of their repentance all the more dramatic. Nor is the story of Zacchaeus alone in this regard. In Luke 3:19, tax collectors respond to John's preaching, and John does not reject them as insincere. Similar in import is the parable of the Pharisee and the tax collector (Luke 18:9-14). And if we accept Tannehill's suggestion that Luke 5:32 and 19:10 form an inclusion that sums up Jesus' ministry, then it is possible to understand "tax collectors and sinners" as the extreme examples of acceptance of the unacceptable and thus as paradigmatic of inclusion. Also, if we translate the conjunction *kai* in Luke 3:12 as "even" (with the NRSV) rather than "also" (with the RSV), the story of the tax collectors' response to John would support this suggestion: "*Even* the tax collectors came to be baptized." Jesus' inclusiveness was so radical that it embraced the least likely persons imaginable.

Pharisees

The portrayal of the Pharisees in Luke, as in the other Gospels, is overwhelmingly negative. They emerge as critics early on (5:17-26), continuing in this role throughout the narrative (for example, 7:39; 11:38; 15:2; 19:34), and in 11:53, they conspire with the scribes to engage Jesus in conversation in order to trap him. Jesus, moreover, is severely critical of them. He pronounces severe woes on them in 11:40-44, warns his disciples against their teaching in 12:1-3, and uses a Pharisee as a negative image in 18:9-14.

There are, nevertheless, reasons to list the Pharisees, in a qualified way, as among the objects of inclusion in Luke-Acts. On three occasions in Luke, we find Jesus eating at the table of a Pharisee: 7:36-50; 11:37-52; and 14:1-4. Each time, a controversy arises. In the third instance, however, Jesus is critical of some lawyers and Pharisees present at the meal, but not of his host. It is to this particular Pharisee that Jesus offers his teaching regarding whom to invite to dinners preliminary to his parable of the great dinner, and there is no indication that the host rejects the teaching. Nor is there sufficient reason to interpret Luke 13:31, where some Pharisees warn Jesus about Herod's intention, as a deception.[4] In addition, Acts 15:5 mentions "some believers who belonged to the sect of the Pharisees." The role of these Christian Pharisees at the meeting in Jerusalem is somewhat negative from the narrator's perspective, because they insist on circumcision for Gentiles. However, when James reaches the decision to forgo this demand, there is no indication of objection from anyone. And in v. 22 it is "with the consent of the whole church" that the apostles and elders commission members of the Jerusalem church to accompany Paul and Barnabas to Antioch with the letter explaining the decision.

At other points, non-Christian Pharisees play positive roles. In Acts 5:34, Gamaliel, whom Paul identifies in Acts 22:3 as his former teacher, convinces the council not to take severe action against the apostles (Acts 5:27-42). His position is in direct opposition to that of the high priest and the Sadducees (Acts 5:17-18). Again, in Acts 23:9-10, some Pharisees side with Paul against Sadducees in a meeting of the council—after Paul has deliberately played the two groups off against each other. Nor should we interpret Paul's tactic in this instance as cynical. Not only is the issue he cites—the resurrection of the dead—a legitimate one from a Christian perspective, but Paul identifies himself on two occasions as a Pharisee. And the use of the present tense in Acts 23:6 indicates that he is not merely referring to his past way of life.[5]

The way in which Acts plays the Pharisees and Sadducees off against each other is related to the theme of the Gospel's creation of a division within the house of Israel. In Luke 3:33-35, Simeon prophesies that Jesus will cause the "rising and falling of many in Israel," and this motif continues in the varying responses to the apostolic preaching to Jews in Acts. The Pharisees, therefore, seem to embody the possibility of a postresurrection acceptance of the Christian proclamation. And there is in fact an emphasis in Acts on the offering of a "second chance" to the Jewish people. Throughout the entire Acts narrative, the apostles' preaching is directed first to Jews. Although the response is mixed, there are continuing reports of some who join the movement (for example, Acts 2:14-42; 5:14-16; 17:1-2; see also 13:13-14; 14:1; 17:1, 16; 18:4; 19:8). There is often virulent opposition, but even in these cases some respond positively (13:43; 14:1; 16:15; 17:4).

According to one interpretation, by the end of Acts the attempt to reach out to Jews has reached its conclusion and given way to an exclusively Gentile mission. The strongest evidence for this is Paul's statement after preaching to the Jewish leaders in Rome at the close of the narrative: "Let it be known to you then that the salvation of God has been sent to the Gentiles; they will listen" (Acts 28:28). However, the description of the reaction of the leaders in 28:24 speaks against this notion: "Some were convinced by what he had said, while others refused to believe." The term "convinced" is a misleading translation of the imperfect *epeithonto*, which we should probably take, with Tannehill, to mean "being persuaded." But if this is so, the statement would be an extremely odd preface to a declaration that the mission to the Jews has ended. As Tannehill argues, "The reference to some being persuaded indicates that there is still hope of convincing some Jews in spite of what Paul is about to say about the Jewish community of Rome" (1990, 347).

If the mission to Jews remains open, with positive references to Pharisees as symbolic of this fact, we must recognize a partial counterweight to the negative portrayal of the majority of the people of Israel in Luke-Acts. It is true that the passion narrative emphasizes Jewish guilt. Three times Pilate tries to release Jesus, and each time the crowd defies him (Acts 23:13-24). It is equally true that Paul encounters virulent hostility from many Jews to his missionary preaching. But to the extent that the process of persuasion continues, we must also take notice of an attempt at a kind of reverse inclusion. The mission that, in the face of great controversy, was opened up to Gentiles without restriction remains open to the people of Israel, who largely rejected it in the past. We can therefore see, now from a different angle, the extent of the inclusiveness of that mission and an additional insight into the ethic of God's plan.

A Polyvalent Example: The Ethiopian Eunuch

Scholars have long recognized that the story in Acts 8:26-40 of the Ethiopian eunuch's acceptance of Christian baptism signifies a type of inclusiveness, because the mutilation of his body would have excluded him from membership in the Jewish community (Deut 23:1). Less attention has been paid to the significance of his Ethiopian origin. As Clarice Martin (1989) has demonstrated, however, a number of Roman texts identify Ethiopia specifically as "the ends of the earth," which suggests that the story stands as an anticipation of the mission to the entire Gentile world. This aspect is easy to miss, Cain Hope Felder argues, because of the attention given in Acts to the Cornelius incident. The Roman-centered character of the narrative, in other words, obscures one of its own emphases (1989, 48).

If the eunuch's place of origin is significant, so also is his "racial" identity. As Martin shows, Greco-Roman texts from the period indicate that the term *Ethiopian* was understood to signify very specifically a dark skin color and other Negroid features (1989, 111–14). Given this evidence, she goes on to draw out its implications for the interpretation of the story in the context of the ideology of Luke-Acts: "We would argue that the story of a *black* African Gentile from what would be perceived as a 'distant nation' to the south of the empire is consistent with the Lucan emphasis on 'universalism,' a recurrent motif in both Luke and Acts, and one that is well known" (1989, 114).

Women

The emphasis in Luke-Acts on the inclusion of women is well recognized. Neither the narrator nor any character in the story, however, thematizes this dimension of inclusiveness explicitly. As Clarice Martin notes, moreover, the narrative as a whole remains within the typical patriarchal framework. Male-exclusive terms dominate, "even when women (who were also recipients of the Holy Spirit and salvation in Jesus Christ) are present (Acts 1:11; 2:5, 14)." Although a remarkable amount of narrative space and significant dialogue are given to women in Luke 1, the same is not true in Acts. There are a number of stories of the conversion of women, but their spoken lines are infrequent and minimal. As Martin comments, "Women are virtually silent in Acts" (1994, 777).

Several considerations, however, justify acknowledgment of the attention given to women as among the most significant aspects of Luke-Acts. Particularly notable is the frequent pairing of stories about women with stories about men throughout the two volumes, which creates a decided sense of women's importance to the story as a whole. Martin provides a convenient listing of examples:

GOSPEL OF LUKE

2:25-28	Simeon and Anna, a priest and priestess
4:25-28	The widow of Sarepta and Naaman
15:4-10	Man with one hundred sheep; woman with ten pieces of silver
23:55–24:35	Women at the tomb; men on the Emmaus road

ACTS

9:32-43	Aeneas and Tabitha
16:11-34	Lydia, the slave girl, and the Philippian jailer. (1994, 777)

To these we should add especially Luke 7:1-17, a particularly dramatic pairing, in which the healing of the centurion's slave is followed by the raising of the widow's son at Nain.

Also, the stories about women sometimes make important contributions either to the plot or to the ideological fiber of the narrative. The strong role given to Mary in chapter 1 is significant in itself, but even more important is the content of her speech. As Tannehill comments, "Mary's hymn suggests a set of expectations about God's character and purpose which guide the reader in understanding what is most important in the subsequent story" (1986, 30). It thus sets the stage for continuing emphases on reversal, God's preference for the poor, and fulfillment of the divine promises to Israel. Later in Luke (10:38-40), the story of Mary and Martha shatters traditional expectations with respect to women's roles. Jesus takes Mary's side against Martha, who objects to her neglecting of household duties to sit and listen to Jesus. And the baptism of Lydia and her household in Acts 16:11-15 signals a new stage in the mission. Not only is she the first convert in Europe, but her apparent social position (see Reimer 1995, 71–130) and the fact that Paul returns to her house after a stint in prison (Acts 16:40) show "the importance of her conversion for the wider Philippian mission" (Wall 2002, 231).

If we turn now from this general description of the importance of women in Luke-Acts to the question of ethics, it is important to recall my earlier comments regarding the ethics of God that is revealed in the narrative's presentation of God's plan. Although Jesus never commands his followers to be inclusive of women, the narrative does so by implication. By assigning important roles to women, it implies that in God's plan of salvation women play an important role, which fractures traditional gender roles. The breakage may be incomplete, but Luke-Acts nevertheless pushes in significant ways against the limitations placed on women in ancient patriarchal societies.

The Nature of Liberation

Immediately following the story of Lydia's conversion, we find the account of the slave girl possessed with a "spirit of divination" (Acts 16:16-18). Despite the judgment of many exegetes, it is probably best not to think of this spirit as unclean or evil. As Ivani Richter Reimer notes, it does not bring with it the ill effects of such spirits, such as illness, pain, and isolation. It does, however, represent a different god, most likely Apollo, and thus engages Paul in a conflict between competing deities. But it is not this spirit that enslaves the girl but her owners, who exploit her gift for profit (1995, 171–73). We hear nothing of the slave girl's conversion, but the invocation of Jesus' name in v. 18 releases her from the captivity in which unscrupulous profiteers had held her. In this way, the story has paradigmatic value, adding nuance to Jesus' definition of his message, in Luke 4:14-19, as bringing "release to the captives."

I argued above that there is a close connection between inclusion and liberation, that Jesus in some way liberates each of the groups that are objects of his inclusion; and the same is true of the extension of his mission in Acts. We have seen this explicitly with respect to the poor and powerless as well as sinners. The former are liberated from the suffering brought on by the oppressive practices and the exclusion from which they suffer and the latter from the effects of their own sin and its social consequences. We may now say that to the extent that barriers based on gender are broken down, women are released from the restrictions imposed by patriarchal systems. Likewise, Gentiles are liberated from the social marker of circumcision that stood between them and the mercies of God available to Israel. Even the Pharisees, who are symbolic of those who rejected the ministry of Jesus, have the potential to obtain, through repentance, liberation from the consequences of this decision.

If we add to this picture the witness of the stories of the slave girl and the Ethiopian eunuch, we can round out our characterization of the liberating character of the mission of Jesus and the apostles. Both terms—inclusiveness and liberation—take on the broadest possible connotations. The Gospel is in fact all inclusive; its intention is to draw all humanity everywhere into the sphere of the mercies of God. And whenever and wherever the power that Jesus manifested is exercised, it liberates those brought into that sphere from whatever it is that stands between them and the blessings God intends for all. The liberation that Jesus engenders is therefore both material and spiritual, embracing every aspect of the lives of human beings.

CHRISTIANS AND THE EMPIRE

How, according to Luke-Acts, should Christians relate to the Roman Empire? And how, conversely, should the empire view the church? A widely influential view on these questions is that of Hans Conzelmann (1961). From his perspective, Luke-Acts is, in Hays's apt summary, an attempt "to show Christianity to be politically harmless within the Roman world" (1996, 126).

There is much evidence that Conzelmann can cite to make his point. We have already noted Pilate's threefold attempt to free Jesus, and this incident is part of a consistent emphasis on innocence—first of Jesus himself and then of Paul (Luke 23:1-4, 13-25, 41, 47; Acts 25:13-27; 26:30-32). Along similar lines, Conzelmann argues that the scenes in which Paul appears before Roman officials demonstrate "what attitude should be taken towards the State, and what the State must take note of if does not wish to sacrifice its own legal position," thus emphasizing that "to confess oneself to be a Christian implies no crime against the State" (1960, 139–40). In addition, the ethical teaching of John the Baptist in Luke 3:10-14 includes instructions for tax collectors and soldiers that imply loyalty to the state. The same is true, according to Conzelmann, of the passage on paying taxes to Caesar (Luke 20:20-26; Conzelmann 1960, 138, 148), and in the Lukan version of Jesus' entry into Jerusalem all political significance is absent: "The concept of the Davidic lordship is replaced by the simple title of king, the non-political sense of which is preserved (xix, 38). Accordingly the Temple is the only goal of the Entry, and the only place of Jesus' activity" (1960, 139).

The persistent theme of innocence is perhaps Conzelmann's strongest point, and it could conceivably serve in some degree to soothe Roman fears about the nature of the Christian movement. It is also possible that the passages about John the Baptist would contribute indirectly to this effect. Some of Conzelmann's other arguments, however, are less convincing. We have already seen that in other contexts the passage on paying taxes to Caesar is by no means an endorsement of loyalty to Rome, and there is nothing in the Lukan version to suggest otherwise. Nor do I see that the removal of the Davidic language from the story of Jesus' entry into Jerusalem significantly undermines the political content of the passage. Over against Mark, the Lukan version lacks "the coming kingdom of our ancestor David" but has "king" in place of "the one who." The difference is minimal.

Conzelmann's argument depends on a focus on passages that appear to have direct political significance. If we broaden our scope to include passages that reveal the social impact of the Christian movement, however, a somewhat different picture emerges. The pattern of radical inclusion discussed above suggests a degree of social disruption that would not have suggested political harmlessness to any Roman official responsible for keeping the peace. Thus, Richard J. Cassidy claims, against Conzelmann, that the new patterns of social existence that Jesus fostered were very much a threat to Roman power. From his perspective, "Jesus pointed the way to a social order in which neither the Romans nor any other oppressing group would be able to hold sway" (Cassidy 1992, 79, quoted by Hays 1996, 126).

Along similar lines, Hays argues that the Gospel is "a threat not just to Jewish authorities but also to the status quo in the Gentile world." He cites as an example the story of Paul's preaching in Ephesus. In Acts 19:23-41, an artisan "who made silver shrines of Artemis" stirs up wrath against Paul and his companions because his preaching against idolatry has affected his business. Paul has done nothing overtly disruptive but has sought only to bring people into the Christian fellowship. "Yet in case after case," Hays argues,

> this sort of community-building seems to introduce an explosive new catalyst into the sociopolitical order. The book of Acts portrays a movement that is turning people in large numbers "from the power of Satan to God" (Acts 26:18) and re-socializing them into a community that lives by very different norms—the norm defined by Jesus' life and teachings. (1996, 128)

Cassidy's point is also reinforced by consideration of the theme of God's rule in Luke-Acts, which is by no means a weak element, as we can see in Matera's summation of the usage of the term:

> Whereas Mark refers to "the kingdom" or "the kingdom of God" 14 times, and Matthew 50 times, these phrases occur in Luke's Gospel 39 times, 21 of which are peculiar to him. Luke also shares 9 sayings from Q with Matthew. In addition to these sayings, one should note the 8 occurrences of the term in the Acts of the Apostles. As was the case with Matthew, Luke seems to understand the term in much the same way as does Mark, from whom he derives 9 sayings about the kingdom: it is the dynamic and powerful reign of God. (1996, 63)

In light of this evidence, the deletion of the term from the entry scene loses much of the weight Conzelmann wants to give it. And Hays is correct in reminding us "that talk about the 'kingdom of God' was potent political language in Jesus' time: it would have been heard as declaring the restoration of Israel free from outside domination" (1996, 127). The political content of the term, moreover, is reinforced by the strong emphasis on the hope of Israel.

We should also note that the depiction of Roman officials in Luke-Acts is not entirely sympathetic. Pilate's attempts to release Jesus may seem exculpatory, but, as Hays shows, Acts 4:23-31 clearly indicates his guilt. Following the appearance of Peter and John before the council and their subsequent release, the gathered Christians say a prayer in which they indict Herod and Pilate, along with "the peoples of Israel," for having "gathered together against your holy servant Jesus, whom you anointed . . ." (vv. 27-28). This indictment, moreover, is preceded by a quotation from Psalm 2 that portrays Gentiles, "the kings of the earth" and "the rulers," as standing "against the Lord and against his Messiah."

In some ways the clearest indications of the sociopolitical disruptiveness of the Christian movement are to be found in the apostles' speeches before the Jewish council in Acts 4–5, which contrast obedience to God to obedience to human beings, and are summed up in 5:29: "We must obey God rather than any human authority" (Greek *anthrōpois*; see also 4:19-20). Conzelmann points out that this axiom appears only when the Christian missionaries are dealing with Jews rather than Gentiles. Even Conzelmann, however, must concede that Jesus counsels his followers to be bold in their testimony before all authorities (Luke 12:11-12; 21:12-13) (1960, 148).

In the end, it would appear that Luke-Acts might tread somewhat lightly when directly portraying relations between Christians and the empire. But to characterize this work as a wholesale attempt to make the movement appear politically innocuous is more than a slight exaggeration. To the extent that there remains a degree of ambiguity concerning how Christians should regard the empire and behave toward it, it should be helpful to recall the concept of the "hidden transcript," discussed in chapter 4. Although the world of the readers of Luke-Acts is far removed from that of Galilean peasants, the Jesus people are still a tiny minority in the Roman empire; and their existence is precarious. If Luke-Acts does not take an explicitly belligerent attitude toward the Roman government, as does the book of Revelation, this does not mean that it counsels simplistic accommodation. Ancient readers would have had no trouble combining the passages in which both Jesus and the apostles defy the Jewish authorities with the subtler indications of God's sovereignty over Rome to conclude that their loyalty to another "empire" and another sovereign makes them a counterculture with alternative values. Nor would they have been unable to understand that although the charges brought by Jews in Acts 17:1-10 are in one sense false, the proclamation of the gospel does in fact turn "the world upside down," and Jesus is indeed an alternative king to Caesar. Certainly, it should be clear to believing readers that their loyalty is first of all to God and that God's rule ultimately brings all human sovereignties to an end.

THE QUALITY OF DISCIPLESHIP

What, finally, does it mean to follow Jesus? So far, we have seen that it means to ally oneself with the plan of God and its inclusive ethic that Jesus conveys in both his deeds and his teaching and to witness boldly in the face of all oppositional powers. It means to embrace all kinds of persons, most especially the poor and powerless and otherwise marginalized, and in some way to enhance their liberation. With all this in mind, it is important now to comment on some additional aspects of discipleship that are central to its meaning.

With respect to the treatment of others, Luke joins Mark and Matthew in presenting the commandment to love one's neighbor as parallel to the commandment to love God (Luke 10:25-28). Luke also concurs with Matthew in counseling love of one's enemies (Luke 6:27-28, 32-36) and in prohibiting judgment of others (Luke 6:37-42). Although this list of passages does not compare to Matthew's explicit emphasis on love and elevation of the love command as the hermeneutical key to the Law (Matt 22:40), it does show that love is an important value in Luke-Acts. And, in its own way, the Lukan introduction to the two great commandments gives it a central place. In both Mark (12:28-34) and Matthew, the question to which Jesus responds has to do with which commandment is the greatest. In Luke, however, the lawyer's question is, "What must I do to inherit eternal life?"

If, as we saw above, the ethic of God and Jesus entails their mercy toward the poor, then Christians are also called to participate in such acts of mercy. And doing so entails, in part, a detachment from personal wealth. In Luke, the most radical passage related to this theme is Jesus' demand that his disciples sell "everything and give alms" (12:33).

In other passages, however, the demand seems simply to involve the sharing of personal wealth, as does the injunction of John the Baptist in Luke 3:16: "Whoever has two coats must share with anyone who has none; and whoever has food must do likewise." Thus, following the parable of the dishonest manager (Luke 16:1-8), Jesus gives such advice as this: "Whoever is faithful in a very little is faithful in much," and "You cannot serve God and wealth" (16:10, 13). The point of the story is that the steward

> will make prudent use of his master's wealth while he still has access to it in order to make friends for the future. Jesus employs the parable to provide his disciples with an example of prudent conduct in the use of wealth, not to approve of the steward's dishonest actions. The disciples should be as prudent in their use of wealth as are the children of this age (12:8b-9); that is, they should share their wealth so they will have treasure in heaven. (Matera 1996, 85)

Also, Jesus' saying following his encounter with the rich ruler shows that "[i]t is not impossible for the rich to enter the kingdom of God, since all things are possible with God (18:27), but the accumulation of possessions makes it more difficult." The story of Zacchaeus is paradigmatic in this regard. "Jesus calls him a descendant of Abraham precisely because he shares his possessions with others" (Matera 1996, 85). It is also significant that almsgiving is what Jesus demands of the Pharisees in Luke 11:37 as a way of counteracting the "greed and wickedness" within their hearts.

This pattern of implicit moderation of Jesus' more radical sayings continues in Acts. The apostles preach a message defined largely in terms of Lukan salvation history, and they perform acts of mercy that parallel those of Jesus. But they do not repeat his concrete teaching. In Acts, instead, we find an emphasis on almsgiving (9:36; 10:2, 4, 31; 24:17).

Acts does present the image of a primitive Christian community in which all material wealth is shared (2:43-47; 4:32-37). There is some ambiguity as to the precise nature of the sharing—that is, whether one's goods were sold on joining the community (as the latter passage seems to imply) or only when need arose (as the former seems to indicate) (see Reimer 1995, 11–14). Either way, the community's practice can legitimately claim to be an implementation of Jesus' advice to the rich ruler in Luke 18:18-25. The question, however, is how the reader of Luke-Acts is expected to use this image in making ethical decisions regarding wealth. As Tannehill observes,

> The community of goods is mentioned only in connection with the early Jerusalem church. It is part of the narrator's picture of the ideal church at the beginning. Already at the time of writing there was probably a clear difference between this ideal picture and the actual practice of Christians. Nevertheless, the ideal is emphasized. We need not suppose that the narrator expected later churches to be transformed into the ideal community described. Such an expectation is not required for the ideal to be relevant. The ideal can function as a critique of a complacent church with narrow vision, content with its own obedience, and constructive criticism may find a response among individuals, if not in a church as a whole. If Jesus' call and this ideal picture of the church lead some Christians with assets to recognize that they can and should give those assets to the poor, something important has happened. Such responses by individuals may not in themselves produce the ideal community of the narrator's vision, but

they do recognize the needs of the poor as a moral claim, as did the early church, according to Acts. (1990, 46; quoted in Beardslee 1993, 228)

In sum, then, a degree of ambiguity prevails when we consider the question of how either the church or the individual reader is supposed to implement the witness of Luke-Acts with respect to the question of personal wealth. Some of Jesus' sayings are radical, demanding complete divestment, and the image of the economic communality of the Jerusalem church in Acts presents a monumentally challenging ideal. When we view the Luke-Acts narrative as a coherent whole, however, there are indications that accommodations to more conventional ways of responding to the needs of the poor are to be accepted. To say this, however, raises important hermeneutical questions that will come under discussion in the final section of this chapter.

One final aspect of discipleship is the demand to accept suffering as a consequence of witness. To begin with, Luke retains all three of Jesus' predictions of his suffering and death in Mark (Luke 9:18-22; 9:43-45; 18:31-34), together with the call to take up one's cross that accompanies the first of these (Luke 9:23-27). Beyond this, in 14:26-27 Jesus reiterates the statement on taking up one's cross. And in this new context it is strengthened with the call to hate one's family and the parables of the tower builder and the king going to war (vv. 28-32). Also, the summary statement in 14:33 links 14:26-27 to the theme of one's attitude toward wealth, making the forfeiting of wealth a subcategory of taking up one's cross: "So therefore, none of you can become my disciple if you do not give up all your possessions" (Matera 1996, 81).

In Acts, this call to suffering on behalf of Christian witness is made more concrete through the exemplary behavior of the apostles and other witnesses. Stephen and James the brother of John are killed (6:8–7:60; 12:1), and Peter is brought before the council in chapter 4 and imprisoned in chapter 12. In 5:17-42, the entire group of apostles is imprisoned. Paul suffers severe opposition from Jews in Thessalonica, who have him imprisoned briefly and then pursue him in Beroea (17:1-15). And, following his arrest in Jerusalem in chapter 20, he remains captive for the rest of the narrative.

Throughout all these accounts of persecution, opposition, and imprisonment, the apostles and other witnesses remain steadfast in their witness. The words of Peter thus hold good for them all: "we cannot keep from speaking about what we have seen and heard" (Acts 4:20). And it is this model that rounds out the ethic of Luke-Acts, defining the extreme cases of what it means to be a disciple of Jesus.

HERMENEUTICAL QUESTIONS

In the preceding section, I raised the question of how the church and the reader are expected to implement the witness of Luke-Acts on the question of wealth and poverty. The problem arises from the fact that there are genuinely radical sayings and images that are significantly moderated by the scope of the narrative as a whole. To this observation we may add a point that Blount borrows from Joel Green: "even though Jesus opens his ministry as one speaking good news to the poor, he does not seem to actually preach directly to poor people per se" (Blount 2001, 80, citing Green 1994, 59). In light of this fact, Blount is motivated to consider the charge that in Luke Jesus actually ministers primarily to the wealthy. He rejects this suggestion, however, on the basis of the strong theme of reversal that is associated with the usage of the term "poor" in Luke-Acts (2001, 80–81); and I can give basic assent to his position. One may still question, however, whether the way in which the theme of rich and poor plays out in the full scope of two volumes does justice to the truly radical character of the first beatitude.

William Beardslee has pursued this question in an article that approaches it from the perspective of deconstruction, and a review of his work on this issue can give us insight into the nature of the problem. Beardslee's argument is that the radical elements resist accommodation to the more moderate elements. Whereas from one perspective the interpreter's job would consist in ordering all textual elements into a coherent and consistent whole, deconstruction focuses on the fissures in the text's system of signification. From this perspective, questions as to the author's intention—including the author's way of resolving this particular tension—are irrelevant. For the fact remains that sometimes a given element can resist accommodation to the whole.

This is precisely what happens, Beardslee argues, when we consider the first beatitude (Luke 6:20) in relation to the moderating effect of the narrative as a whole. "The immediate thrust of the text of Luke-Acts," he states,

> is to integrate the concern for the poor into the practice of the community. The global concern for "the poor," and the bold proclamation that they are "happy" because the kingdom of God is theirs, is structured into the practice of the church, and even there it becomes an ideal that . . . was at best only very imperfectly practiced. (1993, 228)

It is at this point, however, that Beardslee draws on deconstruction to note that the radical character of the first beatitude makes it resistant to such accommodation.

> What happens when we listen seriously to the statement, "Happy are the poor" is exactly the opposite of finding a place for the poor in a structured society. The structure is broken; the line between the hearer and the poor is erased; we find ourselves open to, at times perhaps even identified with, the subjects of the saying. A vivid, shattering awareness of the possibility that there, among the poor, is the place of happiness or blessedness does not produce a plan of action (not even giving away all that one possesses, to say nothing of a plan for restructuring the means of production or the rules of property ownership). It does break the established lines of relatedness by opening up a new and hitherto unrecognized relatedness to the poor. It challenges the structure of power that establishes a place for the poor. (1993, 229–30)

Attention to the radical character of the saying, in other words, deconstructs the pattern into which Luke-Acts integrates it. The point is thus not simply that the saying is more radical in a political sense than is the framework of the narrative but that it calls into question any way of translating its shattering effect into a plan of action. If understanding it this way cuts off any strategy of putting it into practice, the positive effect is that it unleashes the untamable power of the saying in order to challenge the reader at the deepest level and undermine any interpretation that might domesticate it. We may say, then, that the tension between the most radical elements in the text and the overall perspective of the narrative can become the catalyst for recognizing wider potentials for meaning. It encourages and empowers the reader to think beyond all previously sanctioned ways of responding to the tragedy of human poverty and the criminally unjust maldistribution of wealth that have plagued human civilization from its outset.

In the end, of course, those interested in the actual implementation of a biblical ethic will want to ask whether such an irritant, for all its power of provocation, can be of any use in determining appropriate action in relation to the issue of wealth and poverty. How do we appropriate a powerful indictment of injustice if it undermines all attempts at practical response? At some point, those who are motivated by the call must decide on a course of action. This is a legitimate concern, but the question is whether one can move beyond the deconstructive moment without forfeiting the energizing tension it has unleashed. Here again we find a question to be pursued in part 4.

A second point at which our discussion of Luke-Acts leads us into hermeneutical waters is the theme of the hope of Israel. We have seen above that this hope carries with it a worldly, political dimension, which is clearly evident in the speeches in Luke 1. We have no right to excise this dimension from the meaning potential of the signifier "hope of Israel" without good warrant. The narrative, however, seems to leave no concrete mode in which this dimension might be realized. It reports Jesus' prediction of the destruction of the Jerusalem temple but then leaps forward to a prophecy of his return in glory at the end of the age. And yet we find Paul, in the very last chapter of Acts, still speaking of the hope of Israel. So, what can this hope mean in concrete terms? To begin with, the indefiniteness of the text invites the reader's participation in the creation of meaning. It is important, however, to reflect critically on the relative adequacy of the various ways the reader might resolve the ambiguity.

One way to understand what the hope of Israel would mean within the framework of Luke-Acts is to understand it in terms of a theology of the church. By now making available to all people the salvation God promised Israel, the church, as a "purified" Israel, makes good on the hope. And one may guard against the charge of spiritualizing by making clear that in the church the specifically economic dimension of the hope is realized. At least ideally, within the new community the division between rich and poor no longer exists. The problem, however, is that—as we have just seen—the ideology of Luke-Acts actually backs off from the ideal and moderates the more radical elements. The "materialist" dimension of the hope is thus relegated to an eschatological future. When the rule of God comes in its fullness, the great reversal of fortune will take place and the hope of the poor will be realized.

The "ecclesiastical" solution, moreover, comes at the cost of a transmutation of the specifically national hope, which stands in tension with the universalism of Luke-Acts. It is also subject to criticism from the opposite angle of vision. A universalism based on the inclusion of all persons into a salvation history rooted in a national history involves another level of tension. On the one hand, we find resounding affirmations of God's universal care and fragments of a "natural theology" or "universal revelation." In his speech in Acts 17, Paul affirms the common ancestry of all humanity and the possibility of the knowledge of God outside the specific revelations given to Israel. God's ordering of the world has the specific intent that the peoples of the world "would search for God and perhaps grope for him and find him" (Acts 17:27). This knowledge of God beyond the bounds of Israel's history, however, is severely limited in two ways. First, this knowledge is a mere possibility, which is indicated by optative mood, rendered into English in the NRSV by the qualifier "perhaps." Second, the entire pre-Christian era is designated "the times of ignorance" (Acts 17:30 RSV; also 3:17), so that it is only with the Christian missionary preaching that salvation is made available to all in an unqualified way. We must therefore reckon with a tension within the ethics of God's plan as constructed by Luke-Acts. The notion of God's universal care resists accommodation to an understanding of salvation history rooted in special revelation to a specific people, even when that revelation is eventually made universally available. Hermeneutical considerations will thus lead us to evaluate in part 4 the ethics involved in the various theological positions on the relationship of Christianity to the other religions of the world.

CHAPTER 8

the gospel and letters of john

⟲

THE JOHANNINE COMMUNITY

Contemporary scholars are virtually unanimous in identifying the Gospel and letters of John as the product of a distinctive movement, or community of believers, that only gradually merged into what became the mainstream of early Christianity. It is generally held that this movement underwent important changes during its lifetime, including a major schism, and that all the writings did not come from the same author. Also, most scholars are convinced that this literature emanated from a Jewish Christian group that suffered a traumatic separation from the larger Jewish community.

Within this broad consensus, however, disagreements abound. Although the majority of scholars place the letters after the Gospel, a significant minority place them earlier, thus suggesting different accounts of the movement's history.[1] There is also disagreement about whether the same author wrote all the letters and about the unity of 1 John. With respect to the Gospel itself, the disjointedness of the narrative line and tensions among various strains of thought have also led to varying accounts of its redactional history, each of which carries its own implications regarding the community's development.[2]

Differing accounts of this history entail different understandings of both the theological and the ethical dimensions of the various writings. As I hope to demonstrate, however, there is enough similarity among the several writings to identify the broad outlines of a Johannine ethic without tying it to a highly speculative reconstruction of the community's course of development. Some judgments about the specific concerns of the letters over against the Gospel will be necessary, but I am convinced that characterizations of the ethic of the letters as fundamentally contrary to that of the Gospel are, at best, misleading. This is a

190

point I will emphasize below in connection with a discussion of Willi Marxsen's reading of the letters.

More so than the question of the community's developmental history, the discussion regarding the specific character of the Johannine movement takes us to the heart of its ethical outlook. Many scholars regard the group as sectarian, and such characteristics as the negative statements about "the world" and the sharp dualisms of light/darkness, above/below, and spirit/flesh suggest such a provenance. Opinions differ, however, as to what this description means in terms of the community's attitude toward those outside its boundaries. By some accounts, the group is completely closed to and hostile toward the world at large. This evaluation issues not only from such passages as John 17:9 ("I am not asking on behalf of the world, but on behalf of those whom you gave me, because they are yours") but also from the apparent limitation of the obligation of love to those within the community. The object of the love command is always "one another," never "your neighbor," much less "your enemy." When this limitation is seen in light of the Gospel's relentless emphasis on the identity of Jesus as the preexistent Son of God, it is not surprising that some interpreters argue that in Johannine thought ethics is actually undercut by a focus on doctrinal purity.[3] And this impression is underscored by the fact that the command to love, while clearly a central component of the community's outlook, remains largely abstract. As Marxsen comments, "Only in one passage is the imperative, to love one another, filled with a specific content: the disciples are to wash one another's feet (John 13:14)" (1993, 296).

It should be obvious that any responsible treatment of Johannine ethics must entail a judgment as to whether this community's sectarian character led it to a completely hostile attitude toward the outside world. It will also be necessary to identify the broad outlines of the nature of the internal split to which the letters attest—that is, to determine whether the issue was purely doctrinal or involved a genuinely ethical component. On the other hand, it will be equally important to focus on the question of ethics and not get lost in a quagmire of historical reconstruction.

THE JOHANNINE THEOLOGICAL FRAMEWORK: CHRISTOLOGY AND ESCHATOLOGY

Close to the center of the ideology of the Johannine movement were its distinctive views of christology and eschatology. In both cases, the emphasis in the letters differs somewhat from that in the Gospel, which raises the question as to whether the differences have substantial impact on the ethics of the respective writings.

Christology

As noted above, the focus of the Gospel is on Jesus' identity as the preexistent Son of God. This focus is evident as early as the prologue (1:1-18), which identifies Jesus as the incarnation of the Word (*Logos*), who was in the beginning with God, as the agent of all creation and who, in a paradoxical formulation, "was with God" and "was God." Within the ensuing story line, in contrast to all three Synoptic Gospels, the usual subject of Jesus' debates with his opponents is the explicit question of his identity. Thus, even though the initial issue in 5:9b-18 is healing on the Sabbath, the story ends with a reference to Jesus' claims regarding himself: "For this reason the Jews were seeking all the more to kill him, because he was not only breaking the Sabbath, but was also calling God his own Father, thereby making himself equal to God." And Jesus' identity is the primary content of his own teaching. What he demands of those who would follow him is that they believe in him.

The narrator prepares the reader for this emphasis in the prologue: "But to all who received him, who believed in his name, he gave the power to become the children of God" (John 1:13). Then Jesus continually makes the same point, often referring to himself in the third person. In his conversation with Nicodemus, he uses the self-designation "the one who descended from heaven, the Son of Man" (1:13), and then identifies belief in him as the standard of God's judgment: "Those who believe in him are not condemned, but those who do not believe are condemned already" (1:17). Similarly, in 3:36 he tells his disciples, "Whoever believes in the Son has eternal life; whoever disobeys the Son will not see life, but must endure God's wrath" (see also 11:25). At numerous points, moreover, he claims for himself titles that indicate his divine nature: "the bread of life" (6:35, 48), "the living bread that came down from heaven" (6:51; also 6:41), "the light of the world" (8:12; 9:5; also 12:46), "the resurrection and the life" (11:25), and "the way, the truth, and the life" (14:6).

These epithets point in varying degrees to the notion of preexistence, and it is clear in some passages that acceptance of Jesus' preexistence is the standard of true belief. Thus, in 6:41-59, his opponents complain that he speaks of himself as "the bread that came down from heaven." And in a long discussion with "the Jews who had believed in him," the issue of preexistence distinguishes their partial belief from the faith for which Jesus asks. When he says that those who keep his word "will not see death," his opponents accuse him of being possessed by a demon and ask, belligerently, "Are you greater than Abraham who died?" When Jesus eventually brings the discussion to an end with the declaration "before Abraham was, I am," they try to stone him to death.

Alongside this pervasive insistence on Jesus' status as *Logos* incarnate, we also find assertions of his humanity. In the prologue, the narrator makes the bold declaration that "the Word (*Logos*) became flesh and lived among us," and in 20:24-29, Thomas's doubt about Jesus' resurrection leads to Jesus' invitation to touch his wounds, proving that he died a real death but is now alive. The emphasis on Jesus' humanity is not equal to the focus on his divine nature, however. Throughout the entire story, the depiction of Jesus suggests a being with supernatural powers, seemingly devoid of such human passions as fear and anxiety. As is often noted, he strides through the passion account as if he were in full control of the events taking place.

When we turn from the Gospel to the letters, we find once again that christology is central. The First Letter of John, reflecting the disruption caused by the traumatic schism, provides criteria for testing the various prophetic spirits. And these criteria are designed specifically to brand as deviant the group that has separated from the faction represented in the letters. In some formulations, the central criterion appears simply as the confession that Jesus is the Christ. Thus, we find in 1 John 5:1, "Everyone who believes that Jesus is the Christ has been born of God," and in 1 John 2:22, "Who is the liar but the one who denies that Jesus is the Christ?" Regarding the first of these passages, C. Clifton Black makes this observation:

> The governing theme in v. 1 . . . is the significance of faith or belief in Jesus as the Christ. The verb "to believe" (πιστεύω; *pisteuō*), which has already appeared three times in 1 John (3:23; 4:1, 16), occurs in chapter 5 six times (vv. 1, 5, 10 [3x], 13). Throughout these verses the subject matter of faith is christologically concentrated: the entrustment of oneself to Jesus as the Christ (v. 1) or the Son of God (v. 5). (1998, 435)

First John is therefore in accord with the Gospel in making christological confession a central concern. And although we do not find in the letters an explicit emphasis on preexistence, there are subtle indications of this notion in 1 John 1:1-2:

We declare to you what was from the beginning, what we have heard, what we have seen with our eyes, what we have looked at and touched with our hands, concerning the word of life—this life was revealed, and we have seen it and testify to it, and declare to you the eternal life that was with the Father and was revealed to us. . . .

The primary reference of the phrases "what was from the beginning" and "word of life" is to the proclamation that stood at the center of the community's self-understanding. However, against the background of the prologue to the Gospel, they probably echo as well the notion of the preexistent *Logos*, whether or not the Gospel was already in existence. And that is certainly true of two other elements in the passage: "this life was revealed," and "the eternal life that was with the Father and was revealed to us." Thus, as D. Moody Smith concludes, "the 'word of life' is at once a reference to Jesus the Word who is the origin of life and an allusion to the preaching about him" (1991, 36).

We may say, then, that the letters share the Gospel's notion of Jesus as the incarnate *Logos*. Alongside the indication of preexistence, however, is a more explicit insistence on Jesus' humanity. Thus, we find in 1 John 4:2b-3 the declaration that "every spirit that confesses that Jesus Christ has come in the flesh is from God, and every spirit that does not confess Jesus is not of God." And 2 John 7 is equally emphatic: "Many deceivers have gone out into the world, those who do not confess that Jesus Christ has come in the flesh; any such person is the deceiver and the antichrist!"

The identity of those termed "antichrist" as the group that split off from the community represented by the letters is undeniable in light of a parallel passage in 1 John 1:18-27. The writer refers in v. 18 to "many antichrists," whose appearance is a sign that "it is the last hour," and follows this declaration with the comment, "They went out from us, but they did not belong to us; for if they had belonged to us, they would have remained with us." Then in vv. 22-23 the issue of confession of Jesus as the Christ comes to the fore: "Who is the liar but the one who denies that Jesus is the Christ? This is the antichrist, the one who denies the Father and the Son. No one who denies the Son has the Father; everyone who confesses the Son has the Father also."

Clearly, then, in the eyes of the faction represented in the letters, the schismatics are thoroughly evil persons, guilty of denying Christ by failing to give adequate attention to his human nature. And as for the passages that focus simply on the confession of Jesus as the Christ as the criterion for testing the spirits, we must interpret them in light of those that emphasize his having come in the flesh. For it is extremely unlikely that the dissident group, once a part of a community clearly bound together by a very high christology, would have denied Jesus' status as the Christ. The issue must rather have been the emphasis on his human nature. We might therefore approximate the full force of 1 John 5:1, for example, by understanding it this way: "Everyone who believes that *Jesus* (the human being) is the Christ has been born of God. . . ."

This emphasis suggests to some scholars that the dissident faction held a docetic christology, characteristic of later gnostic groups, that denied Jesus' humanity altogether. Others doubt that a full-blown docetism is in view, however. Raymond Brown, for example, argues that the issue turned rather on the *significance* of Jesus' human nature:

> For the secessionists, the human existence was only a stage in the career of the divine Word and not an intrinsic component in redemption. What Jesus did in Palestine was not truly important for them nor was the fact that he died on the cross; salvation would not be different if the Word had become incarnate in a totally different human representative who lived a different life and died a different death. The only important thing for them was that eternal life had been brought down to men and women through a divine Son who passed through this world. (1979, 113–14)

This view, Brown notes, constitutes neither a genuine docetism nor a form of gnosticism. He speculates, however, that the two fragments of the shattered community were eventually "swallowed up respectively by the Great Church and the Gnostic movement" (1979, 145). Thus, the dissident group, although not gnostic in the proper sense, was moving in that direction.

Whatever the specific nature of the disagreement, it seems clear that the question of Jesus' human nature was at the center of the schism and that the dissident group had pushed the larger community's already high christology beyond the bounds that the other faction found acceptable.

Eschatology

Closely related to the distinctively high christology of the Gospel is its emphasis on realized eschatology. In the story of the raising of Lazarus (John 11:1-44), Jesus' correction of Martha's inadequate understanding hinges precisely on this connection. When Jesus tells her that "your brother will rise again" (v. 23), she replies, "I know he will rise again in the resurrection on the last day." Jesus' retort, although not directly critical, implies that her statement falls short of a full grasp of the truth: "I am the resurrection and the life. Those who believe in me, even though they die, will live; and everyone who lives and believes in me will never die" (vv. 23-27). Martha's final statement underscores John's high christology: "I believe that you are the Messiah, the Son of God, the one coming into the world." Part of what she now grasps, in other words, is that Jesus has come from God into the world, that he is in fact the preexistent Son of God. But what has led her to this insight is his assertion that because he is "the resurrection and the life," those who believe in him "will never die." In the context of what is about to happen, and against the background of the implied inadequacy of Martha's belief in the resurrection "at the last day," this can mean only that what she in her incomplete understanding expected at the end of history is in fact available now—resurrection from the dead.

The opening of Jesus' prayer for his disciples in John 17 links this availability of the new life in the present to the theme of "eternal life," which pervades the entire Gospel. For in v. 3, Jesus explicitly defines "eternal life" in terms of quality rather than temporal extension: "And this is eternal life, that they may know you, the only true God, and Jesus Christ whom you have sent." It is therefore no surprise to find throughout the Gospel an emphasis on the present, or realized, dimension of eternal life. In 5:24, Jesus declares that "anyone who hears my word and believes in him who sent me has eternal life, and does not come under judgment, but has passed [*metabebēken*; perfect tense] from death to life." Conversely, Jesus can also speak of the judgment in terms of the present. After defining God's purpose as making eternal life available to those who believe in the Son—to grant them salvation rather than condemnation—Jesus declares that "those who do not believe are condemned already. . . . And this is the judgment, that the light has come into the world, and people loved the darkness rather than the light because their deeds were evil" (3:18b, 19). Likewise, anticipating his death, Jesus says in 13:31, "Now is the judgment of this world; now the ruler of this world will be driven out."

This strong emphasis on the present dimension of eternal life, however, is in some measure balanced by an explicit affirmation of a judgment and resurrection yet to come—that is, a future eschatology. In John 6:54, Jesus says, "Those who eat my flesh and drink my blood have eternal life, and I will raise them up on the last day"; and in the summary of his teaching in 12:48, he speaks of the judgment of the world as in the future: "The one who rejects me and does not receive my word has a judge; on the last day the word that I have spoken will serve as judge." By some accounts, such future eschatology is the product of a later redaction of the Gospel by an editor representing the perspective of the emerging Great Church (for example, Marxsen 1974, 256–57). There is some reason to accept the notion of one or more redactions, but many scholars remain unconvinced that all future elements were absent in the original. And in any case, as we will now see, such an element is definitely present in 1 John.

In 1 John 2:18, the warning about the antichrists who have appeared in the form of the schismatic faction begins with the dramatic declaration, "Children, it is the last hour!" This statement is preceded, moreover, by the observation that "the world and its desires are passing away" (2:17), and in 2:28—3:3 there are references to a future coming (*parousia*) in which Christ will be fully revealed and those who abide in him "will see him as he is." This emphasis on the future by no means negates the sense that eternal life is experienced in the present. For in 3:2a the author gives a dramatic affirmation that those within the community are already God's children in the present: "Beloved, we are God's children now (*nyn*)." This sense of present salvation is also implicit in the language about believers' "abiding" (*menein*) in God/Christ and God/Christ's "abiding" in them that is found in both the Gospel and 1 John (John 6:56; 15:4-7; 1 John 2:6, 24, 27-28; 3:6, 9, 24; 4:12, 15, 16). And it is explicit in the close parallel to John 5:24 found in 1 John 3:14: "We know that we have passed [*metabebēkamen*; perfect tense] from death to life because we love one another."

Summary

Despite important differences in emphasis between the letters and the Gospel with respect to both christology and eschatology, we find substantial similarity. Both manifest a high christology that includes a notion of preexistence, and both affirm the reality of Jesus' existence in the flesh. Both, moreover, reflect a two-dimensional understanding of eschatology: the new life is in some sense present, yet some form of consummation is expected in the future. These are key elements in an understanding of the truth that supports Johannine ethics.

THE JOHANNINE THEOLOGICAL FRAMEWORK: THE LANGUAGE OF DUALISM

The world of Johannine thought is a world of dichotomies. In the prologue to the Gospel, the preexistent *Logos* is named as containing the life that is the light of all persons. The human Jesus, as the *Logos* made flesh, is therefore the light of the world as long as he is in the world (John 9:5). As the light, he gives life to all who come to him. In opposition to this light, however, stands the realm of darkness. Therefore, when the light shines in the darkness—whether in the form of the eternal *Logos* or in the life of the human Jesus—it shines within a dominion fundamentally opposed to it but which is ultimately powerless against it (John 1:5). Because they live in darkness, the people of the world fail to recognize the light (John 1:10-11).

Other pairs of opposites parallel the light/darkness dichotomy—above/below (John 8:23), of this world/not of this world (John 8:23; 15:19; 17:14), spirit/flesh (John 3:6; 6:63), all of which express the dualistic perspective of the Gospel. Jesus and those who follow him exist in one realm, and those outside exist in another. Those in his realm have God as their father (John 1:18; 8:18-19; see also 1 John 2:23), and those outside have the devil as their father (John 8:42-44). There would appear to be no middle ground, and this impression is supported by Jesus' words in John 15 and 17 about the world's hatred. Because the world hated and persecuted Jesus, it also hates and persecutes the disciples, who do not belong to the world (John 15:18-20; 17:14). Thus, Jesus prays for the disciples but not for the world (John 17:9).

Related to this severely dualistic outlook is the fact that much of the language in John suggests a deterministic view of human behavior. In 6:44, for example, Jesus' statement seems to imply that God is in complete control of all decision making: "No one can come to me unless drawn by the Father who sent me." And the classification of people as either "from above" or "from below," "of this world" or "not of this world" (8:23), tends to suggest that actions flow from an unalterable predisposition. In 9:40-41, however, Jesus says to the Pharisees, "If you were blind, you would not have sin. But now that you say, 'We see,' your sin remains." The coming of the light into the world, it would seem, opens up a choice. People can decide to move from darkness into the light and to act either as those who are "from above" or "from below." Thus, moral behavior flows from a fundamental disposition or realm of origin, but those who encounter the light are given the freedom to choose the realm to which they belong.

This freedom is presupposed in the passages in 1 John that reject the claim—presumably made by the schismatics—of sinlessness: "If we say that we have no sin, we deceive ourselves, and the truth is not in us" (1 John 1:8; see also 5:16-17). Here again, we find tension between freedom and determinism. For we also read in 1 John 3:9 (see also 3:6), "Those who have been born of God do not sin, because God's seed abides in them; they cannot sin, because they have been born of God." The probability is that the notion of sinlessness was important in the

Johannine community as a whole and that it was rooted precisely in its dualistic outlook. The dichotomy between light and darkness logically implied that sin was simply incompatible with living in the light. But when the schismatics adopted this claim as their own, this may have forced a more nuanced statement of the matter. The statement of intention in 1 John 2:1 clearly rules out interpreting the claim that those who are born of God cannot sin as a literal, absolute statement: "My little children, I am writing these things so that you may not sin. But if anyone does sin, we have an advocate with the Father, Jesus Christ the righteous." It is also clear that those who abide in God are free from sin, but, as D. Moody Smith comments, this is "a freedom that must be ratified by continually willing and doing what is right . . ." (1991, 36).

In 1 John 2:1-11, the light/darkness dichotomy appears in connection with the "new commandment," and in 2:15-17, the author sets up a relationship of stark opposition between the community and the world and uses it to issue a moral warning:

> Do not love the world or the things of the world. The love of the Father is not in those who love the world; for all that is in the world—the desire of the flesh, the desire of the eyes, the pride in riches—comes not from the Father but from the world. And the world and its desires are passing away, but those who do the will of God live forever.

The theme of hatred by the world appears again in 1 John 3:13, and in each of the other letters we find dichotomizing statements. The Second Letter of John 9 contrasts those who abide in Christ's teaching with those who do not, and 3 John 11 contrasts good and evil, what is from God and what is not.

THE JOHANNINE ETHIC OF LOVE

Sectarian Love and the Outside World

The high Johannine christology, in combination with the dualistic outlook, issues in one of the two most explicit statements of exclusive salvation in the New Testament: "No one comes to the Father except through me" (John 14:6; see also Acts 4:12). It is, therefore, part and parcel with the community's sectarian character, and this exclusivist-sectarian perspective leads to a particular way of framing the group's ethical understanding. The love command, which is prominent both in the Gospel and in 1 John, is issued specifically as a matter of intracommunity relations (John 13:31-35; 15:12-17; 1 John 2:7-11). Thus, a number of critics have interpreted the Johannine love ethic as narrow and ingrown, the corollary of an attitude of hostility to the world outside.

There is some justice to this description, but it is decidedly one-sided. To put the matter in broader perspective, we need first to look more closely at the role of love in the total theological structure of the Johannine literature. The love command is not simply a command; it is an element within a set of relationships defined by reciprocity. Love is first and foremost a characteristic of God. The emphasis in the Gospel is on God's love for the Son (John 3:34; 10:17; 17:24, 26), but God also loves the world (John 3:16) and those whom he has given to the Son (John 17:27). God is in fact the very foundation of love, because "love is from God" (1 John 4:7); and one can even define God's being in terms of love: "God is love" (1 John 4:8, 16).

Jesus, as the Son, loves the Father, who has loved him (John 14:31). He also loves those whom God has given him as a direct response to God's love for him: "As the Father has loved me, so I have loved you . . ." (John 15:9). And in his coming into the world he is the revealer of God's love: "God's love was revealed among us in this way: God sent his only Son into the world so that we might live through him" (1 John 4:9). Those who abide in the Son therefore participate in the same reciprocal relationship. Their love for one another is a direct response to the love God has shown them, as 1 John 4:11 makes clear: "Beloved, since God loved us so much, we also ought to love one another." And the same point appears in 1 John 4:19: "We love because he first loved us." They are called to love God, of course, but the emphasis in 1 John is that one cannot love God without loving the children of God: "Those who say, 'I love God' and hate their brothers or sisters, are liars; for those who do not love a brother or sister whom they have seen, cannot love God whom they have not seen" (1 John 4:20).

In light of this survey, Georg Strecker's summation of the theological framework of the love command in the Gospel would seem to stand for the entire Johannine tradition.

> The special significance attached to agape [love] is explained by the Gospels' focus on the Christ, since the whole Gospel is oriented to the fact that the Father's love is revealed in the Son. The foundation for the ethic of the Gospel of John is accordingly the ἀγάπη θεοῦ [*agapē theou*; love of God] manifest in the Son. (2002, 512)

In summary, we may speak of a Johannine triangle of reciprocity, in which God's love for the Son and for those who follow him is the foundation of the Son's love both of the Father and of those entrusted to him, as well as for the love that community members are called to have for God and for one another. And an understanding of this pattern puts the seeming limitation of love to community members into a somewhat different perspective. Emphasizing the sectarian nature of the Johannine community, Hays explains this limitation as follows: "With the world inexplicably refusing to accept Jesus as the bearer of God's truth . . . the community of faith came to be seen as the only sphere within which life and love could be found" (1996, 147). So it would hardly have occurred to the community to command love outside its boundaries, and its failure to do so would appear less an intentional limitation than a function of its focus on the enabling power of God's love in combination with its alienation from the wider world.

This explanation is only partially valid, however. The perceived impossibility of love occurring in the world outside the community, where God's enabling love was seen as ineffective, need not have prevented one from seeking to love the unloving world. There was never a guarantee that loving one's enemies would result in reciprocity. But recognition of the community's perception that it was the only sphere in which love could flourish is not the only mitigating factor we need to take into account. Alongside the very strong strain of sectarian thought, we also find subtle undercurrents of a different perspective.

In the Johannine vocabulary, "the world" (*kosmos*) from which the community is alienated is not "the creation" but rather human society. The term can refer to the creation, as it does in John 17:24, and in many instances it probably embraces both aspects, as in the passages that refer to Jesus' coming into or being in the world (for example, 3:7; 9:39; 12:46; 16:28). But most often it is clearly the social world of human beings, which is evident in the way in which it is described in terms of agency: it hated Jesus, and it hates his followers (John 15:18; 1 John 3:13). And precisely as the social world of human beings, it is under the present rule of Satan (John 15:30) and is a realm of darkness, which is the source of evil deeds (John 1:5; 3:19).

Such a characterization of society certainly issues from a deep sense of alienation, but we must not neglect the ways in which the world appears in a positive light. We may point first of all to John 1:10, which depicts the world as created by God through the *Logos*. The world is God's creation, and it remains so despite the corruption within it. And it is not only when the term refers to creation that it has positive meaning but also when it refers to the social world. Not only does John 3:16 declare that God's sending of the Son is a sign that God loves the world, but John 6:51 indicates that Jesus' death is for the sake of the world: "the bread that I will give for the life of the world is my flesh." In 4:42, moreover, Jesus is called "the Savior of the world," and in 12:47 he says that he came in order to save the world.

Despite the severe attitude toward the world in many passages, then, it remains redeemable. And this point is underscored by the way in which both the Gospel and 1 John indicate victory over the world. The prologue to the Gospel asserts that the darkness did not overcome the light (1:8), and even before his death Jesus declares, "I have conquered the world" (John 16:33). Likewise, in 1 John 2:8 we read that "the darkness is passing away and the true light is already shining."

Strecker argues, along similar lines, that attention to the comprehensiveness of "the love of God manifest in the Son, a love directed toward the world," shows that the command to love the members of the community carries with it broader implications. Noting that the love of God "precedes all human action," Strecker goes on to assert,

> Whenever people let themselves be determined by this love, they stand completely under its claim, and are called to love even to the point of giving their lives. Every human limitation is excluded. The love of neighbor and the love of enemies are both therefore implied in the agape command, for whoever stands in unity with the Father and the Son is determined by the comprehensive and universal deed of love. (2000, 515)

We may fairly ask, of course, whether it is sound exegetical practice to draw out implications in this way, given the pervasiveness of the negative evaluation of the world and the fact that the Johannine community almost certainly had access to traditions in which love of neighbor and love of enemy were stated more explicitly. Marxsen, in fact, comes to the exact opposite conclusion about the ethic of the Gospel. Although it "has nothing to do with *restricting* love to the small circle of disciples," the reciprocity that underlies love means that it simply "cannot include those who live outside this relationship" (1993, 288).

It would appear, then, quite possible to trace out the logic of Johannine ethics in more than one way, with textual support for contradictory readings. It will therefore be important to return to this problem in a later section on hermeneutical questions.

The Meaning of "Love One Another"

However we are to imagine the scope of the love commandment in relation to the outside world, its primary focus is the internal life of the group; and it is essential to the movement's self-understanding. In John 13:31-35, Jesus issues this "new commandment" to his disciples. They are to love one another, just as he has loved them; and this love marks them as his disciples: "By this everyone will know that you are my disciples, if you have love for one another." Jesus repeats this commandment in 15:12-17, this time calling the disciples his friends and stating that "[n]o one has greater love than this, to lay down one's life for one's friends." In the letters we find reiterations of the commandment in 1 John 3:32 and 2 John 5 and extended statements on love in 1 John 2:7-11, 3:11-17, and 4:7-21.

The passages in 1 John 2 and 4 are distinctive in emphasizing the necessary link between love of one another and love of God. As we have seen, in 1 John 4:20, those who claim to love God but hate others in the community are termed liars, for such hatred is incompatible with loving God. In 1 John 2:15, they are equated with murderers. In all of this, there is virtually nothing about the concrete forms that love might take. However, 1 John 3:11-17 ends with a rhetorical question that makes one form absolutely clear: "How does God's love abide in anyone who has the world's goods and sees a brother or sister in need and yet refuses help?" Here we see that love necessarily entails economic justice within the community.

Hays makes an important observation about the significance of this verse:

Although this admonition is not developed at length, it shows that the Johannine talk of love does have practical implications. Love within the community is not merely a matter of warm feelings; rather, it is a matter of action. The sharing of "the world's goods" is only one example of what it might mean in practice to "love one another." One suspects, then, that a general formulation such as 1 John 3:23 is intended to cover a range of behaviors that are not actually specified: "And this is the commandment, that we should believe in the name of his Son Jesus Christ and love one another, just as he commanded us." (1996, 145)

The very fact of the example would seem to make the case that love is a matter of action, and it appears almost self-evident that the citing of one example implies other ways of making love concrete. To this we may add Georg Strecker's comment that the general lack of specificity is based on the conviction that the gift of agape includes the gift of freedom and responsibility to those who believe. Christians know that they are called to do the right thing at the right time, the time of every new situation in which they are called upon to decide what action is appropriate to that love that proceeds from the Father through the Son and has brought them near to God. (2000, 515)

This point is well taken. It would in fact seem that precisely by concentrating its ethic in the single command to love one another (grounded in the prior love of God mediated through Christ), the Johannine community has already closed the door on any attempt to spell out in advance just what love might demand in any future circumstance.

Having made this point, however, I must also stress that the notion of love does not remain utterly without content in this literature. But just as 1 John 3:23 points to economic justice as one way of making love concrete, so John 13:1-20 provides a graphic illustration of love in action. Jesus' washing of the disciples' feet is rich in meaning. It signifies humble service of one another and an attitude of unrestrained self-giving. And it complements the controlling paradigm of love that underlies the entire Johannine ideology: Jesus' sacrifice of himself on behalf of others. Thus, in John 15:13-14, the love command appears as an imitation of the love Jesus has shown for his disciples, which is spelled out in terms of self-giving to the point of death: "This is my commandment, that you love one another as I have loved you. No one has greater love than this, to lay down his life for his friends. You are my friends if you do what I command you." The Jesus who lays down his life and who washes his disciples' feet is therefore clearly an ethical model for the disciples, even if specific examples of self-giving service are lacking.

In addition, we should not neglect the concrete implications of the demand for sharing "the world's goods" in 1 John 3:17. Granted that it stands for a wide range of possible applications of the love command, as the one specific application chosen for emphasis, it most likely speaks to a live issue within the community's experience. And this observation brings us to the question of the nature of the schism that lies in the background of the letters. The way in which 1 John 4 juxtaposes the discourse on love in vv. 7-21 with the reference to the schismatics in vv. 1-6 shows that the declaration in 4:8 that those who do not love do not know God is directed at this group. Their offense is not only their inadequate appraisal of Jesus' humanity but their lovelessness. From the perspective of 1 John, they are guilty of hating others and of withholding "the world's goods" from those in need within the community.

It is impossible to know how much truth there was to this accusation, since we have only one side of the story. As Raymond Brown notes, the dissident faction probably made the same charge against the group represented in the letters (1979, 131–32). However, if we interpret the statement on "the world's goods" in 1 John 3:17 against the background of the term *koinōnia* in 1 John, it is possible to see in it a hint of a concrete dispute that would lend force to the accusations against the schismatics. This term occurs four times in 1 John 1: twice in v. 3 and twice in vv. 6-7. In each pairing, it refers once to the community's relationship with God and once to the community members' relationship with one another. In the RSV, NRSV, and NIV it is rendered as "fellowship." Thus vv. 6-7 read as follows in the NRSV: "If we say that we have fellowship with [God] while we are walking in darkness, we lie and do not do what is true; but if we walk in the light as he himself is in the light, we have fellowship with one another. . . ." We may ask, however, whether "fellowship" is an adequate translation of the term in the context of 1 John.

The Greek noun *koinōnia* belongs to a family of words related to the broad fields of meaning that embrace the notions of sharing, having something in common, or participating in something. A related verb, *koinōnein*, has a range of meaning including to have a share in something, or to take part in something; and the semantic field of the adjective *koinos* includes the concepts of shared in common, common, public, and general (Liddel and Scott 1995, 440). It is the term that appears in Acts 2:44 and 4:32 to indicate that the early Jerusalem community held all their goods "in common." And the noun itself embraces a wide range of meanings that includes partnership in, communion, association with, and fellowship. It occurs nineteen times in the New Testament, thirteen of these in the letters of Paul; and in three of these latter instances it "signifies a Christian economy" (Rom 15:26; 2 Cor 8:4; 9:13) (Callahan 2005, 22). In 2 Corinthians 8:4, for example, Paul writes specifically of the collection for the impoverished Jerusalem church, noting how the churches of Macedonia begged his entourage "earnestly for the privilege of sharing (*koinōnia*) in this ministry to the saints . . ." (NRSV).

Against this linguistic background, Allen Callahan's contention regarding the meaning of the term in 1 John has significant force: The translation "fellowship," he argues,

> is too weak to carry the weight of *koinōnia* here. Because the issues of practical assistance to brethren in need is central to the ethics in the exhortations of the Elder, we must understand the fellowship referred to here as concrete, even economic. (2005, 18)

This is not to deny the broader connotations of the term in 1 John, but it is to insist that actual community of goods is one dimension of the meaning of the term in this context.

This reading might seem to place too much weight on the one reference to economic justice in 1 John. Callahan's case, however, rests on a broader base than this. The more seriously we take the sectarian character of the movement, the more likely we are to conclude that the Johannine community did in fact involve a communal economic arrangement. As many scholars have noted, the language of dualism in the Gospel and letters is reminiscent of that found in the sectarian documents of the community of Qumran at the Dead Sea. And, as Callahan observes,

> Community of goods was literally the law of Qumran. "And if the lot results in him joining the community," stipulates 1QSa 6.21-22, "they shall enter him in the rule according to his rank among his brothers for the law, for the judgment, for purity and for the placing of his possessions in common." The word for community here and throughout the Qumran literature is *yaḥad*. The noun rarely appears in the Hebrew Bible (Deut 33:5; 1 Chr 12:18). But *yaḥad* is the term of choice in the Qumran documents for describing the association that bound the members to one another as "the community of God" (1 Q 1.12; 1.22). . . . The Greek translation of *yaḥad* is *koinōnia*. (2005, 19–20)

If we accept the Qumran analogy, we may also follow Callahan in his characterization of the nature of the schism in the Johannine community. The passage in 1 John 1 reveals an interest in protecting the community

> against the appeal of less demanding alternatives to their common life. Apparently some members have already deserted the community of goods. The concrete example of the defectors was a threat to the unwavering, concrete commitment that their common life requires. (2001, 21)

Even apart from Callahan's claim that the schism had to do with the issue of a communal economy, there is reason to doubt that it was purely a doctrinal dispute. As argued above, the repeated emphasis in 1 John on love, together with the link between love and economic justice, shows that interest in the proper understanding of Jesus' nature cannot be separated from concrete action in the world. Thus, in Strecker's words,

The correlation of knowledge and action is an essential aspect of Johannine theology. Corresponding to this, fellowship with God and the knowledge of the truth embraced in it calls not only for theoretical acknowledgment but the ethical action that necessarily follows from it. (2000, 430)

To know the truth about Christ was, for this community, also to do the good, specifically in the form of loving one another in concrete ways.

MARXSEN'S VIEW OF THE ETHIC OF THE LETTERS

Marxsen's evaluation of the Johannine letters is worthy of special treatment, because he denies that they share the same perspective as the Gospel. The letters, he claims, issue from a later period in the Johannine movement in which the Gospel's reformation of earlier tradition has now hardened into doctrine. The Johannine school that develops after the Gospel, therefore, fails to do what the author of the Gospel did, which was to deal critically with inherited tradition (1993, 299–309).

To understand Marxsen's point, we must remember that from his perspective the point of investigating New Testament ethics is not to identify specific actions as Christian, since "God's will cannot be concretely determined" (1999, 43). Being Christian is therefore not a matter of following commandments or laws but of being shaped by Jesus. But it is precisely this point, he argues, that is forgotten in the Johannine school. "The author of 1 John is above all interested in having his readers hold to the right creed. The criterion for its rightness is acknowledgement of the real incarnation of Jesus Christ" (1993, 305). And correlative with this focus on doctrine is a misunderstanding of the ethic of the Gospel: "Quite obviously, the author has adopted John's love for one another but understands it in a completely different way. For the 'brothers and sisters' are for him a precisely defined group." This group is comprised only of those "who believe that Jesus is the Christ and therefore the only ones who have been born of God (5:1)."[4]

Marxsen's judgment against the Johannine school is severe. "The self-understanding of the community leads to a strict exclusivity in this area. Those who have fallen away are expressly excluded. They are no longer brothers and sisters. Hospitality may no longer be extended to them (2 John 10)." Thus, "the brotherly love of the Johannine school is bought with a lovelessness that is unparalleled in the New Testament scriptures" (1993, 308). And, for Marxsen, the emphasis on right doctrine apparently entails an abandonment of ethics as being shaped by Jesus. For he argues that the Johannine school severed the link between christology and ethics and thereby "ruined nearly everything John wanted to accomplish with his reformation" (1993, 309).

I have argued above that the emphasis on economic justice in 1 John 3:17 undermines the perception that the dispute between the factions in the community was purely doctrinal. But what of the claim that the letters have departed from the theological foundation of the Gospel by severing ethics from christology? It would be useless to deny that the schism led to an emphasis on right *didachē*, although whether we translate this term as "doctrine" or "teaching" will have some effect on how we understand this shift in emphasis. More important than the issue of translation, however, is the question of how the insistence on adherence to a correct understanding of Jesus' humanity relates to the triangle of reciprocity discussed above.

One way of posing this question is to examine the usage of the verb *menein* (abide or dwell) in the letters as over against the Gospel. In the Gospel, this term is used on a number of occasions as a key expression of reciprocity. Thus in John 14:10, Jesus speaks of the Father's dwelling/abiding in him, and in 15:5 he says to his disciples, "I am the vine, you are the branches. Those who abide in me and I in them bear much fruit." It is therefore clear that the ethical "fruit" of his followers flows precisely from the triangle of reciprocity.

The matter does not appear to be fundamentally different in the letters. In 2 John 9, *menein* refers specifically to abiding in the *didachē*, but we should not reduce "what you heard from the beginning" in 1 John 2:24 to doctrinal content. It is, as Smith comments, "the word of Jesus, the word about Jesus—thus in some sense Jesus himself" (1991, 74). And, in any case, 2:25 links this phrase to the triangle of reciprocity: "If what you heard from the beginning abides in you, then you will abide in the Son and in the Father." This triangle, moreover, is explicitly the focus of other important passages. To be sure, in this and some other cases (1 John 4:12; 4:16) the wording might seem to suggest that God's abiding in believers is the result rather than the cause of God's abiding in them. Such formulations, however, are best understood simply as functions of the paraenetic nature of the letters, because other passages clearly reflect the priority of God's grace. This is particularly clear in 1 John 4:11-12, where God's love appears as the enabling agent, despite the conditional element in the second verse: "Beloved, since God loved us so much, we also ought to love one another. No one has ever seen God; if we love one another, God lives in us; and his love is perfected in us." Also, the language in 1 John about being born of God clearly issues from a sense of the priority and enabling power of God's love: "Those who have been born of God do not sin . . . they cannot sin, because they have been born of God" (3:9; see also 4:7; 5:1, 4, 18).

It may well be the case that the letters reveal a stage in the community's development when definition of sound doctrine is becoming a central concern. We have ample evidence of such a trend in other New Testament writings. But it does not appear to me that in this case the christological foundation of ethics has been undermined.

CONTINUING REVELATION AND ETHICAL DISCERNMENT:
THE ROLE OF THE PARACLETE

To the extent that the Johannine triangle of reciprocity ensures the christological foundation of ethics, it also ensures the inseparability of ethical demand and empowering grace. And this inseparability is further enhanced by the notion of the Paraclete (John 14:16, 26; 15:27; 16:7; NRSV: Advocate; RSV Counselor), which is the special term in the Gospel for the Holy Spirit. This Spirit will abide in the community in Jesus' absence and will not only remind the community of what Jesus has told them but will also teach them "everything" (John 14:26) or guide them "into all the truth" (John 16:13). We must therefore recognize a strong notion of continuing revelation in John, which almost certainly must embrace both the doctrinal and the ethical dimensions. Thus, as Hays observes, "any reflection about Johannine ethics must take seriously the community's expectation of being led by the Spirit. Indeed, that expectation may provide a partial explanation of the near absence of specific moral instruction in these texts." And although Hays is probably correct in thinking that the Spirit's leading should be understood as something that takes place communally rather than in the individual conscience (Hays 1996, 151, citing Smith 1984, 15–17, 30–33), the notion of a Spirit-guided ethics necessarily implies a process of discernment. Thus, while love provides the broad principle on which ethical action is founded, there remains an irreducible open-endedness to ethical reflection: the community must count on the Spirit not only to guide it into deeper understanding of the truth but also to inspire and empower it in the process of discerning the good.

LIBERATION POTENTIAL IN THE JOHANNINE WRITINGS

The Gospel of John has, since very early times, been known as the "spiritual Gospel" and, in the words of David Rensberger, "held to present a more inward or theologically profound side of the New Testament interpretation of Jesus, or even of Jesus himself" (1988, 14). It might thus seem to stand at the opposite end of the spectrum from the interests of liberation theology. However, the rise of interest in the social settings of New Testament writings in recent years has inspired scholars such as Rensberger, and more recently Brian Blount and Allen Callahan, to interpret John against its social background with just such interests in view.

We have already seen one example of how such an approach, when applied to the letters, might affect our understanding of Johannine ethics: Callahan's contention that the emphasis on sharing "the world's goods" in 1 John 3:17 is suggestive of a communal economy. Rensberger's study, however, focuses solely on the Gospel and deals with issues of a somewhat different nature.

Raymond Brown has argued that it is possible to discern within the narrative of the Gospel a spectrum of attitudes, ranging from extreme hostility to a more moderate critique, toward specific groups outside the community's borders (1979, 63–91). The pervasive term "the Jews," used in a thoroughly derogatory way, refers to members of the wider Jewish community who reject the Christians' messianic claims about Jesus altogether (esp. 3:22-26; see also 1:8, 19-28). At a few points we can see hints of an awareness of followers of John the Baptist who are not counted as Christian believers. And there are also passages that seem to take account of Christians who are not in the Johannine fold (12:42-43; 6:66; 7:3-5).

Within this spectrum, we also find a group of secret adherents, symbolized by Nicodemus. These are persons who accept Jesus as Messiah but who will not make a public declaration for fear of expulsion from the synagogue. In examining the story of Jesus' encounter with Nicodemus in chapter 3, Rensberger finds that it has important social implications, since the "new birth" to which they were invited "implied not only personal faith and sacramental initiation but a change of social location as well." Jesus' demand for a "birth from above, the birth from water and the spirit" constituted a criticism of both their "lack of open discipleship" and their failure to accept the Johannine group's high christology. In calling for baptism from above, Jesus was in effect asking for "a choosing of sides at the border between a familiar and secure social setting and the disenfranchised Johannine community." Characterizing this community as an oppressed group by virtue of its expulsion from the synagogue and alienation from society at large, Rensberger interprets the Nicodemus story as a statement of "solidarity with the oppressed" (1988, 113; also chapters 2–4).

It must be said that from the perspective of the religious leadership and the majority Jewish community, the group's high christology would likely have appeared as a threat to the notion of God's unity. Also, we have no independent means of determining to what extent the perceived oppression was real. We must therefore be careful about making facile judgments about the mistreatment of Johannine Christians by other Jews. The alienation, however, is undeniable, and the perception of oppression was undoubtedly a major component of the community's self-understanding.

If we turn our attention to the question of the Gospel's attitude toward the empire, the exchanges between Pilate and Jesus in 18:33-38 and 19:8-11 are crucial. Although Jesus offers no answer to the question, "Where are you from?" (19:9), the reader has been well trained to supply the answer: "from above." Indeed, Jesus' earlier reply in 18:36a has already suggested this: "My kingship is not from this world." The reader can thus discern a sharp contrast between Jesus' kingship and that of Caesar, which Pilate represents; and this point becomes explicit in 19:10-11:

> Pilate therefore said to him, "Do you refuse to speak to me? Do you not know that I have power to release you, and power to crucify you?" Jesus answered him, "You would have no power over me unless it had been given you from above; therefore the one who delivered me to you is guilty of a greater sin."

Although this passage places the greater guilt on Jesus' Jewish opponents, it implicates Pilate and Rome as well, and it completely undermines Roman sovereignty. The reference to Pilate's power being granted from above by no means implies that human governments in general are based on some kind of "divine right." As Hays comments, "God has merely granted Pilate a temporary and limited authority in order that God's own purpose (the 'lifting up' of Jesus by crucifixion) might be fulfilled. . . . The whole dialogue subverts Roman claims of sovereignty and subordinates Roman power to the power of God" (1996, 148). And, in Rensberger's words, "God the creator of the world is by no means the sustainer of the world's religions, states, and economies. Rather, when God the Logos, through whom the world was made, entered the world, the world 'knew him not' and refused the light precisely because its works were evil (John 1:10-11; 3:16-21)." Thus, precisely because it challenges the worldly powers that cause the community's suffering and alienation, the Gospel of John offers "hope to those who are oppressed by the sovereignties of this world by offering them instead the sovereignty of God" (1988, 117).

JOHANNINE DUALISM, ABUNDANT LIFE, AND THE "VOICE OF THE EARTH"

For many Christians with a strong ecological bent, John 1—with its echoes of the positive view of creation in Genesis 1—provides one of the New Testament's most important witnesses to the value of the natural world in itself. For we find here not only the declaration that the *Logos* is the agent of God's creation of the cosmos and the source of all life but also the affirmation that the light of the *Logos* continues to shine in the darkness (v. 5). Thus Paulos Mar Gregorios can claim on the basis of this text that "[t]he creative energy of God is the true being of all that is," that "matter is that spirit or energy in physical form," and conclude that "we should regard our human environment as the energy of God in a form that is accessible to our senses" (1990, 40).

Norman C. Habel, however, questions "whether John 1 rereads Genesis 1 in a dualistic way that tends to devalue Earth and the physical universe" (2002, 77). He finds that the concept of *Logos* suggests "a starting point where Word and God exist without any of the stuff of creation" and thus "a locus that is purely spiritual." The result, he contends, is that John 1 bypasses the fact that in Genesis 1 the earth itself "is the domain from which life emerges" and that life is already "latent in the physical universe" before God calls it into being. The Johannine dualisms of light/darkness and above/below, moreover, reinforce the dichotomy between the spiritual and the material, leaving the cosmos as something in need of redemption by something outside it (2002, 79). And, finally, Habel asks whether the radical declaration in 1:14 that "the Word became flesh" is really an affirmation of the goodness of the material world:

> Is flesh revalued by this action of God from above? Or is flesh but the temporary—and dispensable—abode of Word passing through from "above" to "below" and back to "above" again? Even if the transcendent enters the material, does it continue there? Does it redeem the material world? Is the material accorded the same worth as the spiritual Word who enters human flesh? (2002, 82)

Habel has raised valid questions about the Johannine attitude toward material reality. As I noted above in the discussion of the relationship between the Johannine community and the outside "world," however, the *kosmos* from which this community was alienated was human society rather than the realm of nature. And Vicky Balabanski, in response to Habel, has noted four distinct meanings that the term takes on in the Gospel of John: (1) "the context into which Light comes," which "includes the Earth, but not as subject or agent, rather as an arena in which the drama of salvation is played out"; (2) "the totality of creation"; (3) "the world of human affairs"; and (4) "*kosmos* as 'this world,' and contrasted with the world above." It is therefore relevant to ask which of these meanings is at work in the statement in 3:16 that "God so loved the world." The third sense is clearly the primary reference, because "human beings are the ones who stand under judgment and who are capable of belief" (2002, 91–92). But Balabanski is convinced that the second sense—the totality of creation—is also implied in 3:16 by virtue of the birthing imagery that the Nicodemus passage shares with John 1:

> While the birthing/rebirthing of human beings is the focus of John 1.12-13 and the dialogue with Nicodemus (John 3), the fact that "all things came into being" through Word (John 1.3), and "the *kosmos* came into being through him" (John 1.10) means that the whole of creation/Earth community shares in the love of the one who gave birth to all things. How could God and the creative Word through whom creation came into being/was birthed fail to have compassion on the whole world? (2002, 93)

I would add that the Johannine notion that Jesus came so that human beings might have life "abundantly" (John 10:10), although clearly designating human life in its spiritual depth, implies a positive evaluation of creation in light of the pervasive emphasis in the Gospel on realized eschatology. The fact that true life—authentic life, abundant life—begins in the present must mean that life in the material world is not inherently inimical to spiritual existence. And the very notion of "abundant life" can hardly be grasped apart from an appreciation of the emphasis on human fulfillment in the context of the material world that runs throughout the entire Hebrew Bible. This is not to deny the force of Habel's observations, but it is to identify a significant countercurrent of meaning and therefore a point of tension that is conducive to hermeneutical reflection.

HERMENEUTICAL QUESTIONS

In addition to the tension between competing attitudes toward creation mentioned at the end of the preceding section, I have also identified in the earlier section, "The Johannine Ethic of Love," another question for hermeneutical reflection. Many scholars take at face value the fact that in the Johannine literature love is always commanded as an intracommunity affair. It is the logical corollary of the dualistic and sectarian outlook of the community. Such love simply cannot exist outside the community. It is possible, however, to view the matter otherwise. Since the disciples stand under the absolute command of the God, who loves the world, love cannot be limited to the community.

Any attempt to solve this problem on the basis of exegesis alone is doomed to failure, since both lines of logic make sense in their own terms. One can scarcely doubt that the weight of emphasis is on love as an internal matter. However, the tension created by the passages suggesting a positive attitude toward the world invites the interpreter to reflect more broadly on the issue. And such reflection inevitably brings us to the question of the character of God as depicted in the Gospel. Although the focus on God's love for the Son and the various dimensions of reciprocity that flow from this basic affirmation are dominant, the undercurrents of emphasis on God's love for the world force us to ask how a loving God could in fact remain content with love confined to the triangle of reciprocity.

To raise this question is also to bring to our attention the problematic character of the notion of exclusive salvation that appears in this literature. Although the countercurrent is less prominent in this case, we may point to the prologue of the Gospel for hints of a more inclusive view, such as we found in some passages in Matthew. Not only have all things come into being through the *Logos* (1:2), but the *Logos* is explicitly termed "the light of all people" (v. 4) that "enlightens everyone" (v. 9). Once again, the weight of emphasis is clearly on the exclusivist note. But precisely because the weak countercurrent of inclusivism connects so well with the pervasive characterization of God in terms of self-giving love to the point that one can speak of God *as* love, we have good reason to approach both the dualism and the exclusivism of this literature with a critical consciousness.

The dualistic language in the literature also raises important questions regarding our contemporary appropriation of the Johannine materials with regard to the relationship between church and society. We have seen how the sense of separation from the world can have positive meaning from the perspective of liberation theology by calling all human claims to sovereignty into question. But we must also ask whether it might foster a severely antagonistic attitude that would in the end subvert the Johannine sense of God's love for the world. What attitude should the church take toward the world outside its boundaries? Attention to the Gospel and letters of John lands us right in the middle of this age-old question.

One final hermeneutical question arises when we consider the strong element of discernment in the Johannine ethic. How do we negotiate the tension between an open-ended, Spirit-guided ethic that only rarely gives concrete content to the principle of love and the more definite commandments we find in some other New Testament writings? What value should we place on the notion that the Spirit will guide the community in its quest for the truth and the good? This is an issue, as we will soon see, that also arises in the letters of Paul.

CHAPTER 9

the undisputed letters of paul

⌥

The sharp differences in the ways in which contemporary Christians ground their ethical views in the New Testament reflect, in large measure, variations in their interpretations of Paul's letters. These variations are based partly in disparate hermeneutical approaches, but they are more fundamentally the result of decisions as to which writings one counts as letters of Paul. The inclusion of those letters that many scholars regard as products of later followers of Paul would change significantly our understanding of both his theology and his ethics. I will therefore confine myself at present to the seven undisputed letters—Romans, 1 and 2 Corinthians, Galatians, Philippians, 1 Thessalonians, and Philemon— and deal with the disputed letters, along with Hebrews and the General Letters in the next chapter.

INDICATIVE AND IMPERATIVE:
THE THEOLOGICAL BASIS OF PAULINE ETHICS

Scholars who adhere to the understanding of Paul's thought that reigned among Protestant scholars from the Reformation to recent decades have always had a problem defining the relationship between Paul's theology and his ethics. According to this view, classically promulgated by Luther, the linchpin of Paul's thought is "justification by faith," which means that it is through faith in Christ alone that human beings stand acquitted before God and not through good works. Thus, the problem arises as to how the indicative and the imperative are related—that is, how Paul moves logically from the declaration of acquittal before God to the exhortation to do the good. And because of this apparent lack of connection between theology and ethics, some interpreters have charged that such a view amounts to a "legal fiction," entailing the notion that God pronounces innocent those who are in fact guilty.

Roman Catholic interpreters, on the other hand, have tended to deny the centrality of Paul's concept of justification, viewing it as "one of the many metaphors describing the new Christian existence" (Plevnik 1986, 57) and contending that God's grace does not preclude human cooperation in the process of salvation. However, Protestant and Catholic scholars are far less divided in their readings of Paul today; this is due in part to significant departures by Protestants from Luther's interpretation.

One line of departure stems from E. P. Sanders's retrieval of aspects of Albert Schweitzer's "mystical" reading of Paul (Sanders 1977; Schweitzer 1931/1956). Schweitzer found the center of Paul's thought not in his doctrine of justification but in his understanding of believers' participation in Christ's "body" and their existence "in Christ." Paul's language of justification, he argued, appeared only when he was addressing the issue of the Jewish Law, while the "mystical" terminology—which recent interpreters prefer to term "participationist"—occurs in relation to other important aspects of his thought, including ethics. Thus, it is the believers' incorporation into Christ that provides the motivation for ethical behavior.

We may note, for example, that Paul issues his injunction not to "let sin exercise dominion in your mortal bodies" in Rom 6:12 as a logical complement ("therefore") to his discourse on baptism as dying and rising with Christ in vv. 1-11. And in Galatians 5, after declaring the believers' freedom from the Law, Paul's caution against the misuse of freedom in self-indulgence (v. 13) leads not only to his summation of the Law in the command to love the neighbor (vv. 14-15) but ultimately to an extended discourse (vv. 16-26) on life in the Spirit as the foundation for doing the good. The connection between the Spirit and participation in Christ, moreover, becomes explicit in vv. 24-25: "And those who belong to Christ Jesus have crucified the flesh with its passions and desires. If we live by the Spirit, let us also be guided by the Spirit." The ethical appeal is therefore both grounded in and motivated by the spiritual qualities of the new realm of existence. Far from a "legal fiction," their new status is a new state of being.

Well before Sanders's retrieval of Schweitzer, Victor Furnish addressed the problem of theology and ethics in Paul from a somewhat different perspective, which also helped dispel the impression of a "legal fiction." Furnish identified the fundamental interpretive mistake as a tendency to separate Paul's ethics from his theology, as if they were independent concepts.

Paul understands these two dimensions of the gospel in such a way that, though they are not absolutely identical, they are closely and necessarily associated. God's *claim* is regarded by the apostle as a constitutive part of God's gift. The Pauline concept of God's grace is *inclusive* of the Pauline concept of obedience. (1968, 224; emphasis original)

Furnish therefore finds Rudolf Bultmann's view of the imperative as based on the indicative too weak, since "this suggests that the imperative is designed somehow to 'realize' or 'actualize' what God has given only as a 'possibility.'" To the contrary, Furnish states, "The Pauline imperative is not just the result of the indicative but fully integral to it" (1968, 225).

If we ask precisely how the imperative is integral to the indicative, we come to the heart of Furnish's view and find a point of convergence with arguments made from the "participationist" perspective. Believers who have been justified by God's grace belong to a new "realm"—or, as some later interpreters have termed the matter—a new "force field." They stand "under the aegis and hegemony of a new Sovereign" and are given not just the possibility of new life "but an actually new existence" (1968, 225).

We may go one step further in articulating the unity of indicative and imperative if we draw on recent scholarship regarding Paul's usage of the term *pistis*, traditionally translated as "faith." Although it has long been recognized that Paul does not use it as a mere equivalent of "belief" (a misunderstanding that goes as far back as the Letter of James, as is evident in James 2:14-17), the tendency to view it as separable from outward behavior has persisted. If, however, we accept the judgment that in many cases it is better translated as "faithfulness," it begins to appear more clearly as "an encompassing way of being in the world and not simply an interior attitude of belief or trust . . ." (Cobb and Lull 2005, 17). This contention seems basically congruent with Bultmann's near equation of faith with obedience (1951, 314–24) and Furnish's claim that love also counts as an equivalent (1968, 202), with the added advantage of a more explicit connection with actual behavior. "When *pistis* is understood in this way," John Cobb and David Lull argue, the old debate about whether justification is simply God's acceptance of us in our unchanged sinfulness, or involves some transformation of our character, is largely superseded" (2005, 17–18).

It is possible, then, to understand Paul's juridical language as a facet of his broader participationist perspective. The fundamental theological "fact," for Paul, is God's decisive victory over sin and death by raising Jesus from the dead. By this act, God has made salvation available to human beings, who can participate in Jesus' death and resurrection and be incorporated into his "body" through their faithfulness, understood as "an encompassing way of being in the world." This faithfulness involves an inner attitude of ultimate trust in God's grace; but it cannot be isolated as a discrete moment, since it necessarily embraces concrete manifestation in actual deeds of love.

Just how Paul understands Christ's death and resurrection to effect salvation is a more difficult question. He never gives an account of the "mechanics" of this process (nor does any other New Testament writer). He comes closest to this is in Rom 3:22b-26, a passage whose exact meaning has been hotly disputed. The NRSV translation is as follows:

> For there is no distinction, since all have sinned and fall short of the glory of God; they are now justified by his grace as a gift, through the redemption that is in Christ Jesus, whom God put forward as a sacrifice of atonement by his blood, effective through faith. He did this to show his righteousness, because in his divine forbearance he had passed over sins previously committed; it was to prove at the present time that he himself is righteous and that he justifies the one who has faith in Jesus.

This passage has often been used as the showpiece for a substitutionary theory of the atonement, according to which Jesus stands in as a substitute, "paying the price" for human sin in order to "satisfy" God's need for justice. At the heart of the issue is the meaning of the Greek noun *hilastērion*. It is related to the verb *hilaskesthai*, whose range of meanings includes "propitiate," "conciliate," and "expiate," and to another noun, *hilasmos*, which can mean either "propitiation" or "expiation." The substitutionary/satisfaction theory generally understands *hilastērion* as "propitiation"—that is, Jesus' death propitiates God's wrath by satisfying the legal requirement for punishment. A different tradition, by contrast, understands it as "expiation," a term that connotes atonement for sin but does not carry with it the specific implications of the substitutionary/satisfaction theory. The NRSV translation stands in this latter tradition.

There is little doubt that the passage contains the broad notion that Jesus' death somehow had a conciliatory effect, bridging the gap between God and sinful humanity. The specific way in which this takes place, however, is elusive. The noun *hilastērion* occurs only one other time in the New Testament, in Heb 9:5, where it refers to the "mercy seat," the lid of the ark of the covenant, which is consistent with its usage in the Septuagint. The other noun, *hilasmos*, occurs only in 1 John 2:2 and 4:10, where it refers to Jesus' role in the expiation of sin but without any hint of theological elaboration. The verb also occurs only twice, in Heb 2:17 and Luke 18:13. In the former, it expresses Jesus' atoning act, and in the latter it expresses the tax collector's plea for God's mercy: "God, be merciful to me, a sinner!"

We may say, then, that if one is already committed to a substitutionary theory of atonement, one can perhaps find it in Rom 3:25. The passage by no means requires such an understanding, however, and it is difficult to find explicit support for it elsewhere in Paul. Such support is often claimed for 1 Cor 5:7, where Paul makes a passing reference to the sacrifice of "our paschal lamb, Christ." Here again, however, neither the verse itself nor its context calls for such an interpretation, as David Lull and William Beardslee demonstrate:

> Nothing in the context of 1 Cor. 5:7 suggests that the metaphor interpreted Jesus' death as a *substitutionary* sacrifice whose effect is to set aside divine punishment for sinners, or as the *satisfaction* of divine justice, or as *propitiation* averting God's wrath or anger. . . . None of these atonement theories was associated with the Passover sacrifice in Jewish or "Christian" pre-Pauline traditions. Moreover, these pre-Pauline traditions did not associate the lamb sacrificed at Passover with the suffering servant of Isa. 52:13—53:12, even though this servant is metaphorically called a "lamb" (53:7). Rather, consistent with pre-Pauline Jewish traditions, Paul uses this metaphor in this context to interpret Jesus' death as bringing about the fulfillment of God's promise of *deliverance* from bondage to "wickedness and evil" (1 Cor 5:8, author's trans.). (2007, 41)

An interpretation of Rom 3:25 very different from that of substitution theories is possible, moreover, if we draw again on some recent scholarship with respect to the meaning of *pistis*. We have seen that in many cases it is best translated as "faithfulness." Now we may take account of the argument of many scholars that in some instances the phrase usually translated as "faith in Jesus Christ" (*pistis Iesou Christou*) should rather be rendered as "faithfulness *of* Jesus Christ." In other words, in these passages it is not the believer's faithfulness that is the object of reflection but Jesus' own.

Standard translations of the phrases *dia pisteōs* (literally, "through faith/faithfulness") and *en tō autou haimati* (literally, "in/by his blood") in Rom 3:25 rest on the assumption that the faith mentioned is that of the believer and that the conciliation between God and humanity is effected by Jesus' blood. Hence the NRSV: "whom God put forward as a sacrifice of atonement by his blood, effective through faith." As Luke T. Johnson notes, however, the positioning of the phrase *dia pisteōs* in the Greek text, not at the end of the sentence but between *hilasterion* and "in/by his blood" shows that it "is clearly intended to qualify the manner of Jesus' death." Thus, Johnson, understanding *pistis* as faithfulness, argues that it is Jesus' own obedience that is indicated:

> the two phrases "through faith" and "in his blood" form what in Greek is known as a hendiadys, that is, two phrases that make a single expression. In this case, the two phrases would be the equivalent to "Jesus' faithful death," which is exactly what Paul seems to get at here. (1997, 59)

On this interpretation, the effective agent in the process of conciliation between God and humanity is not Jesus' blood or even his death per se but his faithfulness to God, his obedience "to the point of death" (Phil 2:8). Thus, Cobb and Lull suggest the following paraphrase as expressive of Paul's intended meaning in Rom 3:25: "whom God intended as an act of conciliation in and through Jesus' faithfulness even to death" (2005, 67).

If we are prepared to accept that the phrase *pistis Iēsou* (or *pistis Iēsou Christou*) can refer to Jesus' own faithfulness, then we will likely want to follow Johnson in his reading of v. 26 also. Here, he contends, the Greek phrase simply cannot mean "him who has faith in Jesus." Rather, "[t]he most natural reading would be 'the one who shares the faith of Jesus'" (1997, 60). Thus, as Cobb and Lull argue, "[u]nderstanding *pistis* as faithfulness not only changes the understanding of the relation of *pistis* and works but also provides new ways of understanding the process of salvation" (2005, 17–18). For we may now see that the human faithfulness that leads to justification is itself participation in Jesus' own faithfulness.

This insight also enables us to see more deeply into the logic that undergirds Paul's ethic of *imitatio Christi*. "And you," Paul reminds his readers in 1 Thess 1:6-7, "became imitators of us and of the Lord, for in spite of persecution you received the word with joy inspired by the Holy Spirit, so that you became an example to all the believers in Macedonia and Achaia." As Paul himself imitates Jesus, those in his charge imitate both him and Jesus and thus become models for others. But this process of imitation has a limited focus, for, as Furnish observes, all the passages dealing with imitation share an emphasis on selfless service and an indication of the near inevitability of suffering. And it is always Jesus' humility and obedient love that is the subject of imitation, never any other specific aspect of his human character (1968, 223).

CHRISTOCENTRISM AS THEOCENTRISM:
THE FAITHFULNESS OF ABRAHAM

Paul's theology is clearly christocentric: it is Christ and Christ alone who has effected a reconciliation between God and humanity. And whether we understand *pistis Iēsou Christou* as faith in Christ or Christ's faithfulness, the concept of *pistis* is almost always related specifically to Christ. An important exception, however, appears in Romans 4, where Paul makes the *pistis* of Abraham a major link in his argument for his doctrine of justification. To prove that human beings are justified not by the Law but by *pistis*, he evokes the image of Abraham, whom God accounted righteous on account of his faithfulness before there was a Law. What is interesting in this instance is that Paul presents *pistis* as a generic human possibility that has nothing directly to do with Christ. Abraham is faithful to *God*, and in v. 16 Paul can even speak of later generations sharing in *Abraham's* faithfulness. Paul's christocentrism thus opens into a theocentrism, as we can see also in 1 Cor 15:28: "When all things are subjected to him, then the Son himself will also be subjected to the one who put all things in subjection under him, so that God may be all in all."

Here again, in Paul as in Matthew, then, we find a universalistic element that stands in tension with more exclusivist strains of meaning. If faithfulness to God is possible apart from Christ, then soteriology extends beyond the limits of christology, and we must reckon with an enabling grace that is universally available (see Boers 1971, 74–106, and Pregeant 1978, 148–51).

NOW AND THEN: THE APOCALYPTIC FRAMEWORK
OF PAUL'S THEOLOGY AND ETHICS

The role of suffering in Paul's notion of the imitation of Christ is intimately related to his whole way of thinking. The believers' transfer from one realm of being to another is actually a transfer from one age to another—that is, from the "present evil age" (Gal 1:4), in which human beings have been held under the power of sin (for example, Rom 6:6-14) since the time of Adam (Rom 5:12-14), to the new age inaugurated by Jesus' death and resurrection. Through this pivotal event, God has liberated humanity from the power of sin and made available a whole new way of existence. Just as Jesus' resurrection from the dead freed him forever from death's dominion (Rom 6:9), so those in Christ, having been "buried" with him in baptism, now are free to "walk in newness of life" (Rom 6:4). They are also filled with the empowering presence of the Spirit, so that Paul can appeal to them to "be guided by the Spirit" (Gal 5:25) and expect from them the "fruit of the Spirit," which he defines as "love, joy, peace, patience, kindness, generosity, faithfulness, gentleness, and self-control" (Gal 5:22).

God's victory over the dominion of death, however, remains incomplete, even though the resurrection of Jesus from the dead has won the decisive victory. Thus, believers remain in an in-between time, when the power of the coming age is present but the powers of sin and death have not yet been fully defeated. This is clear, above all, from 1 Cor 15:20-25, where Paul speaks of the resurrection of Christ as the firstfruits of the general resurrection to come and of the final victory over death as still in the future. The present, therefore, remains a time when death has not yet suffered ultimate defeat. Thus, even those who are in Christ and infused with the Spirit remain in a state of incomplete knowledge and are still subject to suffering, death, and temptation. Moral exhortation is therefore not only possible but also necessary, especially since some think that their reception of the Spirit means that they are no longer bound by the restrictions of the present age. Thus, in 1 Corinthians Paul criticizes some in Corinth for their boasting about their wisdom (1:18—2:16) and their spiritual gifts (chapters 12–14). And he ironically contrasts their apparent sense of unqualified membership in the new age with the sufferings he has experienced as an apostle in such a way as to reveal the connection between being in Christ and suffering:

> We are fools for the sake of Christ, but you are wise in Christ. We are weak, but you are strong. You are held in honor, but we in disrepute. To the present hour we are hungry and thirsty, we are poorly clothed and beaten and homeless, and we grow weary from the work of our own hands. When reviled, we bless; when persecuted, we endure; when slandered, we speak kindly. We have become like the rubbish of the world, the dregs of all things, to this very day. (1 Cor 4:10-13)

The suffering that belongs to believers in the present age is in part the suffering that belongs to all persons in that age in which death still reigns. But this passage reveals another dimension of that suffering. When Paul says that he and his entourage are "poorly clothed and beaten and homeless," he points beyond the "normal" suffering that attends this age to the persecution that will almost inevitably attend those who are in Christ. Paul receives a special portion of this persecution by virtue of his role as apostle, but he is clearly inviting his readers to share in this suffering. To be in Christ is thus to be in conflict with the powers that rule the present age; and this is a point that will command attention in a later section. First, however, we must focus on the process by which Paul expects those in Christ to determine God's will.

TRANSFORMATION, DISCERNMENT, LOVE, COMMANDMENT: DETERMINING THE WILL OF GOD

As many scholars have observed, the notion of God's eventual triumph over evil is central to Paul's gospel (see esp. Beker 1980). Thus it is hardly surprising that the apocalyptic outlook also plays a central role in his ethical thinking. As we have seen, those in Christ are capable of receiving moral address because they already participate in the new age. Thus, in Rom 12:1-2, Paul counsels his readers to allow the transformative power of the new age to do its work: "Do not be conformed to this world, but be transformed by the renewing of your minds." And then, presupposing this process of renewal, he indicates how to identify right action: "so that you may discern what is the will of God—what is good and acceptable and perfect." Because of their new existence in Christ, believers have the power of discernment, of puzzling out what God requires of them in any specific circumstance. This is clearly what Paul means when he urges the Galatians to be guided by the Spirit (5:25) and the Philippians to "work out" their "own salvation with fear and trembling" (2:12) in light of the fact that God is enabling them "to will and to work" for God's own "good pleasure" (v. 13).

At its core, then, Paul's ethic is a Spirit-driven ethic of discernment based on his apocalyptic notion of the emerging new age inaugurated by Christ's death and resurrection. It is therefore also a character ethic, with the goal of a spiritual transformation informed by the imitation of Christ and of others who are in Christ. And it is by no means an amorphous ethic. The phrase "fear and trembling" in Phil 2:12 is a reminder both of God's will as the goal of the discernment process and of God's role as judge, just as the reference to God's enabling presence is a reminder of God's grace. Of equal importance, Paul is consistent in giving shape to his expectations regarding the behavior of believers by reference to the love command. Thus, he can state that love is the fulfilling of the law (Rom 13:8-10; Gal 5:14), urge it upon his readers as their most fundamental obligation

(1 Cor 16:14), and lift it up as the primary virtue (1 Cor 13:1—14:1). It is thus clear from the outset that the discernment process of those who are truly guided by the Spirit will lead them in the direction of love.

Paul is also clear that love has specific characteristics. In 1 Corinthians 13, he presents it as the foundation for such other virtues as patience, kindness, hope, and endurance and distinguishes it from all that is "envious or boastful or arrogant or rude." He sees its primary exemplification in Christ's self-sacrifice on behalf of human salvation and continually associates it with humility and a willingness to put others ahead of oneself (Phil 2:1-11). It is, in fact, for him the primary distinguishing characteristic of community in Christ. Thus, in 1 Corinthians his reflections on the issue of eating food offered to idols focus on whether such action harms one's fellows in Christ (1 Corinthians 8; 10:14—11:1), and in his counsel regarding lawsuits within the community he asks his readers to suffer loss rather than take a fellow believer to court (1 Cor 6:7). In neither case does Paul refer directly to love, but the concept is all-pervasive in these discussions. His injunctions make self-giving love concrete, and it is precisely such behavior that defines community membership. For Paul, in fact, the notion of a solitary believer is unthinkable (Sampley 1991, 37–38); to belong to Christ is to be in community, a member of Christ's body, and therefore to love and serve one another.

Paul does not, however, trace all moral behavior directly to love, nor does discernment appear to be completely open-ended. He can issue ethical pronouncements, and he clearly presupposes the immorality of certain behaviors. Thus, he occasionally refers to a teaching of Jesus (for example, 1 Cor 7:10-11; 9:14) and gives standard lists of virtues and vices (for example, 1 Cor 6:9-11). It is therefore clear that he considers such actions and attitudes as fornication, adultery, theft, greed, and drunkenness to be unacceptable.

In the end, however, Paul's ethic remains primarily a Spirit-driven ethic of discernment with love at its center. As Furnish has argued, if we ask about how Paul expects those in his communities to discern God's will, we do not find a systematic approach. "The law is by no means irrelevant to the Christian's practical conduct," and Rom 13:8-10 and Gal 5:14 show that Paul still understands it as in some sense binding for Christians. These very passages, however, reveal that he does not view it as providing concrete rules of conduct, since they state very clearly that the Law is fulfilled precisely through obedience to the love command. And although the teachings of Jesus provide a few concrete rules, they come nowhere near constituting an actual code of conduct (1968, 228).

Thus, Furnish concludes, for Paul, "God's will is finally discerned through the 'knowledge' and 'insight' of which the member[s] of Christ's body [are] capable when [they commit themselves] to the good of others and thus [abound] in love" (1968, 236).

ASSEMBLY, SOCIETY, EMPIRE:
PAUL AND THE WORLD OF HUMAN AFFAIRS

Paul's understanding of believers as incorporated into Christ's body results, as we have seen, in a strong doctrine of community. His focus is generally on the *ekklēsia*, the assembly of believers, rather than the individual. In many ways, then, his ethic is an ethic of community solidarity, so that right and wrong are largely determined by what does or does not "build up" the community (1 Cor 14:4-5). This is not to say that he has no sense of the world outside the assembly and the community's relationship to it. In approaching this issue, however, it is important to make a distinction between the outside world as society and the specific structures and institutions that constitute it as the Roman Empire.

Paul and the Empire

For many, the passage that first comes to mind in relation to Paul's view of the empire is Rom 13:1-7. Here he counsels his readers "to be subject to the ruling authorities," states that these authorities "have been instituted by God," and even says that "whoever resists authority resists what God has appointed. . . ." Because this passage has so dominated discussion of Paul's view of governments in general, many Christians have understood their obligation as obedience to whatever governmental structure might be in place in any given circumstance. And, as a result of this interpretation, there is a long history within the church of opposition to movements on behalf of liberation and support for regimes guilty of domination and oppression. To their shame, Christians have supported slavery, the Nazi regime, and, more recently, murderous governments in Latin America (see N. Elliott 1994, 3–20).

Precisely because many interpreters have allowed Romans 13 to dominate other relevant aspects of Paul's letters, it will be important to begin elsewhere and thus put this passage into a broader context. So let us look first at some key terms in Paul's vocabulary that have political overtones. We have already seen that *euangelion* ("good news," "gospel"), which is central not only to the Gospels but to Paul's letters, was the term that emperors used in announcing their military victories. Even more provocative is the use, in both the Gospels and Paul, of the term *basileia*. The apocalyptic proclamation that God is in the process of setting up a new rule carries with it the implication that all earthly dominions are about to be brought down; and of course in Paul's context this has to mean, above all, Rome itself!

Along similar lines, Helmut Koester finds subtler political significance in some of Paul's language in 1 Thessalonians. With respect to parousia, which Paul applies to Jesus' eschatological return four times in this letter (2:19; 3:3; 4:15; 5:23), he notes "no evidence in pre-Christian apocalyptic literature" for the technical usage of the term in a similar way. "If there is any 'technical' usage of *parousia*, it appears in the terminology for the arrival of a king or an emperor" (1997, 158). In 4:17, moreover, the word *apantēsis*, which Paul uses when referring to believers meeting Jesus in the air, "is a technical term describing the festive and formal meeting of a king who arrives for a visit of the city" (1997, 160). One therefore gets the image of Jesus coming down from heaven, meeting in the air those who belong to him, and then marching triumphantly into the city (rather than returning to heaven). And it is consistent with this rather provocative political imagery that Paul employs the phrase "peace and security" (*eirēnē kai asphaleia*) in an ironic way in 5:3: "When they say, 'There is peace and security,' then the sudden destruction will come upon them, as labor pains come upon a pregnant woman, and there will be no escape." Again finding no parallels to the use of this terminology in apocalyptic language, Koester argues (see also N. Elliott 1994, 189–90) that it is drawn explicitly from the political vocabulary. Thus, he maintains,

> As a political slogan, *eirēnē kai asphaleia* (= *pax et securitas*) is best ascribed to the realm of imperial Roman propaganda. If this interpretation of the phrase is correct, it would imply that Paul points to the coming day of the Lord as an event that will shatter the false peace and security of the Roman establishment. Of course, such a view is entirely in keeping with older Jewish and later Christian apocalyptic protest against imperial establishments. (1997, 162)

It should also be noted that the centrality of the cross in Paul's message has implicit political significance. For, as Neil Elliott notes, Jesus' crucifixion "is, after all, one of the most unequivocally political events recorded in the New Testament" (1994, 93; 1997, 167). As the form of punishment reserved for slaves and the lower classes and the preferred weapon of choice in dealing with insurrectionists, crucifixion carried with it an unmistakable link to the power of Rome, which was ever ready to crush any hint of insurrection. Thus, to proclaim that God has raised a crucified person from the dead was to mock both the power and the morality of the empire itself. Yet, Paul stresses that it is precisely the cross of Christ that is at the very heart of his message (1 Cor 1:23; 2:2; Gal 6:14).

In the eyes of many scholars, however, although Paul made constant use of the imagery of the cross, he emptied it of all political significance. Thus, they emphasize, we do not find in his letters any references to the specific sociopolitical reasons for Jesus' arrest and conviction. So it is possible to come away from his writings with the impression of the crucifixion as a sacrifice initiated by God, without any hint of the human injustice. Such an impression, however, involves a serious distortion, as is evident from 1 Cor 2:6-8, where we find a rather blatant indictment of "the rulers of this age":

> Yet among the mature we do speak wisdom, though it is not a wisdom of this age or of the rulers of this age, who are doomed to perish. But we speak of God's wisdom, secret and hidden, which God decreed before the ages for our glory. None of the rulers of this age understood this; for if they had, they would not have crucified the Lord of glory.

The key question here is what Paul means by "the rulers of this age." Does he refer to cosmic powers or to earthly governments and leaders? Although this issue was once hotly debated, there is a strong tendency in recent scholarship to see it as a false dilemma. As an apocalyptic thinker, Paul viewed earthly dynasties as manifestations of cosmic forces. As Walter Wink notes, regarding the use of the "language of power" in the New Testament and its environment, the writers of this period speak of "the powers" sometimes "as if they were *these* centurions or *that* priestly hierarchy, and then, with no warning, as if they were some kind of spiritual entities in the heavenly places" (1984, 5). Wink thus concludes that in the New Testament "*[t]hese powers are both heavenly and earthly, divine and human, spiritual and political, invisible and structural*" (1984, 11; emphasis original).

This general judgment is borne out by a close look at 1 Cor 2:6-8. On the one hand, as Wink summarizes a point made by Martin Dibelius,

> Herod, Pilate, and the Jewish authorities cannot possibly be made to bear the weight of the phrase "rulers of this aeon." At the time Paul writes,

none of them is still in office; Herod has indeed "passed away," but every mortal must, and his death had no eschatological significance. The statement is extravagant applied to humans, but sensible if it refers to powers considered by his hearers to be *athanatoi*, immortal. (1984, 42; citing Dibelius 1909, 89)

On the other hand, the context shows that Paul does in some sense mean earthly powers here. For in 1 Corinthians 1 he has framed his critique of the Corinthians' claim to wisdom in terms of a contrast between God's wisdom and the wisdom of the world, naming the proclamation of Christ crucified as "a stumbling block to Jews and foolishness to Gentiles" (1:23). When he comes to 2:6-8, then, he has

already spoken of the "wise person" (*sophos*), the "scribe" (*grammateus*) (1:20), the "powerful" (*dynatoi*), and the "well-born" (*eugeneis*) (1:26), whom God is bringing to nothing (1:28). These are the "powers" of this age (*tou aiōnos*, 1:20), and they are all human. (Wink 1984, 41, citing Schniewind 1952, 104–9)

In a similar way, Rom 8:31-37 seems to embrace both a cosmic and an earthly dimension in its naming of the forces that oppose the gospel. "Who will separate us from the love of Christ?" Paul asks in v. 35, and then names earthly forces— such as persecution and famine—as the enemies. But in v. 37 his language seems directed primarily at cosmic forces: "For I am convinced that neither death, nor life, nor angels, nor rulers, nor things present, nor things to come, nor height, nor depth, nor anything else in all creation will be able to separate us from the love of God in Christ Jesus our Lord."

It would therefore seem undeniable that Paul had a strong sense that the earthly political structures involved in the crucifixion of Jesus were manifestations of cosmic powers opposed to the purposes of God. And if we take account of the difficulties Paul faced in his apostolic ministry, it becomes difficult to imagine otherwise. As Elliott observes,

We should doubt that Paul's gospel was a purely "spiritual" matter, socially and politically innocuous, once we recall the efforts of the Nabatean king Aretas IV to arrest Paul in Damascus (2 Cor. 11:32-33) and the apparent regularity with which Paul was hauled before civic magistrates, thrown into Roman prisons, and condemned as a menace to public order (Philem. 1, 9, 13; Phil. 1:7, 12-14, 16; 4:14; 1 Thess. 2:2; 1 Cor. 4:9; 2 Cor. 1:8-9; 6:5; 11:23). (1994, 183)

It is easy enough, of course, to classify the offenses for which Paul was incarcerated as "religious" in the narrow sense, because he can say, for example, that his "imprisonment is for Christ" (Phil 1:13). To do so, however, is to overlook the likely reason for the objections to his missionary activity. Although Rome had for some time tolerated the "oddity" of Jewish monotheism, those in the Christ communities lacked the essential qualification of an ancient heritage. Thus, their refusal to participate in the worship of deities other than the one they knew through Christ was clear evidence of disloyalty to the empire. Not only did their exclusive devotion rule out sacrifices to the emperor, but it also segregated them from the other religious observances that were associated with allegiance to Rome. Thus, as Elliott states, drawing on work by Holland Hendrix,

> Thessalonika, to take one example, secured its "freedom" from Roman subjugation (it remained immune from tribute, if no less dependent economically) by developing an elaborate cultus honoring Augustus. Roman benefactors received official civic recognition and the *imperial pantheon of Rome was incorporated into the official worship of the city* (a temple to Augustus was built; Augustus's head replaced Zeus's head on the city's coinage). The result was a *thorough integration of Roman and local cults into a sacred pyramid of civic worship, the imperial cult assuming priority.* (1994, 188; citing Hendrix 1984; emphasis added)

Therefore, since it is clear from Paul's letters (1 Thess 1:9; 1 Cor 8:5-6; 10:14-22) that his message entailed an aggressive rejection of "idols" and a strict prohibition of participating in pagan worship, we must also imagine that his formation of assemblies of converts was often received as an attempt to undermine imperial theology and with it loyalty to the emperor and to Rome itself. Nor should we imagine that such a reception would be in error, unless we somehow exempt imperial theology from Paul's blatant characterization of pagan worship as sacrifice to demons (1 Cor 10:20-21). Pheme Perkins would therefore seem justified in her speculation about the troubles faced by Paul and other followers of Christ in Thessalonica and Philippi: "The reason for this disturbance and persecution was probably related to the imperial cult" (Perkins 1991, 93; cited by N. Elliott 1994, 196–97).

It would appear, then, that there is much in Paul's authentic letters that promotes an understanding of God's coming *basileia* as subversive of the empire's role as guarantor of peace and security and therefore as a threat to its power. And against this background, Rom 13:1-7 appears not only singular but in fact anomalous. It is strange indeed to hear from one who has condemned the modes of worship that are complicit in the empire's project of self-legitimization and boldly proclaims the advent of an alternative sovereign rule that human authorities have been instituted by God and that those in Christ should be subject to them and not resist. This, however, is precisely what we find in Rom 13:1-7, and the primary challenge in understanding Paul's attitude toward the empire is to make sense of this passage in light of all that we have seen that would seem to suggest a very different view.

The first point to note is that the evidence presented above should leave no doubt that Furnish is on solid ground when he argues that for Paul "*[t]he Christians 'subjection' to the governing authorities is secondary to his or her obedience to the will of God*" (1985, 137; emphasis original). Paul's understanding of human authorities as instituted by God draws on a Jewish heritage that also views those authorities as having responsibilities to God and as subject to God's judgment (1985, 127), and only a few verses later (v. 14) Paul refers to Jesus Christ as "Lord" (*kyrios*). It should therefore be clear that if in any circumstance the members of Paul's assemblies found themselves faced with a choice between their loyalty to Christ and their role as subjects of the empire, Paul would have expected them to choose the former, even under the threat of death.

The second point we should recognize, however, is that Paul did not have such a circumstance in mind in this passage, nor did he apparently think that the assemblies generally existed in such circumstance. In Paul's time "there had not yet been any fundamental confrontation between Rome and the church" (Furnish 1985, 134), and, despite Paul's imprisonments, he actually had reason for a measure of confidence in the Roman judicial system:

> If we are to believe the picture drawn for us by Acts, Paul had more than once been the beneficiary of the law and order that Roman civil and military authority had made a reality throughout the Mediterranean world, even though he had also been its victim. His own continuing confidence in the judicial system was demonstrated when, sometime after the writing of this letter to the Roman Christians, having been arrested in Jerusalem and imprisoned in Caesarea, he appealed his case, as a Roman citizen, to the emperor (Nero) himself. (Furnish 1985, 128)

With these two points in mind, we may now ask why Paul felt it necessary to say what he does about "the authorities" in Rom 13:1-7. A widely current explanation is a broad recognition of Paul's desire to keep the congregation out of trouble as they await Christ's parousia, but in and of itself this does little to explain why Paul should make his point on the basis of such a seemingly uncritical acceptance of the empire's power. A number of scholars, noting that the passage ends with a reference to paying taxes, claim that Paul's concern issued from his fear that the assembly would put itself in jeopardy by engaging in tax resistance. Others, however, reject this suggestion as overly speculative, since Paul does not state explicitly that this issue is at work in the Roman congregation. An alternative view is that the reference to resistance in 13:2 is an indication that Paul's specific concern was to urge the Roman congregation "to renounce the revolutionary cause in Judea"—a concern that grew specifically from the expulsion of Jews from Rome under Claudius.[1]

After considering these and other explanations, Elliott finds that although they offer plausible historical backgrounds for the passage, "they have not connected these historical circumstances with an adequate view of what Paul is trying to do in the rest of the letter" (1994, 221–22). He therefore proposes a specific analysis of the place of these verses in Paul's overall rhetorical strategy.

Having already noted that a major purpose of the letter to the Romans was to urge the Gentile members not to despise the Jewish members (1994, 216)—a point readily evident in chapter 14—Elliott focuses on the relationship of 13:1-7 to chapter 12: "If Paul's remarks in 13:1-7 address specific historical circumstances in Rome," he argues,

> they do so in such a way as to extend to those circumstances the more general ethos Paul has encouraged in the preceding verses: an ethos of mutual accommodation and harmony within the ekklesia (12:3-13) and an ethic of nonretaliation and harmony toward enemies without (12:14-21). As Gordon Zerbe has shown, the wider context of Romans 12 and 13 involves the theme of nonrivalrous love (*agapē anypokritos*, 12:9) and the "apocalyptic conflict between the aeons of good and evil" (12:19-20; 13:11-13). (1994, 224, citing Zerbe 1992)[2]

"Within this context," Elliott continues,

> Paul's exhortation to be subordinate to the authorities (13:1-7) focuses the ethic of nonretaliation on a potentially volatile situation. Just as

Christians are to "live peaceably with all," leaving vindication to God (12:18-20) and thus to "overcome evil with good" (12:21), so they are to "do good" within the city (13:3), cooperating with the authorities as they "diligently pursue the same goal" (13:6). They are not to take the righting of wrongs into their own hands by opposing the present "disposition" (*diatagē*) of earthly power, since *God's redisposition of the powers is imminent anyway* (13:11-14). (1994, 224; emphasis original)

One must still, of course, contend with the fact that Paul claims that the governing authorities derive their legitimacy from God. But Elliott denies that these verses represent Paul's "evaluation of government in the abstract or government officials in particular." For he views them as "mere rhetorical commonplaces, meant only to focus the audience's attention on the discernment of 'the good' (compare 12:1-2), which finds expression in recognizing one's obligation to others (12:2-13)." He can therefore deny that the passage constitutes a "theology of the state," in any sense "beyond the conventional prophetic-apocalyptic affirmation that God disposes the rise and fall of empires and gives the power of the sword into the hands of the ruler (13:1, 4)" (1994, 223–24).

Together with Furnish's insights, Elliott's analysis is helpful in showing that Paul's intention in these verses is not to urge on his readers an uncritical loyalty to the empire or even to promote a sacralization of governmental power in general. One must say, nevertheless, that the rhetoric of the passage stands in some tension with the observations made earlier in this section about the revolutionary aspects of Paul's proclamation of the gospel. Whatever Paul's specific intentions, and however he would have correlated his thoughts here with that broader proclamation, it is not surprising that in later times Christians used them in ways that seriously compromised Paul's own message. So we must, in the end, identify these verses as the source of a question that will demand serious hermeneutical analysis later in this volume.

Paul and the Common Good

Emphasis on Paul's eschatological outlook and those aspects of his message that imply a subversive stance toward the empire can create the impression that he viewed his assemblies as heavenly colonies at odds with all social and political structures. And much of his language would seem to support such a reading. He could remind the Philippians that their "commonwealth is in heaven" (2:20) and characterize the purpose of Christ's self-giving as deliverance from "the present evil age" (Gal 1:4). His letters, in fact, are permeated with sharp distinctions between those in Christ and those outside, such as we find in 1 Cor 2:12: "Now we have received not the spirit of the world, but the Spirit that is from God, so that we may understand the gifts bestowed on us by God."

Despite this dualistic strain in Paul's language, however, Furnish finds aspects of Paul's letters that suggest a more congenial attitude toward the wider social environment. At some points, for example, Paul explicitly urges his readers to do good to "all"—that is, not only to those in Christ but to those outside the community. Thus, in 1 Thess 3:12 he can wish for his readers that God will make them "increase and bound in love for one another *and for all*," and in Gal 6:10 he can urge his readers to "work for the *good of all*, and especially for the family of faith." And an interesting aspect of the latter quotation is that in the first part of the sentence Paul qualifies his injunction with the phrase "*hōs kairon echomen.*" Although the NRSV translates this as "whenever we have opportunity," Furnish notes that the word *kairos* almost always has eschatological connotations for Paul and that he has in fact just used it in this way in v. 9 (NRSV: "at harvest time"; RSV: "in due season"). Thus, Paul's sense of Christ's imminent return results not in a disparagement of worldly action in the present time but in precisely the opposite. So in v. 10 he indicates that "precisely now, in this 'meanwhile' until the Lord's return, in this time that has been both graced and claimed by God's promise, believers are to be working for the good" (2005, 73–74).

Paul's concern for "all," moreover, is not confined to an interest in outsiders as individuals. The NRSV translates the verb *politeuesthai* in Phil 2:27 as "live your life" ("in a manner worthy of the gospel"), but Furnish notes that this reduces its meaning to an equivalent of *peripatein* ("walk"), which Paul frequently uses when enjoining his assemblies to proper conduct. Only here in all his letters, however, does Paul use *politeuesthai*, the core meaning of which is "to live as a citizen." Furnish therefore argues that Paul's use of the term is deliberate and "peculiarly appropriate in a letter to believers who resided in a Roman colony and were under pressure to be upstanding citizens." In addition, this term "coheres with the metaphor of a heavenly 'commonwealth' [*politeuma*: NRSV: citizenship], which Paul also employs in this letter (3:20)." Thus, "[b]y using a recognizably political term, the apostle is pointing specifically to the civic, political context in which believers are called to live in a way that is appropriate to the gospel they have embraced" (2005, 67).

It would seem, then, that any characterization of Paul's understanding of the communities' relation to the outside world as sectarian in an unqualified sense is inaccurate. And it is important to note that, as Furnish comments, "Paul has not chosen to describe believers as either 'resident aliens' (*paroikoi*) or "transients [sojourners]" (*parepidēmoi*) in Philippi, although these very metaphors are used of Israel in the Septuagint" and we do find such terms employed in this way in 1 Pet 2:11 and Heb 11:13; 13:14 (2005, 67–68). Although Paul's eschatological beliefs probably worked against the development of a social ethic in our modern sense, they apparently did not prevent him from expecting the members of his assemblies to have a sense of responsibility to work for the common good in the world beyond their borders.

SOCIAL DISTINCTIONS AND COMMUNITY IN CHRIST

In his dispute with those in Galatia who were attracted to the teaching of a missionary group claiming that (male) Gentiles who accept Christ must be circumcised, Paul draws a sharp contrast between faith and Law. Much of his argument is couched in juridical terms: it sets up a contrast between any attempt to gain justification before God through obedience to the demands of the Law and acceptance of justification as the free gift of God through Christ. At other points, however, Paul makes use of participationist language to make his point. Thus, in Gal 2:19 he speaks of his having "died to the law" and having been "crucified with Christ," so that "it is no longer I who live, but it is Christ who lives in me." Then, in 3:27-28, proclaiming that the coming of Christ put an end to the era in which the Law served as a disciplinarian, he uses similar language to characterize the new status and communal character of those who belong to Christ: "As many of you as were baptized into Christ have clothed yourself with Christ. There is no longer Jew or Greek, there is no longer slave or free, there is no longer male and female: for all of you are one in Christ Jesus." Here, most scholars acknowledge, Paul is probably drawing on an existing baptismal formula; but there is no doubt of its central importance to the argument he is making.

It is apparent, then, that the new status of those in Christ entails the transcendence of various traditional distinctions among persons. From the juridical perspective, the point is that the provision of a means of justification apart from the Law places Jews and Gentiles on the same footing before God. Circumcision is unnecessary because the Law, which requires it and into which it is an entrance rite, is no longer in effect. But Paul's participationist language reveals another aspect of the new life. It is existence within a new "force field," a foretaste of the fullness of the age to come, in which all human distinctions—not just Jew/Gentile, but even slave/free and male/female—are overcome.

The participationist language thus introduces an element into Paul's understanding of the nature of the community in Christ that is not strictly implied in his juridical logic. Justification by faith calls into question the privileged standing of the Jew over against the Gentile with respect to salvation, but it need not imply the obliteration of the other distinctions. Paul's insight therefore reaches beyond the question of access to God's grace and embraces a vision, based on his sense of the nature of the coming new age, that overcomes not only the alienation of humanity from God but also the various forms of alienation within the human community itself. And this line of reasoning, taken to its logical conclusion, implies a radical egalitarianism. As we will see, Paul is not always willing to accept the full implications of the formula he quotes in Gal 3:27-28; but, as we will also see, it does in many ways inform his thinking and give to his message a genuinely progressive flavor.

It is clear, above all, that Paul believes that *all* who are in Christ have equal standing before God. And this means that social status in the outside world must play no role within the assembly, as is evident in his ironical attack on spiritual pride in 1 Cor 1:25-29 that reverses conventional accounts of human worth:

> For God's foolishness is wiser than human wisdom, and God's weakness is stronger than human strength. Consider your own call, brothers and sisters: not many of you were wise by human standards, not many were powerful, not many were of noble birth. But God chose what is foolish in the world to shame the wise; God chose what is weak in the world to shame the strong; God chose what is low and despised in the world, things that are not, to reduce to nothing things that are, so that no one might boast in the presence of God.

Paul and Slavery

As the letter to Philemon shows, Paul took the phrase "no longer slave or free" in Gal 3:28 with full seriousness. Some critics see in Philemon an implicit acceptance of slavery, and it has indeed had a long history of use as a justification for that institution. The rhetoric of the letter reveals, however, that Paul understood the gospel as calling into question the notion that one person in Christ could hold another as slave. As Norman Petersen argues, Paul systematically confronts Philemon with a characterization of the community in Christ as based on a symbolic universe that stands over against the social system of the hierarchically ordered empire. By encircling Philemon with the familial language of community in Christ from the beginning, as well as by addressing the letter to the entire assembly that meets in Philemon's house, Paul challenges his reader to make a distinction between the values of the community and those of the world outside. As Petersen comments,

> In the world, Philemon and Onesimus [Philemon's slave] are related in terms of two unmediated hierarchical structures, those of master and slave and of debtee and debtor. Those relationships are, through Paul's letter, invaded by the church's ultimate mediation, the relationship between brothers, and brotherhood is anti-structurally opposed to the worldly social structures in such a way as to permit no other mediation, only a decision by Philemon as to which domain he is to occupy. (1985, 169)

Although he does not make a direct request for Onesimus's freedom, it is all but explicit in his suggestion that the slave was separated from him "so that you might have him back forever, no longer as a slave but more than a slave, a beloved brother—especially to me but how much more to you, both in the flesh and in the Lord" (vv. 15-16). And by speaking of the implied request as Philemon's duty (v. 8), Paul also indicates that refusal would be a denial of the bond that all parties involved have in Christ. Paul's letter, therefore, precipitates a crisis for Philemon. As Petersen states,

> Previously, he could be "in Christ" while still being and acting like the master of a slave "in the world." Now he finds that "being in Christ" makes a totalistic claim upon him from which there are no exceptions. *If he is to remain in the service of Christ the Lord, he cannot be "in Christ" only when he is "in church."* . . . Because they *are* in Christ, Onesimus cannot *be* both Philemon's slave and his brother, and Philemon cannot *be* both Onesimus's master and his brother. (1985, 269; emphasis original)

Beyond the specific issue of master-slave relationships within the assembly, it is also clear that Paul regarded slavery itself as a violation of the exclusive devotion owed to Christ. Thus, in 1 Cor 7:23 he issues this injunction: "You were bought with a price; do not become slaves of human masters." The verses preceding and following this statement, however, have led many commentators to think that because of his expectation of Christ's imminent return, Paul thought slaves should remain in servitude even if they had the opportunity for freedom. Paul does say in the first part of v. 21 that those who were enslaved at the time of their conversion should "not be concerned about it." And in v. 24, he makes the general statement, "In whatever condition you were called, brothers and sisters, there remain with God." Such a reading, moreover, seems on the surface to be consistent with his related injunctions in this context that have to do with circumcision (vv. 18-19) and marital status (vv. 25-39).

The problem is that this understanding of Paul's view rests on a particular interpretation of the ambiguous Greek wording in the second half of v. 21, reflected in the NRSV translation: "Even if you can gain your freedom, make use of your present condition now more than ever." However, the phrase "your present condition" is not actually in the Greek, and "even if" is not the only way of rendering the opening term *alla*. All we can be sure of is that the sentence says something like, "if you can gain your freedom, rather/all the more make use of. . . ." But make use of what? As Richard Horsley comments,

> The most obvious completion grammatically would be from the nearest substantive term, "freedom," with which the previous clause ends, and not "slave(ry)" from three clauses earlier in verse 21 or "call" from verse 20. In addition, the aorist tense of the verb "use (it)" suggests a single action (even if in the future) rather than the continuous action of "make use of." (1998, 102; see also Lull and Beardslee 2007, 68–70)

Thus the RSV, translating *alla* as "but," renders the sentence, "But if you can gain your freedom, avail yourself of the opportunity." The "but" at the beginning of the sentence, on this reading, indicates that Paul is making an exception to his general rule of "remain as you" are, which is hardly surprising, since in this chapter he has already made a number of exceptions to his general counsels (7:5, 9, 11a, 15, 28) (Horsley 1998, 102).

This reading of v. 21 seems more compatible not only with Paul's injunction against becoming slaves in v. 23 but also with his arguments in Philemon. It does not mean that Paul was inviting his readers to engage in overt social protests against slavery, but it does indicate that he saw it as incompatible with the worldview implied in an acceptance of Christ. When he tells his readers in v. 21 not to be concerned about their status as slaves, he is not approving the institution but only assuring them that their being in Christ transcends the limiting status they have in the world. The point is that their primary concern should be faithfulness to the gospel, not worldly rank or circumstance. Thus, as Paul Sampley summarizes the point of 7:17-24, "The common ground that all believers, no matter their social status or ethnicity, share is that they are now 'owned' by a new master, by Christ as their Lord" (2002, 881).

The Status and Role of Women in the Church

It is important, when characterizing Paul's views on women in the church, to take account of three factors: (1) the differences between the disputed and undisputed letters; (2) Paul's actual practices, as we can observe them in the undisputed letters, with regard to the acceptance of women in leadership roles; (3) the opinion of many scholars that some passages in the undisputed letters are interpolations by a later hand.

Nearly all of the passages in which "Paul" restricts the role of women or makes reference to their subordinate status occur in Colossians, Ephesians, 1 and 2 Timothy, and Titus—all disputed letters. As we will see, much that is in these writings stands in contradiction to what we can learn from the undisputed letters. Since this is particularly so when we pay attention to Paul's apparent practice with respect to leadership roles, I will begin with a review of passages in the undisputed letters that are relevant to this issue.

First, there are a number of references to women that imply their leadership and importance in general terms. In Rom 16:3-5, Paul mentions a woman named Prisca and her husband Aquila as having "worked with me in Christ Jesus," and his description of their work indicates that he considered it significant. His references to Prisca depart from Roman custom in two important ways. As he also does in 1 Cor 16:19, he writes of "the church in *their* house," whereas it would have been more in keeping with the current understanding of property and responsibility to have spoken of Aquila's house. Also, in both passages he mentions Prisca before her husband, whereas convention would have dictated the opposite (Furnish 1985, 105–6). In Phil 4:2-3, Paul refers to two women, Euodia and Syntyche, who, he says, "struggled beside me in the work of the gospel," and in 1 Cor 1:11 he mentions a woman named Chloe and "her people" in such a way as to imply a high degree of importance in her congregation.

The names of several other women whom Paul clearly recognizes as making important contributions to the propagation of the gospel appear in Romans 16. We also find in this chapter two instances in which he names women as holding specific offices that we would today clearly term "ministerial." The history of the translation and interpretation of both passages, however, shows how later interpreters all but erased their witness to the important roles women played in the Pauline congregations.

In Rom 16:1-2, Paul writes, "I commend to you Phoebe, a deacon (*diakonos*) of the church at Cenchreae, so that you may welcome her in the Lord as is fitting for the saints, and help her in whatever she may require from you, for she has been a *prostatis* of many and of myself as well." We do not know the exact nature of the office of "deacon" in Paul's assemblies. Although it is anachronistic to think of an ordained ministry at this early period, the position was undoubtedly one of considerable responsibility. The term *prostatis*, which Paul applies to Phoebe in v. 2, is rendered in the RSV as "helper" and in the NRSV as "benefactor." As Cobb and Lull comment, however,

> The term literally means "one who stands in front" and, in some contexts, it is applied to one who presides at meetings. In classical Greek literature, the word-group to which this word belongs refers to a person of "first rank," a "leader, presiding officer, or ruler," as well as a "protector" and "patron." If it has that meaning here, then Paul was saying that she was a person of higher rank than many in the community, including Paul himself. (2005, 184)

It is the great weight attached to the term *diakonos* that has led some translators to render it as "deaconess," suggesting "a specific order, of female church workers quite different from 'deacons,' which would not be invented for another three hundred years" (Wright 2002, 762). Alternatively, some translations render *diakonos* as "servant"—which is legitimate on one level, but which again reflects an inability or unwillingness to entertain the notion that a woman actually served in a formal leadership capacity.

Along similar lines, in Rom 16:7 Paul sends greeting to Andronicus and Junia, whom he names as "prominent among the apostles." Here, both the history of textual transmission and translation have conspired to obscure the apparent fact that Paul acknowledged a woman, Junia, as an apostle. Although the most reliable manuscripts have Junia, some variants substitute "Julian" in its place. And some translators have used the fact that the name appears in the accusative case, as Junian, to argue that it must be the accusative of a supposed male equivalent, Junias. We have no Greek manuscripts that attest such a male equivalent, however, and it is apparent once again that presuppositions about women's roles in the early church have created distortions in our reading of the texts.

Further evidence of a strong egalitarian element in Paul's thought is found in the remarkable way in which he balances his statements on women and men in his advice regarding marriage and marital relations in 1 Cor 7:1-16. To avoid immorality, he counsels, "each man should have his own wife and each woman her own husband" (v. 2). Each, moreover, should give to the other their "conjugal rights" because each "has authority" over the body of the other (vv. 3-4). Likewise, both husbands and wives are subject to "the Lord's" (that is, Jesus') prohibition of divorce (vv. 10-11), and both husbands and wives with unbelieving spouses get the same advice: do not divorce an unbelieving spouse who is willing to remain in the marriage (vv. 12-16).

Other passages, however, show that Paul's egalitarianism is incomplete, although his differentiation between men and women is not nearly as severe as some interpreters have claimed. In 1 Cor 11:2-16, he lays down different criteria for women and men regarding proper appearance during worship, and he uses language that seems to imply, in some sense, the subordination of women to men; and yet in the same passage we can also observe his efforts to maintain a sense of equality between males and females.

The issue at stake in this passage is whether women who pray or prophesy at a service of worship should have their heads covered. Traditional readings have assumed that Paul is counseling women to wear veils—a view reflected in the common translation of the verb *katakalyptesthai* as "to veil." It simply means "to cover one's head," however, and many recent scholars argue that Paul is not counseling women to wear veils but is asking them to keep their hair done up on top of their heads rather than letting it flow freely. If this is the case, then the reason for Paul's prohibition probably had to do with the sensuousness of flowing hair and the similarity of such practice to that of women in pagan cults (Schüssler Fiorenza 1984a, 226–30).

Whatever the specifics of the issue, Paul makes his case for women covering their heads by appealing first to theological principles (vv. 3-13) and then to what he considers an argument from nature (vv. 14-16). The theological argument begins with the assertion that "Christ is the head of every man, and the husband is the head of his wife, and God is the head of Christ" (v. 3). As some scholars have argued (for example, Furnish 1985, 98), this verse does not necessarily indicate a hierarchy of God-Christ-man-woman, since the Greek term *kephalē*, translated here as "head," can also mean "source" and therefore may not be a metaphor for a position of authority over another. Understood as "source," it would likely be a reference to Eve's creation from Adam's rib (Gen 2:21). There is still more than a hint of subordination even on this reading, however, and it is difficult, in any case, to deny that such a motif is at work in vv. 7-9: "For a man ought not to have his head veiled, since he is the image and reflection of God; but woman is the reflection of man. Indeed, man was not made from woman, but woman from man. Neither was man created for the sake of woman, but woman for the sake of man."

Precisely at this latter point, however, where Paul is in danger of undermining completely the egalitarianism of Gal 3:28, we find him wrestling with the issue by adding an important qualification: "Nevertheless, in the Lord woman is not independent of man or man independent of woman. For just as woman came from man, so man comes through woman" (v. 12). And we should be careful about reading too much into Paul's language about woman as the "reflection" of man in v. 7, since the Greek term (*doxa*) can also mean glory. Although the verse implies an important difference between male and female, it does not imply that the female is created any less in the image of God than is the male (Lull and Beardslee 2007, 99).

Although the theological aspect of Paul's argument dominates this passage, in vv. 14-15 he makes an appeal to nature. Along the way, he has argued for different criteria for men's and women's hairstyles by referring to the unacceptability of men praying with their heads covered and comparing women's praying with their heads uncovered to having their heads shaved. Now he makes explicit the logic behind these earlier verses: nature itself teaches that men should not wear long hair, whereas a woman's long hair "is her glory."

Interestingly, however, this is not Paul's final word on the matter. In v. 16, he rounds out the entire argument by making an altogether different point: "But if anyone is disposed to be contentious—we have no such custom, nor do the churches of God." His final appeal is therefore simply to custom, which is perhaps a sign that he has some sense of the tenuousness of the whole case he is trying to make—a case that stands in considerable tension with the phrase "no longer male and female" in Gal 3:28, as is underscored by his own backtracking in vv. 11-12.

If elements in 1 Cor 11:2-16 stand in tension with other aspects of Paul's thought, 1 Cor 14:33b-36 seems a blatant contradiction of those aspects. For according to the traditional interpretation, Paul prohibits women from speaking during worship. Ironically, however, his attempt to regulate women's appearance in 11:2-16 is clear testimony that he had no such policy, since his whole argument has to do with a woman's proper adornment precisely when she "*prays or prophesies*" (11:5)! And neither the prohibition of women's speech during worship nor the injunction that they should be subordinate and consult their husbands at home when they want to know something (14:33b-34a) can be reconciled with what we have seen above about his recognition of women as leaders. Can we seriously imagine that he expected Prisca to ask Aquila for instruction or that Phoebe the deacon and Junia the apostle could not play a public role in worship?

First Corinthians 14:33b-36, however, clearly prohibits women from speaking in church and demands their subordination. Many scholars have therefore argued that the passage is an interpolation by a later hand, which reflects the tendency found in the disputed Pauline letters to limit the roles assigned to women. And there is good reason to take this position, since if these verses were excised from the text, Paul's argument would flow freely from his statements on keeping proper order in worship by regulating both speaking in tongues and prophecies to his concluding remarks on worship in vv. 37-40. In addition, in some ancient manuscripts vv. 34-35 appear at the end of the chapter. One possible explanation for this is that some early copyists found their content inappropriate in their present context (Metzger 1994, 499).[3]

Some scholars are reluctant to accept a theory of interpolation without stronger manuscript evidence (that is, major manuscripts in which the passage is missing entirely), but the passage seems so completely out of line with what we know of Paul's thought from the other undisputed letters that it is extremely difficult to accept these verses as authentic. There is, however, another way of accounting for them, a theory recently revived by David Odell-Scott and supported with some rather commanding evidence. Many scholars have believed for some time that earlier in the letter Paul quotes slogans of persons in Corinth with whom he is arguing. Since ancient Greek did not have quotation marks, we must determine such instances from the rhetorical development of Paul's arguments themselves. For example, as the use of quotation marks for certain statements in the NRSV rendering of 6:12-13 indicates, it is widely accepted that here Paul is quoting the statements of those who argue that freedom from the Law gives them wide latitude in their behavior. Odell-Scott argues that Paul has made a similar move in 14:34-35. It is some in Corinth who are seeking to silence women, and Paul is disputing their point. Thus, in v. 36, after quoting their statements, he reacts with a firm rejection—a reading quite compatible with the RSV (rather than the NRSV) translation: "What? Did the word of God originate with you, or are you the only ones it has reached?" (Odell-Scott 1991, 184–92; also 1983 and 1987, passim).[4]

Whether this passage is an interpolation or a quotation that Paul refutes, we have good reason to reject the verses that silence women as a statement of Paul's. And without this passage, as long as we confine ourselves to the undisputed letters, the case for Paul as one who sought to limit the role of women in the churches simply collapses. This is not to say that he carried through the egalitari-anism of Gal 3:28 with full consistency, since he wavers on it in 1 Corinthians 11. But we can say with confidence that the primary thrust of Paul's ministry and thought was a significant deviation from the traditional understanding of women's roles in the ancient world. As we will see in our next chapter, however, some of those who followed Paul and claimed his heritage did not simply waver on the principle of "no longer male and female" but came close to undermining it altogether.

Paul and the Poor

We do not find in Paul's letters the emphasis on God's care for the poor that we do in the Jesus tradition, but his interest in economic justice within the com-munities is everywhere apparent. Not only is the collection for the poor in the Jerusalem assembly (Rom 15:26; Gal 2:10; 2 Cor 8:1—9:15) a major concern for him, but in various ways he demonstrates a strong sense of solidarity with those in the communities who were "the least" by conventional standards. In 1 Cor 1:26-28—a passage Neil Elliott names "the first Christian articulation of the preferential option for the poor"—Paul proclaims that "God chose what was weak in the world to shame the strong." And in that same letter he "criticizes the wealthier Corinthians for distorting the life of the community by celebrating their own material advantages as God given (4:6-11) and showing contempt for the poor in their ritual life" (11:21-22) (1994, 87–88). He also expresses a deep empathy for the poor and identification with them when he describes the social circumstances of the itinerant apostles: "To the present hour we are hungry and thirsty, we are poorly clothed and beaten and homeless, and we grow weary from the work of our own hands" (1 Cor 4:11).

PAUL AND HUMAN SEXUALITY

Sex, Marriage, and Divorce

Many people have criticized Paul for his supposedly negative attitude toward sex and marriage, often citing 1 Cor 7:1b as primary evidence: "It is well for a man not to touch a woman." This statement, however, is most likely another example of Paul's quotation of a slogan used by persons in Corinth. It is therefore mis-leading to take it as an indication of Paul's aversion to sex. And it is important to note that his entire discussion of issues pertaining to sex, marriage, and divorce follows on the first part of 7:1: "Now, concerning the matters about which you wrote. . . ." Thus, as Furnish observes, Paul's statements here are by no means "an essay on the Christian family," since the entire chapter "is addressed to a specific dispute about sex in Corinth" (1985, 45). In other words, Paul is treating only those aspects of sex and marriage that relate to the dispute in Corinth and not making a comprehensive statement.

The dispute about sex was rooted in a larger question that arose as the believers in Corinth made their own attempts to appropriate the gospel Paul had originally proclaimed to them. As Lull and Beardslee comment, both Paul and those he addresses in this chapter "believed that it was possible for life to be transformed radically," although "they differed on what that transformation was to be" (2007, 63). As we saw earlier, although Paul believed that the new age was partially present but that its fullness would come only with Christ's return, there were apparently some in Corinth who believed that they were already experiencing the power of that new age in its fullness. And this belief seems to have worked itself out in terms of two opposing views on moral questions. Whereas some thought they were free from moral restrictions altogether and tended toward libertinism (1 Cor 5:9-13; 6:12-20), others adopted the opposite position, believing that the new situation demanded asceticism. "It is above all the concern to correct the ascetic error," Furnish argues, "that moves Paul to write to the Corinthians as he does about marriage and divorce" (1985, 31).

It would be easy to understand Paul himself as an ascetic, since in vv. 7-8 he expresses the wish that all would remain unmarried. And his declaration that "it is better to marry than to be aflame with passion" (v. 9) is hardly a ringing celebration of either sexuality or marriage. However, Paul explicitly names his own preference for celibacy a gift that is not given to all (v. 7b-c). And the greater part of his discourse in 1 Corinthians 7 on sex in marriage is devoted to an injunction *against* celibacy *within* marriage except in the case of a mutual agreement for temporary abstinence for the sake of prayer. To be sure, his stated reason for rejecting this option is the same as his reason for permitting marriage in the first place: the avoidance of temptation (v. 5). But we get no hint in these verses that he considers sexual activity degrading. Nor should we interpret his wish that all had the gift of celibacy as an indication that he thought of the married state as morally inferior; for the broader context of his argument shows that a very different motive is at work.

This motive is rooted in Paul's belief that Christ's return was imminent. After his advice on sex and marriage, he turns to the question of divorce, addressing the general issue in vv. 10-11 and then the specific question of those married to unbelievers in vv. 12-16. In v. 17, he lays down a principle applicable to various questions concerning a change in status: "let each of you lead the life that the Lord has assigned, to which God has called you." Verses 18-24 then address the issues of circumcision and slavery under this rubric, and in the rest of the chapter he turns back to the question of marriage, this time supplying two reasons for his preference that the single remain unmarried: first, "the appointed time has grown short" (v. 29) and "the present time of this world is passing away" (v. 31); second, marriage brings with it anxieties (vv. 28, 32-35). The point is that with Christ's return so imminent, believers should avoid making any changes in circumstance that might divert attention from prayerful preparation. Thus, Paul counsels a kind of internal detachment from anything that might have the potential for distraction. This is the meaning of the injunction in v. 29, "let even those who have wives be as though they have none."

We should not, however, understand such injunctions as a call for total withdrawal from the world. "In none of these cases," Furnish comments,

> does Paul mean that the Christian should opt out of his or her worldly responsibilities. Earlier in this same letter, for example, he had chided the Corinthians for having mistakenly thought it was even possible to "go out of the world" (5:9-10). Therefore, Paul's meaning must be that no ultimate value is to be placed on worldly institutions or relationships. No mundane responsibility, however noble or important in this present age, should be allowed to make an *absolute* claim upon the Christians. The apostle is not denying the *importance* of the responsibilities worldly existence entails, but he is denying their *ultimacy*. (1985, 37; emphasis original)

While Paul gives us no eloquent passages celebrating the goodness of either sex or marriage, then, it is a distortion of his views to accuse him of disparaging either. As noted above, we should not take his reflections on specific questions as comprehensive statements. A devoted Jew such as Paul would almost certainly have accepted both sex and marriage as God's creation and gift; and in fact we find a tacit acknowledgment of this attitude in 1 Cor 7:38a: "So then, he who marries his fiancée does well. . . ." His fervent eschatological hope, however, gave him reason to view sex and marriage in the light of more pressing concerns— which explains why he adds in v. 38b, "and he who refrains from marriage will do better."

When Paul addresses in 7:12-16 the question of whether believers should separate from unbelieving spouses, he reveals other dimensions of an essentially positive view of marriage. In v. 14 he expresses the belief that both the children and the unbelieving spouse, whether husband or wife, are "made holy" through the believing partner. Here, as Sampley comments, Paul shows the reverse side of his point in 5:6-7 that the presence of an unholy person can infect an entire community: "In 7:14 Paul affirms a different, even reverse 'contagion,' but this time a positive one; sin and *porneia* have a corrosive potential; but sanctification—being claimed and set apart by God—also has a rub-off potential that bears on those around . . ." (2002, 877). In addition, these verses illustrate a point that Furnish finds implicit in Paul's whole discussion: his *"concern for the character of the relationship between husband and wife"* (1985, 46; emphasis original). After stating that "if the unbelieving partner separates, let it be so . . . the brother or sister is not bound," he gives this as a reason: "It is to peace that God has called you." In other words, in the specific case of a marriage with an unbeliever, although Paul clearly favors maintaining the relationship, he recognizes the destructiveness of trying to maintain a union that is rent by extreme discord.

On the other hand, Paul's preference for maintaining the relationship is consistent with 7:11, where he alludes to a saying of Jesus as his authority for prohibiting divorce. Just as 7:15 acknowledges that the unbelieving partner may demand a divorce, however, so also we find in 7:11, a statement translators generally place in parentheses, an acknowledgment that even within the community divorce may in fact happen: "but if she does separate, let her remain unmarried or else be reconciled to her husband." Although some commentators think that this part of the verse is an interpolation, there is no manuscript evidence to support this view (Furnish 1985, 41); and it seems inherently probable that such divorces did occur. Assuming the authenticity of the verse, then, Sampley makes the following observation:

> Quite strikingly, Paul acknowledges that believing behavior may sometimes go counter to an explicit teaching of Jesus. Unmistakably, Paul prefers adherence to Jesus' teaching, but equally beyond question he recognizes that . . . there may be times when women and men may need to divorce (see also 7:12-15) and that those who do divorce remain full participants in the fellowship of believers. (2002, 876)

If we can detect a slight equivocation in Paul's views on divorce, this is not the case when we come to certain matters of sexual behavior. In 1 Cor 6:13-20 he makes an impassioned denunciation of sex with prostitutes and fornication (see also 5:9, 13); and in 5:1-5 he passes a severe judgment against a man in Corinth who is "living with his father's wife." The phrase undoubtedly refers to the man's stepmother, but we have no way of knowing whether his father is still alive or whether, presuming his father's death, the son is now married to the woman. What we do know is that both Roman and Jewish law prohibited a son from marrying his stepmother (Lull and Beardslee 2007, 38), so that such a case would have been considered a form of incest. And we also know that Paul's reaction was one of utter shock and outrage, and such behavior would have merited expulsion from the community.

If the designation of a relationship between two persons not biologically related as incest seems strange from our perspective, this serves as a dramatic illustration of the radical difference in social contexts between our world and that of Paul. For, as L. William Countryman has shown, the Torah's prohibition of such a relationship is a function of a combination of purity laws and property rights. As we will see in more detail shortly, the concept of purity had to do with a sense of order, with each element in reality having its assigned roles. For a son to marry his father's wife was an act that incurred impurity because it entailed "an intolerable mixing of roles. An ideal son cannot be the father's sexual rival" (1988, 35). The primary reason for the condemnation of incest, however, had to do with an understanding of the wife as the husband's sexual property. The Torah defined incest not on the basis of "shared genetic endowment" but "as a violation of the intra-family hierarchy," which "was an expression of property relations, a way of exercising ownership over human property, whether slaves or children or wives . . ." (Countryman 1988, 159).

According to Countryman, then, Paul's concern about incest in 1 Corinthians 5 has to do with sexual property rights. Noting that Paul "did not use purity language from Leviticus by speaking of 'lying with' the father's wife," he disputes Jerome Neyrey's contention (1986, 38–42; also Conzelmann 1975, 98) that vv. 6-7, where Paul uses yeast as a metaphor for the way in which the incest infects the entire community, demonstrate a specific concern for purity. Against Countryman, I find it likely that the yeast metaphor does connote purity. However, the property issue is also at work, since the Greek infinitive in v. 1 (*echein*)—translated in the NRSV as "living with"—literally means "to have." The man's offense is thus a transgression of another's rights, specifically "of possessing one who belonged properly to another" (Countryman 1988, 198). And a clear indication that Paul understood sexual ethics partly in terms of property is found 1 Thess 4:3-8, where he couches his admonition against adultery by characterizing it as wronging one's brother—that is, as violating another man's sexual property rights (Countryman 1988, 105).

Homosexuality

No question is more central to the debates among segments of the church in recent decades than the issue of homosexuality, and Paul's letters are the focal point of the division. A few New Testament passages outside the undisputed letters sometimes come into play, as do some in the Hebrew Bible; but it is two passages in Paul that receive the most attention. Before discussing these passages, however, it is important to make seven preliminary points regarding homosexuality in the Greco-Roman world.

Homosexuality in the Greco-Roman World

1. Homosexual relationships of a particular type were widely known and accepted in Greco-Roman culture. This was the love of a man for a boy, known as pederasty. Furnish gives a helpful account of the nature and development of this phenomenon:

> Beginning in the sixth century B.C., homosexual love had a relatively prominent place in Greek social life. As several historians have noted, this coincided with the development of a commercial economy based on the institution of slavery and the use of money in business transactions. It coincided also with the increasingly subordinate role assigned to women in Greek society. Women had come to be valued only for their part in helping to ensure the continuation of the race. In this male-dominated society, even when the young female form became the model for beauty, the youthful male was regarded as embodying the ideal. Thus, the more a youth resembled a female, the more he was admired by older males, and the more he was to become the object of their erotic attentions. (1985, 58–59; see also Scroggs 1983, 29–43)

Although there were variations in the ages of the youth and the older male, Robin Scroggs finds two important constants in the nature of these relationships. First, "[w]hat does seem constant, no matter how much the typical age differential was modified in specific circumstances, is the acceptance of the roles of active and passive by the partners." Second, "[a]part from certain exceptions of an adult male prostitute who retains his passive (or perhaps also active) role well into adulthood and thus may service adults of his age, *I know of no suggestion in the texts that homosexual relationships existed between same-age adults*" (1983, 35; emphasis original). As we will see below, there was ancient testimony to same-age relationships between women, but Scroggs is apparently correct insofar as consciousness of male-male relationships are concerned.

A pederastic relationship—chosen voluntarily by both partners—was often part of a male youth's education. Also widespread, however, "were the various forms of slave prostitution, in which boys would be forced to provide sexual services for the masters or master's friends." In keeping with their "feminine" roles, they were sometimes castrated (Scroggs 1983, 38–39). Yet another type of pederasty, of which Scroggs takes special note, involved what he has termed the "effeminate call-boy": "By 'call-boy' I mean they were *free* (i.e., nonslave) youths, or adults, who sold themselves to individuals for purposes of providing sexual gratification. With 'effeminate' I use the most common description of such persons in the texts themselves" (1983, 40). Significantly, as is shown by many texts from the period, this particular variation of pederasty "was widely excoriated by Greco-Roman culture itself" (Scroggs 1983, 40).

2. There are no terms for "homosexual" or "homosexuality" in either Greek or Hebrew. Such terminology dates back only to the nineteenth century, and it is only since the mid-twentieth century that any English translations have used the term in rendering biblical words (Furnish 1985, 53–54).

3. The absence of the terms, however, does not necessarily mean—as is often claimed—that there was no awareness of the phenomenon of fixed sexual inclinations. Bernadette Brooten finds evidence of "the concept of a long-term or lifelong erotic orientation in ancient astrology and medicine" (1996, 3), and Robert Gagnon notes "considerable testimony in ancient sources to the belief that same-sex passions, at least in some cases, are congenital" (2001, 384).

4. Nevertheless, we do not know whether Paul himself was familiar with the notion of fixed inclinations, and other texts from the period seem to view homoerotic behavior as a simple choice. Paul's own attitude, therefore, is something that we must try to determine from the passages in his letters in which homoerotic sex is mentioned.

5. Although many scholars have prescinded from discussion of female homoeroticism on the grounds that we have insufficient sources from the period, Brooten has amassed a great deal of material that documents both the phenomenon itself and widespread awareness of it (1996, 29–286). Notable in this regard are references to marriages between women (1996, 107, 332–36), a fact that contrasts sharply with Scroggs's finding regarding male homoerotic relationships.

6. Brooten is also able to show that many writers on the subject of female homoeroticism regarded it with extreme horror and disgust. "Unlike the sources on male-male couplings, the ancient sources nearly uniformly condemn sexual love between women." On the other hand, these sources do "testify to a certain level of tolerance for such love, as in their reference to woman-woman marriage, since any kind of cohabitation requires at least a minimal social and economic support." Nevertheless, not only is the negative attitude overwhelmingly predominant, but the condemnations are striking in their severity (1996, 359).

7. We must therefore reckon with a discrepancy between opinions regarding male-male relationships on the one hand and female-female relationships on the other. And another of Brooten's findings goes a long way toward offering an explanation of this divergence. "Gender role transgression emerges as the single most central reason for the rejection of female romantic friendship." Operating on the assumption (which Brooten also attributes to Paul) "that a married woman was 'under a man,'" those who shaped ancient culture "saw homoerotic women as transgressing nature by experiencing pleasure while not under a man." Their point was that "such pleasure was against both nature and the divine will" (1996, 359).

Paul on Homoerotic Sex

Despite attempts to show the contrary, all biblical references to homoerotic sex are negative. Although the precise meaning of many passages remains a matter of debate, there can be little doubt that insofar as the Bible makes reference to homoerotic acts, its attitude is consistently one of rejection. Given the apparent unanimity of the biblical texts, then, for some Christians, the debate is essentially settled. To take this position, however, is to collapse the hermeneutical question into simple exegesis. First of all, it is to circumvent the question of the reasons for the biblical condemnations; and, second, it is to assume without question that biblical proscriptions are without exception applicable to our own time, without regard to the differences between the ancient world and our own or to the possible ways in which other sources of authority—most particularly reason and experience—might legitimately come into play. I will reserve a fuller discussion of these latter issues until chapter 12, although in this and the following section

I will give some indication of the direction of the later discussion. First, however, I turn to the two passages from the undisputed letters.

In 1 Cor 6:9, Paul lists among those who will not inherit the kingdom of God *malakoi* (pl. of *malakos*) and *arsenokoitai* (pl. of *arsenokoitēs*). The basic meaning of *malakos* is "soft," and *arsenokoitēs* is a combination of *arsēn* ("*male*") and *koitē* ("bed"). Translators have generally taken both these terms to refer in some way to persons who engage in same-sex relations. The RSV, for example, conflates the two terms into one as "sexual perverts"; the NRSV has "male prostitutes" and "sodomites," and the NIV has "male prostitutes" and "homosexual offenders." A recent view (Scroggs, Furnish, and others) is that the pairing of the two terms indicates that Paul had in mind relations between youthful male prostitutes, to whom was assigned the stereotypically subordinate/"female"/submissive role, and another male who assumed the stereotypically dominant/"male"/active role. If so, then Paul would have echoed the protests of a number of other Greco-Roman writers who condemned such practice.

Not all scholars are convinced of this reading, however. Gagnon, for example, denies that Paul here condemns only one specific type of same-sex relations. Among his reasons is the fact that Paul could easily have used the term *paiderastēs* if he wanted to refer only to pederasty; also, Gagnon argues, Paul's condemnation of the passive partner as well as the active undermines the notion that his concern was exploitation (2001, 329).

From a very different perspective, Dale Martin argues that we cannot be certain that either *malakos* or *arsenokoitēs* refers to persons who engage in homosexual practice. Noting that the meaning of a compound word is not necessarily equal to the sum of its parts, he cites numerous Greek texts in which the context of *arsenokoitēs* has rather different connotations. For example, in the case of a passage from the *Sibylline Oracles* (2.70–77), he argues that "*arsenokoitēs* here refers to some kind of economic exploitation, probably by sexual means: rape or sex by economic coercion, prostitution, pimping, or something of the sort" (1996, 120–21). Likewise with respect to *malakos*, Martin shows that it was used in a variety of ways and had a variety of connotations that ranged from persons with weak characters to those who "prettied themselves up" in search of sexual pursuits, whether to attract women or other men (1996, 125–26).

We must recognize, then, that the exact meanings of these terms remains uncertain. The sexual content of *arsenokoitēs* seems clear, however, and its pairing with *malakos* does make a reference to the (stereotypically) active and passive participants in male homoerotic sex plausible. It would, of course, appear problematic from our perspective for Paul to blame the victim, if certain forms of pederasty are in view here. This is less so, however, if we recognize that catalogs of vice or categories of immoral individuals such as we find in 1 Cor 6:9-10 were common in the Greco-Roman world and that Paul here, as elsewhere, is simply quoting existing tradition. Hans Conzelmann finds specific evidence of this in the fact that in this passage "the terms of expression (kingdom of god, inherit) are common Christian parlance, not specifically Pauline" (1975, 106).

It is also important to note the subject matter of Paul's wider discourse. The chapter begins with a challenge to members of the community who have taken other members to court to be judged by outsiders. In v. 1, Paul applies to the outside judges a term (*adikos*) that is usually translated "unrighteous" but can also mean "unjust," which would seem to be more apt in this case. His first point is that disputes should be settled by "the saints"—the community members themselves. In v. 7, however, he suggests that those in Christ should not bring lawsuits against one another at all, asking with great rhetorical force, "Why not rather be defrauded?" In v. 8, he ratchets up his rhetoric by expressing astonishment that members actually defraud one another; and only then does attach his list of those who will not inherit the kingdom. The function of his catalog of vices is thus to add force to his judgment against those who take others to court; and, as Alan C. Mitchell has argued, the former were probably more affluent members who sued poorer members to retrieve debts (1993). So if justice is an issue in the broader context, this gives some support to the contention that in 6:9 Paul has pederasty, a highly exploitative type of sexual activity, specifically in mind.

It is even more important to pay attention to Paul's broader rhetorical purpose when we come to Rom 1:26-27. These verses occur within Paul's attempt to show that all human beings "have sinned and fall short of the glory of God" (5:23), a logical correlate of his declaration that all are justified not by the works of the law but by "God's grace as a gift, through the redemption that is in Christ Jesus . . ." (5:24). Paul can hold Jews accountable for their sin, because they are the recipients of the Law (2:12-13, 17-29). However, he perceives the problem in holding accountable those who had no access to Israel's Law. He therefore begins his argument in v. 18 by proclaiming God's wrath against "*all* ungodliness and wickedness" and then asserting in v. 19 that "what can be known about God is plain to them, because God has shown it to them." Since this initial indictment includes "all" wrongdoing, in anticipation of the phrase "all have sinned" in 5:23, it includes the sins of all people. But the force of the argument that follows is precisely to include Gentiles in the indictment, even though Paul does not use the term.

Referring back to those who practiced ungodliness and wickedness, Paul asserts that since "they" had access to the knowledge of God's "eternal power and divine nature" through a type of revelation given in nature itself, "they are without excuse" (1:20). What remains is for him to name their sin specifically, and this he does in vv. 21-25. Although those outside the Law had knowledge of God, they "exchanged the glory of the immortal God for images resembling a mortal human being or four-footed animals or reptiles" (v. 23) and "served the creature rather than the Creator . . ." (v. 25). He names their sin, therefore, precisely as idolatry. Jewish members of the assembly would think of the sin of idolatry as peculiarly Gentile, but in 2:1-10 he turns the tables and accuses those who pronounce judgment on others of being guilty of the same sins. Then he is ready to declare in 2:11-12 that "God shows no partiality," since those "who have sinned apart from the law will also perish apart from the law," while those "who have sinned under the law will be judged by the law."

Between Paul's indictment of idolaters and his proclamation that all have sinned, he declares that God abandoned the idolaters by giving "them up in the lusts of their hearts to impurity" (v. 24), or "degrading passions" (v. 26a). Then follow vv. 26b-27, in which he illustrates this impurity and degrading passion with references to women who "exchanged natural intercourse for unnatural" and men who, "giving up natural intercourse with women, were consumed with passion for one another." Finally, in vv. 28-32 Paul completes his picture of human degeneracy by repeating the phrase "God gave them up," this time naming "a base mind" and "things that should not be done," then moving on to a list of specific vices, such as covetousness, murder, deceit, and craftiness. Clearly, then, Paul considers homoerotic acts not as the sin for which God punished sinners but as the punishment for prior sin. It is, in his mind, one aspect of the state to which God abandoned these persons guilty of the basic sin of idolatry. The function of 1:26-27 in this discourse is therefore not to name a particular sin, whether of "all" or of those outside the Law. It is to illustrate the working out of God's wrath, which was proclaimed in 1:18.

> Paul is not enumerating specific "sins" but listing some representative consequences of sin. Here it is evident that he shares several Hellenistic-Jewish ideas: that "one is punished by the very things by which one sins" (Wisd. Sol. 11:16), that the failure to acknowledge God leads to a fundamental "confusion" about right and wrong (e.g., Wisd. Sol. 14:26), and that sexual immorality is an especially telling symptom of this confusion (e.g., Wisd. Sol. 15:15-17). In short, humanity's refusal to let God be God sets "Murphy's Law" in operation; everything that can go wrong does go

wrong. Alienation from God brings the breakdown and de-formation of every other relationship. (Furnish 1994, 29)

Whether or not Paul had pederasty specifically in view in 1 Cor 6:9, in the Romans passage he accuses both women and men of "unnatural" acts. Although he does not specify these acts in the case of women,[5] the rhetorical parallel with his indictment of homoerotic male relationships in following verses suggests that he means to include same-sex relations as at least part of his accusation against women. And this would indicate that Paul condemns homoerotic sex in principle.

At this point, however, it is important to ask about Paul's reasons; and the first observation to make is that he gives none. In 1 Corinthians he simply includes *malakoi* and *arsenokoitai* in his catalog of sinners, and in Romans he presupposes the agreement of his readers as he uses the fact of homoerotic sex as a sign of sin. His condemnation is therefore based on an assumption and not a point that he makes through argumentation.

So why, then, did Paul reject homoerotic sexual relationships? Gagnon denies that the exploitative character of pederasty was Paul's primary motive (2001, 347–61). One may grant that this was probably not his primary motivation, since his condemnation seems to include other types of relationship. But this does not mean that the extremely negative images of certain types of pederasty did not contribute to Paul's attitude. Such a contribution would undoubtedly have functioned mostly as confirmation of what Paul already believed on other grounds, however, since the most likely source of Paul's views is his Jewish heritage.

There are clear condemnations of male homoerotic relationships in Lev 18:22 and 20:13, and later Jewish texts provide extensive argumentation against such relationships. In the latter, we find parallels to Paul's emphasis on "natural" vs. "unnatural," but in these texts explanations appear. Gagnon summarizes as follows:

First, they drew evidence from the unique capacity for procreation of heterosexual intercourse. Second, they understood the anatomical complementarity or fittedness of the male and female sex organs and the gender-transgressing feminization of the receptive homosexual partners as evidence of homoeroticism's misdirection. Criticisms of homoeroticism, third, as an excess of passion and, fourth, as a form of behavior that even animals have the sense to reject were ancillary to the primary arguments. (2001, 180–81)

The passages in Leviticus offer no similar explanations. However, a number of biblical scholars have found the insights of anthropologist Mary Douglas helpful in understanding the reasoning behind ancient Israel's purity regulations. What is apparently at work is a very tightly constructed sense of order in the universe, the violation of which would bring danger and confusion. Here Brooten summarizes Douglas's explanation of the logic of clean and unclean animals:

> Douglas takes a clue from the first Genesis creation narrative, noting that each type of animal has a form of locomotion proper to its kind: "two-legged fowls fly with wings" through the air; "scaly fish swim with fins" in the water; and "four-legged animals hop, jump or walk" on the earth. Animals that do not fit into these categories are unclean for human consumption. For example, four-footed animals that fly, such as insects (Lev. 11:20, 23), cross the boundary between two-legged animals that fly with wings and four-legged animals that hop, jump, or walk. Since insects' mode of locomotion does not conform to that of one of the delineated categories, insects are impure; touching their carcasses renders an Israelite impure (Lev. 11:24f.). (1996, 234, citing Douglas 2002, 55)

Brooten then goes on to claim that this delineation "fits ancient homoeroticism perfectly," for "homoerotically involved women do not conform to the class of women, since they take on the active sexual roles that many authors of the Roman period describe as unnatural or monstrous for women" (2001, 234). Although she refers here to Greco-Roman literature, the logical extension from the purity/impurity of animals to human sexuality holds for Leviticus as well. Also, Fernando Belo, drawing on another aspect of Douglas's theory, offers a slightly different but complementary explanation that focuses more directly on Leviticus 17–26, which contains prohibitions against cross-breeding of animals, wearing garments made of two kinds of material, and sowing more than one kind of seed in a field (1981, 19). The kinds of mixing here apparently threatened to disrupt the natural order and were therefore dangerous. Belo thus suggests that the logic that rejects homoeroticism involves an inversion of this sense of the incompatibility of diverse elements: "even comparable elements can be joined only if they are different" (1981, 38). And we can explain this latter point more fully by reference to the concepts of confusion of roles and the high pollution potential ascribed to women. As Countryman notes, the discrepancies between laws of purification for women and for men suggest that women are "a more virulent source of the contagion of impurity than men," an attitude that could have contributed to the rejection of both homoerotic acts and cross-dressing (Deut 22:5), "both of which seemed to confuse the purer male with the 'dirtier' female" (1988, 29–30).

If we take the suggestions of Brooten, Belo, and Countryman seriously, and if we add to them what Gagnon reports about Jewish writers' concerns about the anatomical compatibility of sex organs and "the gender-transgressing feminization of the receptive homosexual partners," we can come close to a comprehensive explanation of the logic of the rejection of homoeroticism in ancient Israel and early Judaism. It is rooted in an ancient sense of order that is essentially patriarchal in nature, presupposing sharply defined gender roles that impact the criteria for proper sexual behavior. Thus, as Brooten comments, what is wrong with homoeroticism is that "people are not maintaining clear gender polarity and complementarity" (2001, 235).

Although we cannot be certain that Paul had Leviticus specifically in mind when he wrote Romans 1, his use of the term "impurity" in 1:24 suggests that he did presuppose something like the sense of cosmic order just described. However, this does not mean, as Countryman has argued (1988, 109–23), that Paul viewed homoerotic activity as impurity but not sin. Not only was his inherited Jewish tradition rife with moral condemnation of it, but the clear implication of his terminology of "natural" versus "unnatural" is that homosexual acts are morally wrong. Although the notions of sin and impurity in ancient Israel were distinct concepts, there was also significant overlap; and Countryman himself acknowledges that "uncleanness is a kind of sin, but a recognizably distinct category of it" (1988, 23).

If we cannot point to Paul's use of purity terminology as evidence that he did not consider homosexual acts sinful, it nevertheless reveals an aspect of his presuppositions that cries out for hermeneutical reflection. It would seem that in this particular instance a traditional notion of impurity has been determinative in Paul's definition of what is sinful and what is not. And this has to raise, from our contemporary perspective, the issue of the extent to which Paul's views on this matter are tied up with a particular culture and the worldview it presupposes.

One remaining question about the logic behind Paul's assumption that homoeroticism is sinful is whether he had any sense of sexual orientation. Gagnon makes a great deal of the texts that attest an ancient awareness of fixed sexual identity in order to refute the argument that Paul, lacking any understanding of sexual orientation, tacitly assumed that all persons were heterosexual (2001, 380–95). As stated above, the texts do seem to indicate that some people acknowledged a fixed sexual identity, but they do not prove that such a recognition was widespread or that Paul himself was aware of such a concept. So the question is whether Romans 1 itself can give us help in this regard.

Furnish argues that Paul's use of the verbs "exchange" (*metallassō*) and "gave up" (*aphiēmi*) in vv. 25-27 to indicate a turn from "natural" to "unnatural" relations implies "a conscious decision to act in one way rather than another." He therefore concludes that Paul viewed homoerotic behavior as something "freely chosen" (1985, 73). Hays disputes this conclusion, however, on the grounds that Paul is thinking not of individuals but of humanity collectively:

> Paul is not describing the individual life histories of pagan sinners; not every pagan has first known the true God of Israel and then chosen to turn away into idolatry. When Paul writes, "they exchanged the truth of God for a lie," he is giving a global account of the universal fall of humanity. (1994, 9)

One may readily grant that Paul thinks collectively here. Since, as we have seen, he understood all humanity to be enslaved to sin, he could not regard sinful behavior, for those apart from Christ, as a simple matter of choice. Human enslavement to sin, however, does not mean a complete inability to choose, and it is necessary to recognize a paradoxical aspect of Paul's logic with respect to sin and freedom. Whether we think in terms of individual or humanity collectively, the whole point of Rom 1:19-32 is to document universal sin precisely by proving that the choice of idolatry was made in the face of a clear alternative presented in a kind of revelation in the natural world. If that is in tension with Paul's statements about the power of sin, this is a tension we will simply have to live with. Verses 25-27 do in fact seem to presuppose that both idolatry (v. 25) and homoerotic behavior (vv. 26-27) were in some measure matters of human choice.

In any case, as Dan Via argues, even if Paul "did in fact know about and believe in some kind of homosexual nature or orientation, he could not *with logical consistency* have said that homosexual practice was against nature" (Via and Gagnon 2003, 16). Gagnon disputes Via on this point, arguing that "even some of the Greco-Roman texts theorizing biological influence designated the activity as contrary to nature," so that "[n]ot everything *given by nature* is constituted *according to nature*" (Via and Gagnon 2003, 102; emphasis original). This distinction makes sense, however, only insofar as we consider so-called freaks of nature, which is certainly not what Paul had in mind in describing those whose actions he considered "unnatural." If Gagnon wants to claim that Paul believed in a given homosexual orientation but also condemned homoerotic acts, then he will have to argue that we must simply accept the paradox in Paul's thinking. To be sure, there is biblical precedent for paradoxes such as this. However, it is precisely such tensive elements in the texts that drive us to hermeneutical reflection that entails tracing out the logical implications of competing lines of reasoning.

A HINT OF COSMIC EMPATHY:
THE GROANING OF CREATION IN ROMANS 8:18-25

In another context, I have employed the phrase "cosmic empathy" to characterize an aspect of the prebiblical worldview: the presupposition of the organic inter-relatedness of all components of the natural world. "In this view, the universe is pervaded by feeling; what affects one part affects all others. Human beings, animals, trees, mountains, moon and stars—all alike participate in the same life-giving power" (Pregeant 1995, 45). Characteristic of biblical thought, however, is a partial break with this very ancient view. The development of the notion of a transcendent God who acts within human history was a step toward the demystification of nature. Thus, the typical emphasis in the mid-twentieth-century school of biblical theology on God's redemptive acts and the correlative deemphasis of creation motifs had some justification. However, the notion of God as creator remained as a strong theme alongside that of God as redeemer, and the break with cosmic empathy was in fact only partial. We can see this, for example, in the purity code and also in the way apocalyptic texts mark the transition from the old age to the new with descriptions of the empathic responses of the natural world such as we find in Joel 2:31: "The sun shall be turned to darkness, and the moon to blood, before the great and terrible day of the Lord comes" (see also Rev 6:12b-14).

In texts such as this, the motifs of creation, redemption, and cosmic empathy come together; and it is just such a blending that we find in Rom 8:18-25, where Paul contrasts the sufferings of the present time with the glory of the new age. Alluding to the curse on the ground in Gen 3:17-18, in Rom 8:21, Paul envisions the eventual release of creation from "its bondage to decay" and places it in direct correlation to the expected "freedom of the glory of the children of God." He can therefore depict creation itself as waiting "with eager longing for the revealing of the sons of God" and as "groaning in labor pains" (v. 22)—that is, experiencing the birth pangs of the age to come—and again make a connection to the experience of human beings, who also "groan inwardly" (v. 22) as they await redemption. In Robert Jewett's words, Paul thus uses language that "reflects an ancient view of the world as a living organism" (2007, 512). And this language is particularly striking in light of the way in which Paul usually contrasts the new being in Christ with humanity under the power of the present age. As Gerd Theissen comments, "Whereas elsewhere Paul always emphasizes the contradiction between nature and the new [person], here he uncovers a profound correspondence—a common longing that joins 'nature' and the Spirit" (1987, 333; quoted in Jewett 2007, 516).

In the midst of a discourse informed largely by apocalyptic categories, then, we find an intriguing hint of cosmic empathy within the natural world and an empathic relationship between human beings and other components of that world. And Jewett notes an equally intriguing relationship between the theme of cosmic empathy and Paul's sense of salvation history. Placing this passage in the missional context assumed by the letter to the Romans as a whole, he interprets "the revealing of the children of God" (v. 19) as containing "a clear reference to God's glory advancing the world, in this instance, through the advance of the gospel." And, reflecting upon the missional work expected of such persons, he goes on to relate their task to the problem of a natural world defaced by human sin:

> As the children of God are redeemed by the gospel, they begin to regain a rightful dominion over the created world (Gen 1:28-30; Ps 8:5-8); in more modern terms, their altered lifestyle and revised ethics begin to restore the ecological system that had been thrown out of balance by wrongdoing (1:18-32) and sin (Rom 5–7). (2007, 512)

On Jewett's reading, then, the passage not only suggests a strong sense of human relatedness to the natural world but also authorizes human action in defense of the integrity of creation. Of course, Paul could not have envisioned a corps of environmental activists in the modern sense. His thought remains thoroughly apocalyptic in character, so that the ultimate restoration of the universe comes through God's own action; and the task of the mission he envisions is to spread the gospel of Jesus Christ. But precisely by spreading this message, those who labor on Christ's behalf bring the people of the world under the aegis of God's rule, which means that God's dominion is in fact restored through the new communities they establish. And wherever that dominion is restored—wherever God's ultimate reign is proleptically established—the grand reconciliation that involves God, humanity, and the natural world is in process.

HERMENEUTICAL QUESTIONS

I have already mentioned two aspects of Paul's undisputed letters that call for hermeneutical reflection: (1) the tension between Paul's statement on the governing authorities in Romans 13 and aspects of his letters that imply that the gospel is inherently subversive of "the rulers of this age"; (2) the implicit reasoning behind his negative presuppositions regarding homosexual acts. To these I now add these additional points of tension: (3) Paul's inclusive attitude toward women versus his occasional departure from it; (4) Paul's apocalyptic outlook versus our contemporary worldview; (5) the hint of cosmic empathy in Romans 8 versus the disjunction between humanity and nature implied in other aspects of biblical thought, including Paul's; and (6) Paul's ethic of discernment, centered on the love command, versus his tendency to pronounce moral absolutes in some instances.

The first of these issues will necessitate bringing Paul into conversation with what we found earlier regarding the social ethic of the Jesus movement. It will also lead to further theological reflection not only on the question of the nature of the church and its relation to society but, more fundamentally, on how God relates to the world. In relation to the latter, moreover, it will overlap with the question of how Christians in our time can appreciate apocalyptic thinking—a question I have raised at several points already. Attention to the problem of apocalypticism will also relate to the question of how to value the sparse hints of ecological thinking in the New Testament, and the ambivalence in Paul's attitude toward women will foster reflection on both the divine nature and God's relationship to the world.

The second and sixth issues, which I consider the most crucial for appropriating Paul's ethics in our contemporary situation, call for more comment at this point. I begin with the second, which is narrower in scope but which leads naturally into the sixth. If I am correct in arguing that Paul's negative attitude toward homosexual acts is rooted in thinking tied to a worldview that presupposes both a specific sense of order that underlies the purity code and a hierarchical understanding of sexual property rights, then we are forced to ask whether we must also accept these presuppositions in order to appropriate Paul's message. If we answer yes, then are we prepared to appropriate all the laws in Leviticus? And, if we are not, what is our principle of selection, and how do we meet the challenge posed by Kathryn Greene-McCreight's statement on the issue?

If we are to argue for an interpretation which contradicts that of the tradition, we must make a move analogous to that of the tradition. It will therefore not be adequate to sweep aside an item within the "Holiness Code" on the basis that Christ has set us free from the burdensome old yoke of Torah. This is the antinomian danger of a flat-footed relating of the covenant. Far more pernicious and pervasive, however, is a modernist version of this: Israel's law is ancient; we are moderns; and no self-respecting person in his or her right mind would follow those ridiculous laws. This is ethnocentric, theologically suspect, and borders on anti-Semitism. If one finds the traditional venue for reinterpreting Old Testament law unacceptable, one must find another venue which at least allows for the integrity of the Old Testament witness. (2000, 250–51)

Part of what is at stake in our attempt to deal with these issues is the question that occupied so much of mid-twentieth-century theology: if we are to speak of the Bible as the vehicle of God's revelation, what is it that is *revealed* in this revelation? With respect to the issue at hand, it is necessary to ask whether and to what extent a loyalty to the Bible entails acceptance of the specific cultural patterns that are presupposed in its various witnesses.

The final issue is how we can understand the relationship between Paul's ethic of discernment/love to the passages in which he presents (whether explicitly or implicitly) moral absolutes. From one perspective, we might say that the absolutes simply define the boundaries of discernment. Both a discernment ethic and the love principle, however, point to a deeper insight, which has to do with the ongoing, open-ended character of human experience. Consideration of the open-endedness of experience, moreover, brings us back to reflection on the divine nature, God's relationship to the world, and the meaning of revelation. The question is whether and in what sense *specific* moral absolutes are possible once one recognizes the historicity of human existence and the relationship between such absolutes and the cultural contexts in which they were formulated.

CHAPTER 10

the post-pauline letters

—⊙—

In this chapter, I have adopted the term *post-Pauline* as a broad designation for a diverse group of writings that likely appeared after Paul's lifetime. Most have some connection to the Pauline tradition. Those I treat as Deuteropauline—Ephesians, Colossians, and the Pastoral Letters (1 and 2 Timothy and Titus)—all bear Paul's name but are widely considered pseudonymous. First Peter, which bears marks of a period late in the century, is often considered a product of the Pauline school. The same is true of Hebrews, the text of which mentions no author; some early church leaders believed Paul to be the author, but its thought world differs significantly from that of Paul. The letter of James, on the other hand, seems in some ways a reaction against a particular understanding of Paul's theology. Second Thessalonians, which I also consider Deuteropauline, is a special case among the letters attributed to Paul, because the evidence for pseudonymity is quite different and much less certain than is the case with other disputed letters. Because neither it nor Jude or 2 Peter contains anything that would add substantially to our understanding of New Testament ethics, I will confine my treatment of them to brief comments that have some bearing on the general purpose of this book; and I will consider only selected aspects of 1 Peter, Hebrews, and James.

THE DEUTEROPAULINE LETTERS

Hays makes an important observation in his treatment of the Deuteropauline letters (although he considers Colossians to be authentic):

Even if Paul is the author of these letters, their portrayal of the church and of the faithful Christian life diverges so significantly from the picture

263

drawn by the other letters that they would in any case demand separate consideration, perhaps as the vision of the "late Paul" as opposed to the "early Paul" of Galatians, the Corinthian correspondence, and Romans. (1996, 61)

From my own perspective, I could have chosen to treat aspects of the Deutero-Pauline letters as undercurrents within the mainstream of the Pauline corpus as a whole. Nevertheless, I find it important to treat the Deuteropaulines separately, partly to preserve Paul's distinctive voice. There is, however, no a priori reason that we should regard Paul's views as more authoritative than any others in the canon. Thus, another consideration is of even greater importance. Although it is no more my intention than it is Hays's (1996, 9, 14) to write a history of New Testament ethics, I believe that awareness of the trajectories of development have some bearing on hermeneutical questions. As will become clear below, in the Deuteropauline letters we can observe the Pauline assemblies at two different stages of development; and to speak of a trajectory is different from speaking merely of two competing voices. For awareness of developments in the Pauline tradition raises the question as to whether they represent a salutary extension of Paul's thought into new times and places or are, at least in some measure, betrayals of Paul's authentic legacy. I therefore begin my analysis with a brief statement of the arguments for pseudonymity.

The Case for Pseudonymity

Some scholars accept the Pauline authorship of some or all of these writings, but in many instances their reasoning involves special pleading—accepting explanations for the ways in which these letters diverge from the undisputed letters that carry weight only to someone with a strong bias in favor of authenticity and demanding a level of proof seldom attainable in historical study.

The arguments for the pseudonymity of the Pastorals are overwhelming. They presuppose a period in the development of Christianity later than Paul's lifetime, when leadership in the communities has become more formalized. We can see this in the discussions of the qualifications for specific offices (1 Tim 3:1-13; Titus 1:9) as well as in a reference to ordination (1 Tim 4:14). We can see it also in the use of terminology, not found in the undisputed letters, that is characteristic of second-century Christianity, along with the extensive use of such Hellenistic forms of presentation as philosophical maxims and household codes. Likewise significant are shifts in the meaning of *faith* from a dynamic appropriation of God's mode of life-orientation to a body of doctrine and the absence of key elements of Paul's thought—the designation of Christ as "son," the formula "in Christ," and emphasis on the cross. In addition, these letters are "clearly documented only in later sources" and are missing from many important manuscripts (Boring and Craddock 2004, 655). And, finally,

> It is difficult to understand the letters as appropriate communications from an actual Paul to a historical Timothy and Titus. They were seasoned missionaries . . . but are addressed as young and inexperienced. It is also difficult to understand such elementary instruction given in letter form from a Paul who is only temporarily absent, but who had already spent an extensive amount of time with them. (Boring and Craddock 2004, 656)

Colossians and Ephesians also manifest significant variations in vocabulary, but more important is the inclusion of lengthy and cumbersome sentences highly uncharacteristic of the undisputed letters. And although both letters retain Paul's basic theological foundations, there are significant departures. They compromise Paul's careful distinction between justification as something available in the present and salvation as something attained only in the future, and they revise Paul's image of the *ekklēsia* (assembly/church) as Christ's body by making Christ the "head" of the body. Neither letter, moreover, conveys any sense of the imminence of Christ's return—an important theme in the undisputed letters. Also uncharacteristic of the undisputed letters is the use of the phrase "forgiveness of sins/trespasses" (Eph 1:7; Col 1:14), which stands in some tension with Paul's language about freedom from the power of sin.

Ephesians, moreover, gives evidence of a later period with its terminology regarding the apostles as the foundation of the church (2:20) and the reverential reference to "the *holy* apostles and prophets." And part of the reason Colossians and Ephesians are so similar is that the author of Ephesians has apparently drawn heavily on Colossians, something it is difficult to imagine Paul himself doing.

The arguments for the pseudonymity of Colossians are generally considered weaker than is the case with Ephesians and the Pastorals, but when we add one final observation that applies to all these writings, the cumulative case becomes very strong. All depart significantly from the undisputed letters with respect to the status and role of women; and in all cases this particular departure is accompanied by a general weakening of Paul's egalitarianism. The particular form that the departure from the undisputed letters takes with respect to women is, moreover, significant in its own right. Citing Max Weber's observation that the death of a charismatic leader can foster efforts on the part of the leader's "staff" to insure a community's survival, Margaret Y. MacDonald proposes that the "household code" in Col 3:18—4:1 shows that the writer is speaking to just such a crisis (2000, 7–8). This code is unparalleled in the undisputed letters but mirrors similar codes in the broader culture in defining the obligations of persons in various social roles. Thus, although many scholars have argued that there are no signs of a late date for the composition of Colossians, there is a strong likelihood that it was written after Paul's death.

The Social Development of the Pauline Assemblies

In line with the observation just made, Margaret MacDonald has suggested a model based on social-scientific insights for understanding the developments within the Pauline communities. On this model, Paul himself functioned as a charismatic leader who fostered a limited degree of the formalization of leadership. MacDonald terms this stage of development, which is a first step beyond the initial Jesus movement, "community building institutionalization" (1988, 17).

The death of a charismatic leader, however, can produce a crisis that leads to a second stage of institutional development, since the community will likely be threatened by the emergence of competing interpretations of the leader's teachings. Colossians represents an initial attempt to come to terms with Paul's death, and "the household code is an integral part of the author's response to a type of false teaching that threatens to undermine tenuous relations with the outside world." Ephesians, which draws heavily on it, represents a later effort along similar lines that "reveals a stronger introversionist sectarian response than the other Pauline epistles, including Colossians." Thus, "[b]ecause of a perceived threat by "spiritual powers that shape the outside world," the author urges believers "to set themselves apart from those around them as saints (holy ones)—in essence to turn into the church and away from the non-believing world" (M. MacDonald 2000, 8, 21). Despite this difference, however, Colossians and Ephesians belong to the same general stage of community development, which MacDonald terms "community stabilization institutionalization." And the Pastoral Letters constitute a third stage, which she names "community-protecting institutionalization," in which "[t]he severe threat posed by false teaching results in more radical transformation of the symbolic universe" (2000, 18).

The institutionalization of leadership is therefore in part a response to threats posed by what are perceived as false teachings within the community and corrupting forces from outside. MacDonald also draws on her social-scientific model to suggest another motivation that she considers even more determinative: the interests of the leadership "staff" to maintain their own positions and power (2000, 13). However we might weigh the relative influence of these two factors, it seems undeniable that on the one hand the texts themselves attest the interest in maintaining sound teaching and strong community boundaries, while history attests the consolidation of power in an increasingly institutionalized and hierarchical pattern of leadership. And although the ethical norms that arise in the course of this development must be judged on their own merits, this insight gives us a perspective that could legitimately come into play in our reflections on hermeneutical questions.

Colossians and Ephesians

The basic structure of Paul's theological and ethical reflections remains intact in Colossians and Ephesians to the extent that they retain his correlation of indicative and imperative: God's raising of Jesus from the dead has placed believers in a new situation that both demands and enables ethical action. In Col 3:1-6, for example, we read, "So if you have been raised with Christ, seek the things that are above, where Christ is. . . . Put to death, therefore, whatever in you is earthly: fornication, impurity, passion, evil desire, and greed (which is idolatry)." And Ephesians first addresses the readers as those who, although once "dead through trespasses and sins" (2:1) have now been saved by grace and raised up" (2:4-9), and then includes them, with a moral twist, in this ringing celebration of the new life: "For we are what he has made us, created in Christ Jesus for good works, which God prepared beforehand to be our way of life" (2:10).

In addition to this basic theological structure, both letters include an element of Paul's emphasis on spiritual discernment in their approach to ethical behavior. As Wolfgang Schrage comments,

In view of the increased importance attached to the apostle, as well as to apostolic teaching and tradition, it is surprising that, like Paul, Colossians and Ephesians often enjoin the reader explicitly to test the divine will. Colossians 1:9-10 prays that the recipients of the letter may be filled with the knowledge of God's will "in all spiritual wisdom and understanding," that they may lead lives worthy of the Lord and bear fruit in every good work. Here again the argument moves in a single direction: from knowledge, through reason renewed by the Spirit (cf. also Eph. 4:23), to action. (1988, 246–47)

Particularly worthy of mention in this regard is Eph 5:10: "Try to find out [*dokimazein*, the same word used in Rom 12:2] what is pleasing to the Lord."

As Frank Matera notes, both letters also "repeat important Pauline themes . . . such as the moral implications of being God's people, the communal aspect of morality, the centrality of love, and the example provided by Christ's own life." He therefore finds that "Colossians and Ephesians represent an organic development of the Pauline tradition" (1996, 208), and Schrage similarly concludes that "by no means are they a sellout of the Pauline heritage," adding that "[b]oth in theology and in ethics, the two letters are fully on a level with the heights of genuinely Pauline thought" (1988, 244). It will be important, as we look more closely at these writings, to ask whether these judgments are fully justified.

The Argument in Colossians

In a lengthy thanksgiving in 1:3-14, the author of Colossians declares that God "has rescued us from the power of darkness and transferred us into the kingdom of his beloved Son" and then goes on in vv. 15-20 to quote a hymn celebrating Christ's sovereignty over all cosmic powers. This sets the stage for an attempt in 2:8-20 to combat a teaching that apparently demanded specific regulations regarding food and calendrical observances: "Therefore do not let anyone condemn you in matters of food and drink or of observing festivals, new moons, or Sabbaths." The logic of the appeal is that such observances entailed some sort of obeisance to cosmic powers, but that this is unnecessary, because Christ is sovereign over these powers and has in fact triumphed over them (2:15).

From the beginning, the ethical ideal of love is evident. In 1:3, the author praises the recipients' "love for all the saints." And in 1:8 and 2:2 we find references to their "love in the Spirit" and the author's wish for the hearts of the believers in Laodicea "to be encouraged and united in love." In chapter 3, the author engages more explicitly in moral instruction, condemning typical vices and exalting love as the hallmark of community solidarity: "Above all, clothe yourselves with love, which binds everything together in perfect harmony" (3:14). Verses 10-11 stress the indicative that supports the imperatives, concluding with a modulation of Gal 3:28: "In that renewal there is no longer Greek and Jew, circumcised and uncircumcised, barbarian, Scythian, slave and free; but Christ is all and in all." Although this formulation expresses the unity of all in Christ, as does the Galatians passage, the final phrase, by emphasizing the sovereignty of Christ, creates a more explicit link to the earlier discussion of the defeated cosmic powers. The unity theme nevertheless remains and is even strengthened by the addition of "barbarian" and "Scythian" to the list, since the Greeks considered "barbarians," or non-Greeks, uncivilized and Scythians "the lowest kind of Barbarians" (Lincoln 2000, 644). Interestingly, however, Paul's "not male and female" has disappeared in Col 3:11, and, more importantly, the "household code" in 3:18—4:1—with which the author brings the moral instruction to a climax—introduces important qualifications to the theme of unity in Christ. I will delay comment on this passage, however, until after a preliminary discussion of Ephesians.

The Argument in Ephesians

Although Ephesians makes passing reference to the dangers of false teachings (4:14), it shows no evidence of a specific theological controversy such as we find in Colossians; and the absence of a destination in some manuscripts suggests that it was a circular letter originally intended for a number of churches. According to Matera's analysis, it consists of two parts. "The first (1:3—3:21) . . . recalls and celebrates the divine election of the addressees," while the remainder is an exhortation "intended to persuade the addressees to conduct themselves in accordance with their elected status" (1996, 215). This letter is distinctive in its highly developed theology of the church as a unified body, founded on the witness of the apostles, that completes God's plan for a new humanity by bringing Jew and Gentile together (2:11-22) and functions as an organic community.

The ethical content of the letter is intimately related to the ecclesiology. The unity of all members in Christ is the grounding for the fundamental virtue of love, which is the motivation both for the truthfulness with one another that opposes false teaching and for the mutual care that builds up the community: "But speaking the truth in love, we must grow up in every way into him who is the head, into Christ, from whom the whole body, joined and knit together by every ligament with which it is equipped, as each part is working properly, promotes the body's growth in building itself up in love" (5:16).

The series of exhortations in 4:17-20, which warn against typical vices, is interspersed with references to community solidarity and love (4:29, 32; 5:2). And near its conclusion the author adds an injunction to "be filled with the Spirit" (5:18) as a direct antidote to the "unfruitful works of darkness" (5:11) that have been enumerated at length. Following all this, the author injects a household code in 5:21—6:9 before continuing with an appeal to "put on the whole armor of God" in 6:10-18 and final words in 6:18-23.

Indicative and Imperative

It should be apparent that both Colossians and Ephesians do in fact preserve Paul's union of indicative and imperative and his sense of the importance of community. They also present love as the primary virtue and hallmark of existence in Christ and make room for discernment in ethical decision making. There is therefore some reason to conclude, with Matera and Schrage, that they represent a faithful adaptation of Paul's thought to new circumstances. This judgment, however, stands in need of serious qualification in light of the household codes.

The Household Codes in Colossians and Ephesians

Although the specific background of the New Testament household codes has been the subject of debate, David Balch (1981) has argued that the theme of "household management" found in Greco-Roman writings is a direct antecedent. And Margaret MacDonald (1988, 106) cites the following passage from Aristotle that discusses the relationships that make up a household "under the rubrics of ruling and being ruled," as the most important parallel to the New Testament codes:

> Hence there are by nature various classes of rulers and ruled. For the free rules the slave, the male the female, and the man the child in a different way. And all possess the various parts of the soul, but possess them in different ways; for the slave has not got the deliberative part at all, and the female has it, but without full authority, and the child has it, but in an undeveloped form. (Aristotle, *Politics* I 1260a 9–14)

MacDonald goes on to note that New Testament codes are closely parallel to Aristotle's delineation by virtue of "the presence of the three pairs of relationships: wives/husbands, children/parents and slaves/masters" and the fact that "in both cases the pairs are treated expressly as relationships of superiors to subordinates" (1988, 106).

The theme of ruling/being ruled is clear in Col 3:18—4:1: wives should be subject to their husbands, children should obey their parents "in everything," and slaves should obey their masters. These standard themes have, however, been adapted to the ethos of the communities in Christ. It is distinctive as over against the Greco-Roman parallels that not only the dominant members of the pairs but also the subordinate "are treated as moral agents" and "as equally accountable in the Lord" (Lincoln 2000, 654). The emphasis on the superiors' authority, moreover, is tempered by reciprocal injunctions: husbands should love their wives and not treat them harshly, fathers should not provoke their children, and masters should not mistreat their slaves. And, finally, the entire code is given explicit theological foundation. Children's obedience is their "duty in the Lord," that of slaves is linked to "fearing the Lord," and masters are reminded that they "also have a Master in heaven."

The exhortations to slaves are the lengthiest. Verses 23-24 elaborate on the basic injunction, urging wholeheartedness in the performance of duties and promising both an inheritance from Christ for the slave and retribution for wrongdoing, the latter of which may have served as a warning not only to the slave but also to the master (Lincoln 2000, 658).

The code in Ephesians 5:22—6:9 elaborates on the themes in Colossians. In 5:21, the author provides a preface, although it is unclear whether it applies only to the wife-husband section or to the whole code: "Be subject to one another out of reverence for Christ." Either way, it introduces a note of mutuality that sets the general tone for what follows.

What follows immediately, however, in some ways strengthens the distinction between male and female roles, so that the mutuality is more explicitly defined within the limits of a patriarchal social structure. Verse 23 declares the husband to be the head of the wife. This echoes 1 Cor 11:2, but goes beyond it in making her subject to him in all things. This verse also replaces Paul's accounting of the God-Christ-husband-wife relationships with an analogy between the subordination of the church to Christ and the wife's subordination to her husband. Interestingly, the author expands the injunctions to the husband even more profusely (vv. 25-28), drawing on the motif of Christ's sacrifice for the church as a model for the husband's love for his wife and elaborating at great length on the nurturing quality of such love. The net effects of this elaboration are a much more positive evaluation of the institution of marriage than is found anywhere in the undisputed letters, a brief reiteration of the strong doctrine of the church presented earlier (esp. 2:11-21; 2:5, 10, 21; 4:1-16), and a strengthening of the patriarchal theme.

The patriarchal character of moral instruction is thus more pronounced in Ephesians than in Colossians, but it is undeniably present in both, and it is considerably stronger than in the undisputed letters. And although, as we saw, the addition of "Scythians" in Col 3:11 to Paul's formula strengthened the theme of inclusiveness, the attachment of the household has the effect of circumscribing the concrete forms that inclusive love can take. In both Colossians and Ephesians, Paul's emphasis on love survives, but it is now defined explicitly within the limits of a patriarchal social structure. We may therefore say that in a profound sense the term *love* takes on a rather different meaning in these writings than it has in the undisputed letters.

Hays (1996, 65) aptly applies the term "love patriarchalism" (used by Theissen 1982, 107 and Schüssler Fiorenza 1984b, 218) to the ethos of these codes. Margaret MacDonald uses it also of the Paul of the undisputed letters (1988, 43). As we saw in the preceding chapter, however, Paul has departed in significant ways from the patriarchal ideology, while in Colossians and Ephesians we see a reversion to elements of it. This is not to deny that the explicitly christological grounding of the codes gives them a twist that cuts against the grain of the traditional social order. Hays is perfectly justified in these observations regarding Ephesians:

> When masters are told to stop threatening their slaves because "you have the same Master in heaven, and with him there is no partiality" (6:9), a theological image is invoked that unsettles the conventional patterns of master-slave relations. Similarly, if marriage is a metaphor for the relationship between Christ and the church, the exalted ecclesiology of Ephesians must deconstruct static patriarchal notions of marriage. (1996, 65)

Granted these qualifications, however, we must still say that both letters depart from Paul by strengthening the patriarchal sanction for social roles. If we see in the Jesus movement and the authentic letters of Paul glimpses of a challenge to ancient patterns of subordination, in Colossians and Ephesians we find the beginnings of a reaccommodation to those patterns. Neither letter constitutes a complete betrayal of Paul, and both in some ways continue his legacy by applying it to a new situation. But in some important ways both dull the edges of the blade with which he cut against social convention in the name of oneness in Christ.

Ephesians 3:10: The Church's Witness in the "Heavenly Places"

I considered in the preceding chapter Walter Wink's contention that when Paul mentioned the various "powers" that control the present age, he had in mind earthly governments and structures of authority as manifestations of cosmic forces. Similar language about "the powers" appears in Eph 3:10, where the author writes of the church's witness "to the ruler and authorities in the heavenly places." The use of the term "the heavenly places" or "the heavenlies" (*ta epourania*) here and elsewhere in Ephesians is distinctive, however, and its meaning is not immediately apparent. If it were simply a synonym for "heaven," it is unclear just what would be meant by the church's witness. But it does not in fact seem simply to be a reference to heaven. In 1:3, we read that God has blessed the church "with every spiritual blessing in the heavenly places," and in 2:6 the author informs the readers that God has already "raised us up with [Christ] and seated us with him in the heavenly places." Thus, Wink concludes that "we must think of 'the heavenlies' as a dimension of reality into which believers already while on earth have been admitted yet in which unredeemed powers still exercise dominion and must be fought with, preached to, and made to know the manifold wisdom of God" (1984, 89). The role of the church in relation to "the powers" is therefore to convert them. Created good, but now fallen, they have the potential to become once again part of God's cosmic rule.

If "the powers" still exercise dominion, however, we must clarify an important aspect of the theological differences between the undisputed letters and Colossians and Ephesians: the claim in the latter two that the cross has *already* defeated these powers. In Eph 1:22, we read that God "*has put* all things under [Christ's] feet and has made him the head over all things. . . ." And in Col 2:15, the author states that "[God] disarmed the rulers and authorities and made a public example of them, triumphing over them in it." Paul, too, can speak of the cross as in some sense a victory, but he is clear that the *final* victory is yet to come. This is evident, above all, in 1 Cor 15:20-30. Although the powers have been in some sense subjected to Christ already, he must nevertheless still "reign until he has put all enemies under his feet" (v. 25). It would thus appear that the difference is only partial, at least with respect to Ephesians.

Nevertheless, an important difference between Eph 3:10 and Paul's view of the powers in the undisputed letters remains, for Neil Elliott has argued convincingly that it is wrong to attribute to Paul himself the notion that the role of the church is to rehabilitate the powers. Not only do they remain in active opposition to God, but Paul in no way speaks of their conversion or rehabilitation but only "of their defeat" (Elliott 1994, 122). We must reckon, then, with an important difference between the authentic letters and Colossians and Ephesians on the nature of the church's calling with respect to worldly authorities.

Christ, Church, and Cosmos in Colossians and Ephesians:
Implications for a Theology of Nature

Scholars have generally recognized that in Col 1:15-20 the author edited a preexisting version by adding references to the church in v. 18 and the cross in v. 20. In its presumed original form, the hymn celebrated Christ's role in creation and redemption, his supremacy over all powers in the universe, and his unique status as the one in whom God's "fullness" dwells and in whom all things hold together. The edited version serves a complex purpose in the overall argument. We have already seen that it stresses Christ's supremacy to show that deference to other cosmic powers is unnecessary. In addition, by interpreting Christ's body as the church, it creates the image of an organic community, with Christ as the head, and thus serves "at the level of social interaction . . . to encourage cohesion and integration" in the community. The interpolations, moreover, "give solid historical reference to a hymn with a clear cosmological flavor," reminding the readers that "the reconciliation of the whole cosmos took place through *the death of Christ*" (M. MacDonald 2000, 69, 66; emphasis original).

Important in the present context is whether the historical emphasis created by the interpolations negates the cosmological content. According to Eduard Lohse, the additions prevent "any attempt to utilize the hymn for the purposes of a natural or cosmic theology" (Lohse 1971, 60, quoted by Santmire 1985, 265). It would be strange, however, for the author to quote something with such a strong cosmological flavor if the intention were only to negate it. And it would have been easy enough to excise the phrases that seem so clearly to imply some sort of cosmic theology. Even if one were to grant that the author intended to negate such a theology, moreover, we would still have to recognize that the cosmological portions remain in the text. So if (with literary critics, in opposition to early redaction critics), we define the exegetical task as interpretation of the text itself rather than the mind of the author, we cannot simply ignore these elements.

At the very least, then, we can say that there is a cosmological strain that stands in tension with the historical. But, in truth, there is little reason to find significant tension here. As H. Paul Santmire writes, "we can appropriately interpret this hymn . . . in the sense of both/and: both cosmos and church, both exalted lord and crucified Savior, both strophe one (on creation) and strophe two (on redemption)" (1985, 205). Christ therefore "has an imminent cosmic role akin to Wisdom in Hebraic and later Judaic thought" and appears as "the vital principle of creation" and "its source of unity." We may therefore think of Christ's wisdom and power as "permeating all things, as Wisdom did in the thought of Hellenistic Judaism" (Santmire 1985, 205).

Drawing out the implications of this notion, Santmire observes that the "things" in creation "surely are not mechanical, self-contained, eternally determined by fate—or Christ would not be their creative principle." This does not mean that the passage is pantheistic, since "there is no doubt whatsoever about [Christ's] transcendence of all things. . . ." But Santmire does suggest that "Christ can be thought of—precisely because he is transcendent Lord of all—in the vision of this hymn as the transcendent divine whole, which is greater than the sum of its parts" (1985, 206). The latter claim may be something of an overstatement, but it seems undeniable that we have here a strong sense of nature itself infused with a quality of the divine.

Similar themes appear in Ephesians. This writing presents God's plan as "to gather up all things" in Christ (1:10) and "depicts Christ as descending through all levels of the universe, so that he might ascend far above the universe and then 'fill all things' (4:10)" (Santmire 1985, 206). Thus, Henry Chadwick can claim that in Ephesians, Christ "is the linchpin of the great chain of being, transcendent over it and at the same time imminent within the whole" (Chadwick 1962, 859a; quoted by Santmire 1985, 206).

THE PASTORAL LETTERS

The Social Setting

As I noted above, on Margaret MacDonald's model, the Pastoral Letters date from a time in which the Pauline assemblies had begun to feel the need for stabilization. This accounts for the pervasive emphasis on sound teaching and proper behavior. Their agenda, however, was not severe separation from the outside world, nor were the teachings perceived as false or the behavior perceived as disruptive threats to internal solidarity alone. For it is clear that the community was concerned not to give offense to the larger society. In 1 Tim 3:7, we read that a bishop "must be well thought of by outsiders," and "[i]n 1 Tim 6:1-2 and Titus 2:9-10 slaves are instructed with a view to the impression of outsiders" (M. MacDonald 1988, 168). MacDonald also detects an interest in evangelization, which fed into this desire for social acceptability, and she argues that the specific instructions in the letters were a response to outside criticisms "for departing from values that were highly esteemed by members of the Greco-Roman society . . ." (1988, 170). The image of the later Pauline assemblies that emerges from MacDonald's study is that of communities that are by no means isolated from the outside world, but in constant interaction with it. They know themselves, however, to be in a somewhat precarious situation, subject to criticism and therefore the potential object of ostracism.

They were not communities made up entirely of persons of lower rank. Arguing that they included members who were "relatively well-to-do," along with those of much lower status, including "slaves and needy widows," Mac-Donald contends that "it is the values and norms of the well-to-do which are dominant in the Pastorals, even though such members may have been greatly in the minority" (1988, 190–91). We therefore find in both the moral instruction and the regulations regarding community life an essentially conservative ethic, in many ways reflective of views of the elite strata in the surrounding Greco-Roman culture.

This picture of the later Pauline communities should not be surprising. Even in Paul's time, we find diversity in the sociological makeup of the assemblies and a degree of concern with respect to offending outsiders. The desire to fit into society seems to have increased exponentially, however, possibly because of the waning of imminent eschatological expectation and the increase in relatively wealthy members. Nor should the adoption of the values of the elite be surprising, since it is a well-known sociological axiom that those in the lower strata often accept the moral outlook of the ruling class. It is the elite, after all, who were "the bearers of the Great Tradition (the norms and values which gave continuity and substance to the ideals of society)" (M. MacDonald 1988, 190, citing Malina 1983, 73–74).

The Theological Framework

Because the Pastoral Letters are concerned primarily with the regulation of behavior and the qualifications for leadership, we do not find in them the intricate weaving together of theology and ethics that is characteristic of the authentic letters, Colossians, and Ephesians. Thus many critics conclude that they contain no theology at all. Frances Young, however, argues that the Pastoral Letters "may not make sense as Pauline theology, but they do have a theology of their own" and summarizes this theology in six themes:

(1) the Saviour God, with the divine grace, kindness and forbearance, (2) the Saviour Christ, God's representative, who died to save the human race making his own confession before the hostile world, (3) salvation for the life of goodness in this present age, (4) membership of God's people,

(5) the hope for the second "epiphany" and (6) the chain of authority insuring that people keep faith (1994, 73)

Young also argues that theology and ethics are intimately related in the Pastorals, despite the long-standing contention to the contrary. In 1 Tim 1:8-9, we read that "the law is good, if anyone uses it legitimately. This means understanding that the law is laid down not for the innocent but for the lawless and disobedient. . . ." Such a statement, Young argues, is in line with Paul's own affirmation in Rom 7:12 that the law is "holy, just, and good" and does not negate his understanding of justification. For the point is not that the law is in itself salvific; the notion of salvation by grace is evident, for example, in 2 Tim 1:9-11 and Titus 2:11-14; 3:4-8a. The law is necessary "to regulate antisocial behavior" but is "irrelevant to the 'righteous one,' since such a person will keep it all anyway just by being a good citizen and a loyal Christian." On the other hand, the list of prohibited behaviors in 1 Tim 1:9-10 seems to reflect the Decalogue, which consisted of God-given "guidance on how life was to be lived." The moral injunctions in the Pastorals therefore have a clear theological basis (1994, 25–29).

This theological basis, moreover, provides the author a standpoint from which to criticize and modify the Greco-Roman values that play a part in the letters' moral exhortation. Drawing on Reggie Kidd's study on wealth and beneficence in the Pastorals, Young notes that although some aspects of the Pastorals' teaching on wealth are merely conventional, the author departs from convention in rejecting the correlation between wealth and moral behavior and in avoiding "the typical language of making 'friends' through generosity" (1994, 34, citing Kidd 1990, 157).

The Specific Instructions

Warnings against false teachings bracket the entirety of 1 Timothy (1:3-11; 6:20-21), and a passage in the middle (4:1-5) denounces erroneous doctrines. Against these, the author holds up "sound teaching" (1:10; 4:6), "the mystery/words of the faith" (3:9; 4:7), "the gift that is in you" (4:14), "the commandment" (6:11), and "the mystery of our religion" (1:14) as the antidote. Similarly, 2 Timothy commends "sound teaching" (1:13), "the good treasure entrusted to you" (1:14), "sound doctrine" (4:3), and "the word of truth" (2:15); and in Titus we find references to "the word that is trustworthy" (1:9) and "sound doctrine" (2:1).

The descriptions of the teachings deemed heretical suggest an early form of gnosticism, with Jewish components. The author ridicules "what is falsely called knowledge (*gnosis*)" in 1 Tim 6:10 and "myths and endless genealogies" in 1 Tim 1:4 (also 2 Tim 3:4), and in Titus 1:3 he attacks "Jewish myths." He also criticizes the prohibition of marriage and the demand for "abstinence from foods," countering with the declaration that "everything that God created is good, and nothing is to be rejected, provided it is received with thanksgiving, for it is sanctified by God's word and by prayer" (1 Tim 4:4-5). And, finally, he accuses the purveyors of false teachings of bad character and innumerable vices (1 Tim 4:1-2; 2 Tim 3:1-10; Titus 1:10-16).

Women in particular, in the author's view, are vulnerable to the heretical doctrines. In 1 Tim 4:7, he describes the false doctrines as "profane myths and old wives' tales," and in 2 Tim 3:6-7 he adds this to the list of the offenses of the false teachers: "For they make their way into households and captivate silly women, overwhelmed by their sins and swayed by all kinds of desires, who are always being instructed and can never arrive at a knowledge of the truth."

Against such a background, the author offers specific instruction regarding the communities' qualifications for leaders and the comportment of the members occupying various social stations. There are no stipulations regarding a specific form of community organization, but the statements on the qualifications for bishops and deacons (1 Tim 3:1-13), together with references to an early form of ordination (1 Tim 3:14; 5:22; 2 Tim 1:6) indicate the beginnings of clerical authority. And 1 Tim 1:18 suggests that some officers received some sort of compensation. There are also references to elders (1 Tim 5:17-19; Titus 1:5), but there is no clear indication of how these offices differed from one another.

The qualifications for bishops presuppose male candidates only. The same is likely true for deacons, although it is unclear whether the phrase "women likewise" in 3:11 refers to female deacons or to the wives of the deacons. If female deacons are permitted, it is probable that their duties were limited to caring for the needy and related tasks (M. MacDonald 1988, 188). And, in any case, the author expects all real authority to rest with males, as we can see in the instructions for women in 1 Tim 2:11-12: "Let a woman learn in silence with full submissiveness. I permit no woman to teach or have authority over a man; she is to keep silent." It is often debated whether the "real widows" mentioned in 1 Tim 5:3-8 constituted some kind of office, but in light of 1 Tim 2:11-12, whatever authority they might have had was undoubtedly limited to the spheres of human service and the instruction of younger women. Thus in Titus 2:3, "Paul" tells Titus to enjoin the older women to teach the younger ones to love their husbands and children, and to be chaste, self-controlled, and submissive to their husbands.

The prohibition of women teachers is accompanied by special instructions on women's dress and comportment. They must be devoted to prayer and "should dress themselves modestly and decently in suitable clothing, not with their hair braided, or with gold, pearls, or expensive clothes, but with good works, as is proper for women who profess reverence for God" (1 Tim 2:8-10). The author is particularly concerned about the younger widows, whom he singles out for pointed criticism and instruction. They should not be put "on the list" of widows, since their sensual desires will eventually lead them to want to marry and thus violate a vow of celibacy, which was apparently required for those granted the status (1 Tim 4:11-12). Charging them with being idle and "gadding about from house to house" and naming them busybodies and gossips, he recommends that they "marry, bear children, and manage their households, so as to give the adversary no occasion to revile us" (1 Tim 5:14-16). This latter injunction is indicative of the author's understanding of the status and role of women, and it is reinforced in 1 Tim 2:13, where—after blaming Eve for the deception of Adam—he states the terms of women's salvation: "Yet she will be saved through childbearing, provided they continue in faith and love and holiness, with modesty."

Slaves also receive special attention. The author counsels Titus (2:9-10) to tell them to be submissive to their masters, not to talk back, not to pilfer, and "to show complete and perfect fidelity"; and in 1 Tim 6:1-2 the writer commands that they should "regard their masters as worthy of all honor" and makes a special point that slaves of believing masters should not use their relatedness in Christ as an excuse for disrespect.

Throughout the letters, the author condemns typical vices and exalts typical virtues. And in 6:3-10 a discourse on such matters culminates in a condemnation of greed. In v. 9 he criticizes "those who want to be rich" and closes with the maxim that "the love of money is a root of all kinds of evil. . . ." Interestingly, however, vv. 17-19 take a rather different tack on the matter of wealth. Beginning with the advice to "command [the rich] not to be haughty, or to set their hopes on the uncertainty of riches," the author closes the section with this summation of the proper use of wealth: "They are to do good, to be rich in good works, generous, and ready to share, thus storing up for themselves the treasure of a good foundation for the future, so that they may take hold of the life that really is life." These two attitudes toward wealth seem somewhat in tension, but their juxtaposition becomes intelligible when we consider the social function of the teachings.

The Social Function of the Instruction

Drawing on the work of Bruce Malina, Margaret MacDonald offers an explanation for the apparent discrepancy in the teaching about wealth in 1 Tim 6:3-10. The key to understanding these verses lies in the concept of "limited goods," the perception, common in the ancient world, that there is a fixed quantity of resources, which means that any increase in a person's wealth must come at the expense of another's. Thus when the author condemns "those who *want to be* rich" in v. 9, he thinks specifically of those who seek an increase in their present financial status, which would be perceived as a threat to the wealth of others. When in vv. 17-19 he treats wealth as something legitimate that must be used responsibly, however, he has in mind those who are *already* rich. He thus "appears fully to support the preservation of inherited status," so that "[c]ommunity harmony and stability becomes inextricably linked to maintenance of existing arrangements and statuses" (1988, 192–93, citing Malina 1983, 75).

This interpretation can help us understand the social function of all the teaching in the Pastorals. A main purpose of the letters is to create stability within the community, characterized by personal behavior that is acceptable in general society. The movement toward formalized channels of authority regulates acceptable teaching, but it also ensures internal coherence with respect to social roles. The intent of defining women's roles in terms of marriage and childbearing or official widowhood is to bring all women under the supervision of males. The reason for enjoining slaves to obedience and respect for their masters is to reinforce the hierarchical social structure. And the purpose of the caution against seeking wealth is to perpetuate the existing social distinctions.

It is often argued that the Pauline communities felt the need for greater organization because of the threat of heretical teachings. This is not false, but it is no more than a half truth. For it is apparent that a social agenda, which overlaps only partly with this concern, was also at work; and that was the desire of a male leadership, with a concern to relate positively to the hierarchical and status-conscious larger society, to maintain their own power and privilege.

The Pastoral Letters and the Pauline Legacy

We can appreciate the point just made if we look again at the harsh statements about women in the Pastorals and think beyond the issue of protognostic teachings. There is reason to think that some form of gnostic thought was in fact in the background. Dennis MacDonald, however, has also argued that the barbs directed at women are best explained if the author is seeking to undermine the stories about Paul that we find in the apocryphal *Acts of Paul and Thecla,* which recounts the adventures of a bold woman who defies male authority and social convention in order to follow Paul. She breaks with the patriarchal system by refusing two suitors, baptizes herself, dresses like a man, and follows after Paul. And although Thecla is the stronger character, Paul himself—who ordains her to teach—is no model of conformity. "Nothing in the legends suggests that Paul or any other Christian could be characterized as moderate or dignified; rather, they are proudly presented as socially deviant, impudent, and incorrigible" (D. MacDonald 1983, 72). It is just such images of Christians that the author of the Pastorals was anxious to dispel.

The subtitle of Dennis MacDonald's book—*The Battle for Paul in Story and Canon*—contains an important insight. The legacy of Paul was diverse. When Marcion constructed a form of Christian teaching that denied that the God of the Hebrew Bible was the God revealed in Christ, he edited Paul's letters in order to remove all positive references to Judaism. Gnostics picked up Paul's teaching and accommodated it to their own systems, interpreting his phrase "the likeness of sinful flesh" (Rom 8:3) to mean that God's Son had no physical body, since the flesh is evil. Others, perhaps women, told tales such as are found in the Thecla cycle. And, of course, still others transformed Paul's teachings into the defense of the patriarchal system that we find in the Pastorals.

Continuity or Discontinuity?

Young is largely convincing in her argument that the Pastorals do not disconnect ethics from theology and in finding a degree of continuity with Paul with respect to his understanding of grace. The reassertion of patriarchy, however, is a major departure from Paul's inclusiveness, and when we look more closely at how theology and ethics are united in the Pastorals a serious question arises. Although we can find one passage that points to the indwelling of God's Spirit (2 Tim 1:14) and another that mentions "renewal by the Holy Spirit," which God "poured out" through Jesus Christ (Titus 3:5-6), we find no hint of Paul's ethic of discernment. Granted the partial "Christianization" of conventional Greco-Roman moral teaching, it is difficult to imagine that the author could have endorsed Paul's injunctions to his readers to puzzle out God's will (Rom 12:2) and work out their "own salvation with fear and trembling" (Phil 2:12).

Along with a degree of continuity between the Pastorals and Paul, then, we must reckon with significant discontinuity, considerably greater than that found in Colossians and Ephesians.

HEBREWS AND 1 PETER

Hebrews and 1 Peter share the use of the term *parepidēmoi* ("strangers, exiles, foreigners") as a designation for those belonging to the community of Christ. In 1 Peter, it occurs in the address (1:1): "To the exiles in the dispersion." In Hebrews, it comes in the author's rehearsal of the heroic figures of the Hebrew Bible, who remained faithful in their hope for the fulfillment of God's promises, even though they all died before the promise was realized in Christ: "They confessed that they were strangers (*xenoi*) and foreigners (*parepidēmoi*) on the earth, for people who speak this way make it clear that they are seeking a homeland" (11:13).

The Ethics of the Pilgrim People in Hebrews

The meaning of the Hebrews passage is clear. The Hebrew forerunners were foreigners or exiles on earth, since their true home was in heaven, as becomes explicit in vv. 15-16a: "If they had been thinking of the land that they had left behind, they would have had opportunity to return. But as it is, they desire a better country, that is, a heavenly one." One rhetorical function of this description of the heroes of faith who preceded Christ is to support the author's appeal for faithfulness on the part of those who have now actually received God's promise. "Therefore, since we are surrounded by so great a cloud of witnesses, let us also lay aside every weight and the sin that clings so closely, and let us run with perseverance the race that is set before us, looking to Jesus the pioneer and perfecter of our faith. . . ." In addition, the rehearsal of the faith of those who preceded Christ also is a partial model for those who follow Christ. For in 13:12-14, the realized eschatology of the earlier chapters gives way to an element of future eschatology (Hughes 1979, 2–3): "Therefore Jesus also suffered outside the city gate in order to sanctify the people by his own blood. Let us then go to him outside the camp and bear the abuse he endured. *For here we have no lasting city, but we are looking for a city that is to come.*" The fulfillment that the faith community experiences thus remains partial.

This sense of alienation is reinforced by the author's recognition that the readers have apparently experienced some form of persecution (10:32-34; 13:33), although no members have as yet forfeited their lives (12:4). In addition, we find a sharp distinction between the earthly sanctuary of the Hebrew people and the heavenly sanctuary, where Christ functions as high priest (8:1-7). The notion that the earthly sanctuary is but "a sketch and a shadow of the heavenly one" (v. 5) is indebted to Platonic thought, which understands the material world as inferior and derivative from the true world of pure ideas. In this author's terms, the present world, which can be shaken, must pass away "so that what cannot be shaken may remain" (12:27).

The cumulative effect of these themes is what many scholars have termed a "pilgrim theology." The author understands the recipients of God's promise as a band of exiles—strangers in a strange land—who exist uneasily in the present world as they await the eschatological future. The ethics of Hebrews is thus, in Schrage's words, "an ethics of the people of God," according to which "[t]hose who are on their way to the heavenly rest journey in company with other members of the people of God" (1988, 327).

The ethics of Hebrews might also be termed an "ethics of endurance," because *pistis* (faith/faithfulness) in this writing seems to connote faithfulness in the face of ostracism on the one hand and sheer weariness on the other. The author explicitly defines it as "the assurance of things hoped for, the conviction of things not seen" (11:1). It is not, however, merely autonomous human courage but issues from a christological foundation. The fundamental logic of the argument is that because Christ has brought completion to the partial revelation of former times as well as making the once-for-all purification from sins (1:3; 4:14—5:10; 8:1-13), the people of God should not "neglect so great a salvation" (2:3a). And the parenesis that comprises much of the writing is directed precisely toward that goal: to encourage the readers to "keep the faith."

Christology also supports ethics through the author's version of *imitatio Christi*. Throughout the writing, as Schrage notes, the author employs models for the reader to imitate. The prime example is chapter 11, which rehearses Israel's history. But "[i]t is not by chance that the example of Jesus culminates the series." Jesus, in fact, serves as "the great paradigm," particularly as an example of obedient suffering, so that "we may speak of a paradigmatic ethics in which Christ serves as the true model" (1988, 324–25).

As the pilgrim people of God who are called to endurance in suffering, the readers are expected to maintain rigorous moral standards, and the author defines these in fairly conventional terms. Community solidarity is central, however; and the ideal of love is not only in the background of the demands, such as the calls to practice hospitality and remember those who are in prison or are tortured

(13:2-3) as well as to share (13:16), but becomes explicit at several points: 6:10 and 10:24 (*agapē*) and 13:1 (*philadelphia*).

In presenting the ethics of the pilgrim people as an ethics of internal solidarity, however, the author has little or nothing to say of the community's relationship to the outside world. As Schrage comments, "there is no mention of being sent into the world or of any relationship to the world other than passive suffering." Schrage also claims that "[e]ven the injunction to 'strive for peace with all' (12:4) is probably limited to the members of the Christian community," citing "the exhortation to love of the brethren in 13:1" and the exhortation "to exercise *diakonia* [service] toward 'the saints' in 6:10" as evidence (1988, 327). In any case, the emphasis is overwhelmingly on maintaining the integrity of the people of God as such, who remain in a strong sense aliens in the world.

The Ethics of God's Holy Nation in 1 Peter

Whether the use of the term *parepidēmoi* in 1 Peter also connotes a pilgrim theology as in Hebrews—a sense of alienation from the present world—is a matter of debate. The author clearly thinks of the recipients as in some sense "strangers in a strange land." In addition to 1:1, the term appears in 2:11 in conjunction with *paroikoi* ("aliens, strangers, exiles"), and in various ways the readers get a strong sense of separateness from the larger society. The author calls them "a chosen race, a royal priesthood, a holy nation, God's own people," and refers to those on the outside as "Gentiles" (2:12; 4:3). In 1:4, moreover, we find a reference to "an inheritance that is imperishable, undefiled, and unfading, kept in heaven" for them. Thus, given the reference to a "fiery ordeal" in 4:12, many interpreters have thought that the letter addresses persons undergoing active persecution. John Elliott, however, argues that the alienation has a sociological rather than a metaphorical force. He believes that the recipients are noncitizens, resident alien workers who are powerless and probably economically deprived; they are alienated not from their true home in heaven but from the society in which they live (1981, 87). A third position is that of David Bartlett, who suggests that they are natives of the culture in which they live but are now "a slandered minority," alienated by virtue of their newfound faith (1998, 236).

Whatever the cause of the alienation, the community members are in some sense a "pilgrim people" suffering because of their identity (1:6-7; 3:13-18; 4:12-19). They are also converts from paganism (1:18), and the author uses this fact as a way of stating the indicative that grounds the imperatives that abound in the letter. They have been "ransomed from the futile ways" of their ancestors (1:18) and "have come to trust in God, who raised [Christ] from the dead . . ." (18:21). They have purified their souls and have been "born anew" (1:22-23; 2:1) and are recipients of a baptism that saves them (3:21). The link between indicative and imperative, moreover, is explicit. In 1:22, it is the purification of the recipients' souls that enables mutual love (*philadelphia*) and grounds the command to "love (*agapan*) one another deeply from the heart," and in 2:34 the author declares that Christ "bore our sins in his body on the cross, so that, free from sins, we might live for righteousness' sake; by his wounds you have been healed."

The community is thus a distinct people within an alien environment, freed from sin, purified, and born anew by their baptism into Christ. Much of the moral exhortation is therefore directed internally. In 4:7-11, for example, the counsels on mutual love and hospitality are clearly calls to group solidarity. In contrast to Hebrews, however, 1 Peter also manifests a strong emphasis on the community's dealing with the outside world. The lyric description of the role of the community as "God's own people" in 2:9ff. includes an explicit reference to mission as the distinctive task of this community: "in order that you may proclaim the mighty acts of him who called you out of darkness into his marvelous light." The author also counsels the readers to conduct themselves "honorably among the Gentiles" (= non-Christians) so that "though they may malign you as evildoers they may see your honorable deeds and glorify God when he comes to judge" (2:12).

In 2:13-17, the author addresses the community's relationship to the secular government. Verses 13-14 make it clear that they should "accept the authority" of the emperor and governors, but v. 16 introduces a subtle qualification: "As servants of God, live as free people, yet do not use your freedom as a pretext for evil." The designation "free people" indicates that believers' ultimate loyalty is to God, which means that they "must maintain their freedom also within the context of the state" (Schrage 1972, 277). But the caution against using freedom as a pretext for evil reveals the substance of the author's advice: do not provoke the authorities unnecessarily. Thus, v. 17 closes with injunctions regarding what is owing to both God and Caesar: "Fear God. Honor the emperor." It is appropriate to honor the human, secular authority, but it is God alone that one should "fear" (*phobeisthai*)—that is, render reverence in the deep, religious sense.

The NRSV translates the first part of v. 13 as, "For the Lord's sake accept the authority of every human institution," and some interpreters find in this verse an endorsement of the state itself "together with its divine origin" (Schrage 1972, 277–78). The term rendered as "institution" here, however, is *ktisis*, the literal meaning of which is "creature." And, as Schrage comments,

Nowhere else does *ktisis* mean "institution," either in secular Greek or in the LXX. Since 2:13-14 and 17 use personal terminology [governors, emperor] to expand on it and since 2:18a (cf. also 3:1 and 5:5) also speaks of subjection in personal terms, the translation "creature" is more likely. (1988, 278)

Schrage thus concludes that the obedience the author counsels is "owed concretely to individual human beings, who are still 'creatures' even when acting as agents of civil authority." And he notes that there is nothing here corresponding to Rom 13:1b-2, which refer to God's *institution* of secular authorities. In 1 Peter, then, neither the emperor nor the imperial governors are *"eo ipso* appointed by God or even possessed of divine dignity; their authority is the authority of creatures . . ." (1988, 278). As Bartlett comments, moreover,

> [h]ere the reasons for loyalty are much more simply pragmatic. Emperors and governors are one example of those "human creatures" to whom Christians are called to show humble honor. Moreover they are useful because they uphold at least minimal standards of behavior. The description of the relationship of God to emperor to governors does not imply any divine chain of command, as if God authorizes the emperor, who then authorizes the governors. Rather, God creates the emperor and the governors, and the emperor gives authority to the governors for the sake of good order. (1998, 275)

Members of the community thus owe their ultimate allegiance to God but should be obedient to the secular authorities just as they should live "honorably among the Gentiles" (2:12). In doing so, they will "silence the ignorance of the foolish" (2:15)—that is, discredit the false charges made against them by those who accuse them of evil deeds and perhaps lead them to glorify God (2:12).

We must remember that the author gives this advice against the background of the community's suffering and a lively eschatological hope. The eschatological motif pervades the letter. In 1:5, we read of "a salvation ready to be revealed in the last time," and in 1:13 there is instruction to "set all your hope on the grace that Jesus Christ will bring you when he is revealed." The counsel to live honorably among the Gentiles in 2:12, moreover, is supported by a reference to God's coming judgment, and in 4:7 the author refers to the imminence of "the end of all things." Also, in 5:13 we find what Schrage terms "the apocalyptic codeword 'Babylon'" as a reference to Rome (1988, 278). This is a subtle promise that in the coming judgment, God will bring Rome to account. In the meantime, the community must seek to live amicably under that rule, even though it is destined ultimately to fall.

If the commands to honor imperial authority remain problematic in our time from some perspectives, this is also the case when it comes to the household code in 2:18—3:7. In this table of instructions, the author counsels slaves to accept their masters' authority "with all deference," whether they are kind or harsh, promising God's approval to those who endure the pain of unjust suffering and presenting Christ as the model for such endurance (2:18-25). We also find injunctions to wives to accept their husbands' authority, even if they are not members of the community, so that they might be "won over with a word by their wives' conduct . . ." (3:1-2). Husbands should "show consideration" for their wives, "paying honor to the weaker sex," because "they too are also heirs of the gracious gift of life . . ." (3:7). Notably, there are no injunctions to masters such as we find in Colossians and Ephesians. The latter fact probably indicates that there were few, if any, slaveholders among community members, but it is undeniable that the code is even more patriarchal than those in Colossians and Ephesians.

Despite this fact, many interpreters have sought to put this element of the writing into context. M. Eugene Boring and Fred B. Craddock, for example, make a number of observations along these lines, of which I will mention three. The first is based on the fact that the instructions to slaves and wives can be seen as part of a larger section that begins with 2:11, which is directed to the community as a whole. But because "2:13—3:7 does not cover all cases and classes, instructions to slave and wives are to be taken as illustrative," so that "[t]he whole community is to learn from what is said" to them. The second point is that "*[t]he text of the whole letter is oriented to the weak and vulnerable*; it sees the world from the underside." That is to say, the slaves and women in the community "have already shown that they *are not submissive*" by their "courageous decision to join a despised foreign cult that is not the religion of their non-Christian masters and husbands" (2004, 731; emphasis original). The third point is that

> [m]ission, not submission, is the focus of this text. The challenge is to remove a false stumbling block, so that people may decide for or against the truth of the Christian message without being put off by [their perception of] the cultural forms associated with it. (2004, 731–32)

These observations are in my estimation valid, but the turn that we can see in both the Deuteropauline letters and in 1 Peter is unmistakable. Whatever the circumstances, and whatever the motivations, the fact remains that we find the communities in Christ toward the end of the first century abandoning the more egalitarian spirit of both Paul and the Jesus movement and reverting to the patriarchal structures of the wider society. The point in saying this, however, is not to pass judgment on those who made these decisions but to bring to the fore the question of whether and in what sense the writings that manifest this decisive change have validity in our own time.

RICH AND POOR IN THE LETTER OF JAMES

"No other document is as dominated by ethical questions as is James." Thus Schrage begins his treatment of the letter of James. Then, in the course of his discussion, he contends that although there are hints of the author's knowledge of a Christian understanding of salvation (for example, 1:17-18), such knowledge does not really function "as a foundation for ethics" (1988, 281). He acknowledges that the characterization of wisdom as a gift from God in 3:17 and 1:5 serves as "an indicative motivation for realizing God's will," but he concludes that "this perspective is not maintained." Thus "[t]he imperative stands in relative isolation, without motivation" (1988, 282). These judgments are not without foundation, but to some extent they evaluate James on the basis of a Pauline standard. In what follows, I will explore the letter's ethical perspective by relating it to its own theological framework.

Theology and Ethics in James

That frame of reference is, first and foremost, theocentric. God is the giver not only of wisdom but of "every perfect gift" as well as "birth by the word of truth" (1:17-18). Whether the latter phrase refers to creation and the Law or to regeneration in Christ through the gospel is unclear, but in either case the point is that God is the benevolent creator who grants life and all its blessings. And the author reinforces this notion of divine benevolence in 1:12-16 by denying that God is the source of temptation and promising "the crown of life" to all who endure the temptation that comes from their own desires. God is also the source of the power to resist evil. After proclaiming that "friendship with the world is enmity with God," the author quotes Ps 3:34—"God opposes the proud, but gives grace to the humble"—and then promises the divine presence to those who humble themselves before God. It is God, moreover, who is the object of the believers' faith, as the example of Abraham's faithfulness shows (2:23-26). And, finally, God is the eschatological judge who holds persons accountable for their deeds (5:9), who can both save and destroy (4:12), who hears the cries of the oppressed and punishes the oppressor (1:10; 5:4), and who dispenses or withholds mercy according to a principle of reciprocity (2:13).

Law is also central to the theological framework. The word *nomos* (law) occurs ten times in this short letter, proportionately much higher than in any New Testament writing other than Romans and Galatians. In 1:22-25, the author seems to equate the Law with "the word," refers to it as "the perfect law, the law of liberty," and names it a blessing to those who do not merely hear it but also do it. This passage also helps support the author's condemnation of partiality toward the rich in 2:1-13. Immediately after the injunction on doing as well as hearing the Law, 1:26-27 provide a definition of true religion (*thrēskeia*) that ends with a strong focus on social justice: "to care for orphans and widows in their distress, and to keep oneself unstained from the world." Immediately after this comes the discourse on partiality/impartiality, which is followed by another commendation of the Law in 2:8: "You do well if you really fulfill the royal law according to the scripture, 'You shall love your neighbor as yourself.' But if you show partiality, you commit sin and are convicted by the law as transgressors." The author thus brackets the teaching on partiality/impartiality with references to the Law, showing both that it is the Law that grounds this ethic of justice and that justice is central to the ethic based on law. As 2:8-13 shows, James reflects the long-standing Jewish notion of the Law as an indivisible unity. In practice, however, it is clear that only the moral law matters. As Victor Furnish comments on 1:26-27,

> "Religious" service is not cultic action but moral action . . . ; to approach God with clean hands means to approach [God] with a pure heart, in full sincerity and with humility (4:8-9). Thus while it is true that this ethic has a nomistic structure, the author understands that Christians have been given a new kind of law to follow. (1972, 177)

Schrage reinforces this point by referring to the latter part of 4:8: "Cleanse your hands, you sinners, and purify your hearts, you double-minded." For here the author has taken a theme originally related to cultic purity and made it "a call to single-minded obedience" (1988, 288).

There is considerable debate as to what is meant by the reference to the "royal law" in 2:8. The first question is whether this phrase designates the whole Law or the love commandment (Lev 19:18) specifically. Many interpreters contend that it is the love commandment. Wesley Wachob (2000, 92), however, follows Martin Dibelius (1976, 142) in stressing that the term *nomos* that appears here generally refers to law, whereas *entolē* is the usual term for individual commandments. The point of the ensuing verses (2:10-12), moreover, is that the breaking of one commandment is a rejection of the Law in its entirety, so that it is the issue of Law per se that is really at stake. As to the specific connotations of "royal" [*basilikos*], some commentators have treated this epithet as merely "decorative." To say that a law is "royal," however, is to say that it is a king's law. Thus, Wachob argues that it "suggests both that the law originates with God and that it is also applicable to [God's] kingdom" (2000, 92).

Although accepting Dibelius's view that the "royal law" means the whole Law, Wachob challenges his contention that the love commandment is "only a part" of the Law. It is rather the "author's basic expression for or summary of the whole law" (2000, 121). As evidence, Wachob notes the abundance of both Jewish and Christian writings that cite Lev 19:18 "as a summary of the whole law" and quotes Hans Dieter Betz's observation that "the evidence indicates that early Christianity was historically united on the fact that Jesus taught the fulfillment of the Torah in the love-commandment" (Betz 1985, 37; Wachob 2000, 122).

It is true that James does not explicitly name the love commandment a summary of the Law, but 2:10-13 make a correlative point. Assuming the well-known Jewish notion of the unity of the Law, the logic of these verses is that since those who break one commandment violate the entire Law, those who fail to keep Lev 19:18 are guilty in terms of the whole Law. The logic would work with any other commandment, but one could argue that since the chosen example is a verse that was traditionally used as a summary of the Law, the reverse logic is also implied: to keep this one commandment, precisely because it is the very heart and soul of the Law, is also to keep the Law in its entirety.

The strongest point, however, is the fact that Jesus' use of Lev 19:18 was so well known. As Wachob argues, "it is hard to imagine that judgments connecting the poor, the promised kingdom, the royal law, and the love-commandment could have been heard without thinking of Jesus' words and deeds" (2000, 122). And this observation brings us to a central point in the discussion of the theological perspective of James. It has been long recognized that there is a very close relationship between James's moral teaching and the sayings of Jesus, with most scholars linking James to the precanonical tradition. To be sure, the author never cites Jesus directly in presenting ethical maxims, and there are scant references to Jesus himself. It would be wrong, however, to think that the ethics of James therefore has no christological foundation. What we should rather conclude is that the letter has a very distinctive way of relating ethics to christology.

The NRSV translation of Jas 2:1 is as follows: "My brothers and sisters, do you with your acts of favoritism really believe in our glorious Lord Jesus Christ?" The RSV, however renders it, "My brethren, show no partiality as you hold the faith of our Lord Jesus Christ, the Lord of glory." The crucial point is that the NRSV understands the phrase *pistin . . . Iēsou Christou* as faith *in* Jesus Christ. As we saw in chapter 8, however, it is very likely in Paul's writings that this phrase often means "the *faithfulness of* Jesus Christ." And Wachob makes a convincing case for a similar reading of Jas 2:1, contending that in this verse "the audience is admonished to hold (*echein*) a faith-obedience that in quality is like the faith-obedience of Jesus Christ." To begin with, in James the verb *echein* is almost always associated with faith. "Moreover," Wachob continues,

> there is nothing in the thoroughly theocentric letter of James that plainly suggests a faith *in* Jesus in the sense of the Pauline kerygma. Salvation in James is fundamentally a matter of faith-obedience to God (see James 2.14, 17, 22, 26; 1.21, 25, 27; 4.12a; 5.19-20). The verb *pisteuein*, "to believe," occurs twice in James and in both instances it is directed toward God. . . . (2000, 65)

Understanding 2:1 as a plea for the reader to hold the faith of Jesus, then, Wachob argues that this reference "functions as a 'global allusion,' that is, it evokes the whole of what our author perceives Jesus to have believed, said, and done" (2000, 122).[1] And the author's counsel to obey Lev 19:18 because to transgress one commandment is to transgress all (2:10) "not only corroborates the theme that Jesus' faith is antithetical to acts of partiality (2.1) but also intimates an inherent connection between holding Jesus' faith and fulfilling the whole law" (2000, 122).

Building on Wachob's thesis, I would argue that James has a christological foundation for his ethics, although it is decidedly different from Paul's. The author's "failure" to cite Jesus as the source of the moral teaching is a sign not of the lack of such a foundation but of a specific strategy in the use of the Jesus material. What the author has done, in a sense, is to pass on this teaching, not in the form of references to the past but as a living word for the present. The re-presentation of Jesus' teachings, in other words, becomes the vehicle for expressing Jesus' own faith-obedience, or faithfulness, so that it can find its way into the lives of the readers. Thus, the theocentric and Law-centered ethic of James is also in its own way a christocentric ethic that depends on the generative power of Jesus' own faithfulness.

The author's adoption of the persona of James the Just and passing on sayings from the Jesus tradition as those of James is, moreover, an important tool in implementing this strategy rather than a hindrance to it. For the presentation of James as the *doulos* ("slave"; NRSV: "servant") of God and Jesus Christ was a way of forging a connection between the authorial voice and that of Jesus. In the Greco-Roman context, Wachob argues, "the 'slave' metaphor was . . . employed by persons who desired to present themselves as spokespersons and representatives of their master patron" (2000, 136).[2]

The christological element in James's theology compromises neither the writing's theocentrism nor its focus on law. Not only does the letter present God as the giver of all good gifts, but, as Cain Felder notes, there is "an implicit *imitatio Dei*" in 2:13: "For judgment will be without mercy to anyone who has shown no mercy; mercy triumphs over judgment." Whereas the first part of the verse reinforces v. 12, with its eschatological sanction for good deeds, the final clause introduces the notion "that mercy is ultimately descriptive of God" (1989, 133). The point is that human beings should be merciful because God is merciful. Of course, we encounter here a problem similar to that observed in Matthew—the sanctioning of mercy with a threat of withholding mercy—but it is important that the final emphasis is clearly on God's mercy, as it is in 5:11: "you have seen the purpose of the Lord, how the Lord is compassionate and merciful."

If the christological element does not negate James's emphasis on law, we must nevertheless say that the implicit theme of *imitatio Dei* in 2:13 puts that focus in a slightly different light in a way reminiscent of the discussion of John Barton's work on the ethics of the Hebrew Bible (see chapter 3 above). For, as Felder comments, the *imitatio Dei* actually "introduces another motive for 'doing' beyond that of the moral law" and indeed "perhaps gives substance to the moral law in the first place . . ." (1989, 133). As subtle a point as this is, it is an important reminder of the difference between law as arbitrary command and law that expresses a standard of right and wrong inherent in the nature of things.

The Teaching on Rich and Poor

The teaching on rich and poor is central to the letter's concerns. It appears at three different points, is dispersed throughout the letter, is interwoven with other themes, and is presented in rhetorically powerful language. According to Patrick

J. Hartin's analysis, moreover, the two later and longer sections on this theme bracket the body of the letter, which is arranged chiastically (1991, 30).

The first instance is 1:9-11, which echoes Isa 40:6-8 as well as the theme of the eschatological reversal of fortune, which pervades the Jesus tradition:

> Let the believer who is lowly boast in being raised up, and the rich in being brought low, because the rich will disappear like a flower in the field. For the sun rises with its scorching heat and withers the field; its flower falls, and its beauty perishes. It is the same way with the rich; in the midst of a busy life, they will wither away.

The NRSV rendering of *adelphos* ("brother") as "believer" correctly presumes that the reference is to a community member; and although the term "lowly" *(tapeinos)* does not literally mean "poor," the contrast with "rich" shows that it refers to a person in economic distress. It is unclear whether the rich person is a member of the community or not, but this much-debated issue is not of ultimate importance. As Pedrito U. Maynard-Reid comments, to the author, "all rich fall in the same category" (1987, 44). In any case, attempts to understand *lowly* in the sense of spiritual humility rather than economic deprivation founder on the later passages about poverty and wealth.

Also inadequate are the spiritualizing interpretations of the counsel to the rich to boast in their being brought low that understand this in the sense of a voluntary humbling of oneself before the poor. The more likely reading, especially in light of the later passages, is that "James's language regarding the economically rich person has an ironic twist—a device that is utilized to underscore the humiliation in which the rich person lives and . . . that is similar to Luke's use of the rich fool (Luke 12:13-21)" (Maynard-Reid 1987, 44). The suggestion that the rich should boast is, in other words, a taunt: "The rich man has had his day; all he can expect from the future is humiliation; that is the only thing left for him to 'boast about.' This would be some 'boast'!" (Maynard-Reid 1987, 42; quoting Dibelius 1976, 85).

The passage is thus a condemnation of the rich, and it establishes a rich/poor dichotomy on which the later passages will build. It is more than this, however; as Peter H. Davids notes, "the proverbial statement" on the flower in the field "invites us to consider the meaninglessness of wealth" (1982, 77). And the weaving together of these two elements illustrates how the letter as a whole combines motifs from the wisdom and the prophetic traditions.

The second passage on rich and poor is 2:1-13. Whereas the first was primarily a reflection on the ways of the world—that is, an observation on the respective fortunes of rich and poor—this passage takes the form of an admonition to the community against showing partiality to the rich. As such, it builds on 1:22-25, where the author exhorts the readers on the themes of hearing and doing the word and on what it means to be truly religious. It also leads naturally into the section on faith and works in 2:14-26, so that it constitutes a major example of good works.

The first part of the passage (vv. 1-7) warns specifically against partiality, while the second (vv. 8-13) buttresses this teaching by connecting it to the love commandment and showing that violation of this one commandment is a rejection of the entire Law. The author also signals the centrality of the teaching on rich and poor by choosing the beginning of this passage (2:1) to introduce the concept of the faithfulness of Jesus. Partiality toward the rich—described in graphic terms in vv. 2-4—thus appears as a prime example of spurning that faithfulness as the guide to one's own life.

In v. 5, the author refers to the poor as chosen to be rich in faith and heirs of the kingdom. We must beware, however, of spiritualizing or sentimentalizing this point. It is true that in some strains of Jewish and Christian piety, as Davids comments, "the term 'poor' picked up a religious quality, and this can be seen in our present passage." The logic is that "[t]he world sees only their poverty; God sees their exalted state because of [God's] election of them to eschatological exaltation, for they are those who love [God] and thus receive [God's] promise. . . ." However, the term "poor" does not thereby lose the "quality of material poverty, for it is a materially poor person who has been discriminated against" (1982, 112). The crucial point is that God did not choose the poor *to be* poor but chose them rather *because they were poor*. Their poverty, as Elsa Tamez writes, "is the result of a scandalous act of oppression" (1990, 28). The point becomes clearer later in the letter, but it is evident enough in vv. 6b-7: "Is it not the rich who oppress you? Is it not they who drag you into court? Is it not they who blaspheme the excellent name that was invoked over you?"

The intention of the passage, however, is not merely to condemn the rich but to call the recipients of the letter to account for the deference they pay to the rich while they discriminate against the poor. If we can assume, as do most scholars, that the community is itself made up largely, and perhaps even exclusively, of the poor, then we have another situation in which persons near the bottom of the social scale have adopted the values and prejudices of the ruling class. Thus the force of v. 5, which refers to God's "option for the poor," is actually a call to solidarity among those who have been excluded from power and privilege.

The third segment of teaching on rich and poor is 4:11—5:6, where the author addresses the rich directly, ratchets up the rhetoric, and focuses on specific acts of economic oppression. Here the dichotomy between rich and poor, established in 1:9-11, reaches its apex. The first part, 4:13-16, is an attack on the rich. Their business ventures reveal a false sense of security, since they do not know what tomorrow will bring. The author condemns the arrogance of their failing to acknowledge God's sovereignty over all outcomes and ends by proclaiming their attitudes evil. The second part (5:1-6) focuses on their exploitation of their workers and describes God's judgment on them. They have withheld wages by fraud, "and the cries of the harvesters have reached the ears of the Lord of hosts." They are in fact murderers who have "fattened [their] hearts in a day of slaughter." It would be difficult to imagine a more severe indictment than this.

In addition to these passages that deal directly with the poor, 2:14-26 not only contributes to the bracketing of 2:1-13 with references to the Law but complements 2:8-13 by stressing social justice as central to the Law. Arguing that "faith by itself, if it has no works, is dead," the author illustrates the point by injecting the theme of the plight of the poor in vv. 15-16: "If a brother or sister is naked and lacks food, and one of you says to them, 'Go in peace; keep warm and eat your fill,' and yet you do not supply their bodily needs, what is the good of that?" Justice for the poor is thus the primary example of keeping the love commandment. It should also be noted that the phrase "or a sister" in v. 15 is not a translator's effort to make the text more acceptable to modern sensibilities but is actually in the Greek. This is quite remarkable, given the patriarchal environment and general linguistic usage, so that Tamez's comment seems fully justified: "It is very probable, then, that the needy were commonly women" (1990, 25).

In sum, we find in James a document largely focused on issues of social justice, reminiscent of the Hebrew prophets as well as of a significant element in the Jesus tradition. In keeping with earlier tradition, moreover, it does more than merely condemn. As Tamez shows, its focus on oppression is matched by emphases on both hope and praxis. Hope appears in 1:11-12, for example, in eschatological joy over the coming reversal, in God's identification with the poor in 2:5, and in the theme of judgment in 5:1-6 (1990, 33–50). But Tamez also finds that "hope is not sufficient; there is also need for praxis, deeds" and that in James the emphasis on praxis takes three forms: militant patience, integrity, and genuine prayer (1990, 33–51).

Examining the use of the noun *hypomenē* ("patient endurance, steadfastness") and the verb *hypomenein* ("to remain, stand one's ground") in 1:3-4; 1:12; and 5:11, she concludes that they have active meanings: "Here to be patient means to persevere, to resist, to be constant, unbreakable, immovable" (1990, 53). In 5:7-8, 10, the author uses another term for patience that has a slightly different range of meanings: *makrothymia*. Although it does not have an active meaning, "neither is it passive in the traditional negative sense." The analogy of the farmer in 5:7 says to the oppressed community that "its difficult situation is going to change, that judgment has been pronounced in favor of those who suffer." But this does not mean that the oppressed should wait passively for the action of God. It is rather "a question of doing everything possible not to despair in spite of the desperate situation, relying on the future that will put an end to sufferings" (Tamez 1990, 55–56).

"For James," Tamez states, "the core of praxis is integrity" (1990, 56). The author introduces the notion of integrity at the very beginning—"so that you may be mature and complete, lacking in nothing" (1:5)—and in 1:8 and 4:8 we find condemnations of double-mindedness. Since the world at large represents values antithetical to the justice-oriented values of the community, incarnated in the care for widows and orphans as commanded in 1:27, the readers "must avoid accommodation to this unjust world and not fall into the trap laid down by its value system" (1990, 62). They must also avoid a duplicitous spirit in the third form of praxis—prayer. The author condemns the wrong kinds of prayer in 1:6 and 4:3, that which is either plagued by doubt or asks for the wrong things. In contrast, we find in 5:13-18 a commendation of authentic prayer, which "will comfort them in their oppression, will exalt them in their hope, and will help them to achieve integrity in the practice of justice, as Christians faithful to God" (1990, 72).

COMMENTS ON JUDE, 2 PETER, AND 2 THESSALONIANS

Both Jude and 2 Peter, which scholars generally agree is highly dependent on Jude, are strident attacks on teachings perceived to be at odds with the gospel. The strategy in both cases is to assert the authority of tradition, impugn the character of those who teach the deviant doctrines, reaffirm God's eventual eschatological judgment, and counsel moral behavior as the readers await the end. While the authors do not engage in theological argument, by referring to the apostolic faith they invoke the broad contours of an accepted body of belief as the theological sanction for ethics. As to the specifics of moral behavior, Schrage's summary is apt:

> Primary emphasis is on vitriolic polemic against heretical libertinism (cf. 2 Peter 2). The major charges include worldly pleasures and lawlessness, debauchery and greed. The recommended remedies are escape from the world (2 Pet. 2:20), virtue, and morality, supported by recourse to the "holy commandment" delivered by the apostles (2 Pet. 21:21). (1988, 278)

While neither of these letters adds anything substantial to our survey of New Testament ethics, their presence in the canon underscores a question that arises also in relation to the Pastoral Letters. Although the invocation of the apostolic tradition provides a theological basis in one sense, we see in all these letters an approach to doctrine that depends primarily on formalized definitions. So the question is whether the church is better served by attempts to set doctrinal boundaries in precise terms once and for all or by continuing the process of creative reexpression that is evident in both the Jesus tradition and the undisputed letters of Paul. How one answers this question will have an important impact on how one understands the authority of ethical traditions as well.

Turning now to 2 Thessalonians, in 3:10b we find a statement that is often used in political debates over the proper role of government in meeting human need: "Anyone unwilling to work should not eat." The statement, however, clearly has to do with a situation internal to the community and nothing whatsoever to do with public policy. Although many interpreters have thought that the issue was the idleness of some members who were caught up in eschatological expectations, Boring and Craddock suggest a more likely possibility. In vv. 6-9, the author presents Paul as a model of a missionary who worked with his hands to earn his keep when he was present in the assembly. Paul's practice is probably presented as a contrast to the behavior of later traveling missionaries "who went from church to church designating themselves as 'apostles' (= missionaries) and 'prophets' (= spokespersons for the risen Christ), teaching and preaching and expecting the churches to support them." In vv. 6 and 11, the author uses the adverb *ataktos*, which the NRSV translates as "in idleness," to describe the behavior. The more literal meaning of the term has to do with "disorderly" or "disruptive" behavior. The point is, therefore, that the author considers the presence of missionaries who demand to be supported by the labors of others to be a disruptive force. And the controversy is a glimpse of an early struggle between older and newer models of ministry (2004, 652–53). To use such a passage in a debate over contemporary public policy is to ignore its historical context, and to view it as a sanction for punitive governmental policies is a mean-spirited travesty of biblical ethics.

HERMENEUTICAL QUESTIONS

The most evident hermeneutical question raised by the materials examined in this chapter is how to deal with the tensions between some of these materials and both the letters of Paul and the Jesus tradition on issues related to the patriarchal system and the hierarchical arrangement of power and privilege. Whatever the reasons for the reversion to the traditional patterns, it is clear that some of the later writings have significantly curbed the trajectory toward a more egalitarian understanding. We are thus left with the question of how to appropriate these disparate witnesses when relating these traditions to the contemporary church.

The various models of the relationship between church and world also raise important questions. The differences among Paul's undisputed letters and the various post-Pauline materials on this point are by no means absolute, and all are clear that the believer's first loyalty is to God. But 1 Peter goes beyond Paul's statement in Romans 1 by affirming the authority of governments, and the pilgrim theology in Hebrews makes the body of believers much more of an alien entity in the world. Ephesians, moreover, seems to embrace a notion of the conversion of "the powers," which we do not find in the authentic letters. Thus, we are left with a tangle of overlapping but to some extent competing perspectives.

We have already observed tension within Paul's undisputed letters regarding the relationship between his Spirit-driven ethic of discernment and his promulgation of specific rules, but the tension is increased exponentially when we come to the Pastoral Letters, Jude, and 2 Peter. Also, the tendency to understand salvation as present in Colossians and Ephesians contrasts with Paul's careful delineation of the present as a time of only partial fulfillment, and the comparison of the two views raises interesting questions for believers at a time in which the whole apocalyptic way of thinking has become questionable. The letter of James, moreover, presents a contrast to the authentic letters of Paul with respect to how christology grounds ethics. Law apparently retains a kind of validity that it does not have for Paul, a phenomenon that recalls aspects of Matthew in which ethics extends beyond christology.

Another issue that emerges from the letter of James is how the church in our time should relate to its radical condemnation of wealth and seemingly unqualified indictment of the rich. The voices of both the Jesus movement and the Hebrew prophets take on new life in this writing, issuing a bold challenge to an institution that long ago made its peace with both wealth and worldly power. What message does it have for a worldwide association of communities of believers whose lot in the world ranges from affluence or great wealth to stark poverty? Can it in any way reconcile, or must it only further separate, those who profit from the existing structures of economic power and those who are completely alienated from such systems? Does it have any potential at all as a vehicle for Paul's vision of genuine community in Christ or Jesus' proclamation of the rule of God in which all human barriers are broken down?

One final issue deserves mention. In discussing Colossians and Ephesians, we have once again come upon elements of ecological thinking (see above, 139–41, 212–13, 259–61). But these two writings, which seem to offer such promise for an ecologically sensitive ethic, are problematic from the perspective of gender equality. We have already seen that Paul's venture into an argument from nature in relation to women's head coverings runs counter to his egalitarian declarations such as Gal 3:28. And so, even though the cosmological language in Ephesians and Colossians is christologically grounded, we must ask whether there is an inherent tendency in references or allusions to the created order to reinforce entrenched cultural patterns that are often oppressive in character.

CHAPTER 11

the revelation to john

⤴

To many readers of the Revelation to John, any talk of this document's ethics seems an oxymoron at best and a cruel irony at worst. Is it not a self-indulgent panegyric to revenge, a virtual house of horrors filled with grotesque images of death and destruction? And does it not replace the witness of the Jesus tradition to God's love, mercy, and forgiveness with the image of a cruel and punitive tyrant who subjects his enemies to torment, terror, and torture? It was not without reason that D. H. Lawrence dubbed this writing the "Judas" of the New Testament (1932, 14–15) or that Alfred North Whitehead found it illustrative of "the barbaric elements" in Christianity that work against the best intuitions of the faith (1967, 170). From another perspective, of course, the writing fares quite differently. To those who have no problem with images of God as violent despot, the lurid details of the implementation of divine wrath are perhaps to be celebrated as the just desserts of the disobedient. There are, however, other possible evaluations of the work, and a more nuanced approach to its moral significance will have to begin by taking account of the nature of the language it employs.

THE FUNCTION OF THE APOCALYPTIC LANGUAGE

Although there is a long history of attempts to view this writing as a prediction of the future course of human history, all versions of this approach founder on the simple fact of the book's own insistence that the end of the present world order is in fact "near"—near, that is, to the time in which the author wrote (1:3; 3:11; 21:10, 12, 20). Thus to the extent that the author's language refers to the actual world at all, its focus is on the time in which he lived and the immediately expected future.

300

It is only in a qualified sense, moreover, that we can speak of references to the actual world. The author employs the highly imaginative and symbolic language of the apocalyptic tradition to "describe" the "events" associated with the end of the old age and the beginning of the new. And although one school of interpretation tries to find an exact referent for each symbolic term, as M. Eugene Boring comments, "[m]any of the scenes John describes simply cannot be imaged." Thus a better appreciation of the nature of that language understands the symbols employed as "tensive, evocative, and polyvalent" (Boring 1989, 54). Elisabeth Schüssler Fiorenza therefore terms the language of Revelation "mythopoetic" and compares it to poetry and drama. The power of its images lies in their "evocative power" that invites "imaginative participation," its ability to elicit "emotions, feelings, and convictions that cannot, and should not, be fully conceptualized." This latter point is of great significance, because some interpreters who view the language as symbolic and poetic have nevertheless "attempted to relegate apocalyptic language to mere form from which the historical or theological content can be distilled." And this tendency to reduce the text's imaginative symbolism to conceptual content is often associated with "the theological evaluation of Revelation as a myth of revenge and a drama of resentment which is deemed incompatible with a Christian theology of love and forgiveness" (Schüssler Fiorenza 1981, 18–19).

If we are to give a fair hearing to the moral potential of this writing, then, we must allow it to speak with its own voice and hear it in a way commensurate with the character and purpose of its language. And to do that, we must give some attention to the historical context of the writing. The author, who identified himself as John, wrote in the face of considerable danger from the Roman Empire to Christians who refused to participate in the cult of emperor worship. Most recent scholars assign the writing to the reign of the emperor Domitian (81–96 C.E.) and do not find sufficient evidence to support the earlier theory of a systematic, "*official, government-sponsored* persecution" of the church during this period (Farmer 2005, 16; emphasis original). When accused by their neighbors of disloyalty to the empire, however, Christians could be required to refute the charge by proclaiming Caesar as Lord; and persistent refusal could result in the threat of death. Nor were such accusations hypothetical. In addition to the tensions with their neighbors caused by their "suspicious beliefs and practices," the socioeconomic situation made their situation particularly precarious. Food shortages often caused "tensions between rich and poor," and "Christians, generally poor and disenfranchised, probably sympathized with the poor in the conflicts, which again brought them into confrontation with the authorities" (Farmer 2005, 17).

Given this situation, when directly confronted with the demand to worship the emperor, John's readers had only two realistic options. They could either comply with the empire's requirements or they could refuse and risk death. From the perspective of Revelation, then, "[t]he present situation was an opportunity to bear witness to the reality and meaning of Christian faith in the one God and Jesus as the only Lord, even if it meant dying at the hands of the Romans as had Jesus himself. John affirms this as the only Christian response" (Boring 1989, 23).

Against this background, John composed his work in highly symbolic and evocative language to give encouragement to readers in a dire situation. He used a few symbols that had direct referents. For example, drawing on the current Jewish practice of symbolizing Rome as Babylon, the ancient enemy that had once destroyed the temple, he constructed an "alternative universe" in which Babylon/Rome meets its eventual demise (chapters 17–18). Beyond a few such definite references as this, however, John employed a multitude of symbols whose mode of signification is more open-ended and evocative. Thus, the point of the rehearsal of "events" is not to give an outline of actual happenings expected in the future but to make the point in an imaginative way that the oppressive power that rules the world in the present is not the ultimate power in the universe but will someday come under the judgment of God. And even the symbols with definite referents take on the ability to speak to situations far removed from the author's specific situation.

The purpose of the lurid descriptions of God's punishment of the wicked, then, is to dramatize the author's belief that God will vindicate the righteous who have remained faithful in the face of the demands of an evil empire. "Babylon/Rome in its splendor," Schüssler Fiorenza writes,

> symbolizes imperial power and cult. In Rev. it is the powerful incarnation of international exploitation, oppression, and murder. Babylon/Rome is intoxicated not only with the blood of saints but with that of all those slaughtered on earth. Rome's ruthless power and exploitative wealth are enormous and its decrees are carried out in the provinces that support Roman oppression. (1985, 7)

Thus to symbolize God's judgment of Babylon/Rome is to give poetic expression to the human hope for justice, the hope for a time in which all forms of violence and oppression are brought to an end and human beings are free to live the lives that God intended for them, recognizing God as their sovereign and living in peace and concord with one another.

MORAL INSTRUCTION IN THE SEVEN LETTERS

The apocalyptic framework of Revelation provides a context of ultimate hope within which the author addresses his audience with ethical demands, which are found primarily in chapters 1–3—the letters to "the seven churches that are in Asia" (1:4). Far from a mere preface, these chapters are essential to the author's purpose, because it is here that he states the implications of the theological point he makes in the "alternative universe" described in chapters 4–22. And it is largely because of the opening chapters that we can legitimately think of Revelation not merely as an apocalypse—a revelation of "things to come"—but, in keeping with the author's own description of the work (1:3; 22:7), as prophecy. For here John, in the tradition of the Hebrew prophets, addresses his audience in the present with moral imperatives on the basis of his understanding of God's will for their lives and intentions for the immediate future.

These imperatives, however, are limited in scope. As Wolfgang Schrage observes, "[a]lthough there are hints of how life was lived in the Christian community and the world, the seer scarcely touches on concrete ethical problems besides this conflict with the state and emperor worship, which keeps him in suspense and threatens him with death" (1988, 341). The letters to the churches are thus dominated by the motifs of faithfulness and endurance. "Be faithful unto death" (2:10) is the command that the Son of Man in the vision issues through John to the church at Ephesus, and there are repeated promises to those who "conquer" (*nikan*; 2:7, 11, 17, 26; 3:5, 12, 21; also 21:7)—that is, those who remain faithful. We also find several calls to repent (*metanoein*; 2:5, 16; 3:3; also 2:21, 22), severe condemnations of those who justify eating food sacrificed to idols (2:14-15, 20), and the use of fornication as a metaphor for idolatry (2:21).

Not all injunctions in these chapters relate specifically to idolatry, however. The Son of Man also issues compliments to or criticisms of individual churches' performance with respect to their "works" (*erga*; 2:2, 5, 23; 3:2), and in 2:4 and 2:19 he uses the criterion of love as one of the standards for judging their spiritual status. However, all fall under the more general motif of wholeheartedness, which, as Schrage notes, is closely associated with the call to repentance and is particularly well illustrated by the word spoken to Laodicea: "I know your works;

you are neither cold nor hot. I wish that you were either cold or hot. So, because you are lukewarm, I am about to spit you out of my mouth" (3:15-16). "The basic evil," Schrage comments, "is indifference, compromise, the indecisive, lukewarm, vague Christianity that the seer describes as arousing the Lord's loathing" (1988, 34). We may therefore speculate that it is precisely this half-hearted kind of commitment that, as John sees the matter, has led some to compromise with the idolatrous demands of the empire. And in 3:17 he links this half-heartedness to the community's economic situation: "For you say, 'I am rich, I have prospered, and I need nothing.' You do not realize that you are wretched, pitiable, poor, blind, and naked." Apparently, then, as Hays writes,

> The church has been lulled to sleep by the hypnotic power of affluence and co-opted by the economic system of the Roman Empire. John regards this as a back door into idolatry; the materially wealthy community is de facto compromised and therefore spiritually poor. Thus, although there are no specific commandments or teachings about possessions in Revelation, there is a clear symbolic correlation between wealth and idolatry. (1996, 177)

If we accept Hays's reasoning on this point, it would appear that John's condemnation of idolatry extends beyond the external act of emperor worship. Since the empire makes this idolatrous demand, any degree of participation in its life would in itself compromise the Christians' commitment to God alone. Thus, later in the work, John calls for explicit withdrawal from the larger society: "Come out of her, my people, so that you do not take part in her sins . . ." (18:4).

In summary, "[t]he overall message of the seven letters is to call for sharper boundaries between the church and the world" (Hays 1996, 177). This message is based on the perception that participation in the life of the empire is in itself an idolatrous compromise with the faith professed by those who name themselves followers of Christ. And the result of such compromise is manifest in what John sees as the more blatantly unfaithful practice of eating food offered to idols. It is clear that some members of the churches justify this practice, and, as Hays suggests, "perhaps some even argue that Christians can accommodate the emperor cult as a civic obligation without betraying their faith in Jesus." In any case,

> Against such thinking, John sounds an alarm. It is no accident that the Letter to Laodicea comes as the climax of this section. There can be no compromise, John insists, and the church that thinks it can live

comfortably within the empire's economic system is in spiritual danger. (Hays 1996, 177)

THE NATURE OF THE EMPIRE'S EVIL[1]

What is it, in John's eyes, that is so evil about the evil empire? Certainly, the persecution of Christians is a central factor. Early on, in 1:9, he mentions persecution as something he shares with the recipients, and in the vision of the fifth seal in 6:9-11 he sees "under the altar the souls of those who had been slaughtered for the word of God and for the testimony they had given." These souls are crying out to God, "how long will it be before you judge and avenge our blood on the inhabitants of the earth?" They are given white robes and "told to rest a little longer," until the empire's bloodbath comes to an end. But the reader does not have to wait beyond chapters 18–19, which finally depict God's judgment. And that judgment appears explicitly as vindication of the martyrs, for in 19:2, we read that God "has judged the great whore [Babylon/ Rome] who corrupted the earth with her fornication, and he has avenged on her the blood of her servants."

One point that those who criticize Revelation as nothing more than a call for revenge tend to miss, however, is that John's condemnation of Rome's violence is not limited to its actions against the church. In 18:24, an angel directs in more general terms these words against "Babylon" that indict its violence: "And in you was found the blood of prophets and of saints, *and of all who have been slaughtered on earth.*" No reader in the Greco-Roman world could read this passage without thinking of all of Rome's wars of conquest and vicious suppression of revolts against its rule. The specific charge of murdering the prophets, moreover, shows that the identification of "Babylon" with Rome is not absolute, since it was not Rome who put Israel's prophets to death. It therefore invites the reader to understand "all who have been slaughtered on earth" as a much broader reference to imperial violence—a phenomenon that had plagued Israel in many incarnations over the centuries. Thus, as Boring comments, "[r]uthless use of violence by every empire is here included in 'Babylon'" (1989, 187).

The author's critique also extends beyond violence and persecution per se. The arrogant and luxurious lifestyle of the empire's elite, built on the exploitation of others, is also the subject of prophetic condemnation. In 18:7a-b we find this broad indictment of Roman affluence: "As she glorified herself and lived luxuriously, so give her a like measure of torment and grief." Even more poignantly, in

18:12-13 the judgment extends to those merchants throughout the world who participated in the empire's exploitative practices:

> And the merchants of the earth weep and mourn for her, since no one buys their cargo anymore, cargo of gold, silver, jewels, and pearls, fine linen, purple, silk and scarlet, all kinds of scented wood, all articles of ivory, all articles of costly wood, iron, and marble, cinnamon, spice, incense, myrrh, frankincense, wine, olive oil, choice flour and wheat, cattle and sheep, horses and chariots, slaves—and human lives.

The final phrase (*kai sōmatōn kai psychas anthrōpōn*) has been translated in several different ways. The NRSV has "slaves—and human lives" but gives "and human bodies and souls" (see also NIV) as an alternative. The RSV, however, has "and slaves, that is, human souls." Despite these variations, the phrase is an unmistakable reference to slavery and a clear condemnation of this practice. The use of *sōmatōn* (bodies), rather than the actual word for "slaves," moreover, underscores the gross insensitivity that allows societies to engage in such practice. As Christopher C. Rowland remarks, "slaves were just bodies, mere commodities to add to the long list. But John cannot allow that to pass without glossing the word: They are human lives" (1998, 694). Also, the reference to slavery forges a close link between imperial affluence and imperial violence, because slavery is an inherently violent institution. Here again, John transcends the specific issue of the persecution of the church. And the same may be said of his indictment of economic exploitation: "Rome's economic policies of living in luxury at the expense of the poor are condemned as such, quite apart from its direct religious consequences" (Boring 1989, 188).

Finally, the empire is guilty of blasphemy, idolatry, and self-glorification. In 13:8 the "whole earth" worships the beast, and in 13:5 the beast utters "haughty and blasphemous words." In 18:7c-8, moreover, the angel elaborates on "Babylon's" self-glorification with this indictment of its self-deluding arrogance and moves from that point to a pronouncement of final judgment:

> Since in her heart she says,
>   "I rule as a queen;
> I am no widow,
>   and I will never see grief,"
> therefore her plagues will come in a single day—

pestilence and mourning and famine—
and she will be burned with fire;
  for mighty is the Lord God who judges her.

JOHN'S VISION OF VINDICATION AND RENEWAL

Another point that those who see in Revelation only death and destruction tend to overlook is the character of the new world John envisions. And the first point to make in this regard is that the charge that John is guilty of an actual hatred of civilization (Lawrence 1932, 14–15) involves a rather flat reading of some important passages. As Boring observes,

> not everything about the "Great City" was evil. There is some genuine pathos in the lament that the sound of music, skilled fashioners of civilization, the voice of bride and bridegroom are to vanish (18:21-23) and be replaced by a dead and haunted city (18:2). John himself has some admiration for the great city (17:6-7), even in its perverted state. (1989, 188)

Of equal importance is the fact that in John's vision of ultimate renewal, "[a]ll that is good and valuable will be redeemed and will be present in the Holy City . . ." (Boring 1989, 188). Although it is easy for a reader to be so alienated by the grotesque images earlier in the writing, chapters 21–22 envision "a new heaven and a new earth" characterized not only by an end to death and suffering (21:4) but also by a rehabilitation of human institutions. Although in 19:17-18 we find a ghoulish image of birds "eating the flesh of kings, the flesh of captains, the flesh of the mighty," in the vision of the holy city to come a different image appears.

> And the city has no need of sun or moon to shine on it, for the glory of God is its light, and its lamp is the Lamb. The nations will walk by its light, and the kings of the earth will bring their glory into it. Its gates will never be shut by day—and there will be no night there. People will bring into it the glory and the honor of the nations. (21:22-26)

In John's final vision, moreover, we have a powerful image of ultimate reconciliation:

Then the angel showed me the river of the water of life, bright as crystal, flowing from the throne of God and of the Lamb through the middle of the street of the city. On either side of the river is the tree of life with its twelve kinds of fruit, producing its fruit each month; and *the leaves of the trees are for the healing of the nations.* (22:1-2)

The end of the old age, effected by God's violent overthrow of an empire built on violence, oppression, idolatry, and blasphemy, will therefore be a re-creation of the peacefulness of the Garden of Eden, where the tree of life grew. The reference to "the nations," however, shows that this is not a mere return to the beginning but "a recovery of the goodness of creation by the redemption of the historical process rather than its elimination" (Boring 1989, 22). Ultimately, then, John's vision of the eschatological future is an affirmation of the world and even of the human institutions he has criticized so severely. Neither nations nor civilizations are in principle evil. They have become evil through their alliance with Satan, but in the new world they can and will be redeemed.

If the destruction of Babylon/Rome is vindication for all those murdered, enslaved, oppressed, and mistreated by the imperial powers that have ruled the earth, the final chapters of Revelation nevertheless put that vindication into a broader context. It is not God's punishment that is the final word, but rather God's re-creation of the world as a place of ultimate well-being—a point that has significance in light of the current ecological/climatological crisis.

CREATION AND RE-CREATION IN REVELATION

A text as heavily imbued with the apocalyptic outlook as Revelation would hardly seem a likely place to look for ecological sensitivity. Not only biblical literalists who await a cosmic catastrophe but ecologically minded scholars with a very different perspective have often read the apocalyptic strains in the Bible as denying that earth is "the true human home."[2] There is much material in these writings that lends itself to such interpretation, but a nuanced reading of some important passages can yield some surprising results in this regard. One might, of course, conclude that the re-creation of the cosmos implied in John's vision in 21:1 of "a new heaven and a new earth" replacing "the first heaven and the first earth" that have "passed away" entails a negative judgment on creation itself. However, the obvious allusion to Eden (Gen 2:9) in 22:2 clearly signifies a restoration of creation rather than a demolition followed by the appearance of something totally new. And the vision of the new Jerusalem "coming down out of Heaven from God" in 21:2 shows that the restoration takes place not by destroying earth, or even by lifting it up to heaven, but by a uniting of the two spheres. The poetic section in 21:3-4, moreover, strengthens this point by proclaiming that God's dwelling is now "among mortals." Echoing Ezek 37:26, where God promises to make an everlasting covenant with the people and to establish among them the divine sanctuary itself, these verses comprise a rather striking affirmation of the integrity of the earth as God's good creation.

A passage that has been particularly problematic from an ecological perspective, however, is Rev 12:12:

> Rejoice, then, you heavens
> > and those who dwell in them!
> But woe to the earth and the sea,
> > for the devil has come down to you
> with great wrath,
> > because he knows that his time is short.

If we understand the pronouncement of "woe" here as a curse, it easy to conclude that God condemns the earth. As Barbara Rossing points out, however, the Greek word that the NRSV renders here as "woe" (*ouai*) can also be translated as "alas"—that is, not as a curse but as a lament. The word is in fact generally rendered this way in 18:10: "Alas, alas, the great city, Babylon, the mighty city!" And there is good reason to think that the same sense is operative in 12:12. Here the term is contrasted not with a blessing but with rejoicing. And it is followed not by an indirect object (dative case), as it is in Luke 6:20-26 and other texts in which it signifies a curse in contrast to a blessing, but rather by a direct object (accusative case). The preposition "to" in the above translation is therefore misleading, and Rossing suggests that the grammatical construction is an accusative of reference that would be well rendered by "'Alas, Earth!' or 'Alas for Earth' (that is, 'Alas with reference to Earth')" (2002, 182). Understood in this way, *ouai* expresses not God's condemnation of the earth but rather divine sympathy for it as the devil (not God!) visits wrath upon it.

As to the reason for such a lament, Rossing argues that "Rev. 12.12 and other negative references to 'Earth' (*Ge*) in Revelation can be understood as part of the book's political critique against Roman imperial exploitation" (2002, 184). Central to this reading is 11:18, which announces God's wrath as directed in part toward "destroying those who destroy the earth." There can be little doubt, in light of the condemnation that pervades the entire writing, that "those who destroy the earth" are Rome and those in league with it—a point that becomes particularly clear when we read 12:18—13:10 in context. The "woe" that comes upon the earth in 12:12 is the direct result of Satan's expulsion from heaven in 12:9 and consequent activity on earth; and, since in 12:18—13:10 Satan is associated with the beast, which represents both the Roman emperors and the empire, we can see that it is Rome itself through which "Satan's presence is manifested" in the earthly sphere. Thus, given the sharp economic critique of the beast's activities in 13:17—"expanded in Revelation 18 with an indictment of Rome as a world trade center whose unjust cargoes from Earth and sea enrich the elites while exploiting the rest of the world"[3]—we may identify Rome's economic practices as an example of how it destroys the earth. As Harry Maier comments, "The detailed listing of merchant cargo (Rev 18.11-14, 16) describes the way Earth is mined, slaughtered, logged, spun and sold for the sake of profit" (2002, 176).

There are, to be sure, passages that seem to attribute actions destructive of nature to divine agency. In 8:6—9:12, it is the trumpets of the seven angels that unleash the first of a series of "woes"; and in 9:12 and 11:14 the term *ouai* is used as a noun and clearly refers to acts of destruction. In the visions of the seven bowls in 15:1—16:21, moreover, the angels launch attacks on land, waters, air, and the sun. In all of this, however, a redemptive intent is operative. The purpose of the horrors initiated by the bowls is evident in the notation that the people did not repent (16:9, 11), and the entire array of catastrophes in the natural world is punctuated with allusions to the plagues in Exodus that God sent to convince Pharaoh to release the people from captivity (Rev 8:7; 16:8-9, 19-21//Exod 9:22-26; Rev 8:9; 16:3-7//Exod 7:17-21). It is also clear that it is the abusive power of Rome that has made these cosmic catastrophes necessary. In 15:10-11, the angel pours out a bowl not against nature but against the throne of the beast, shrouding its kingdom in darkness; and in 16:6 the third angel acknowledges before God the justice of turning rivers and springs into blood: "because they shed the blood of saints and prophets, you have given them blood to drink."

If, then, we read these passages against the background of Revelation's severe critique of Rome's exploitative practices on the one hand and the depiction of its eventual destruction in chapters 18–19 on the other, they begin to appear in a somewhat different light. As Maier states,[4]

The Roman Empire was notorious for its extinction of animals and exhausting of Earth resources to feed its hunger for entertainment and luxury. The *mise-en-scène* for the laments in Rev 18 is the desolate and abandoned Babylon whose ecological desolation (Rev 18.2) becomes the potent symbol of the broken Earth relationships between peoples, plants, animals and natural resources that the imperial greed lets loose upon the world. . . . The vision of the destruction of Earth is a hallmark of the ancient apocalypse genre's rhetorical-literary strategies of persuasion. In Revelation, divine agents announce the destruction of Earth, but it is debatable whether the destruction originates with God. (2002, 176)

It is nevertheless undeniable that within the framework of Revelation's rhetoric God appears as the proximate cause of the destructive forces that are visited upon the earth. We must therefore recognize a degree of tension between God's ultimately redemptive purposes and the steps that are necessary, within that rhetorical framework, to achieve the divine ends. It is clear, however, that this same rhetorical framework leads finally to a vision of blessed renewal in Revelation 21–22. And it is equally clear that God's eschatological justice embraces both the socioeconomic order and the natural word. As Rossing comments, drawing on Leonardo Boff's call to bring together the Bible's parallel interests in ecology and justice,

The book of Revelation is a biblical text that brings the two discourses together, setting its vision for Earth within an overall anti-imperial political context. Revelation gives voice to two parallel cries of lament: the cry of the poor and the cry of the earth. (2002, 192)[5]

COMMUNITY, EMPIRE, AND WORLD

The images of ultimate well-being in the final chapters of Revelation should not mislead us into minimizing John's condemnation of the empire. In his eyes, it is evil through and through, indeed an agent of Satan. It is murderous, oppressive, and blasphemous. The calls to repentance in the seven letters are directed to the churches, not the empire or the world in general. And the references to the refusal of repentance by evildoers in the face of the various plagues visited upon the earth (9:20-21; 16:9-11) illustrate the intransigence of those given over to evil, not the actual possibility of change on their part.

We must say, then, that the peace and concord that characterize the eventual renewal of creation remains a purely eschatological vision. For the present, the community of faith remains alienated from both the empire and the world at large. It is the faithful remnant in a world controlled by the powers of death and destruction. John's understanding of the church in relation to the world is therefore fundamentally different from the views of the authors of 1 Peter and Ephesians and to some extent of Paul himself. Neither 1 Peter's injunction to accept the authority of the emperor and governors (2:13-14) nor Paul's statement in Rom 1:1-2 that the "governing authorities" are instituted by God would have a place in Revelation. Nor would Ephesians 3:10, which suggests that it is the role of the church to make God's wisdom known "to the rulers and authorities in the heavenly places."

In chapter 9, I argued that, Romans 13 notwithstanding, Paul expected the dismantling of Rome's power in the new age. We also saw, however, that he had a degree of openness to the wider culture and a sense that those in Christ had a responsibility to contribute to the common good. And in this latter respect it appears that Revelation conveys a rather different attitude. Efforts toward the common good would seem irrelevant in light of the thoroughly corrupt state of the world, and any degree of positive interaction with the world beyond the community would suggest betrayal.

Symptomatic of the sharp difference between Paul and Revelation on this point is the discrepancy between their views on eating meat offered to idols. Whereas for Paul the issue was whether the practice would harm either the individual or the community, for John it was idolatry. The perceived threat of persecution and martyrdom undoubtedly accounts in part for John's adamant position, but there is another dimension to the issue. In the course of Paul's discussion of the matter, he mentions the possibility that a member of the assembly might accept an invitation to a meal at the home of an unbeliever (1 Cor 10:26). There is nothing in Revelation that forbids such a practice, but its sense of alienation from the outside world makes the discussion of such matters irrelevant. For not only the empire but also society at large appears in an exceedingly negative light. Having said this, however, I must reiterate a point made in the preceding section. John's alienation from the empire and even society as a whole does not constitute a hatred of civilization per se. Nor does it signify a rejection of humanity or of the essential goodness of God's creation.

Neither does the pervasive negativity of John toward the world outside the community result in a consistent doctrine of exclusive salvation—that is, the notion that it is only believers who will survive the eschatological judgment. For, despite the denials of many an interpreter, there are (as we will soon see) some passages that actually suggest universal salvation, even though many others present images of myriads of human beings subjected to eternal punishment or death. The view of final salvation in Revelation is therefore paradoxical. This is a matter, however, that is best discussed under the heading of hermeneutical questions.

HERMENEUTICAL QUESTIONS

Indications of the loss of eternal salvation for some persons are not hard to find in Revelation. Ronald Farmer (1997, 164) identifies two types of passages that convey this idea—final judgment scenes and what he calls exclusion texts. One of the former is 14:9-11, which describes the fate of the followers of the beast: not only will they "be tormented with fire and sulfur in the presence of the holy angels and in the presence of the Lamb," but "the smoke of their torment goes up forever and ever." Another judgment passage is 20:11-15, the famous scene depicting the opening of "the books," which ends with the statement that "anyone whose name was not found written in the book of life was thrown into the lake of fire." Among the exclusion texts is 21:8, which lists those who will not inherit salvation. "But as for the cowardly, the faithless, the polluted, the murderers, the fornicators, the sorcerers, the idolaters, and all liars, their place will be in the lake that burns with fire and sulfur, which is the second death."

As Farmer comments, there is nothing surprising about the presence of texts portraying limited salvation in Revelation, "given the general tone of apocalyptic writings" (1997, 170). What is surprising is the presence of passages that "picture salvation as a universal gift." Some of these stand in the tradition of texts in the Hebrew Bible that envision a time in which the Gentiles would be included in the worship of Israel's God. Thus, in Rev 15:3-4, John quotes a passage from Exodus 15 that includes the declaration that "[a]ll nations will come and worship before you," and in Rev 5:13 he describes the worship that takes place around the throne of God as rendered by "every creature in heaven and on earth and under the earth and in the sea, and all that is in them. . . ." Among the other passages that imply universal salvation are those that depict the eschatological renewal of God's creation. Thus, as noted earlier, in 21:22-26, even "the nations and the kings of the earth—the very ones destroyed in chapters 6–20—are part of the new order" (Farmer 1997, 173). Likewise, the reference to "the healing of the nations" in 22:2 tends to imply an ultimate reconciliation and inclusion.

We are therefore faced with the fact that Revelation includes some passages that indicate limited salvation and others that indicate universal salvation, which suggests that, as Boring contends, "John has no *one* consistent view" and that "[n]either group of texts can be subordinated to the other." The interpreter must therefore conclude that John's view is fully paradoxical, and I can agree on one level with Boring's view that our task "is not to seek ways to reconcile the tension in the text" but rather "to find the thrust of Revelation's message precisely in this tension" (1989, 228). Indeed, the tension in Revelation on this point is a sterling example of the fragmentary, open-ended character of language that I stressed in chapter 2. In that chapter, however, I also proposed a hermeneutical model that goes beyond descriptive exegesis by making two additional interpretive moves. The first of these is to trace out the ultimate implications of the conflicting strains of meaning within a text, and the second is to propose a "reconstruction" of meaning designed to speak to the situation in which the interpreter lives. Farmer approaches John's paradoxical language regarding salvation on the basis of a similar hermeneutic and seeks a "transformation" of the paradox (1997, 184–93). I treated the related issue of exclusive vs. inclusive salvation in my examination of Matthew in chapter 5, and I will return to it in chapter 12.

Farmer brings a similar approach to another paradox that he finds in Revelation. Apocalyptic literature in general differs from prophetic literature in part because of the former's strong tendency toward historical determinism. That is to say, the visions of the future that are so pervasive in such works give the impression that God is in unilateral control of the course of human events, which is fixed in stone. Revelation is, for the most part, no exception on this point. In chapters 4–5, however, we find a surprising note of contingency. In 5:2, when the Lamb receives a scroll with seven seals from the figure seated on the throne, an angel thunders out the question, "Who is worthy to open the scroll and break its seals?" Then follows a period of suspense, because "no one in heaven or in earth or under the earth was able to open the scroll or look into it," and John himself begins to weep bitterly because of this. He is comforted, however, by one of the elders around the throne who proclaims that "the Lion of the tribe of Judah, the Root of David, has conquered, so that he can open the scroll and its seven seals" (5:5). The impression is that it is the worthiness of the Lamb— the fact that he "conquered," or remained faithful—that qualifies him for this task. Thus, Farmer concludes, "God's ability to implement the divine purpose is contingent on finding a worthy human agent." And, further, the bracketing of "the whole drama" of eschatological events with "exhortations to faithfulness addressed to the readers (1–3; and 22:6-21)" shows that "[f]or the Word of God to accomplish the New Creation, the followers of the Lamb must bear faithful testimony" (1997, 157).

This undercurrent of contingency stands in marked tension with the dominant strain of historical determinism. And the contrast between the elder's designation of the Lamb as the Lion of the tribe of Judah and the way John describes the Lamb in 5:6 create another point of tension: "I saw between the throne and the four living creatures and among the elders a Lamb *standing as if it had been slain*." This obvious allusion to the crucifixion forces the reader to place in juxtaposition an image of power and an image of weakness and vulnerability. But if it is through the death and resurrection of the Lamb that God redeems the world, the reader is forced to reexamine traditional understandings of the power of God. The presentation of the redeeming Lamb as weak and vulnerable invites us to think of God's power not as unilateral or coercive but as relational and persuasive, even as other aspects of the text imply the contrary. Here again, Farmer applies a hermeneutic similar to my own that will inform my later treatment of the issue.

The two hermeneutical issues identified so far have focused on the theological dimension of Revelation, and they both relate to the questions I have raised throughout this volume with respect to the problems entailed in making use of apocalyptic materials in our contemporary situation. There are other issues that arise from a reading of Revelation, however, that have more clearly moral implications. The first of these is the potential of the descriptions of God's eschatological violence to foster on a human level a thirst for revenge, which is based on a simplistic dichotomy between good and evil persons. Granted the final images of "the healing of the nations" and the peaceable life in the eschatological holy city, one still has to ask whether the violent imagery might so outweigh the other elements as to render them ineffective.

Not only do interpreters remain divided on this issue, but some feel compelled to give highly nuanced accounts that weigh very carefully the positive and negative aspects of the work. One of these is Adela Yarbro Collins, who approaches Revelation from a social-psychological perspective, arguing that its function was to speak to "the unbearable tension perceived by the author between what was and what ought to have been." The author's intention was "to create that tension for readers unaware of it, to heighten it for those who felt it already, and then to overcome it in an act of literary imagination" (1984, 141). On one level, the work served to create a kind of catharsis, the process of cleansing of emotions that Aristotle attributed to Greek tragedies. On another level, it encouraged the readers to imagine an alternative reality in which God's victory over evil was complete—that, in other words, "what ought to be *is*" (1984, 154). It also offered two strategies for dealing with the resentment Christians must have felt in the face of their extreme alienation and vulnerability. The first is transference. Revelation does not encourage its readers to take up arms against their oppressors, but in graphic and emotional terms it envisions Christ as accomplishing the defeat of the enemy. The second strategy is internalization. Thus, John idealized sexual continence on the one hand and glorified martyrdom on the other (1984, 157–60).

We must ask, however, whether such a strategy is psychologically healthy and whether it is a worthy way of applying to a situation of oppression the values that informed the Jesus movement and the major writings of the New Testament. Yarbro Collins can in fact find positive value in this work:

> The strength of the Apocalypse is the pointed and universal way in which it raises the questions of justice, wealth, and power. Revelation serves the value of humanization insofar as it insists that the marginal, the relatively poor and powerless, must assert themselves to achieve their full humanity and dignity. (1984, 171)

On the other hand, she notes, it is also "a book that expresses anger and resentment and that may elicit violence. Its achievement is ambiguous insofar as aggressive feeling and violence can be destructive as well as constructive." Indeed, it "works against the values of humanization and love insofar as the achievement of personal dignity involves the degradation of others." Therefore, although "the imagery and tone of Revelation may embody attitudes that are necessary in the struggle for justice under certain conditions," these same attitudes "have a dark side of which interpreters of the Apocalypse must be conscious and whose dangers must be recognized." Awareness of the serious flaw in this writing does not, however, lead Yarbro Collins to reject the work altogether. Instead, she argues that insight into the violent side of the text and of ourselves might allow us to "move to a personal reinvolvement with the text on a new level"—that is, to engage in a "postcritical" reading "in which a partial, imperfect vision can still speak to our broken human situation" (1984, 171–72).

Another problematic aspect of this writing is the misogyny evident in its use of female images. Tina Pippin notes, for example, the extreme nature of the language used to describe the destruction of the Whore (= Babylon/Rome): "Three times (17:16; 18:8, 9) her burning is mentioned, and once we read that she will burn forever (19:3); three times it is mentioned that the destruction occurs in one hour (18:10, 17, 19)." The vengeance wreaked on the Whore, moreover, is marked by a combination of violence and eroticism that heightens the misogyny. Commenting on 17:16, Pippin writes,

> In this scene the erotic tension is heightened; the whore is literally stripped naked of her fine garments and jewels. Nakedness equals helplessness. Like the dragon goddess Tiamat in the Enuma Elish, the Whore is disembodied. The erotic tension here points to the ultimate misogynist fantasy! All the world's hatred of oppression is heaped on the Whore. Although the Roman Empire is not a scapegoat, the female symbol is a scapegoat. (1992, 67)

A similar dynamic is found in John's account of the punishment of Jezebel, the symbolic name given to the woman identified in the letter to Sardis as one who claims prophetic status and teaches that eating food offered to idols is acceptable:

> I gave her time to repent, but she refuses to repent of her fornication. Beware, I am throwing her on a bed, and those who commit adultery with her I am throwing into great distress, unless they repent of her doings; and I will strike her children dead. (2:22-23a)

There is a positive image of woman in chapter 12—the "woman clothed with the sun" who wears "a crown of twelve stars" (12:1). Her actual role, however, is limited and passive. After giving birth to the Messiah child, all she does is to flee to the wilderness where she remains under God's protection. Thus, as Pippin comments,

> The Woman Clothed with the Sun is a goddess subdued, tamed, and under control. The traditional female values that accompany the act of mothering (nurture and caretaking) are suppressed; the child is taken to live in heaven, and traditional male values of competition and separation come into the foreground. The Woman Clothed with the Sun, Jezebel, and the Whore are all hunted; only the Woman Clothed with the Sun escaped, but her escape is banishment from the center of power. The female is decentered even when held as an ideal woman. (1992, 76)

Along similar lines, Schüssler Fiorenza—who is otherwise a strong defender of the liberating potential of Revelation—gives this succinct statement of the hermeneutical problem that arises from the female imagery in Revelation:

Rev. engages the imagination of the contemporary reader to perceive women in terms of good or evil, pure or impure, wife or whore. Rather than instill "hunger for justice," the symbolic action of Rev. therefore can perpetuate prejudice and injustice if it is not "translated" into a contemporary "rhetorical situation" to which it can be a "fitting" rhetorical response. (1985, 199)

One final question to be raised regarding Revelation, in which the theological and moral dimensions come together, brings us back to the problematic character of the apocalyptic genre in general. In treating the Gospel of Matthew, I noted the tension involved in the notion of God's refusal to forgive those who do not themselves practice forgiveness as well as the broader problems raised by the notion of a God who punishes human violence with divine violence. I have also raised the question, as early as my treatment of the Jesus movement, as to whether the whole notion of a final judgment might tend to subvert the tradition's own emphasis on forgiveness and redemptive love. And even though we have found good reason to question the notion that Revelation takes a negative attitude toward the earth, we also found it necessary to recognize a degree of tension between the ultimate renewal John foresees and his visions of cosmic destruction. It would thus seem that the problems raised by the whole apocalyptic mode of discourse reach a fever pitch in the writing that concludes the New Testament canon, so that a treatment of this work is a natural lead-in to a fuller discussion of the hermeneutical issues we have encountered along the way.

PART IV

engaging new testament ethics

CHAPTER 12

knowing truth, doing good:
the new testament and contemporary
christian ethics

A REVIEW OF THE HERMENEUTICAL METHOD

In chapter 2, I proposed a hermeneutic grounded in Alfred North Whitehead's understanding of language. On this view, language is characterized by open-endedness on the one hand and a systematic thrust on the other. It cannot signify with absolute exactness, but all statements presuppose a systematic universe and therefore invite conceptual clarification on the broadest possible level.

I also characterized the basis of my hermeneutical method as an alternative form of postmodernism. In agreement with "deconstructive" postmodernism, this hermeneutic recognizes tensions within and among texts and acknowledges that competing strains of meaning "deconstruct" one another. It goes beyond this, however, in seeking to bring the disparate strains of meaning together in a higher unity in order to "negotiate" a reconstruction of meaning; but it acknowledges that it is not always possible to find a place for every element in the strains of meaning it integrates. It also differs from the deconstructive school in its insistence that texts not only open up potentialities for meaning but also place constraints on the creation of meaning. A text can mean many things, but it cannot mean "just anything" we want it to.

In terms of a practical approach to biblical texts, I proposed a model of the interpretive process involving five steps: (1) employing the historical-critical method; (2) determining the basic patterns of meaning potential; (3) attending to signs of wider meaning potential; (4) tracing out ultimate implications;

(5) proposing a reconstruction of meaning. I also noted that the final three steps are not applicable to every text. And I defined the reconstruction of meaning as involving a process of mutual challenge in which we allow the text to question the presuppositions that undergird our contemporary point of view even as we reserve the right to question the text on the basis of our own perspective. If we take the former aspect seriously, we must be open to the possibility of rethinking our own presuppositions; and if we take the latter seriously, we must be prepared to revalue some strains of meaning and perhaps reject some altogether.

My treatment of the various New Testament writings involved the first three steps only. In identifying specific hermeneutical questions for further reflection, however, I have laid the groundwork for the final two steps and for explicit conversation between worldviews. One way to approach this task would be to take up each writing again individually. My hope, however, is that the attention I have given to each writing has shown significant variety in both theology and ethics within the New Testament and that my decision to treat the hermeneutical issues in a way that cuts across the various writings will not appear as an attempt to deny this variety.

In the end, how we apply New Testament ethics to our contemporary situation depends on how we weigh competing strains of meaning and how we deal with the tensions between the worldviews in the texts and our own worldview. It depends also on the relative weight we give to Scripture on the one hand and tradition, reason, and experience on the other. It is my intention to bring all these factors into play as I consider the relevance of various aspects of the New Testament for life in the church today. Before turning to a discussion of the hermeneutical questions that have arisen so far, however, there is an assumption behind the whole notion of biblical ethics that I want to make more explicit.

"UNDER THEIR OWN VINES AND FIG TREES": THE ASSUMPTION BEHIND THE QUEST FOR THE GOOD

In chapter 3, I took note of Erhard Gerstenberger's contention that in the ancient world the original provenance of both religious observances and ethics was the small, autonomous kinship network or clan, each with its own deities. In this context, the values embraced by the group served the basic needs of survival and prosperity, and ethics enhanced internal cohesion and solidarity. In Israel, the formation of tribes and, eventually, a tribal alliance, led to the acknowledgment of a common deity, Yahweh. At another stage, the formation of a monarchy,

Yahweh became a state deity represented by the king. And although the king was theoretically accountable to Yahweh for the welfare of the whole people, the official, royal theology in many ways remained far removed from the actual lives of ordinary people. In particular, the poor and marginalized had few avenues through which to express their concerns. Therefore—to supplement Gerstenberger's insights with those of Richard Horsley and others—alongside the Great Tradition represented by the royal theology, a Little Tradition, passed on orally at the local level, continued to flourish. And it was this subterranean Little Tradition—focused on the principle of solidarity—that informed the great prophets' opposition to the policies of the royal houses and aristocracy. In this way, the original function of ethics as a means toward survival, prosperity, and internal cohesion lived on in the hearts and minds of the people.

It should therefore be clear that ethics in the Israelite tradition is not a matter of divine command in the simplistic sense. The point of moral action is not obedience to an arbitrary set of rules but action for the common good. As the work of John Barton shows, at many points the ethical demands of the Hebrew Bible are based either on standards to which even God is held accountable or the imitation of God's own actions. And insofar as New Testament ethics represents modulations on the basic structure of Israelite ethics, it is also, at base, an ethic of the common good.

Having said this, it is important to recognize that any ethic of the common good presupposes aesthetic value: the moral obligation to act for the good of the community and the individuals within it rests on the assumption that life itself is good and is to be enjoyed. In the Hebrew Bible, this presupposition is clear above all in the creation stories in Genesis 1–2. In Genesis 1, God pronounces all creation "good," and in Genesis 2 God places the man and the woman in a lush garden, obviously designed for enjoyment. Likewise, in Micah 4 we find a stirring vision of God's future *shalom* that draws on an image of the good life as enjoyment not only of peace and security but also of the bounty of the earth itself. Following a passage parallel to Isa 2:2-4, which envisions the nations of the world streaming to Jerusalem and beating their swords into plowshares and forswearing war, we find these words: "but they shall sit under their own vines and fig trees, and no one shall make them afraid; for the mouth of the LORD of hosts has spoken" (Mic 4:4).

A similar presupposition is at work in the New Testament stories of Jesus' healings and exorcisms: their result is the restoration of suffering people to the life of the community. And passages such as Matt 7:7-11 and 6:24-34 testify to God's desire for the material well-being of people and recognition that they do in fact "need all these [material] things" (6:3). In the Gospel of John, moreover, Jesus defines his mission in aesthetic terms: "I came that they might have life, and have it abundantly" (10:10). And Paul's vision of life in Christ is one of joy, as we see in Phil 4:1: "Rejoice in the Lord always; again I will say, rejoice" (4:1). It is also a vision of peace, so that he can plead with the Corinthians to "live in peace" (2 Cor 13:11) and pronounce this blessing on the Philippians: "And the peace of God, which surpasses all understanding, will guard your hearts and your minds in Christ Jesus" (4:7). Playing this theme out more fully, Paul defines the ideal for the assembly's life as combining moral and aesthetic qualities:

> Finally, beloved, whatever is true, whatever is honorable, whatever is just, whatever is pure, whatever is pleasant, whatever is commendable, if there is any excellence and if there is anything worthy of praise, think about these things. Keep on doing the things that you have learned and received and heard and seen in me, and the God of peace will be with you. (Phil 4:8-9)

As this passage makes clear, the aesthetic presupposition behind biblical ethics is not any sort of hedonism. The good life is life in fellowship with God, as we can also see in John 17:3: "And this is eternal life, that they may know you, the only true God, and Jesus Christ whom you have sent." Here eternal life is primarily a quality of life, hence aesthetic in character, but its value is inseparable from its religious base. It is the knowledge of God that makes life good and enjoyable. The fact remains, however, that the experience of life as good—the experience of abundant life, within a community of persons bound together in solidarity—is the presupposition of moral behavior. Knowledge of God is indeed the heart and soul of the biblical ethic, but rote obedience to arbitrary commands is not. For the purpose of command, like the call to the imitation of God or Christ and the development of character, is the enhancement of abundant life in relation to God and the neighbor. And for this reason, calls to self-sacrifice, such as we find so powerfully stated in Mark, must always be bracketed by an affirmation of the goodness of creation. In fact, the very logic of self-sacrifice makes no sense apart from the recognition that life is valuable and meant to be enjoyed.

A DISCUSSION OF HERMENEUTICAL QUESTIONS

In this section, I have divided the hermeneutical questions defined earlier into questions concerning truth and questions concerning the good. It is debatable whether ethics is derived from a prior understanding of the truth—that is, from a system of beliefs about the nature of reality—or whether our understanding of the truth about reality is projected from our prior sense of right and wrong. My own view is that in terms of human experience the two questions—"What is the truth?" and "What is the good?"—are fully reciprocal: each presupposes the other. In terms of logic, however, the question of truth seems prior. Our inclination is generally to derive our understanding of the good from our understanding of the truth, even if on the experiential level the relationship is often reversed. Thus, although our understanding of what is true is largely influenced by what we take to be good (so that one major reason for belief in God is to provide a grounding for ethics), I will begin by examining the questions relating to belief, or theology proper, before turning more explicitly to questions of the good, or ethics.

As I turn to this task, I add these final words of clarification about the nature of the third, fourth, and fifth hermeneutical steps. To attend to signs of wider meaning potential means to look for gaps, ambiguities, and undercurrents that take the reader beyond the dominant strains of signification. To trace out ultimate implications means to follow each strain of meaning in a text to its logical conclusion and to compare it with the logical conclusions of the other strains. And to propose a reconstruction of meaning is to weigh the competing strains, in conjunction with insights drawn from the interpreter's worldview, and to find coherent ways of rereading the text while honoring as many aspects of the various strains as possible. Although such a rereading will necessarily weigh the various strains differently, and not all will withstand critical scrutiny, the intention is to produce a reading that takes up significant aspects of the text's basic pattern of signification and not to replace that pattern with another that is more to one's liking. Yet a reconstructed reading is by nature a rereading and not a mere replication or even "translation."

Questions concerning the Truth

There is one major theological issue that has run like a thread throughout my analyses of the various New Testament materials. It has to do with a complex of notions surrounding eschatology: a cataclysmic end to human history, the literal return of Christ in glory, and God's final judgment. Although this apocalyptic scenario appears in the New Testament as a way of enforcing justice, it stands in considerable tension with other important strains of meaning in the various writings as well as with aspects of our contemporary worldview.

Regarding this latter tension, for many persons in the modern/postmodern world the notion of an apocalyptic end to history is simply incomprehensible.

To begin with, it is inherently wed to supernatural intervention, a notion that is notoriously difficult to reconcile with important aspects of our contemporary experience. This judgment depends neither on a "scientistic" reductionism that rules out any talk of God or the spiritual dimension nor on a view of the "laws of nature" as mechanical and immutable. The point, rather, is that the notion of God's exercise of external force to bring the world process to a close suggests a blatant violation of the way in which God seems to have related to that process throughout the history of our planet. And even more important than this objection is the fact that history has already disconfirmed this apocalyptic scenario *in the specific form that the New Testament writings understood it.* For an unbiased reading of these texts shows that, despite some minor variations, the writers expected the culmination of history in *their* near future.

At least as significant are the ways in which apocalypticism clashes with other aspects of the New Testament and the materials that lie behind it. We saw this first in the Jesus movement. The proclamation of the coming of God's rule entailed a notion of judgment that implies the violent action of God, which is difficult to reconcile with the portrayal of God's kindness toward "the ungrateful and the wicked" (Q 6:35) as well as the demand for radical nonviolence on the part of human beings. This same tension is visible in Matthew, especially in the parable of the unforgiving servant, in which God refuses forgiveness to those who will not forgive. Indeed, the problem is evident throughout the New Testament, but I took particular note of how it plays out in Mark and Revelation. It is possible to read both works as saying that the nonviolence to which human beings are called in the present is justified by the hope that God will eventually bring violent retribution on the perpetrators of injustice. In such a scenario, vengeance becomes God's means of enforcing justice.

Currents of meaning that run counter to this theme, however, are abundant. The New Testament materials consistently portray God as manifesting radical love and offering forgiveness freely, and this is especially the case insofar as they present Jesus as God's representative. It is therefore a major hermeneutical task for the interpreter to bring these two competing strains of meaning into conversation.

The traditional way of dealing with this problem is to deny that it exists by saying that eschatological judgment simply represents the limit on God's forgiveness. God graciously grants the opportunity for repentance but justly rejects those who refuse it. This line of reasoning, however, undermines the New Testament themes of God's love, grace, forgiveness, and mercy. For when these divine attributes are limited, they are no longer radical and therefore unworthy of the

God whom the New Testament depicts as represented by the compassionate and nonviolent Jesus.

Barring this solution, which sacrifices love for the sake of justice and nonviolence for the sake of eschatological judgment, it becomes necessary to trace out the implications of each strain of thought. And if we do this, the love-grace-forgiveness-mercy strain appears more fundamental to the overall New Testament proclamation. For the justice-punishment-vengeance strain is clearly dependent on it, rather than vice versa. Whereas God's love makes sense whether or not one speaks of any sort of divine punishment, God's punishment makes sense only on the basis of an understanding of God as one who loves and cares for creatures in the world. But insofar as a final judgment cuts off the processes of mercy and forgiveness, it subverts what is clearly the more important, indeed indispensable, strain of meaning. If we take the theme of God's infinite love and forgiveness to its logical conclusion, it would seem to rule out the notion of the final exclusion of any being from God's grace. But if we start with the notion that God is primarily a God of judgment or vengeance, we have seriously compromised what the New Testament says about divine love.

The theme of final judgment has a legitimate function, however, as a graphic signification of God's disapproval of all behavior that is unjust, oppressive, unforgiving, unloving. But since a literal rendering of this theme flies in the face of the New Testament's presentation of God as loving, we will have to appropriate it in another way, remembering that all language is fragmentary and open-ended. I therefore propose that we understand all references to God's eschatological judgment as imaginative representations of God's active opposition to all that is evil. Such a valuation is in many ways quite traditional, in that it understands God's wrath as the other side of God's love and mercy; and it preserves the biblical emphasis on justice in a way that stands as a bold challenge to the value systems in our contemporary world. For it emphasizes that God always stands on the side of the oppressed. Thus, to the extent that our social and economic systems breed inequalities in power, privilege, and wealth, apocalyptic imagery is a powerful witness against those systems. And to the extent that the church has been co-opted by those systems, it signals also God's judgment on the church as well.

This issue of eschatological judgment opens into two closely related questions. The first is the problem of exclusive vs. inclusive salvation. I noted a corollary of this issue in the Jesus movement, whose focus on the renewal of Israel without explicit reference to the wider world seemed in tension with passages suggesting God's universal care. As we saw, the community probably presupposed the eschatological inclusion of Gentiles, but at some points in the New Testament salvation is clearly limited to those in Christ. Most notably, John 14:6b states that "[n]o one comes to the Father except through me," and in Acts 4:12 we read that there is "no other name" than Christ's "by whom we must be saved." At other points, however, we find a more inclusive view. Matthew 25:31-46 implies the salvation of all who perform deeds of mercy, and in Rom 4:3, Paul treats faith(fullness) generically—as directed specifically toward God, rather than toward God as mediated by Christ. And, as we saw in chapter 11, Revelation contains a number of passages that present salvation as not only inclusive but universal.

Here again, one strain of thought is dependent on the other in a way that cannot be reversed. As I argued long ago in relation to Matthew, a universal standard of judgment logically takes precedence over an exclusivist standard.

> Now there is nothing problematic about the notion of a particularistic application of a universal standard. But the notion of an *exclusive representative* of a universal standard is self-contradictory. If the standard is in fact universal, and if the corollary assumption of the universal possibility of adherence is accepted, then the real possibility of other representatives cannot be logically denied. (Pregeant 1978, 123)

The strain of thought that assumes that all who perform deeds of mercy are acceptable in God's eyes thus outweighs the strain that limits salvation to those who follow Christ, even though the latter is quantitatively dominant.

This insight is strengthened by considerations emanating from our contemporary situation. The encounter among world religions that has developed in the modern/postmodern period has forced open-minded adherents of the different faiths to view the "other" faiths in a new light. Sometimes this has meant recognizing significant points of contact among religions, so that what once seemed alien now appears to share some of the basic patterns of understanding in one's own faith. In other cases, it has meant an appreciation of the "other" faiths on their own terms—as patterns of understanding that differ from one's own faith by asking different questions and purporting a different *kind* of salvation. How to process the fruits of this encounter among religions is a complex problem, but the point is that it has rendered exclusivist understandings of salvation highly suspect.

In assessing the New Testament witnesses, however, we need not deny any place at all to the exclusivist strain of thought. For we can find value in it if we look beyond its surface meaning and pay attention to what it might have to offer on a more imaginative level. That is, we can understand the New Testament's claim regarding an exclusivist salvation offered in Christ "as a kind of confessional hyperbole that gives dramatic weight to the claim that is made" (Pregeant 1978, 157). As such, it can serve as an important reminder that not just *any* pattern of faith and action is acceptable but that all such patterns are accountable to a God who loves and values all life. And it must also be said that not just any pattern that names itself Christian is acceptable, since not all who name the name of Christ think or act in the spirit of Christ.

The final theological issue brings us back to apocalyptic thought. As we saw in chapter 11, there is a tension in Revelation between a dominant strain of historical determinism, typical of apocalyptic thought, and a subtler strain of contingency, more characteristic of the prophetic mode. This tension reflects a broader tension regarding the nature of God's power. On the one hand, the New Testament presents God as wielding coercive power in order to exercise full control of human history. On the other hand, the image of Jesus as the suffering Messiah suggests a different model of power—power as persuasion exercised through God's relatedness to the world, which makes the divine vulnerable by virtue of the world's resistance.

The majority of Christian theologians throughout history have understood God's power as coercive, and many have thought of God's relationship to the world as deterministic. A full-blown determinism, however, logically renders the entire theological enterprise incoherent. Within a deterministic schema, neither calls to repentance nor God's judgment makes logical or moral sense. And if we choose to revalue the deterministic aspects of the biblical tradition, there is reason to rethink the nature of God's power also. I would therefore propose that we understand the biblical presentation of God's relationship to the world in terms of determinism and coercive power as imaginative and hyperbolic representation of God's active persuasion of the world in the direction of the good. If we can free ourselves from a literal understanding of this representation, we can find positive value in it. Imaging God as acting within the world stands as an important challenge to a dogmatic secularism that rules out any sense of divine presence in the world or objective meaning in human existence.

In summary, then, I offer the following reconstruction of the theological framework that grounds New Testament ethics as one way of grasping its meaning for our time. The world itself is the creation of a beneficent, gracious, and forgiving God who is active in the world through the persuasive power of love. This God is represented to the world in the figure of Jesus, whose teachings and whose self-sacrificing life in obedience to God unto death not only serve as a model for imitation but offer an opportunity to human beings to reconcile with God and thus experience new life. The opportunity is not, however, the exclusive property of the followers of Jesus. Whether we understand what is offered to those outside this particular community in terms of an inclusivism (according to which all who relate to God in a way formally parallel to the Christian way are included in God's mercy) or in terms of a pluralism (according to which God's mercy is available in ways that are not formally parallel to the Christian), all human beings have access to that life. Not all, of course, embrace the abundant life they are offered; and insofar as they fail to do so they stand under God's judgment. God's mercy is such, however, that God's judgment never negates it or brings it to an end.

Against this background, New Testament ethics appears as a way of living out in practice the new life that is offered in Christ. This life, moreover, is abundant life—life lived in communal solidarity with other human beings, in harmony with the whole created order, and in faithfulness to God.

Questions concerning the Good

Assessing Various Approaches: Rules, Principles, Discernment, Virtue

Throughout this study, we have observed important differences in the modes of ethical reflection in the New Testament. We have encountered specific rules, but we have also noted ways of thinking about ethics that stand in at least potential conflict with the rule approach. We have identified broad principles and have observed the importance of the process of discernment in some writings, and we have seen that the interest of some texts is less in the rightness or wrongness of specific actions than in the development of virtue or character. It is therefore important to try at this point to assess the value of such differing approaches.

There is an understandable tendency, among many readers of the Bible, to look to specific rules as the surest guide to the moral witness of Scripture. Earlier in this text, however, I argued that rules are often bound so tightly to their original cultural contexts that they have scant potential for transcending that context and becoming relevant in different times and places. Victor Furnish, who takes a similar view, has formulated what he calls "the law of diminishing relevancy": "The *more specifically applicable* an instruction is to the situation for which it was originally formulated, *the less specifically applicable* it is to every other situation" (1994, 32; emphasis original). I do not take this to mean that rules are useless in moral reflection. Given what I have argued regarding the fragmentary quality of language, there is much more to be found in any statement than its seemingly bare and literal signification. We can, in other words, value a rule in many ways other than understanding it as a literal prescription for behavior in all times and circumstances. But its very specificity calls its universal applicability into question.

Broad principles, on the other hand, have often been criticized precisely for their lack of specificity. As we saw earlier, the love commandment has come under attack as far too vague and therefore subject to misuse as a way of blunting the force of more specific modes of moral reasoning. We have also seen that Richard Hays denies the long-standing claim that it stands at the very heart of the New Testament, arguing that it is central only in a limited number of writings. Principles are in fact subject to misuse, but I have argued earlier that the love command is not nearly as vague as some interpreters have charged; and I have also tried to show that this command is considerably more central to the New Testament than Hays allows. It is, for example, more important in the structure of Mark than Hays grants; and if we allow the Jesus movement a place in New Testament ethics, its position is strengthened exponentially (see above, 103–5, 155–57).

Finally, given the undeniable centrality of the love command in the witness of the Jesus movement, Matthew, the Gospel and letters of John, and the undisputed letters of Paul, one can legitimately ask whether we should understand its diminished presence in some other materials as a limitation on its importance or a sign of a deficiency in the writings that fail to grant it a significant place. Since the New Testament consistently presents God as revealed in Christ as a God of radical love and often understands ethics in terms of *imitatio Dei* or *imitatio Christi*, the love command would seem to be a peculiarly appropriate foundational statement of what God requires of human beings. Beyond this, there is an intuitive point we should not overlook: the inherent moral appeal of love as a motivation for moral action. Aside from how widespread it is or is not within the writings of the New Testament, for those whom the love command grasps existentially, it claims a central place by the sheer force of its appeal to intuition.

Another principle (also rejected by Hays as central to the New Testament) that has solid grounding in a variety of New Testament texts is that of liberation. Here again, Hays's objection is, in part, that it is absent in some important canonical writings; and he cites Matthew, Ephesians, and the Pastoral Letters as examples. I consider this judgment somewhat ill founded in the case of Matthew, as I believe my treatment of the Matthean beatitudes shows. On the other hand, Hays is correct in citing Ephesians and the Pastorals. As in the case of love, however, it is legitimate to ask whether this disqualifies the liberation theme or is a sign of an inadequacy in these writings. Given the centrality of liberation to the witness of the Jesus movement and its presence in various forms in the Gospels and the letters of Paul, the latter option would hardly seem unreasonable. The Jesus tradition is filled with stories and sayings that bespeak Jesus' solidarity with the oppressed, and Luke in particular places enormous emphasis on inclusiveness. Likewise, Paul's radical proclamation that incorporation into Christ obliterates the distinctions between Jew and Greek, slave and free, and male and female (Gal 3:28) is anything but peripheral to his message. If our choice is between judging the witnesses of Ephesians and the Pastorals as "off message" on this point and allowing them to blunt a theme so central to what would seem more important New Testament witnesses, then I, for one, have little trouble in making the former choice.

One of the hermeneutical issues that arose in chapter 9 had to do with the tension between Paul's statement of absolute rules and his ethic of discernment. As I noted in that context, one way of resolving this tension would be to understand Paul's absolutes as defining the boundaries of the discernment process. If we take seriously Furnish's "law of diminishing relevancy," however, we can see that such an approach risks undercutting central aspects of Paul's ethical reflection: his emphases on the love commandment, the process of discernment, the work of the Spirit, and the development of virtue through the *imitatio Christi*. For what is most important about these latter aspects is that they are able to transcend the limitations of specific cultures and situations. And to place an absolute limit on the direction that discernment might take would stifle the work of the Spirit and thus limit the freedom of God in the process of revelation.

This does not mean that rules have no place at all in hermeneutical reflection on the New Testament's moral teaching. But, as in the cases discussed above, it means that our wider reflection might lead us to value a rule in a nonliteral way or, in some cases, reject it as incompatible with what we can learn from other aspects of the biblical witness and/or contemporary experience. For if we take seriously the dimensions of Paul's ethics mentioned above, then we simply cannot allow a specific rule, bound as it likely is to a specific cultural context, to set, unilaterally, the boundaries of hermeneutical reflection. These dimensions, in fact, work in concert to invite us to look beyond Scripture, and especially to reason and experience, for guidance in our ethical reflection grounded in the New Testament.

Paul is not, of course, the only ethical witness in the New Testament. But there are parallel and analogous elements in other materials we have examined. The love command is strongly represented in other sources; and the same is true of virtue ethics. In addition, Jesus' freedom in interpreting the law, visible throughout the Jesus tradition, is in some ways similar to a process of discernment. And, finally, the *imitatio* theme is paralleled in the Gospels to the extent that Jesus appears there as a model for behavior. Of equal importance, moreover, is the intuitive appeal of these more open-ended approaches to the question of ethics. I say this not because such open-endedness offers a way of circumventing the content of specific commands but because it is a powerful avenue through which the challenge of New Testament ethics can make itself felt in a time far removed from that of Jesus and the early church.

Specific Issues

It is time now to turn to a treatment of specific moral issues, relevant to life in our contemporary world, in light of the various New Testament witnesses and the hermeneutical reflections I have offered throughout this text. In keeping with the discussion in chapter 2, I would remind the reader of my characterization of all interpretations as "reading proposals," which reflect the life situations of different interpreters. And I would now add that such a characterization is doubly appropriate when we come to the task of determining how to apply those readings to concrete concerns in the present.

Gender and Status in the Community in Christ

The New Testament is by no means consistent in its witness concerning the status and role of women; there is a residual element of patriarchy that never quite disappears. There are, however, dramatic fissures in that structure. We may point, for example, to various elements in the Jesus tradition, including Jesus' willingness to interact with women and the important roles of women in Luke. The undisputed letters of Paul, moreover, disclose his practice of including women in leadership positions; and his inclusive statement in Gal 3:28 is nothing short of astonishing. Patriarchal presuppositions, however, limit Paul's egalitarian tendencies, as we can see in his insistence on some differentiation in male/female standards regarding hairstyles (1 Cor 11:2-16). And when we turn to the Deuteropauline letters, we find a strong resurgence of patriarchal standards. The household codes clearly consign women to a subordinate status, and 1 Tim 2:8-15 not only forbids women to teach but commands them to learn in silence and defines their social role solely in terms of motherhood.

It is remarkable how some interpreters who come down on the progressive side of this particular issue—that is, who argue for the inclusion of women in the church's ministry on an equal basis—fail to take full responsibility for the hermeneutical moves necessary to reach such a conclusion. Robert Gagnon, for example—in attempting to undermine the analogy some interpreters make between a progressive position on women's ordination and acceptance of homo-erotic relationships—notes a trajectory within the Bible itself on this and other issues (2001, 442) and then goes on to argue that

> there are so many positive examples of women in leadership positions in the Old Testament (e.g., Miriam, Deborah, Huldah, Esther), of women involved in the ministry of Jesus, and of women serving as co-workers with Paul in the proclamation of the gospel (Romans 16, among other texts), that the Bible contains within its own canonical context the seeds for liberating women from oppressive male structures. . . . On this point the Bible is often its own critic and inspiration for change. (2001, 443)

I find this to be an excellent statement in itself, and my own way of dealing hermeneutically with this question is in many ways parallel. However, it leaves an important question unanswered—one that could challenge the way Gagnon plays the issue of women's status off against that of homoerotic relationships. The question is why, given the conflicting attitudes represented in the Bible, and within the New Testament itself, the church is justified in choosing the progressive strain over the conservative. If we try to answer this question by reference to a "trajectory," the results will be disappointing from a progressive standpoint. For if we view the changes in attitude chronologically, what we find in the post-Pauline writings is a strong turn back in a conservative direction. The trajectory does not in fact take us where many of us think it should!

When we are faced with competing strains of meaning in a text, our attempt to work hermeneutically with them necessarily involves appeals beyond the text to both reason and experience. We must, in other words, both trace out the implications of each strain, making use of reason, and draw on contemporary experience as a factor in the assessment of the biblical witness.

There is nothing self-contradictory about understanding God as the enforcer of a hierarchical, patriarchal system of social relationships. It is impossible, how-ever, to accommodate the sometimes radical egalitarian strains in the biblical witness to such a system. They simply stand there as anomalies and irritants. Nor is it possible to reverse the logic and accommodate the patriarchal strain to the egalitarian elements or even to find much to value in the former within an understanding based on the latter. In this particular case, the interpreter must simply make a choice, and I can envision no basis for such a choice other than contemporary experience. Yes, the Bible is indeed on this point "its own critic and inspiration for change," but the ultimate sanction for such change must come from outside the texts themselves. It is finally the hard-won modern experience of the full humanity of women and their full equality with men that have led many individuals and some denominations to reject all requirements based on gender for leadership in the church. In this particular instance, then, it appears that contemporary experience authorizes us to challenge those aspects of the biblical worldview that have lent support to the subordination of women and fostered misogynist images such as we find in Revelation. The presence of the seeds of change within the New Testament are important, however; for, along with the presence of the broad principle of liberation, they stand as important testimony to the fact that our contemporary experience does, after all, remain in significant continuity with the ancient tradition.

I would argue similarly regarding other issues related to the patriarchal and hierarchical elements in the biblical witness. We can find no New Testament texts explicitly prohibiting slavery, but there are several that seem to tolerate it. There are strong hints of disapproval in the undisputed letters of Paul, however; and broad principles such as liberation and oneness in Christ provide links with sensibilities that have developed over the centuries and have helped us to see this inherently oppressive institution as a gross violation of the human person. Rejection of class and ethnic (and, at least by implications, racial) distinctions, on the other hand, has stronger grounding in the texts than does rejection of slavery, and the texts relating to class issues make a major contribution to the broad theme of liberation. Since class issues overlap significantly with economic issues, however, I will reserve further comment on this point for the section on wealth and poverty. But it is important to make one additional observation regarding patriarchy and hierarchy. As I noted earlier (see above, 26, 61, 62), the biblical writings are conditioned not only by the social circumstances of their composition but by the power relationships at work within those social situations. Texts that support the subordination of any given group are almost inevitably the products of the dominant groups, whose interests are served by the maintenance of the existing social system. As the early assemblies of Jesus people moved toward institutionalization and men regained the degree of power they had been in danger of losing, they inscribed their positions of power and privilege into the texts that became Scripture.

Divorce and Remarriage

In the chapter on Mark, I noted that Dan Via finds a subtle tension within this Gospel between 10:9 and 10:11-12. Whereas the former passage seems to condemn divorce as such, in the latter the only problem has to do with remarriage. Although it is unclear whether the original form of the prohibition, passed on in the Jesus movement, prohibited divorce itself or only remarriage after divorce, it is undeniable that the tradition has undergone modulation within the New Testament itself. Matthew 5:32 and 19:9 make an exception with respect to infractions of a sexual nature, and Paul seems to allow divorce from unbelieving spouses (7:15) and to recognize that divorce is sometimes inevitable (7:11). Since we do not have any passage that actually approves of remarriage after divorce, however, we cannot really speak of a countercurrent of meaning when it comes to this aspect of the issue. If we confine ourselves to the "choices" given in the various disparate texts, we are left with two alternatives: an absolute prohibition of divorce or permission to divorce only in the case of adultery. But in no case would remarriage after divorce be acceptable.

To put the matter differently, the variations in the texts may authorize hermeneutical reflection on the issue in a very broad sense, but they do not give explicit permission to consider remarriage as an option. To move in that direction involves an appeal beyond the particular texts in question. And that is precisely what has taken place, as various denominations and individuals have wrestled with this issue over the centuries.

One important consideration is the likely reason for the prohibition: as we have seen, there is good reason to think that it was originally intended as a way of protecting the rights of women. As I noted in chapter 6, marriage in the ancient world was a very different institution from the one we know today. In many societies, it has been disconnected from its patriarchal roots and has become much more a union of two individuals than of a contract between families, and divorce is no longer primarily a male prerogative. Thus, the dissolution of a marriage no longer has the same social meaning that it did in biblical times.

In the end, however, the strongest arguments for moving away from the prohibitions of divorce and remarriage have to do with considerations based on broader biblical principles in combination with contemporary experience. In the second section of this chapter, I argued that in the biblical tradition ethics presupposes an aesthetic base, which means that God wills for all human beings a life that is abundant and joyful. I have also argued that liberation is a central principle in the biblical witness. If we take these points seriously, we will have to pay attention to the negative effects these prohibitions have often had on human lives. To ask people to remain in relationships that simply do not work, that often bring intense psychological pain, and that are sometimes characterized by various degrees of abuse hardly seems compatible with the promise of abundant life. Nor does the prohibition of remarriage after divorce, if we affirm the essential goodness of intimate relationships.

Hays concedes—on the basis of the New Testament's own "process of reflection and adaptation of the fundamental normative prohibition against divorce"—that neither divorce nor remarriage can be totally ruled out as valid options. Along the way, however, he has much to say in opposition to the line of reasoning I presented above; and his argument is partially dependent on his insistence that "[w]e should not override the witness of the New Testament in one mode [of authority] by appeal to another mode" (1996, 310). He thus notes that the New Testament deals with divorce not in terms of "formal principles such as justice or personal wholeness" (1996, 368) but "primarily in the *rule* and *symbolic world* modes" (1996, 369). Mark 10:2-9, for example, "reframes the debate about divorce by shifting attention to the symbolic world set in place by the creation story." Against this background, Hays makes this judgment against an appeal to principles in this case:

> Those who try to justify divorce among Christians—for reasons beyond those allowed by the New Testament—tend to appeal to general principles (e.g., "fullness of life," . . .) and to disregard the New Testament's specific rules. But . . . these rules are deeply grounded in the New Testament's symbolic world. Thus, in order to justify the dismissal of the rules, interpreters must also construct (or simply adopt) a different symbolic world. (1996, 369)

I have already given my reasons for believing that rules are the aspect of the New Testament's moral teaching that are most tightly bound to a specific culture and situation and therefore the least able to transcend their original environments. Now it becomes important to respond to Hays's use of the category "symbolic world." By this he means a thought complex "that creates the perceptual categories through which we interpret reality." By way of example, he offers the following:

> Romans 1:19-32 offers a diagnosis of the fallen *human condition* without explicitly articulating any moral directives, and Matthew 5:43-58 proffers a characterization of God (who makes his sun rise on the evil and the

good, and sends rain on the just and on the unjust) in order to establish a framework for his discipleship. (1996, 209)

My first question is whether Hays thinks that a text's symbolic world is somehow immune to criticism. Symbolic world, after all, is as much an outgrowth of a cultural environment as is a rule. My intention is not to sanction wholesale rejection of the various expressions of symbolic world in the New Testament, but I do suggest that they are part of a whole network of meaning-creating significations and cannot claim absoluteness any more than can rules. And if we take seriously the fragmentary, open-ended character of language, then the symbolic world represented in any given text—perhaps considerably more than many other modes of signification—must be understood as polyvalent and therefore capable of being appreciated in many different ways. The symbolic world of Genesis to which Mark 10:2-9 points, for example, does not lead inexorably to the absolute prohibition of divorce and remarriage, even though the Marcan text makes use of it for this purpose. And if we move from the world of the text to our contemporary world, with a very different institution of marriage in effect, then alternative ways of appropriating the Genesis story may well emerge.

However we assess Hays's use of the category of symbolic world, the question remains as to why he thinks it impermissible to override a witness made in one mode by reference to another. As best as I can determine, the point is that we are somehow bound to a text's own mode of signification; but such a restriction, it seems to me, places an unbearable burden on the hermeneutical process. The Bible draws on a wide range of modes of signification. To say that we cannot challenge one with another is to set an arbitrary boundary on how a conversation is to take place; and it is, in the end, a prescription for protecting the most culture-bound aspects of the biblical witness from the life-giving process of the modification of tradition.

Once again, a combination of contemporary experience and strains of meaning within the ancient texts leads us to challenge an aspect of the biblical worldview. In this instance, however, it is also important to acknowledge the challenge to contemporary values that the biblical texts authorize. Although the church can, in my estimation, legitimately depart from the literal application of the New Testament's teaching on divorce and remarriage, this teaching should also serve as a prophetic indictment of the casual way in which both the covenant of marriage and sexual relationships have come to be regarded by large segments of contemporary society. The point is not, however, the breaking of rules but the cheapening of intimate human relationships and the consequent devaluation of human persons.

Homosexuality

In chapter 9, I argued that Paul's negative attitude toward homoerotic relationships was rooted in his inherited worldview, which was presupposed in both a sense of order that grounded the purity codes of ancient Israel and in a hierarchical understanding of sexual property rights. In making this assessment, I also asked whether it was necessary to accept these presuppositions in order to appropriate his message in our own time. This question, moreover, is linked to a broader hermeneutical issue, which I discussed earlier in the present chapter: the tension between Paul's pronouncement of absolute judgments on a few specific issues and his ethic of Spirit-guided discernment, grounded in love. As I have tried to show, we cannot legitimately protect a specific rule from challenges brought on the basis of discernment or broader principles such as love and liberation.

This does not, however, automatically give precedence to discernment or a principle over a rule or a judgment based on a symbolic world on any particular issue. Thus, I will eventually want to make reference to the specific arguments made by those who advocate acceptance of homosexual relationships by the church. First, however, we must take account of the most important arguments against allowing contemporary experience to overrule the testimony of Scripture on this point.

Scripture vs. experience. Hays seeks to counteract the view that contemporary experience should authorize the acceptance of homosexual relationships by drawing limits on how the appeal to experience can function. His first argument is "*that claims about divinely inspired experience that contradicts the witness of Scripture should be admitted to normative status in the church only after sustained and agonizing scrutiny by a consensus of the faithful*" (1996, 399; emphasis original).

This stipulation may sound reasonable, but it is important to consider how social change actually takes place. Consensus seldom, if ever, comes at the beginning of a process of change; nor does significant change generally take place until after some visionary and courageous souls have taken the risk of dissenting against the majority. Having grown up in the American deep South during the civil rights movement, I can testify that it was long after the dismantling of the major structures of segregation—gained at the price of enormous suffering on the part of those who challenged "the system"—that anything approaching a consensus within the white community emerged that the change was just. Certainly, any departure from scriptural norms should come only as the product of "sustained and agonizing scrutiny." But to demand consensus on such a volatile issue as this is strikingly similar to the "not-yet" argument of supposed moderates on the issue of segregation in the mid-twentieth century—which, in practical terms, was the equivalent of "never." Of course, consensus should always be sought; but there are times when it can reasonably be expected only after significant change has been brought about.

Hays's second argument is "that experience must be treated as a hermeneutical lens for reading the New Testament rather than as an independent counterbalancing authority." Given this stipulation, he can reject any rereading of the New Testament that understands homosexual relationships "as a fulfillment of God's design for human sexuality as previously revealed in Scripture" (1996, 399). Here we come to the nub of the issue. As we have seen (see above, 22–23), Hays rejects all attempts to disqualify any aspect of Scripture on the grounds that it is socially conditioned, giving as his reason that all Scripture is conditioned by the situation of its composition. My question, however, is how one can invest such a *degree* of authority in material that one admits is conditioned in this way. Here again, Furnish's "law of diminishing relevancy" is to the point. The biblical condemnation of homoerotic acts, bound as it is to the purity code, an ancient sense of order, and a patriarchal worldview, would seem to be one aspect of Scripture that should be open to reconsideration on the basis of broader scriptural principles and the testimony of contemporary experience. To demand that experience automatically bow to Scripture on every issue is to ignore Scripture's own grounding in prior experience, as well as its rootedness in a particular situation, and also to risk interference with the work of the Spirit.

Experience and principles vs. explicit norms. As we have seen, the explicit testimony of Scripture with respect to homoerotic acts is negative. So on what grounds do some contemporary Christians, including many biblical scholars, justify departure from this particular scriptural norm? The argument is relatively simple. On one level, it is an argument from experience. Despite a long history of misinformation and prejudice with respect to gay and lesbian persons, what has emerged in our time is the coming to light of homosexual persons who are involved in deep, loving, long-term, committed relationships; who are nurturing parents; who manifest sincere religious devotion and concern for other human beings and all forms of life; who make positive contributions to society;

and who—when we get beyond the a priori assumption of homosexuality as inherently pathological—exhibit psychologically healthy personality traits.

On another level, the argument finds scriptural support by reference to broad principles, such as that of inclusion. On both the precanonical and canonical levels, Jesus appears as exercising a radical, prophetic acceptance of all persons; and Paul's declaration in Gal 3:28 stands as a classic and dramatic testimony to the unacceptability of divisions within the body of Christ. It would thus seem that the burden of proof should fall on those who advocate any type of exclusion. A typical response to such an appeal to the ideal of inclusiveness, of course, is that those who deny that homoerotic sex is acceptable for Christians reject only the practice, not the person. For those who experience homosexual orientation as a part of their identity, however, such a distinction is meaningless.

Nonscriptural arguments for the traditional position. Aside from the biblical witness, then, what arguments are there for the perpetuating the church's traditional attitude toward homosexual relationships? These arguments tend to fall into two broad categories: appeals to nature and appeals to personal and social consequences. Because Gagnon makes much of both of these, I will treat them by taking account of his arguments.

With respect to nature, Gagnon argues that "[s]ame-sex intercourse represents a suppression of visible evidence in nature regarding male-female anatomical and procreative complementarity" (2001, 488). Arguments such as this are undoubtedly convincing to many people, and I suspect that a sense of what is natural and what is unnatural is at least as strong a factor in the social rejection of homoeroticism as is Scripture. Appeals to nature, however, can be extremely deceptive. Paul invokes nature in his prescriptions regarding hairstyles, but it is clear that what he regards as natural law is in fact mere custom. Segregationists in the South (and North!), many if not most of whom were church members, were absolutely convinced that mixing of the "races" is a violation of nature's ways. And yet today it has become commonplace to acknowledge that the notion of "race" itself is a social construct. There are more genetic differences within so-called racial groups than between groups; and rather than absolutely distinct groupings of persons according to physical traits, what we can actually observe are broad spectrums of differentiation with respect to such traits.

Also relevant to the question of natural law is the fact that homoerotic acts are frequent in the nonhuman animal world. Gagnon acknowledges this point but dismisses it on the grounds that we have no evidence of animals that form long-term homosexual relationships or that would qualify as exclusively homosexual (2001, 180 n. 25). One might argue, however, that the incidence of *any* homoerotic behavior in the animal world should give us pause with respect to the question of what is "natural." Beyond that, his rejection of the analogy between homosexual acts in the nonhuman and human world is far too facile in light of Bruce Bagemihl's documentation of the astonishing frequency and variety of homosexual activity among animals (1999, passim). Nor does Gagnon take account of the possibility that judgments of researchers who have played down the significance of homoerotic relationships in the animal world might be skewed by their own presuppositions—a point that Bagemihl discusses at length (1999, 122–67). In any case, Gagnon reveals his a priori judgment against homoerotic acts with the comment that "we human beings should emulate not the worst of animal behavior but the best" (2001, 180).

In sum, then, appeals to nature are simply unable to bear the burden of proving that homoerotic relationships are an aberration. We are therefore left with claims regarding the negative consequences of homoerotic sex. Such claims, however, are just as problematic as appeals to nature. Regarding Hays's comparison of homosexuality to alcoholism, for example, Via makes the following comments:

> Hays clearly regards homosexual practice as sinful, and by making homo-sexuality analogous to alcoholism he is also implying that it is harmful or injurious. Everyone knows that it is harmful for an alcoholic to drink. But that begs the question, for the question at issue is whether homo-sexual practice is in fact harmful *in itself.* (2003, 24; emphasis added)

Here again, we come to a crucial aspect of the issue. There are sexual practices that are self-evidently harmful *in themselves.* Pedophilia and rape violate the rights, the dignity, and the humanity of the victims; bestiality violates the rights of animals. But is there in fact evidence that homosexual practice is similarly "harmful in itself"?

Gagnon makes a concerted effort to show that homosexual relations do have negative consequences. Some of his points seem utterly misdirected as, for example, when he notes that homosexuality brings with it "[a] significantly decreased likelihood of establishing or preserving a successful [heterosexual] marriage" (2001, 471). Others at least border on "blaming the victim," as when he cites the high rates of depression, suicide, and substance abuse among homosexuals (2001, 472, 475). Gagnon is aware of arguments that trace the problems among the homosexual population to rejection by society. He plays this factor down, however, and tries to demonstrate that homosexuality fosters psychological difficulties that have nothing to do with social rejection. Thus, we find, at the end of a list of negative effects, this item: "shame and guilt over one's abnormal and unnatural sexual practice (a realization that stems from visible evidence of same-sex discomplementarity or the inability to relate properly to the opposite sex, not from 'internalized homophobia')" (2001, 476). To begin with, the use of the terms "abnormal," "unnatural," and "properly" again testifies to an a priori rejection of homoerotic relations. Second, it is highly doubtful that we can in fact separate a sense of shame and guilt experienced apart from homophobia from that which results from social rejection. And, third, even if we could make such a separation, the remaining shame and guilt would not in principle be different from the similar feelings of persons who stand outside the statistical norm in other ways. Should we reject everything that makes people feel different from their peers? In fact, we have taken some steps to make persons who in some way stand apart from the majority feel "normal" and acceptable. How would greater efforts in this direction, with specific attention to homosexuals, affect the sense of shame and guilt that Gagnon emphasizes?

Essentialism vs. mutability. Gagnon goes to great lengths to refute the widespread view that homosexuality is innate. Through detailed examination of evidence typically cited to make the case for biological determinism of sexual orientation, he raises legitimate questions about some of these claims. He also gives a detailed account of studies that suggest that environmental influences play a part in the development of sexual orientation as well as evidence of a degree of mutability of orientation (2001, 395–429). The matter of biological determinants is by no means settled, one way or the other, however. And, it must be added, if we accept (as most current researchers do) the notion of a spectrum of orientations running from exclusively heterosexual to exclusively homosexual, we must also accept that in many cases the possibility of change is nil, whatever the determinants might be. Thus, despite the cogency of some of what Gagnon says on this particular issue, his use of the evidence is highly misleading. The fact remains that there are many persons who experience their homosexual orientation as a given, and many whose repeated efforts to change this orientation have brought them nothing but grief and extreme frustration.

The issue of mutability, in any case, may not be as important as many who participate in the debate over the acceptability of homoerotic sex assume. It is significant that much of what Gagnon says in opposition to claims of biological determinants is accepted by some who argue for the full acceptance of homosexual practice. And this is particularly true of those who approach the issue from a sociological perspective. It therefore becomes important to raise two questions. The first is why so many, on both sides of the issue, consider biological, but not sociological, determinants as possibly "justifying" homosexual relations. And the second is why a homosexual orientation should be considered more acceptable if beyond the control of the individual than if in some sense a choice? Is there not, perhaps—lurking behind the arguments on both sides—the a priori view that homosexuality is, after all, so abnormal as to call for some sort of "excuse"?

The case for the transformation of tradition. The crux of the issue, I would reiterate, is whether it can be demonstrated that homosexual practice is harmful *in itself.* Despite the best efforts of Gagnon and others, I do not see that it can; and if it cannot, then the burden of proof shifts from those who accept homosexual practice to those who reject it. My own conclusion, then, is that contemporary experience is leading the church, through a process of Spirit-guided discernment—which makes use of broad scriptural principles such as God's inclusiveness, love for all creatures, and promise of abundant life—to transcend the traditional position on homosexual practice.

I realize, of course, that the arguments I have presented will remain unconvincing to many whose views of the authority of Scripture differ from mine. I will return to the broad question of scriptural authority later in this chapter, but at present I want to speak to charges made by Kathryn Greene-McCreight, which I mentioned in chapter 9. The first of these is that those who believe that the Holiness Code is no longer valid for Christians are guilty of antinomianism. The second is her branding as "ethnocentric, theologically suspect," and bordering on anti-Semitism the view that modern persons can no longer accept Israel's Law, emanating as it does from an ancient context.

With respect to the first point, the plain fact is that the same Paul who made pronouncements on homosexual relations also preached a gospel without the Law and argued adamantly against requiring the rite of circumcision for Gentiles who accepted Christ. Equally indisputable is the fact that the church as a whole ultimately dispensed with many of the requirements of the Holiness Code. To be sure, Paul also pronounced the Law as a whole "holy, just and good" (Rom 7:12), and the church has often retained aspects of the Levitical law. But this is by no means justification in itself either for the continuing validity of any specific requirement of this code for Christians in the present or for accusing of antinomianism those who drop any specific requirement.

Regarding the second point, the hermeneutic I have outlined does not rest on the wholesale rejection of Israel's Law on the basis of modern presuppositions. What I have presented, to the contrary, is a dialogical model according to which the presuppositions of both worlds of thought—that of the text and that of the interpreter—are allowed to question each other. And the ancient/modern distinction is tangential to the main issue, which has to do with the differences between the text's presuppositions and those of any interpreter in *any* age or circumstance removed from that of the text's production. I certainly do not see that such a process constitutes anything like anti-Semitism or anti-Judaism, since it could theoretically apply to Jewish as well as Christian interpreters. And, in fact, the history of Judaism itself is filled with examples of interpreters who have argued against the literal application of certain requirements of the Torah.

In the end, I would argue that the dialogical model I propose entails not the rejection of scriptural teaching or church tradition but rather their transformation through continuing interaction with every new situation that arises in the experience of the community. With respect to the issue of homosexuality, as with that of divorce, I have argued that experience gives sound reason for the revision of biblical tradition. But in the present case, as in the other, I would also add that there are ways in which the ancient presuppositions constitute a challenge to our contemporary worldview. There is, in fact, a disposition in our time toward total sexual permissiveness that issues from a kind of self-centeredness that has little regard for the welfare of the other and pays even less attention to the deep questions about the meaning and quality of life in this world. To the extent that beneath Paul's pronouncements about homoerotic practices we can discern a more fundamental set of concerns, his statements on this issue can serve as an appropriate antidote to a deep sickness in our own time. As Furnish remarks,

> When Paul referred to homosexual behavior he was illustrating the wretchedness of the human condition where there has been no acknowledgment that life is God's gift and that one's existence stands always under God's claim. To Paul it represented a rebellion against the Creator . . . , a surrender to one's own lusts, the debasement of one's true identity and the exploitation of another's. It is no longer possible to share Paul's belief that homosexual conduct always and necessarily involves all these things. But it can be said with certainty that whenever a homosexual *or* heterosexual relationship does involve one or more of these, it stands under the judgment of scripture. (1985, 80; emphasis original)

Vines and fig trees in the community of the new creation. In his treatment of divorce and remarriage, Hays makes much of the fact that the New Testament does not appeal to categories such as "fullness of life" (1996, 373), and this observation could easily be applied to the issue of homosexuality. What arguments along these lines ignore, however, is the point I have tried to make with respect to the origin and purposes of ethics. If Gerstenberger is correct that ethics is rooted in the desire for community solidarity, and if I am correct in identifying an aesthetic presupposition behind biblical ethics in general, then notions such as "fullness of life," "abundant life," and "self-fulfillment" or "self-realization" should have some place in our deliberations after all.

Hays argues against this line of reasoning on the basis of Paul's eschatology, charging many who advocate "unqualified acceptance of homosexuality" with having "a realized eschatology that equates personal fulfillment with sexual fulfillment and expects sexual 'salvation' now" (1996, 402). Although Paul's eschatology has a futuristic aspect, the Gospel of John manifests a strong strain of realized eschatology and promises "abundant life" in the here and now. And if there is danger in an uncritical acceptance of realized eschatology, there is danger also in allowing the apocalyptic expectation to subvert the thoroughly biblical hope for the blessings of God's rule in the present world. To yearn for such blessings is not to reduce the meaning of life to sexual or materialistic fulfillment but rather to honor the biblical understanding of the person as a psychosomatic whole. Any human desire can become an object of idolatry, but there is no sin in the desire for one's own vine and fig tree or for the happiness that can be found in intimate relationships when such desires are submitted to the guidance of the Spirit.

Along similar lines, within the Roman Catholic tradition of natural law, a "revisionist" position has developed that places less emphasis on what appears to be "natural" as this is usually understood than on what promotes human flourishing. Stephen J. Pope thus contrasts this view with a more traditional position:

> Whereas the revealed natural law approach identifies the normatively human as what is given in the Scriptures and revelation and taught by the magisterium, the revisionist relies, *in addition* to these very important sources, on what it takes to be reasonable interpretations and judgments of what actually constitutes human flourishing in lived experience. Human flourishing is conceived much more strongly in affective and interpersonal terms than in strictly natural terms. Interpersonal love is here the locus of human flourishing. (1997, 111; emphasis original)

Church, Society, State, and Empire

The New Testament presents no consistent model of the relationship between the communities of faith on the one hand and the state or empire on the other. To be sure, Revelation explicitly names the empire as evil, counseling complete withdrawal from the society under its control. And if we look behind the canonical texts to the Jesus tradition, we find explicit challenges to the leadership of the Judean vassal state and implicit challenges to the empire that stood behind it. In addition, there is much in the undisputed letters of Paul that implies a critical attitude toward imperial authority. There is, however, a degree of tension between this strain of thought in Paul and the rhetoric of Romans 13, even though this passage is by no means his "theology of the state." In 1 Peter, moreover, we noted an endorsement of governmental authority that goes considerably beyond Romans 13. And although Luke-Acts is not, as some have claimed, an attempt to show the political harmlessness of the movement, neither is it a forthright challenge to imperial authority. Nevertheless, its endorsement of the hope of Israel suggests a vision of restoration that contains an implicit threat to the ruling powers, even though the reader is left without a concrete way to imagine the form of that restoration. In sum, there are many conflicting strains of thought within the New Testament when it comes to the issue of church and state/empire.

These differences are in large measure the products of significantly different authorial situations. For example, the radicalism of Revelation issues from the threat of persecution, whereas Paul's letters reflect times and circumstances in which such a threat was less pervasive. These differences in life situations, however, do not alter the fundamental fact that it is impossible to abstract from the various writings a consistent set of principles beyond the basic presupposition that those who follow Jesus owe their ultimate loyalty to God and not to the emperor or the empire. The process of discernment leads different writers and communities to work out the details of retaining this basic loyalty in the face of a hostile environment in different ways.

A similar tension appears when we turn our attention from governmental authorities to society itself. Both the pilgrim theology in Hebrews and aspects of the Johannine writings—their inward-looking understanding of love and their dualistic language—suggest a fairly strong sense of apartness from the world. The undisputed letters of Paul, on the other hand, present a more nuanced view. Paul's apocalyptic framework and inherently subversive language with respect to "the rulers of this age" presuppose a group with strong boundaries, in some sense separated from the world. We have noted, nevertheless, that Paul had some sense of the responsibility of those in the community of Christ to work for the common good in society as a whole. And if we turn to the Jesus movement, we find that in its own way it combined sharp social criticism, which presupposed an interest in the quality of life of the people, with a strong sense of eschatological expectation. As in the case of church and empire, then, we encounter a certain ambiguity in the New Testament's witness regarding the community of faith and the larger society in which it exists.

So how can we work hermeneutically with this set of ambiguities? My first point is that the New Testament is consistent in subordinating loyalty to any government or social system to obedience to God and loyalty to God's rule. And once that principle is accepted, we cannot shrink from the implication that when a choice between loyalties becomes necessary, Christians must choose God over Caesar, even if that choice means civil disobedience or actual rejection of the authority of a given state altogether. The line of logic that claims divine sanction for all governments simply cannot hold up against the dominant and self-consistent insistence on the absolute sovereignty of God, which is an indispensable element in the biblical witness as a whole.

My second point is that the differing perspectives represented in the New Testament should caution us against assuming that there is only one faithful pattern of interaction between the community of faith and either government or society. Differences in circumstance will necessitate differing ways of honoring God's rule in the face of social and political institutions that in various ways and degrees compete with that rule. During the Soviet era, the church in East Germany found in 1 Peter a precedent for its way of surviving within an essentially hostile system (Boring 1999, 115–19, 142–43). If the community's first allegiance is to God, however, it will necessarily define itself as in some sense a counterculture and must ever be on guard against manipulation by any social or political system with which it makes provisional accommodations. Indeed, it must be ready to accept the role of a martyr church when the very core of its faith and values are threatened. In other words, if it cannot find some way, however clandestine, to make its witness—not just on matters of faith but on matters of social justice as well—then it has in fact lost its reason for existence. It is also possible, however, to carry the notion of counterculture to such an extreme as to subvert the doctrine of the goodness of creation by consigning the ideals of peace and justice that define God's rule solely to an eschatological future. And if we accept the rootedness of biblical ethics in a concern for the common good, then to deny the New Testament's sanction for action on behalf of that ideal is to deny its own inner logic.

It would appear, then, that the matter of how a given community is to relate to its social and political contexts is very much a matter of discernment. To say only this, however, is to remain on a highly abstract level. And although I cannot comment in detail on the many complex situations in which the various manifestations of the church finds itself today, it seems important to make some statement on the political situation of the church in the United States in the twenty-first century. For I find it undeniable that Christian bodies in this country have generally erred, and grievously so, on the side of accommodation— and this is a judgment I would apply to a wide spectrum of denominations and theological perspectives. At the root of our problem is the widespread notion of American exceptionalism—the belief, held so dogmatically as to call forth extreme condemnation on anyone who questions it—that this country stands far above all others in the history of the world in terms of morality of purpose and faithfulness to God. And the result of the uncritical acceptance of this notion is that the vast majority of Christians in this country are unable to see the parallels between the ancient Roman Empire and the status of the United States as the sole undisputed superpower in our time.

This is not to deny that in many situations the United States has made positive contributions to the welfare of the community of nations in the world. It has fashioned a credible alternative to authoritarian, hierarchical rule and has sometimes taken important stands in defense of human rights. Simple honesty, however, demands that we recognize the ways in which this nation has also acted out of narrow self-interest and has allowed the legitimate concern for self-protection to sanction a quest for exclusive power on the world stage that has led to an equally legitimate resentment on the part of other nations. Although it is possible to point to instances in which this power has fostered peace and stability, it is instructive to remember that Rome also justified its never-ending quest for domination on the grounds that it brought "peace to the provinces." There was some truth to that claim, but this does not negate the fact that the very purpose of the empire entailed the economic exploitation of those provinces. And no one familiar with the long history of the relationship between the United States and Latin America in particular can deny the exploitative character of that relationship. One glaring result of foreign investment in the southern continent is that land once used to grow staple crops is expropriated to create large plantations to grow luxury crops for North American and European markets, while peasants migrate to urban centers in an often futile search for work and are consigned to lives wracked with poverty and disease in shantytowns. A new managerial class emerges, and some peasants become workers and improve their lot. Many do not find jobs, however, and in any case the gap between rich and poor increases exponentially, while the lion's share of the profits goes outside the country. In both ancient Rome and more modern manifestations of empire, of course, the ruling classes of the exploited regions have often been complicit in the maintenance of domination. But real power always lies in the imperial center, and its rule is always supported by military force.

The vast majority of U.S. citizens would undoubtedly reject the notion that this country is in any sense an empire, and some government officials in recent times have made repeated denials of this claim. It was not always so, however; for the term empire was often used unapologetically in earlier periods. And the reality is difficult to deny if we take a serious look at American history. European settlers came to this continent under the auspices of empires, and when they had gained their freedom they acted very much like an empire as they slowly took the remaining land from the native peoples. As the new country gained economic strength, it did so partly on the basis of a slave economy that involved the kidnapping of persons from a distant continent. In 1823, the Monroe Doctrine asserted that Latin America belonged to its sphere of influence, not that of Europe, and this document became the prelude to later imperialist actions. In the Mexican War, the United States gained half of Mexico's territory. And at the end of the nineteenth century, when it sent troops to help Cuba win its freedom from Spain, it withdrew those troops only after insisting on a clause in the Cuban constitution granting it the right of intervention. In the process of the war, the United States annexed Hawaii, and the peace treaty negotiated with Spain entailed the "purchase" of Guam, the Philippines, and Puerto Rico. In the twentieth century, during the Soviet era, it intervened regularly in the affairs of nations around the world under the rubric of fighting Communism. In Vietnam, it picked up the mantle of French colonialism and brought devastation to the entire country as it sacrificed thousands of its own young citizens. In Latin America, it regularly helped suppress the revolutionary movements that were fed by its own exploitative practices. This involved supporting brutal and murderous local governments and helping to topple the democratically elected—left-leaning, but non-Communist—government of Chile.

With the fall of the Soviet Union, the United States remained as the sole superpower, now largely unrestrained in its ability to intervene in the affairs of other nations. And in the administration of George W. Bush it took a genuinely ominous turn. Defining its enemy as "terrorism," this administration drew on neoconservative ideology to justify a preemptive war in Iraq (based on the distortion of evidence), serious compromises in the nation's historic legal traditions, such as the right of habeas corpus, and an almost unrestrained right to effect "regime change" in any nation in the world. And, despite the denial of imperial designs at the official level, many neoconservative ideologues have openly and unapologetically proclaimed the United States to be an empire. They are, it would seem, quite correct in that usage. And to the extent that this country has in fact acted as an empire, it has also made a mockery of its own claim to the title of a champion of human rights.

The point of this excursus into American history is to call attention to the way in which large segments of the church in this country have accommodated to the imperial designs and actions of their nation without allowing the biblical witness to call their implicit or explicit support of these designs and actions into question. There have, of course, been significant protests against U.S. imperialism from various quarters within the various church groups. Some religious bodies have issued bold and prophetic statements on one specific issue or another, and individuals have engaged in demonstrations—sometimes civil disobedience—and in various ways made their dissenting opinions known. It is nevertheless true that far too many in this country who stand within biblically based faith communities have allowed themselves to be misled by a cynical rhetoric that couches an uncritical nationalism in religious terms and plays on human fears.

To some extent, admittedly, it is lack of information that has made the manipulation of the public relatively easy. Management of the news by administrations of all political stripes, together with intimidation of the media, have often kept the general public ill informed about the facts of complex situations and the true motives of governmental action. What percentage of the U.S. public, for example, knows that the invasion of Iraq in 2003 was part of a neoconservative strategy for reshuffling the power relationships in the entire Middle East, *hatched long before the events of September 11, 2001*? It is nevertheless the responsibility of all, both individuals and communities, who claim loyalty to a transcendent God to inform themselves on public affairs as best they can and refuse to take the pronouncements of any worldly authority at simple face value. To do otherwise is clearly to render to Caesar what rightly belongs to God.

The tendency to allow worldly political loyalties to compromise the exclusive worship of God has, of course, broader and more ancient roots than American exceptionalism. Ever since the church gained a favored position in the Roman Empire under Constantine, it has found itself wavering among several different patterns of church-state relationship. Sometimes the church has wielded political power directly, and sometimes it has been manipulated by governmental structures; at other times it has embraced a doctrine of two realms that places it in a parallel relationship to worldly authorities. In none of these patterns, however, has it escaped the temptation of allowing the values of the state or society as such to distort its commitment to the peace and justice of God's rule as presented in the biblical witness. And for just this reason, there is an inherent appeal in the position of those groups that have opted for various forms of withdrawal from the larger social and political environments as much as possible. The question, of course, is whether such withdrawal forfeits the ability to work, against the prevailing systems, for the common good. Given the ease with which the more interactive options have embraced uncritical nationalism and have sanctioned imperial designs, however, one must view with profound respect the witness of those groups that position themselves more closely to the stance H. Richard Niebuhr named "Christ against culture" (1951, 45–82).

The vast majority of Christians nevertheless remain within traditions of greater interaction with society, state, and empire, and the choices they face are exceedingly complex. The biblical tradition, however, is clear in demanding worship of God alone, and there is no question but that Christians throughout the world today are faced with competing loyalties that we can only term idolatrous. To take one's stand for God's rule rather than any human institution is necessarily to take a stand for peace and justice in this world. In some situations in the world today, this necessarily means opposing the oppressive policies of one's own government. In some situations—most particularly those of the developing nations—it may mean asserting the needs of one's own group against exploitative powers from the outside, as liberation theologians have argued with great eloquence. In the United States, I would argue, it means support for governmental actions that in fact make for justice and peace on a global scale but concerted opposition to those that issue from imperial design and serve to enrich the "haves" at the expense of the "have nots." But for the church as a whole in this country to embrace such a stance will take a revolution in consciousness engendered by a dramatic reencounter with fundamental aspects of biblical teaching.

In conclusion, with respect to an issue raised in relation to the Johannine writings, I would argue that, although it is impossible to mandate a single pattern of interaction between the church on the one hand and society and government on the other, we must hold together two fundamental affirmations: (1) as God's creation, the world itself is good and contains within it the potential for love and justice; (2) the moral vision of the church (at its best) nevertheless stands in stark opposition to many aspects of the value systems at work in the world that invade the church's own life. As the broader of the two, the first affirmation must finally be the controlling element, just as inclusivism trumps exclusivism and images of God's love are more fundamental than images of God's retribution. Those who claim the name of Christ must love the world, as God also loves it (John 3:16). The second remains absolutely indispensable, however, so that Christians must also maintain a sense of their own distinctive worldview and be on guard never to be overcome by the seductive forces that threaten to undo it. They need not, and should not, deny the possibility and reality of love and moral action on the part of those who adhere to other creeds; and indeed they should be willing to join with others in the quest for the common good. But their vision must nevertheless be fed primarily from their own tradition, and they must never lose a sense of their distinctive identity and calling.

Violence, Vengeance, and Justice

One of the more blatant ways in which our contemporary compromise with empire distorts our biblical heritage is the ease with which so many Christians buy into the notion that military action is the only solution to difficult international situations and will respond to any call to arms, however misdirected, that is wrapped in ·the rhetoric of patriotism and national defense. Few themes are so consistently played out in the New Testament, however, as the prohibition of violence. And although I argued earlier that we should probably not take Jesus' strong endorsement of nonviolence as indicative of a systematic and absolute pacifist stance, it should go without saying that the burden of proof is always on the shoulders of anyone claiming the name of Christ who argues for the use of violence in any situation.

My own view, which I state only with great hesitation and trepidation, is that there are in fact some extreme circumstances in which that burden of proof can be met. And I would justify this judgment on the grounds that Hays rejects—the use of a principle to override a specific command. In some cases, the more loving action, the action that best serves the common good, is a limited use of violence in defense of justice (to borrow Hays's phrase) and in order to prevent further violence. It is, for example, difficult to imagine a functional society, at least under the present circumstances in the world, which does not have the option of police action to protect its citizens. And I believe that a case can be made, when all other options have been exhausted, for participation in wars that are purely defensive on the one hand or are waged for the sake of liberation from extreme oppression on the other.

Having said this, however, I must acknowledge that the principle I have stated is clearly vulnerable to misuse. A glaring example is the U.S. invasion of

Iraq in 2003. Although this conflict was packaged as a war of defense against terrorism, it has been shown conclusively that Iraq had no significant connection to the group that carried out the 2001 attack on the United States and that claims regarding "weapons of mass destruction" were based on intelligence that the government had good reason to question from the beginning. It is undeniable, moreover, that the usual result of violence—even violence in defense of justice—is in fact additional violence.

And it is the general unacceptability of violence that I would want to stress far more than my concession that it may sometimes be the lesser evil. The truth is that violence ostensibly waged on behalf of justice, most particularly that which is waged by a state, almost always has a subtext, a hidden motive beneath the cloak of moral purpose, whether this be manipulation of economic markets or the maintenance of power within a world of national entities struggling competitively against one another. The burden of proof must always be on any Christians who advocate violence. And the stunning words of Jesus on nonretaliation must always be the starting point in the process of discernment. I therefore honor the pacifist witness, although I cannot fully endorse it, as a powerful reminder of those words.

At the very heart of the New Testament's ethic of nonviolence is the renunciation of revenge, and adherence to this renunciation would by itself draw severe limits to any claims that violence is necessary. For revenge is something very different from defense, and the typical justifications for retaliation, such as teaching the other side a lesson or honoring the need for an abstract standard of justice, simply do not hold up in the face of the inner logic of nonretaliation. For this logic is an outright repudiation of both these motivations; to demand nonretaliation is to ask the injured party to absorb the violence and thereby put an end to its spiraling effects. Any justification for violence will have to be made on very different grounds. And one particular type of violence, quite often justified by Christians on the basis of passages in the Hebrew Bible, would seem impossible to justify: the practice of capital punishment. Here I would argue, as Hays does with respect to the holy war texts, that "the New Testament vision trumps the Old Testament" (1996, 336). Neither the extremity of a crime nor any abstract principle seems relevant as a way of justifying this barbaric practice, at least insofar as we are thinking of situations within organized societies that have other means of insuring the safety of its citizens.

In a chapter entitled "Violence in Defense of Justice," Hays employs his three images of community, cross, and new creation to argue for what is apparently an absolutist stance against the use of violence. There is much that I can appreciate in his discussion, although I find it necessary to make some qualifications. I begin with a theme that appears in relation to both community and cross—the vocation of the Christian community to bear suffering. In relation to community, Hays comments as follows: "the community is called to the work of reconciliation and—as a part of that vocation—suffering even in the face of injustice" (1996, 337; emphasis original). In relation to cross, he makes this statement:

> Not only the teaching but, more important, the example of Jesus is determinative for the community of the faithful. The passion narrative becomes the fundamental paradigm for the Christian life. This means that the community is likely to pay a severe price for its witness: persecution, scorn, the charge of being irrelevant. When the New Testament canon is read through the focal lens of the *cross*, Jesus' death moves to the center of attention in any reflection about ethics. The texts cannot simply be scoured for principles (the imperative for justice) or prooftexts ("I have not come to bring peace, but a sword"); rather, all such principles and texts must be interpreted in light of the story of the cross. (1996, 338; emphasis original)

Assuming that the church's suffering in any given instance is the result of opposition to its work of reconciliation, I can approve both statements as fair characterizations of what faithful witness will likely entail. I would qualify this endorsement, however, with the stipulation that we should understand paradigms, no less than spoken language, as open-ended, evocative, and imaginative. Thus, while it is valid to lift up Jesus' death as a paradigm for Christians who face rejection, oppression, and even the threat of death for their witness, there is a danger in assuming that the only faithful way of honoring the paradigm is a slavishly literalistic imitation. Without such a qualification, we run the danger of adding to the burdens of powerless groups yet another level of oppression and of turning the New Testament ethic of discernment into an ethic of absolute rules.

With respect to the image of the new creation, my dissent is somewhat stronger. Hays contends that "[n]one of the New Testament's witness makes any sense unless the nonviolent, enemy-loving community is to be vindicated by the resurrection of the dead" (1996, 33). Although it would be foolish to deny the importance of eschatology to New Testament thought, this formulation verges on turning an essentially moral demand into a merely practical one. If I understand the deeper logic of the New Testament's call to love the enemy and forgo violence, its point is not that those who do so will be rewarded in the end. It is rather that obedience to God demands that we do the good because it is in fact the good. The Hebrew tradition contained a strong sense of obligation to God and one's neighbor, even in the face of the loss of life, long before the notion of the resurrection of the dead appeared on the scene; and I do not see that the addition of that belief should be understood as forfeiting that basic insight. To the extent that the New Testament's demand for nonviolence is compelling, it is so on its own merits, not because of any secondary justification.

Wealth and Poverty: Economics and the Rule of God

Economic issues lie at the very heart of the biblical ethic. The Torah proclaims that "there will . . . be no one in need among you" (Deut 15:4) and provides for periodic remission of debts and the restoration of ancestral lands lost through financial failures (Deut 15:1). It also forbids collecting interest on loans (Exod 22:25) and commands farmers to leave a portion of their crops for the poor to glean (Lev 19:9-10). The writings of the prophets, moreover, abound with condemnations of economic injustice. Isaiah demands justice for widows, orphans, and the oppressed (1:17, 23) and rails against those who own too much land (5:8). Jeremiah likewise speaks on behalf of widows and orphans (7:5-7) and condemns those who have shed "the lifeblood of the innocent poor" (2:14). In Micah, we find a stringent indictment of rulers who "abhor justice and pervert equity" (3:9), defining God's requirement as "to do justice, and to love kindness, and to walk humbly with your God." And then there is the book of Amos, which ridicules the rich with bitter satire, pronounces God's judgment on them, and relentlessly takes the part of the poor:

> For three transgressions of Israel, and for four, I will not revoke the punishment; because they sell the righteous for silver, and the needy for a pair of sandals—they who trample the head of the poor into the dust of the earth, and push the afflicted out of the way. (2:6-7)
>
> Therefore because you trample on the poor and take from them levies of grain, you will build houses of hewn stone, but you will not live in them; you have planted vineyards, but you shall not drink their wine. (5:11)

Economic justice and God's "preferential option for the poor," which often takes the form of a promise of the reversal of fortunes in the coming age, are likewise central to the Jesus movement and are strongly represented in the Synoptic Gospels. Paul's sense of community solidarity, moreover, demands sharing within the assemblies, and there is some indication of an ethic of common goods in the Johannine writings. The economic exploitation that lies at the heart of the Roman Empire's reason for being is a central justification for the indictment rendered against it in Revelation, and the letter of James replays in dramatic terms aspects of the Jesus movement's views on wealth and poverty. Economic concerns are therefore no less central to the New Testament ethic than they are to that of the Hebrew Bible.

Tragically, however, the same forces that have seduced the church into idolatrous accommodations to empire have also compromised its inherent affinity with movements dedicated to economic justice. Ecclesiastical support was central to the feudal system of medieval times, and in the modern period large segments of the church have supported the elite classes in societies marked by outrageous discrepancies between rich and poor, even siding with murderous dictators such as Spain's Francisco Franco and Chile's Augusto Pinochet. In the modern West—and, one must say, most particularly in the United States—many Christians have allied themselves closely with a particular version of capitalist ideology that functions in practice as a tool for increasing the wealth and power of the ruling class and driving the poor into ever-deeper poverty.

There is a particular irony in this latter phenomenon, since the theoretical underpinnings of capitalism are firmly grounded in the presuppositions of the Enlightenment, an intellectual current that many conservative Christians repudiate with unbridled passion. The oddity is that to some extent they accept what was bad in this movement but repudiate what was good. On the one hand, they reject not simply the rightly suspect "scientism," which claims science as the only valid means of knowing, but also well-established results of scientific inquiry, such as evolution. On the other, however, they embrace uncritically an economic doctrine that is basically mechanistic and deterministic in orientation. Treating the workings of the economy as a kind of "given," rooted in unexamined beliefs about human nature and behavior, they accept a system that developed in a particular point in history as somehow grounded in the very nature of things.

This theory, well known to any schoolchild in the United States, is that the economy is strongest when subjected to the least government "interference"—that if all persons are allowed to work for their own individual good with the least possible restraints, economic productivity will produce such wealth that all members of society will eventually profit, albeit in differing degrees. The presupposition is that human beings are motivated almost entirely by narrow self-interest and will therefore work productively only for the sake of personal gain.

Another irony in the conservative Christian support of laissez-faire capitalism is that many in this camp embrace an extreme individualism and predatory motivation for profit that Adam Smith, the great theorist of capitalism, actually rejected. His interest was always in the common good, and although he argued that the pursuit of self-interest could serve that good, a far more important emphasis in his writings was the concept of the "impartial spectator," a voice from within that promotes consideration of others and condemns the practice of injuring others in order to benefit oneself.[1]

Whether or not one thinks it possible or desirable to recover a version of capitalism more in line with Smith's ideal, no one need deny a measure of truth in the theory itself; even Karl Marx was impressed with the ability of capitalist economies to produce great wealth. Equally impossible to deny, however, is the great discrepancy in wealth and income that such economies produce if they are allowed to proceed without significant restraints. And the argument that a laissez-faire policy will eventually make everyone better off is patently absurd, as the ill effects of such policy on the most vulnerable persons in society have demonstrated over and over again. As I noted in the preceding section, some do profit, but many others are far worse off and the gap between rich and poor grows ever greater. And even if we could believe that unrestrained economic activity might in time lead to a better life for all, we would still have to reckon with the immense suffering on the part of millions of human beings that would take place as the world waits for this supposed golden age.

To the extent that reigning economic theory treats human beings primarily as individuals motivated almost entirely by selfish interests and understands the economy as a mechanism that operates on the basis of unalterable laws, it runs counter to fundamental presuppositions of biblical thinking. The Bible values individual persons, but it also understands them as members of a community. In the Hebrew Bible, God's overriding concern is for the people of Israel collectively, and in the New Testament the believer's life-in-community is primary. The Bible recognizes a human propensity toward selfishness and sin, but at the heart of its message is the declaration that under the guidance of the Spirit a different kind of life is possible. It was only through an understanding of "original sin" pushed so far as to deny both the goodness of creation and the moral freedom of human beings that Christianity—most particularly a type of Protestantism—adopted such a pessimistic and destructive evaluation of the human possibility. And, finally, as for the notion of the economy as mechanistic and deterministic, such a view clearly undermines the biblical image of God as a sovereign agent who is active in the world, toppling empires and disrupting entrenched social patterns. How odd, indeed, to argue that God has the power to free an enslaved people from Pharaoh's grip and bring the Roman Empire to naught but is somehow powerless in the face of impersonal economic forces that work against the welfare of so many people!

Given the fundamental incompatibility of the dominant capitalist ideology with biblical thought, one is inclined to ask whether the real religion of many who name the name of Christ in the United States today is not in fact capitalism itself, sometimes in its rawest and most predatory form. It is true, of course, that many Christians of all theological stripes supplement their allegiance to the economic system with an emphasis on charitable giving. Both liberal and conservative Christians can be remarkably generous in responding to disaster relief, world hunger, and the needs of the homeless. Many of these same persons, however, stand in steadfast opposition to virtually all efforts to change the social, political, and economic conditions that give rise to poverty and hunger.

The biblical emphasis on economic justice has not always gone unheard, however. There are and always have been individuals and groups within the larger church community that have spoken, acted, and poured out their lives for the sake of such justice. St. Francis cast his lot with the poor, as did Dorothy Day in modern times; and Martin Luther King Jr.'s prophetic witness for racial equality embraced the economic sphere as well. There is also a long history of Christian socialism, although there are few in our time willing to acknowledge it.[2] This is to some degree understandable, given the horrible abuses that have taken place under the banner of Stalinist and Maoist ideologies. And yet it is testimony also to the church's accommodation to the larger culture that so few in its ranks have been able to distinguish between genuinely democratic socialist options and the essentially fascist perversions that have made use of the term. Christians who have embraced those perversions must share some of the blame, but their tiny numbers pale before the throngs who worship at the feet of capitalist ideology.

The majority of Christians in the United States, I suspect, think of themselves as neither "right" nor "left" on the spectrum of political and economic theory, however, but somewhere in the middle. The problem, though, is that this penchant for moderation has its own pitfalls, since those who inhabit this space allow a predefined spectrum of possibilities to define what the mid-point is. Since the middle is always shifting, to gravitate to it automatically is to lack a moral compass. And on the current scene, splitting the difference between the Republican and Democratic parties in the United States will certainly not deliver us from economic exploitation, imperialist foreign policy, or ecological disaster. Persons of faith, moreover, have no business giving uncritical allegiance to any of the options offered by secular society. If they are serious about the doctrine of the sovereignty of God, their reflections on this matter, no less than any other, must be based in their own religious tradition.

That tradition, however, can serve only as a starting point. The New Testament cannot deliver a specific economic theory, form of government, or social system for our own time and place. Our world is far too different from that of the first century, and in any case the New Testament has no comprehensive theory to offer. In addition, as I noted in chapter 7, the deconstructive power of Luke's first beatitude, which proclaims the blessedness of the poor, tends to call into question any specific plan for addressing the issue of poverty. I therefore raised the question as to whether this beatitude can be of any practical use to us regarding this problem. I would argue at this point that precisely by calling all plans of action into question, while at the same time confronting us with the stark reality of the poor, the disruptive saying serves as a reminder that all solutions on the human level are provisional. The loyalty of the faith community is not to a political ideology but to the rule of God, which transcends all human social, political, and economic systems. But this by no means negates the fact that the biblical tradition does witness to a set of values by which we can evaluate the various approaches to the economy that human wisdom delivers. And those values clearly demand economic systems designed not simply to increase productivity but to achieve equity in the distribution of wealth and income and maximize the possibility of a good life, in material terms, for all. The biblical witness can give us only a starting point, but that starting point is all important.

"Race" and Ethnicity

Insofar as direct exegesis is concerned, the issue of "race" has come to the surface in this book only in relation to Luke-Acts. This is not surprising, since "racial" distinctions did not play the same role in the ancient world as they did in later times. Ethnic divisions, however, were a source of intense hatred, and to the extent that the New Testament presents a consistent witness to the radical inclusiveness of the body of Christ it provides the basis for an ethic that demands the rejection of any ideology that sets one group of persons above another or demeans any human being on the basis of origin. And, given the sordid history of raced-based genocide, slavery, prejudice, and oppression in the United

States—together with the discouraging setbacks in the long and arduous process of addressing the results of discrimination in recent years—it seems important to reiterate this point, however obvious it might seem. Current concerns regarding racial injustice overlap with those relating to class and economic status, but we must nevertheless recognize a residual problem based specifically on racial prejudice, whether conscious or unconscious, and take note of the sad fact of the complicity of Christian individuals and groups in perpetuating it. Against such prejudice and the atrocities it breeds, the New Testament testifies to God's judgment on the one hand and, on the other, the image of a community in which all human barriers are broken down.

Eco-Justice and Creation Theology

Paul Santmire's assessment (1985, 8 and passim) of the Christian tradition's ecological promise as ambiguous is borne out, insofar as the New Testament is concerned, by the passages I have treated in this volume. On the positive side, there are hints of the "voice of the earth" in the references to God's care for the natural world in Matthew, significant elements of a cosmological theology in Colossians and Ephesians, and the startling affirmation in John 1 that the eternal *Logos* takes on flesh in Jesus of Nazareth. Even the apocalyptic aspects of the New Testament can manifest a positive attitude toward the earth and creation. In addition, we have observed a sense of cosmic empathy in Rom 8:18-25 and a strong indication in Revelation that the new creation takes the old up into itself rather than destroying it. One can hardly argue, however, that ecological sensitivity is a major strain of thought within the New Testament; and the dualism in the Gospel of John forces us to qualify our optimism about the significance of the theme of incarnation. In our treatment of Ephesians and Colossians, moreover, we had to face the question of whether the reversion to a hierarchical social structure in these writings means that creation theologies have a necessary tendency toward social conservatism that runs counter to the more liberative elements in the early Christian witness.

Despite these ambiguities, the earth-sensitive elements of the New Testament are real, and the broader liberative themes reinforce rather than diminish their significance. Concern for social justice and the environment is a "worldly" matter. This is not to say that it manifests material concerns to the exclusion of the spiritual, but rather that its spiritual dimension is present precisely in its attention to the material realm as the sphere in which God's love and care are manifest. We have already found good reason to deny the literal force of the New Testament's apocalyptic witness, and the revaluation of this strain of thought along the lines

I have suggested opens the way for the earth-sensitive undercurrents to come into their own in support of an unqualified endorsement of the goodness of creation. And even apart from the nascent ecological witness, the New Testament's overriding concern for economic justice and human well-being demands attention to this issue in light of the current crisis. The entire human community will eventually suffer from inattention to the environment, but the poor will suffer disproportionately as the crisis worsens. Beyond all this, moreover, the elements of a genuinely cosmological theology in the New Testament can also serve as textual backing for an earth sensitivity that transcends a concern for the earth as the home of human beings and views the natural world as valuable in itself as the creation of a just and loving deity.

On one final note, if it is true that cosmological theology is sometimes allied with an endorsement of hierarchical social arrangements, we should note that the cosmological witness does not stand alone in the tradition but is accompanied by christological and covenantal themes. Although I have argued that the New Testament's christological exclusivism is trumped by more inclusivist undercurrents of meaning, it is not my intention to deny the indispensable character of the "particularist" element in the biblical witness. The truth is that there is no necessary connection between natural theology and hierarchicalism. And the strength of themes grounded in covenantal and christological thought—such as love, liberation, and inclusiveness—gives ample warrant for hermeneutical moves that deconstruct that connection. In the end, sensitivity to the nonhuman world should strengthen rather than weaken a commitment to justice in human society, because human beings and the other forms of life that inhabit the earth have been victimized by the very same forces of oppression.

THE AUTHORITY OF SCRIPTURE, THE NATURE OF REVELATION, AND THE ACTION OF GOD

I am well aware that the approach I have taken to the biblical writings will strike some readers as subversive of biblical authority, since it sanctions a process of reconstruction of meaning on the one hand and outright rejection of some elements in the tradition on the other. So I want to make one final statement on this issue. In chapter 2, I advanced the thesis that we should understand all interpretations of texts as reading proposals. By this I meant that we should view them not as claims to objective truths but as suggestions, enabled but also limited by the interpreter's circumstances. To name these readings *proposals* is to admit an element of subjectivity, but it is not to deny that they are attempts to represent the text in an accurate way. I want to suggest now that we understand the biblical texts themselves in an analogous way—that is, as proposals for understanding something as revelatory. To clarify this point, I will need to take brief note of the traditional claim that the Bible is "the revealed word of God."

The basic issue has to do with the nature of revelation. In what precise sense is it meaningful to say that in the Bible one finds a revelation of God? For fundamentalists, this means verbal inspiration, but such a view is easily refuted by reference to the well-known contradictions and historical inaccuracies that inhabit these texts. There are, however, many theologians and ordinary Christians who hold to a much less rigid understanding of revelation and biblical authority on a theoretical level but who cite Scripture in such a way as to imply a very direct connection between the text and the mind of God. And what this latter view seems to share with the former, at least by implication, is a particular view of the action of God. The more direct one understands the relationship between the mind of God and the Bible to be, the greater degree of control over the biblical text one must imagine God as exercising.

The fundamentalist position is intelligible in its theoretical structure; it simply runs aground when confronted with the actual content of the texts. It is less clear, however, that some of the more moderate versions of the conservative view are fully coherent. One sometimes hears arguments to the following effect. "We are justified in departing from the biblical subordination of women, because the Bible itself contains differing perspectives. Since the Bible is consistent on the matter of homosexuality, however, a similar move is ruled out in this case." This formulation might seem reasonable on the surface, but insistence that consistency on a given issue binds the church to a specific view suggests a very direct relationship between the Bible and the mind of God. And such a relationship in turn implies a high degree of control over the content of the text. If one accepts such a degree of control, however, the problem arises as to how to account for the differing perspectives within the Bible when we come to other issues.

I see no way out of this problem other than to accept the fundamentalist position and suffer the consequences or, alternatively, to give up the notion of God's direct control over the content of the text and understand the process of revelation as indirect and therefore highly subject to error. To take the latter position is not to deny that the Bible is a vehicle of revelation, but it is to deny that one can move simplistically from the text to the mind of God. I can therefore endorse this statement by Marcus Borg:

I see the Bible as a human response to God. Rather than seeing God as scripture's ultimate author, I see the Bible as the response of these two ancient communities to their experience of God. As such, it contains their stories of God, their perceptions of God's character and will, their prayers and praise of God, their perceptions of the human condition and the paths of deliverance, their religious and ethical practices, and their understanding of what faithfulness to God involves. As the product of these two communities, the Bible thus tells us about how *they* saw things, not about how *God* sees things. (2001, 22–23; emphasis original)

I do not believe that to put the matter this way is to deny the revelatory power of Scripture; it is rather to understand revelation as a dialogical rather than a unilateral process, as indirect rather than direct. It is to understand God's relationship to the text not as external control but as persuasive effort. And it is to understand the biblical writings as human proposals, offered as possible avenues to the truth and the good that must continually be validated in the court of ongoing human experience.

CONCLUSION: THE BIBLE IN BABYLON REVISITED

The legacy of the Bible in the realm of ethics is mixed. In the hands of some interpreters, it has served as a cruel weapon for bludgeoning those who dare to resist the oppressive forces of power and privilege. Used in this way, it has held back the movements for peace, justice, the integrity of God's creation, and the acceptance of all persons as children of God. It has also fostered arrogance toward persons of nonbiblical religions, and in some Christian circles it has been employed in the service of a virulent hatred of Jews and Judaism. Yet it has also inspired many persons to live far ahead of their times as prophetic activists for economic justice, radical inclusiveness, and care for the natural world. It has spawned courageous witnesses against war, violence, slavery, and oppression based on race, ethnicity, gender, or social class. And it has called countless persons to live lives of deep spiritual devotion and self-sacrificial service to their neighbors. The difference between these two ways of appropriating the biblical witnesses is, in the end, less a matter of technical hermeneutical method than of the intuitive hearing of the heart. But method can play important roles. On the exegetical level, it can help establish the parameters of legitimate meaning in texts and show that some construals are simply false. On the hermeneutical level, it can aid the reader in sorting through the many strains of meaning by identifying their presuppositions, tracing out their implications, bringing them into conversation with the readers' worldview, and thus clearing the way for intuition to do its work.

So, then, finally: Of what use is the New Testament in making ethical decisions or living a moral life? My hope is that this book has contributed to the sense that it has much to offer in this regard, although not as a compendium of concrete moral rules but rather as a fund of provocative proposals capable of enhancing deep reflection. To approach the biblical writings as I have suggested will not issue in a hard-and-fast statement of theological truth or a rigid definition of the specifics of moral behavior. What it should do, on one level, is to push behind the question of right and wrong actions to the prior question of character and virtue and confront the reader with a message of grace and demand that calls for a process of discernment rooted in attentiveness to the guidance of the Spirit.

On another level, however, the approach I am commending is intended as a way of evaluating the specific ethical demands and conflicting strains of meaning that we find within the biblical witnesses. Some of these, whether they appear as mainstreams or undercurrents, seem indispensable to the biblical witness as a whole when it is viewed from our contemporary perspective. These are the strains whose implications can be carried through with full consistency without damage to the central affirmation of the character of God as infinitely loving and just. And it is precisely these aspects of New Testament ethics that set the authentic community of faith to some extent in opposition to the world around them. Biblical values such as peace, justice, and the acceptance of all persons cut against the grain of many aspects of contemporary societies. To stand for these values is to run afoul of the ideologies that inform much of our lives together—ideologies based on uncritical nationalism, racial or ethnic superiority, and the desire for the concentration of political and economic power. And to read the New Testament without experiencing a challenge to these modes of thought is to read with stunted imaginations and hardened hearts.

For those who have the ears to hear, however, the New Testament makes a powerful witness, within a christological framework, to the Spirit's work of liberation and of love. And nowhere does this witness receive more eloquent expression than in the summation of Jesus' mission in Luke 4:18-19: "to bring good news to the poor . . . to proclaim release to the captives . . . to let the oppressed go free. . . ."

notes

⟋꯭

2. MAKING MEANING IN THE MISTS OF BABYLON

1. I draw here on Parker Palmer, *The Courage to Teach: Exploring the Inner Landscape of a Teacher's Life* (San Francisco: Jossey-Bass, 1998).

3. THE CONTEXT OF THE JESUS MOVEMENT

1. On the concepts of "Great" and "Little" or "popular" traditions, see Horsley 1996, 25, and 1995, 148f.

2. See Fredricksen 1999, 176–84, for the view that the temple was universally revered in both Judea and Galilee; for an opposing view, see Horsley 1995, 144–47, 155–57.

3. Although rejecting the traditional view that the tribes of Israel were formed in Egypt and that Israel entered Canaan as an already-established national entity, Gerstenberger finds insufficient evidence for the alternative models of the formation of the nation—the slow immigration of groups from outside the land or the internal revolt by the landless classes. All that we can conclude is that "there were tribes and tribal alliances in Israel in the period before the state" and that "Yahweh, the warrior, plays an important role in the few tribal alliances that have been preserved" (2002, 111–20; quotation from 120). His account presupposes the gradual inclusion of groups, formerly dedicated to their local deities, into the Yahwistic faith.

4. Gerstenberger 2002, 22, citing Winfried Thiel, *Die Entwicklung Israels in vorstaatlicher Zeit,* 2nd ed. (Neukirchen-Vluyn: Neukirchener, 1985), 110 n. 1.

5. Barton 2003, 34, citing F. Horst, "Naturrecht und Altes Testament," *Evangelische Theologie* 10 (1950–51): 253–73.

4. THE ETHICS OF THE JESUS MOVEMENT

1. The qualification "roughly" is necessary, since there are some passages shared by all three Synoptic Gospels that contain significant agreements of Matthew and Luke against Mark, which would tend to indicate the influence of Q. Because of such passages, some scholars think that the author of Mark must have known Q but made scant use of it.

2. On the theme of collective responsibility, see Horsley 1987, 197–98, who cites both of these passages.

3. For differing views on whether the people as a whole were loyal to the temple and the significance of the symbolic destruction, see Horsley 1987, 287–91, and E. P. Sanders 1985, 61–90.

4. See the article by Herzog and Horsley's introduction in Horsley ed., 2004, which apply Scott's work to biblical studies, and Scott 1977 and 1990.

5. Mark 15:42-47 and parallels; Mark 16:1-8 and parallels; Luke 8:1-3.

6. For example, the teachings on divorce in Mark 10:1-12 and parallels, on making friends with one's accuser on the way to court in Matt 5:22-26, and on almsgiving, prayer, and fasting in Matt 6:1-6. See Wolfgang Stegemann 1984, and Horsley 1987, 228–31, for critiques of Gerd Theissen's claim that the Jesus movement was made up primarily of wandering charismatics.

7. Mark 2:13-17//Matt 9:9-13//Luke 5:27-32; Matt 11:16-19//Luke 7:31-35; Luke 15:2.

8. For example, Mark 1:29-31 and parallels; 5:21-34 and parallels; 7:24-29//Matt 15:21-28; Mark 14:3-9 and parallels; Mark 15:40-41//Matt 27:55-56; Luke 10:38-42; 13:10-17; John 4:7-30 (note v. 27); 11:17-27; 20:11-18.

9. For example, the stories in Genesis 1–11 depict God's caring relationship to generic humanity, before the call of Abraham and the establishment of the Israelite community; Isa 2:1-4 envisions a time when all nations will stream to Jerusalem to learn of God, which will also be a time of universal peace; and Isa 49:6 speaks explicitly of God's salvation extending "to the end of the earth."

10. Seen primarily in the addition of Matt 22:11-14, which depicts the dismissal of some guests because of their improper attire.

11. Matt 9:10//Mark 2:15-16//Luke 5:29-30; Matt 11:19//Luke 7:34; Luke 15:1-2.

12. Note, e.g., Matt 5:17-19, where Jesus affirms the continuing validity of the entire Law.

5. THE GOSPEL OF MATTHEW

1. The five discourses are (1) 5:1—7:27; (2) 10:1—11:1; (3) 13:1-52; (4) 18:1-35; (5) 23:1 (or 24:1)—25:46. The end of each is indicated by a formulary statement, "rendered in the NRSV as 'When Jesus had finished. . . .' In each of these instances, the clause ends by referring to some kind of teaching that Jesus has been engaged in, and

in each case the formula is preceded by an extended discourse that has thematic unity" (Pregeant 2004, 10).

2. See Pregeant 1978, 64–72, and the extensive references cited there.

3. See, for example, Benno Przybylski, *Righteousness in Matthew and His World of Thought* (Society for New Testament Studies Monograph Series 41; Cambridge: Cambridge University Press, 1980), 79–99.

4. Some manuscripts lack the phrase "against you," but the content of the pericope clearly has to do with an affront against a community member.

5. See, however, Pregeant 1978, 96–100, for the argument that the exclusivism here is "kairological" rather than ontological. That is to say, it excludes from salvation those who reject Jesus during his lifetime and perhaps those who later reject the Christian message, but does not mean "that no person in the history of the world ever has known or ever will know God apart from Jesus."

6. Many interpreters reject this "inclusivist" reading of 25:31-46, arguing that those who receive the acts of mercy are Christian missionaries and those who minister to them are "outsiders." See, e.g., Lamar Cope, "Matthew XXV.31-46: The Sheep and the Goats Reinterpreted," *Novum Testamentum* 11 (1969): 32–44. Even on this interpretation, the passage constitutes a break with exclusivism; and for a defense of the inclusivist reading, see Pregeant 1978, 115–20.

6. THE GOSPEL OF MARK

1. For example, 1:21-28; 2:13; 4:1-2; 6:2; 8:31; 9:31; 14:49; 12:35. See Vernon K. Robbins, *Jesus the Teacher: A Socio-Rhetorical Interpretation of Mark* (Philadelphia: Fortress Press, 1984), chapter 4.

2. The Greek phrase is *hoi dokountes archein. Hoi* is translated as "those" and *archein* as "to rule"; *dokountes* is a participial form of a verb that means "to think/seem/suppose/believe." The literal sense is thus something like "those who seem to rule" or "those who are supposed to rule" (RSV).

7. LUKE-ACTS

1. For example, Luke 7:30; Acts 2:32; 20:27 (Greek: *boulē tou theou*; sometimes translated "purpose (or counsel) of God."

2. See Tannehill's index for his treatments of "Paul and the hope of Israel" (1990, 396).

3. See, esp., Terence L. Donaldson, *Paul and the Gentiles: Remapping the Apostle's Convictional World* (Minneapolis: Fortress Press, 1997), 68–74, citing, e.g., Tobit 13:11; 14:5-7; and numerous passages from the *Testaments of the Twelve Patriarchs*.

4. Tannehill 1986, 178; note, however, his footnote indicating the Pharisees' misunderstanding of Jesus' mission.

5. That Paul continues to think of himself as a Pharisee is not contradicted by the use of the aorist tense (*ezēsa*: "I have lived") in Acts 26:5, which is rightly translated by the RSV and NRSV with the English present perfect. On the complexive, or constative, aorist, which indicates a completed linear action viewed as a whole, see C. K. Barrett, *A Critical and Exegetical Commentary on the Acts of the Apostles*, vol. 2 (International Critical Commentary; London and New York: T&T Clark, 1998), 1152; and F. Blass and A. Debrunner, *A Greek Grammar of the New Testament and Other Early Christian Literature*, trans. and rev. Robert W. Funk (Chicago: University of Chicago Press, 1961), 332.

8. THE GOSPEL AND LETTERS OF JOHN

1. See, e.g., Brown 1979 and Smith 1984 and 1991 for the view that the Gospel preceded the letters; for opposing views, see Strecker 2000, 419–505, and Callahan 2005.

2. For differing views, see Rudolf Bultmann, *The Gospel of John: A Commentary*, trans. G. R. Beasley, gen. ed. R. W. N. Hoare and J. K. Riches (Philadelphia: Westminster, 1971); and Brown 1966.

3. For example, J. L. Houlden, *Ethics and the New Testament* (New York: Cambridge University Press, 1973), 36; and Jack T. Sanders, *Ethics in the New Testament: Change and Development* (Philadelphia: Fortress Press, 1975), 1, 100; cited by Hays 1996, 139.

4. 1993, 305; Marxsen's translator follows the NRSV in rendering "brothers" as "brothers and sisters."

9. THE UNDISPUTED LETTERS OF PAUL

1. See references on all these positions in N. Elliott 1994, 218–21; also Furnish 1984, 130–34.

2. Citing Gordon Zerbe, "Paul's Ethic of Nonretaliation and Peace," in *The Love of Enemy and Nonretaliation in the New Testament*, ed. Willard M. Swartley (Louisville: Westminster John Knox, 1992), 177–222.

3. For alternative explanations for the textual variation, see Antoinette Clark Wire, *The Corinthian Women Prophets: A Reconstruction through Paul's Rhetoric* (Minneapolis: Fortress Press, 1990), 149–52, who accepts the verses as genuinely Pauline and thinks they form an important link in his rhetorical strategy (on the strategy, see 31–35, 152–58).

4. Odell-Scott's case rests largely on his evaluation of the force of the particle *ē* (ἤ) that begins v. 36, noting that it "is capable of conveying a spectrum of negative conjunctions ranging from the simple noting of a difference by comparison to the refutation of one thing by another" (1991, 185). Understanding the force of the particle in the latter

sense, he observes that Paul uses it in an identical way in 1 Cor 11:20-22, where the NRSV renders v. 22 as "What! Do you not have homes to eat or drink in?" (1983, 90). In 14:36, it introduces an interrogative sentence to indicate "that the rhetorical questions to follow will serve to refute the sentences which preceded it" (1991, 185).

5. Since v. 26 does not refer explicitly to same-sex relationships as does v. 27, some scholars think that what Paul has in mind in the former case are practices such as bestiality or heterosexual acts such as anal or oral intercourse. See, e.g., James F. Miller, "The Practices of Romans 1:26: Homosexual or Heterosexual?" *Novum Testamentum* 36 (1995): 1–11. Brooten (1996, 248–53), however, gives compelling reasons against these claims; see also Gagnon 2001, 297–99.

10. THE POST-PAULINE LETTERS

1. Citing Robert Alter, *The Pleasures of Reading in an Ideological Age* (New York: Simon & Schuster, 1989), 123–24.

2. Citing Dale B. Martin, *Slavery as Salvation: The Metaphor of Slavery in Pauline Christianity* (New Haven: Yale University Press, 1990), 54–58.

11. THE REVELATION TO JOHN

1. Broad outlines of this section are dependent on Boring 1989, 187–88, and Yarbro Collins 1980, 203.

2. Theodore Hiebert, *The Yahwist's Landscape: Nature and Religion in Early Israel* (Oxford: Oxford University Press, 1996); quoted by Rossing 2002, 181.

3. Rossing 2002, 185, citing Rossing 1999; and Richard Bauckham, "Economic Critique of Rome in Revelation 18," in *Images of Empire* (Journal for the Study of the Old Testament Supplement Series 22; ed. Loveday Alexander; Sheffield: JSOT Press, 1991), 47–90.

4. Citing Rossing 1998, 491–94.

5. Citing Leonardo Boff, *Ecology and Liberation: A New Paradigm* (Maryknoll, N.Y.: Orbis Books, 1997), 104.

12. KNOWING TRUTH, DOING GOOD

1. See, e.g., John E. Hill, *Democracy, Equality, and Justice: John Adams, Adam Smith, and Social Values,* 2d ed. of *Revolutionary Values for a New Millennium* (Lanham, Md.: Lexington, 2007), 90–93, 114, 142–46.

2. See John C. Cort, *Christian Socialism: An Informal History* (Maryknoll, N.Y.: Orbis Books, 1988).

works cited

Adam, A. K. M. 1995. *Making Sense of New Testament Theology: "Modern" Problems and Prospects.* Studies in American Biblical Hermeneutics 11. Macon, Ga.: Mercer University Press.

Bagemihl, Bruce. 1999. *Biological Exuberance: Animal Homosexuality and Natural Diversity.* New York: St. Martin's.

Balch, David L. 1981. *Let Wives Be Submissive: The Domestic Code in 1 Peter.* Society of Biblical Literature Monograph Series 26. Chico, Calif.: Scholars.

———, ed. 2000. *Homosexuality, Science, and the "Plain Sense" of Scripture.* Grand Rapids: Eerdmans.

Bartlett, David L. 1998. *The First Letter of Peter: Introduction, Commentary, and Reflections.* In *The New Interpreter's Bible.* Vol. 12. Nashville: Abingdon.

Barton, John. 2003. *Understanding Old Testament Ethics: Approaches and Explorations.* Louisville and London: Westminster John Knox.

Bassler, Jouette M., ed. 1991. *Pauline Theology I: Thessalonians, Philippians, Galatians, Philemon.* Minneapolis: Fortress Press.

Beardslee, William A. 1993. "Poststructuralist Criticism." In *To Each Its Own Meaning: An Introduction to Biblical Criticisms and Their Application,* ed. Steven L. McKenzie and Stephen R. Haynes. Louisville: Westminster John Knox.

Beker, J. Christiaan. 1980. *Paul the Apostle: The Triumph of God in Life and Thought.* Philadelphia: Fortress Press.

Belo, Fernando. 1981. *A Materialist Reading of the Gospel of Mark.* Translated by Matthew J. O'Connell. Maryknoll, N.Y.: Orbis Books.

Betz, Hans Dieter. 1985. *Essays on the Sermon on the Mount.* Philadelphia: Fortress Press.

Black, C. Clifton. 1998. "The First, Second, and Third Letters of John: Introduction, Commentary, and Reflections." In *The New Interpreter's Bible.* Vol. 12. Nashville: Abingdon.

Blount, Brian K. 2001. *Then the Whisper Put on Flesh: New Testament Ethics in an African American Context*. Nashville: Abingdon.

Boers, Hendrikus. *Theology out of the Ghetto: A New Testament Essay concerning Religious Exclusiveness*. Leiden: Brill.

Borg, Marcus J. 2001. *Reading the Bible Again for the First Time: Taking the Bible Seriously but Not Literally*. San Francisco: HarperSanFrancisco.

Boring, M. Eugene. 1989. *Revelation*. Interpretation: A Bible Commentary for Teaching and Preaching. Louisville: Westminster John Knox.

———. 1999. *1 Peter*. Abingdon New Testament Commentaries. Nashville: Abingdon.

———. 2006. *Mark: A Commentary*. New Testament Library. Louisville and London: Westminster John Knox.

———, and Fred B. Craddock. 2004. *The People's New Testament Commentary*. Louisville and London: Westminster John Knox.

Boswell, John. 1980. *Christianity, Social Tolerance, and Homosexuality: Gay People in Western Europe from the Beginning of the Christian Era to the Fourteenth Century*. Chicago and London: University of Chicago Press.

Brawley, Robert, ed. 1996. *Biblical Ethics and Homosexuality: Listening to Scripture*. Louisville: Westminster John Knox.

Brooten, Bernadette. 1982. *Women Leaders in the Ancient Synagogue*. Chico, Calif.: Scholars.

———. 1986. "Jewish Women's History in the Roman Period: A Task for Christian Theology." *Harvard Theological Review* 79:22–30.

———. 1996. *Love between Women: Early Christian Responses to Female Homoeroticism*. Chicago: University of Chicago Press.

Brown, Raymond E. 1966. *The Gospel according to John I–XII: A New Translation with Introduction and Commentary*. Garden City, N.Y.: Doubleday.

———. 1979. *The Community of the Beloved Disciple: The Life, Loves, and Hates of an Individual Church in New Testament Times*. New York: Paulist.

Bultmann, Rudolf. 1958. *Jesus Christ and Mythology*. New York: Charles Scribner's Sons.

———. 1984. *New Testament Mythology and Other Basic Writings*. Selected, edited, and translated by Schubert M. Ogden. Philadelphia: Fortress Press.

Cadbury, Henry J. 1958. *The Making of Luke-Acts*. New York: Macmillan. First published in 1927.

Callahan, Allen Dwight. 2005. *A Love Supreme: A History of the Johannine Tradition*. Minneapolis: Fortress Press.

Carter, Warren. 2000. *Matthew and the Margins: A Sociopolitical and Religious Reading*. Maryknoll, N.Y.: Orbis Books.

Cassidy, Richard J. 1978. *Jesus, Politics, and Society: A Study of Luke's Gospel.* Maryknoll, N.Y.: Orbis Books.

Chadwick, Henry. 1962. "Ephesians." In *Peake's Commentary on the Bible*, ed. Matthew Black and H. H. Rowley. London: Thomas Nelson.

Cobb, John B., Jr., and David J. Lull. *Romans.* Chalice Commentaries for Today. St. Louis: Chalice.

Conzelmann, Hans. 1961. *The Theology of St. Luke.* Translated by Geoffrey Buswell. New York: Harper & Row.

————. 1975. *1 Corinthians: A Commentary on the First Epistle to the Corinthians.* Translated by James W. Leitch. Hermeneia. Philadelphia: Fortress Press.

Countryman, William L. 1988. *Dirt, Greed, and Sex: Sexual Ethics in the New Testament and Their Implications for Today.* Philadelphia: Fortress Press.

Davids, Peter H. 1982. *The Epistle of James: A Commentary on the Greek Text.* Grand Rapids: Eerdmans.

Davies, W. D., and Dale C. Allison Jr. 1991. *A Critical and Exegetical Commentary on the Gospel according to Saint Matthew.* Vol. 2. International Critical Commentary. Edinburgh: T&T Clark.

Dibelius, Martin. 1909. *Die Geisterwelt im Glauben des Paulus.* Göttingen: Vandenhoeck & Ruprecht.

————. 1976. *James: A Commentary on the Epistle of James.* Revised by H. Greeven. Translated by M. A. Williams. Edited by H. Koester. Hermeneia. Philadelphia: Fortress Press.

Douglas, Mary. 2002. *Purity and Danger: An Analysis of the Concept of Pollution and Taboo.* With a new preface by the author. London: Routledge.

Elliott, John H. 1981. *A Home for the Homeless: A Sociological Exegesis of 1 Peter: Its Situation and Strategy.* Philadelphia: Fortress Press.

Elliott, Neil. 1994. *Liberating Paul: The Justice of God and the Politics of the Apostle.* Maryknoll, N.Y.: Orbis Books.

————. 1997. "The Anti-Imperial Message of the Cross." In *Paul and Empire: Religion and Power in Roman Imperial Society*, ed. Richard A. Horsley. Harrisburg, Pa.: Trinity Press International.

Farmer, Ronald L. 1997. *Beyond the Impasse: The Promise of a Process Hermeneutic.* Studies in American Biblical Hermeneutics. Macon, Ga.: Mercer University Press.

————. 2005. *Revelation.* Chalice Commentaries for Today. St. Louis: Chalice.

Felder, Cain Hope. 1989. *Troubling Biblical Waters: Race, Class, and Family.* Maryknoll, N.Y.: Orbis Books.

————, ed. 1991. *Stony the Road We Trod: African American Biblical Interpretation*. Minneapolis: Fortress Press.

Fredriksen, Paula. 1999. *Jesus of Nazareth, King of the Jews: A Jewish Life and the Emergence of Christianity*. New York: Knopf.

Friedrich, G., W. Pöhlmann, and P. Stuhlmacher. 1976. "Zur historischen Situation und Intention von Röm 13:1-7." *Zeitschrift für Theologie und Kirche* 73:131–66.

Funk, Robert W. 1966. *Language, Hermeneutic, and Word of God: The Problem of Language in the New Testament*. New York: Harper & Row.

————, Roy W. Hoover, and the Jesus Seminar. 1993. *The Five Gospels: The Search for the Authentic Words of Jesus*. New York: Macmillan.

Furnish, Victor Paul, 1968. *Theology and Ethics in Paul*. Nashville and New York: Abingdon.

————. 1972. *The Love Command in the New Testament*. Nashville and New York: Abingdon.

————. 1985. *The Moral Teaching of Paul: Selected Issues*. Second edition. Nashville: Abingdon.

————. 1994. "The Bible and Homosexuality: Reading the Texts in Context." In *Homosexuality in the Church: Both Sides of the Debate*, ed. Jeffrey S. Siker. Louisville: Westminster John Knox.

————. 2005. "Uncommon Love and the Common Good: Christians as Citizens in the Letters of Paul." In *In Search of the Common Good*, ed. Dennis P. McCann and Patrick D. Miller. New York and London: T&T Clark.

Gagnon, Robert. 2001. *The Bible and Homosexual Practice: Texts and Hermeneutics*. Nashville: Abingdon.

Gerstenberger, Erhard. 2002. *Theologies in the Old Testament*. Translated by John Bowden. Minneapolis: Fortress Press.

Green, Joel B. 1994. "Good News to Whom? Jesus and 'the Poor' in the Gospel of Luke." In *Jesus of Nazareth: Lord and Christ: Essays on the Historical Jesus and New Testament Christology*, ed. Joel B. Green and Max Turner. Grand Rapids: Eerdmans.

Greene-McCreight, Kathryn. 2000. "The Logic of the Interpretation of Scripture and the Church's Debate over Sexual Ethics." In *Homosexuality, Science, and the "Plain Sense" of Scripture*, ed. David Balch. Grand Rapids: Eerdmans.

Gregorios, Paulos Mar. 1990. "New Testament Foundations for Understanding the Creation." In *Liberating Life: Contemporary Approaches to Ecological Theology*, ed. Charles Birch, William Eakin, and Jay B. McDaniel. Maryknoll, N.Y.: Orbis Books.

Griffin, David Ray. 1989. *God and Religion in the Postmodern World: Essays in Postmodern Thought.* Albany: SUNY Press.

Habel, Norman C. 2002. "An Ecojustice Challenge: Is Earth Valued in John 1?" In *The Earth Story in the New Testament,* ed. Norman C. Habel and Vicky Balabanski. Sheffield: Sheffield Academic Press.

———, and Vicky Balabanski, eds. 2002. *The Earth Story in the New Testament.* Sheffield: Sheffield Academic Press.

Hagner, Donald A. 1993. *Matthew 1–13.* Word Biblical Commentary. Dallas: Word Books.

Harrington, Daniel, S.J., and James Keenan, S.J. 2002. *Jesus and Virtue Ethics: Building Bridges between New Testament Studies and Moral Theology.* Lanham, Md., and Chicago: Sheed & Ward.

Hartin, Patrick J. 1991. *James and the Q Sayings of Jesus.* Journal for the Study of the New Testament Supplement 47. Sheffield: JSOT Press.

Hays, Richard B. 1994. "Awaiting the Redemption of Our Bodies: The Witness of Scripture Concerning Homosexuality." In *Biblical Ethics and Homosexuality: Listening to Scripture,* ed. Robert Brawley. Louisville: Westminster John Knox.

———. 1996. *The Moral Vision of the New Testament: Community, Cross, New Creation: A Contemporary Introduction to New Testament Ethics.* San Francisco: HarperSanFrancisco.

Hempel, Johannes. 1964. *Das Ethos des Alten Testaments.* Beiheft zur Zeitschrift für die alttestamentliche Wissenschaft 67. Second edition. Berlin: A. Töpelmann. Original ed. 1938.

Hendrix, Holland. 1984. "Thessalonians Honor Romans." Th.D. thesis, Harvard Divinity School, 1984.

Herzog, William R., II. 2004. "Onstage and Offstage with Jesus: Public Transcripts, Hidden Transcripts, and Gospel Texts." In *Hidden Transcripts and the Arts of Resistance: Applying the Work of James C. Scott to Jesus and Paul,* ed. Richard A. Horsley. Semeia Studies 48. Atlanta: Society of Biblical Literature.

———. 2005. *Prophet and Teacher: An Introduction to the Historical Jesus.* Louisville: Westminster John Knox.

Hooker, Morna D. 2005. *The Gospel According to St. Mark.* Black's New Testament Commentaries. London: A & C Black. First published in 1991.

Horsley, Richard A. 1987. *Jesus and the Spiral of Violence: Popular Jewish Resistance in Roman Palestine.* New York: Harper & Row.

———. 1995. *Galilee: History, Politics, People.* Valley Forge, Pa.: Trinity Press International.

———. 1996. *Archaeology, History, and Society in Galilee: The Social Context of Jesus and the Rabbis*. Valley Forge, Pa.: Trinity Press International.

———. 1998. *1 Corinthians*. Abingdon New Testament Commentaries. Nashville: Abingdon.

———, ed. 2004. *Hidden Transcripts and the Arts of Resistance: Applying the Work of James C. Scott to Jesus and Paul*. Semeia Studies 48. Atlanta: Society of Biblical Literature.

Hughes, Graham. 1979. *Hebrews and Hermeneutics: The Epistle to the Hebrews as a New Testament Example of Biblical Interpretation*. Cambridge: Cambridge University Press.

Iser, Wolfgang. 1974. *The Implied Reader: Patterns of Communication in Prose Fiction from Bunyan to Beckett*. Baltimore: Johns Hopkins University Press.

Jeremias, Joachim. 1955. *The Eucharistic Words of Jesus*. Translated from the second German edition by Arnold Erhart. New York: Macmillan.

Jewett, Robert. 2007. *Romans: A Commentary*. Assisted by Roy D. Kotansky. Edited by Eldon Jay Epp. Hermeneia. Minneapolis: Fortress Press.

Johnson, Luke T. 1997. *Reading Romans: A Literary and Theological Commentary*. New York: Crossroad.

Käsemann, Ernst. 1964. *Essays on New Testament Themes*. Translated by W. J. Montague. Studies in Biblical Theology 41. London: SCM.

Keck, Leander E. 1984. "Ethics in the Gospel according to Matthew." *Iliff Review* 41/1 and 2:39–56.

———. 1996. "Rethinking 'New Testament Ethics.'" *Journal of Biblical Literature* 111/1:3–16.

———. 2000. *Who Is Jesus? History in Perfect Tense*. Columbia: University of South Carolina Press.

Kidd, Reggie M. 1990. *Wealth and Beneficence in the Pastoral Epistles: A "Bourgeois" Form of Early Christianity?* Society of Biblical Literature Dissertation Series 122. Atlanta: Society of Biblical Literature.

Kloppenborg, John S. 1990. "Alms, Debt and Divorce." *Toronto Journal of Theology* 6:182–200.

Kloppenborg Verbin, John S. 2000. *Excavating Q: The History and Setting of the Sayings Gospel*. Minneapolis: Fortress Press.

Koester, Helmut. 1997. "Imperial Ideology and Paul's Eschatology in 1 Thessalonians." In *Paul and Empire: Religion and Power in Roman Imperial Society*, ed. Richard A. Horsley. Harrisburg, Pa.: Trinity Press International.

Lawrence, D. H. 1932. *Apocalypse*. New York: Viking.

Leske, Adrian M. 2002. "Matthew 6.25-34: Human Anxiety in the Natural World." In *The Earth Story in the New Testament*, ed. Norman C. Habel and Vicky Balabanski. Sheffield: Sheffield Academic Press.

Liddell, Henry G., and Robert Scott. 1995. *An Intermediate Greek-English Lexicon Founded upon the Seventh Edition of Liddell and Scott's Greek-English Lexicon*. Oxford: Clarendon Press.

Lincoln, Andrew T. 2004. *The Letter to the Colossians: Introduction, Commentary, and Reflections*. In *The New Interpreter's Bible*. Vol. 11. Nashville: Abingdon.

Lohse, Eduard. 1961. *Colossians and Philemon*. Hermeneia. Translated by William R. Poehlmann and Robert J. Karris. Edited by Helmut Koester. Philadelphia: Fortress Press.

Lull, David J. 2007. *First Corinthians*. Revised and expanded edition of William A. Beardslee, *First Corinthians: A Commentary for Today*. Chalice Commentaries for Today. St. Louis: Chalice.

Lundeen, Lyman T. 1972. *Risk and Rhetoric in Religion: Whitehead's Theory of Language and the Discourse of Faith*. Philadelphia: Fortress Press.

Luz, Ulrich. 1989. *Matthew 1–7: A Commentary*. Translated by Wilhelm C. Linss. Minneapolis: Augsburg Fortress.

Mack, Burton L. 1988. *A Myth of Innocence: Mark and Christian Origins*. Philadelphia: Fortress Press.

———. 1993. *The Lost Gospel: The Book of Q and Christian Origins*. San Francisco: HarperSanFrancisco.

MacDonald, Dennis Ronald. 1983. *The Legend of the Apostle: The Battle for Paul in Story and Canon*. Philadelphia: Westminster.

MacDonald, Margaret Y. 1988. *The Pauline Churches: A Socio-Historical Study of Institutionalization in the Pauline and Deutero-Pauline Writings*. Society for New Testament Studies Monograph Series 60. Cambridge: Cambridge University Press.

———. 2000. *Colossians and Ephesians*. Sacra Pagina. Collegeville, Minn.: Liturgical.

Maier, Harry O. 2002. "There's a New World Coming! Reading the Apocalypse in the Shadow of the Canadian Rockies." In *The Earth Story in the New Testament*, ed. Norman C. Habel and Vicky Balabanski. Sheffield: Sheffield Academic Press.

Malina, Bruce J. 1983. *The New Testament World: Insights from Cultural Anthropology*. London: SCM.

Martin, Clarice J. 1989. "A Chamberlain's Journey and the Challenge of Interpretation for Liberation." *Semeia* 47:105–35.

―――. 1994. "The Acts of the Apostles." *Searching the Scriptures, Volume 2: A Feminist Commentary*. New York: Crossroad.

Martin, Dale B. 1996. "*Arsenokoitēs* and *Malakos*: Meaning and Consequences." In *Biblical Ethics and Homosexuality: Listening to Scripture*, ed. Robert Brawley. Louisville: Westminster John Knox.

Marxsen, Willi. 1968. *Introduction to the New Testament: An Approach to Its Problems*. Translated by G. Buswell. Philadelphia: Fortress Press.

―――. 1993. *New Testament Foundations for Christian Ethics*. Translated by O. C. Dean Jr. Minneapolis: Fortress Press.

Matera, Frank J. 1996. *New Testament Ethics: The Legacies of Jesus and Paul*. Louisville: Westminster John Knox.

Maynard-Reid, Pedrito U. 1987. *Poverty and Wealth in James*. Maryknoll, N.Y.: Orbis Books.

McCann, Dennis P., and Patrick D. Miller, eds. 2005. *In Search of the Common Good*. New York and London: T&T Clark.

Metzger, Bruce M. 1994. *A Textual Commentary on the Greek New Testament*. Second edition. Stuttgart: Deutsche Bibelgesellschaft and United Bible Societies.

Mitchell, Alan C. 1993. "Rich and Poor in the Courts of Corinth: Litigiousness and Status in 1 Corinthians 6:1-11." *New Testament Studies* 39/4:562–86.

Neyrey, Jerome H. 1986. "Body Language in 1 Corinthians: The Use of Anthropological Models for Understanding Paul and His Opponents." *Semeia* 35:129–70.

Niebuhr, H. Richard. 1951. *Christ and Culture*. New York: Harper & Brothers.

Odell-Scott, David W. 1983. "Let the Women Speak in Church: An Egalitarian Interpretation of 1 Cor 14:33b-36." *Theology Bulletin* 13/3:90–93.

―――. 1987. "In Defense of an Egalitarian Interpretation of 1 Cor 14:34-36: A Reply to Murphy-O'Connor's Critique." *Theology Bulletin* 17/3:100–103.

―――. 1991. *A Post-Patriarchal Christology*. American Academy of Religion Academy Series. Atlanta: Scholars.

Pearson, Birger A. 2004. "A Q Community in Galilee?" *New Testament Studies* 50/4:276–94.

Perkins, Pheme. 1991. "Philippians: Theology for the Heavenly *Politeuma*." In *Pauline Theology I: Thessalonians, Philippians, Galatians, Philemon*, ed. Jouette M. Bassler. Minneapolis: Fortress Press.

Petersen, Norman. 1985. *Rediscovering Paul: Philemon and the Sociology of Paul's Narrative World*. Philadelphia: Fortress Press.

Pippin, Tina. 1992. *Death and Desire: The Rhetoric of Gender in the Apocalypse of John*. Louisville: Westminster John Knox.

Plevnik, Joseph. 1986. *What Are They Saying about Paul?* New York: Paulist.

Pope, Stephen J. 1997. "Scientific and Natural Law Analysis of Homosexuality: A Methodological Study." *Journal of Religious Ethics* 25:89–126.

Porter, Jean. 1999. *Natural and Divine Law: Reclaiming the Tradition for Christian Ethics*. Grand Rapids, and Cambridge, England: Eerdmans.

Powell, Mark Allan. 1995. *God with Us: A Pastoral Theology of Matthew's Gospel*. Minneapolis: Fortress Press.

Pregeant, Russell. 1978. *Christology beyond Dogma: Matthew's Christ in Process Hermeneutic*. Philadelphia: Fortress Press; Missoula, Mont.: Scholars.

———. 1995. *Engaging the New Testament: An Interdisciplinary Text*. Minneapolis: Fortress Press.

———. 2004. *Matthew*. Chalice Commentaries for Today. St. Louis: Chalice.

Przybylski, Benno. 1980. *Righteousness in Matthew and His World of Thought*. Society for New Testament Studies Monograph Series 41. Cambridge: Cambridge University Press.

Reed, Jonathan L. 2000. *Archaeology and the Galilean Jesus: A Re-examination of the Evidence*. Harrisburg, Pa.: Trinity Press International.

Reimer, Ivoni Richter. 1995. *Women in the Acts of the Apostles: A Feminist Liberation Perspective*. Translated by Linda M. Maloney. Minneapolis: Fortress Press.

Rensberger, David. 1988. *Johannine Faith and Liberating Community*. Philadelphia: Westminster.

Rhoads, David, Joanna Dewey, and Donald Michie. 1999. *Mark as Story: An Introduction to the Narrative of a Gospel*. Second edition. Minneapolis: Fortress Press.

Ricoeur, Paul. 1974. *Conflict in Interpretations*. Edited by D. Ihde. Evanston: Northwestern University Press.

Robinson, James M., et al. 2000. *The Critical Edition of Q*. Hermeneia. Minneapolis: Fortress Press.

Rodd, C. S. 2001. *Glimpses of a Strange Land: Studies in Old Testament Ethics*. Edinburgh: T&T Clark.

Rossing, Barbara R. 1998. "River of Life in God's New Jerusalem: An Ecological Vision for Earth's Future." *Currents in Theology and Mission* 25:487–99. Also in *Christianity and Ecology*, ed. Rosemary Radford Ruether and Dieter Hessel. Cambridge: Harvard University Center for World Religions.

———. 1999. *The Choice between Two Cities: Shore, Bride, and Empire in the Apocalypse*. Harvard Theological Studies 48. Harrisburg, Pa.: Pilgrim.

———. 2002. "Alas for Earth! Lament and Resistance in Revelation 12." In *The Earth Story in the New Testament*, ed. Norman C. Habel and Vicky Balabanski. Sheffield: Sheffield Academic Press.

Rowland, Christopher C. 1998. "The Book of Revelation: Introduction, Commentary, and Reflections." In *The New Interpreter's Bible*. Vol. 12. Nashville: Abingdon.

Saldarini, Anthony J. 1994. *Matthew's Christian-Jewish Community*. Chicago: University of Chicago Press.

———. 2001. *Pharisees, Scribes, and Sadducees in Palestinian Society: A Sociological Approach*. Second edition. Grand Rapids: Eerdmans.

Sampley, J. Paul. 1991. *Walking between the Times: Paul's Moral Reasoning*. Minneapolis: Fortress Press.

———. 2002. "The First Letter to the Corinthians: Introduction, Commentary, and Reflections." In *The New Interpreter's Bible*. Vol. 10. Nashville: Abingdon.

Sanders, E. P. 1977. *Paul and Palestinian Judaism: A Comparison of Patterns of Religion*. Philadelphia: Fortress Press.

———. 1985. *Jesus and Judaism*. Philadelphia: Fortress Press.

———. 1993. *The Historical Figure of Jesus*. London: Penguin.

Santmire, H. Paul. 1985. *The Travail of Nature: The Ambiguous Ecological Promise of Christian Theology*. Minneapolis: Fortress Press.

Schniewind, Julius. 1952. *Nachgelassene Reden und Aufsätze*. Berlin: Töpelmann.

Schottroff, Luise. 1984. "Human Solidarity and the Goodness of God." In *God of the Lowly: Socio-Historical Interpretations of the Bible*, ed. Willy Schottroff and Wolfgang Stegemann. Maryknoll, N.Y.: Orbis Books.

Schottroff, Willy, and Wolfgang Stegemann, eds. 1984. *God of the Lowly: Socio-Historical Interpretations of the Bible*. Translated by Matthew J. O'Connell. Maryknoll, N.Y.: Orbis Books.

Schrage, Wolfgang. 1988. *The Ethics of the New Testament*. Translated by David E. Green. Philadelphia: Fortress Press.

Schüssler Fiorenza, Elisabeth. 1981. *Invitation to the Book of Revelation: A Commentary on the Apocalypse with a Complete Text from the Jerusalem Bible*. Garden City, N.Y.: Doubleday.

———. 1984a. *Bread Not Stone: The Challenge of Feminist Biblical Interpretation*. Boston: Beacon.

———. 1984b. *In Memory of Her: A Feminist Theological Reconstruction of Christian Origins*. New York: Crossroad.

———. 1985. *The Book of Revelation: Justice and Judgment*. Philadelphia: Fortress Press.

———. 1994. *Jesus: Miriam's Child, Sophia's Prophet: Critical Issues in Feminist Christology*. New York: Continuum.

Schweitzer, Albert. 1956. *The Mysticism of the Apostle Paul.* Translated by William Montgomery. New York: Macmillan. Originally published in 1931.

Scott, Bernard Brandon. 1989. *Hear Then the Parable: A Commentary on the Parables of Jesus.* Minneapolis: Fortress Press.

Scott, James C. 1977. "Protest and Profanation: Agrarian Revolt and the Little Tradition." *Theory and Society* 4:1–38, 211–46.

———. 1990. *Domination and the Arts of Resistance: Hidden Transcripts.* New Haven: Yale University Press.

Scroggs, Robin. 1983. *The New Testament and Homosexuality: Contextual Background for the Contemporary Debate.* Philadelphia: Fortress Press.

Siker, Jeffrey S., ed. 1994. *Homosexuality in the Church: Both Sides of the Debate.* Louisville: Westminster John Knox.

Smith, D. Moody. 1984. *Johannine Christianity: Essays on Its Setting, Sources, and Theology.* Columbia: University of South Carolina Press.

———. 1991. *First, Second, and Third John.* Interpretation. Louisville: John Knox.

Stegemann, Ekkehard, and Wolfgang Stegemann. 1999. *The Jesus Movement: A Social History of the First Century.* Translated by O. C. Dean Jr. Minneapolis: Fortress Press.

Stegemann, Wolfgang. 1984. "Vagabond Radicalism in Early Christians?: A Historical and Theological Discussion of a Thesis by Gerd Theissen." In *God of the Lowly*, ed. Willy Schottroff and Wolfgang Stegemann. Maryknoll, N.Y.: Orbis Books.

Strecker, Georg. 2000. *Theology of the New Testament.* German edition edited and completed by Friedrich Wilhelm Horn. Translated by M. Eugene Boring. Berlin: de Gruyter; Louisville: Westminster John Knox.

Swartley, Willard M., ed. 1992. *The Love of Enemy and Nonretaliation in the New Testament.* Louisville: Westminster John Knox.

Tamez, Elsa. 1990. *The Scandalous Message of James: Faith without Works Is Dead.* Foreword by Mortimer Arias. New York: Crossroad.

Tannehill, Robert C. 1975. *The Sword of His Mouth.* Semeia Supplements 1. Philadelphia: Fortress Press; Missoula, Mont.: Scholars.

Theissen, Gerd. 1978. *Sociology of Early Palestinian Christianity.* Philadelphia: Fortress Press.

———. 1982. *The Social Setting of Pauline Christianity: Essays on Corinth.* Edited and translated and with an introduction by John H. Schütz. Philadelphia: Fortress Press.

———. 1987. *Psychological Aspects of Pauline Theology.* Translated by John P. Galvin. Philadelphia: Fortress Press.

Tolbert, Mary Ann. 1989. *Sowing the Gospel: Mark's World in Literary-Historical Perspective.* Minneapolis: Fortress Press.

Trilling, Wolfgang. 1974. *Das wahre Israel: Studien zur Theologie des Matthäusevangeliums.* Munich: Kösel.

Vaage, Leif E. 1994. *Galilean Upstarts: Jesus' First Followers according to Q.* Valley Forge, Pa.: Trinity Press International.

Via, Dan Otto. 1967. *The Parables: Their Literary and Existential Dimension.* Philadelphia: Fortress Press.

Via, Dan O., and Robert A. J. Gagnon. 2003. *Homosexuality and the Bible: Two Views.* Minneapolis: Fortress Press.

Wachob, Wesley Hiram. 2000. *The Voice of Jesus in the Social Rhetoric of James.* Society for New Testament Studies Monograph Series 106. Cambridge: Cambridge University Press.

Wall, Robert M. 2002. "The Acts of the Apostles: Introduction, Commentary, and Reflections." In *The New Interpreter's Bible.* Vol. 10. Nashville: Abingdon.

Weems, Renita J. 1991. "African American Women and the Bible." In *Stony the Road We Trod: African American Biblical Interpretation*, ed. Cain Hope Felder. Minneapolis: Fortress Press.

Whitehead, Alfred North. 1967. *Adventures of Ideas.* New York: Free Press. Originally published in 1933.

———. 1978. *Process and Reality.* Corrected edition. Edited by David Ray Griffin and Donald W. Sherburne. New York: Free Press.

Williams, Delores. 1993. *Sisters in the Wilderness: The Challenge of Womanist God-Talk.* Maryknoll, N.Y.: Orbis Books.

Wink, Walter. 1984. *Naming the Powers: The Language of Power in the New Testament.* The Powers: Volume 1. Philadelphia: Fortress Press.

Wright, N. T. 2002. *The Letter to the Romans: Introduction, Commentary, and Reflections.* In *The New Interpreter's Bible.* Vol. 10. Nashville: Abingdon.

Yarbro Collins, Adela. 1980. "Revelation 18: Taunt Song or Dirge?" In *L'Apocalypse Johannique dans le Nouveau Testament*, ed. Jan Lambrecht. Gembloux: J. Duculot and Leuven University Press.

———. 1984. *Crisis and Catharsis: The Power of the Apocalypse.* Philadelphia: Westminster.

Young, Frances. 1994. *The Theology of the Pastoral Letters.* Cambridge: Cambridge University Press.

Zerbe, Gordon. 1992. "Paul's Ethic of Nonretaliation and Peace." In *The Love of Enemy and Nonretaliation in the New Testament*, ed. Willard M. Swartley. Louisville: Westminster John Knox.

index